D0742547

BEAUTIFUL UNTRUE THINGS

Forging Oscar Wilde's Extraordinary Afterlife

Beautiful Untrue Things

Forging Oscar Wilde's Extraordinary Afterlife

Gregory Mackie

UNIVERSITY OF TORONTO PRESS
Toronto Buffalo London

Toronto Buffalo London
utorontopress.com
Printed in the U.S.A.

ISBN 978-1-4875-0290-4

Printed on acid-free, 100% post-consumer recycled paper.

Library and Archives Canada Cataloguing in Publication

Title: Beautiful untrue things: forging Oscar Wilde's extraordinary afterlife / Gregory Mackie.
Names: Mackie, Gregory, 1976– author.
Description: Includes bibliographical references and index.
Identifiers: Canadiana 20190084162 | ISBN 9781487502904 (hardcover)
Subjects: LCSH: Wilde, Oscar, 1854–1900 – Influence. | LCSH: Fan fiction – History. | LCSH: Literary forgeries and mystifications.
Classification: LCC PR5827.I52 M33 2019 | DDC 828/.809—dc23

Carnation image used for epigraph: Kang Ha / shutterstock

This book has been published with the help of a grant from the Federation for the Humanities and Social Sciences, through the Awards to Scholarly Publications Program, using funds provided by the Social Sciences and Humanities Research Council of Canada.

University of Toronto Press acknowledges the financial assistance to its publishing program of the Canada Council for the Arts and the Ontario Arts Council, an agency of the Government of Ontario.

Canada Council for the Arts
Conseil des Arts du Canada

For my parents
and for Vin Nardizzi

Contents

Illustrations

Acknowledgments

This book is the product of over a decade's worth of research and writing, and during that period I accumulated a number of debts to the kindness, imagination, and generosity of others. My interest in book history and my enthusiasm for archival research are the product of training I received as a graduate student at the University of Toronto. For encouraging me on this research and career path I thank Gillian Fenwick and the late Richard Landon, who kindled my interest in the enigmatic world of literary forgery. This particular project first took shape during a research fellowship I held at the William Andrews Clark Memorial Library at the University of California, Los Angeles, during the summer of 2008. It was there that I blundered into an archival goldmine of Wilde forgeries that kept me coming back over several years for briefer research trips when time and funds permitted. My time at the Clark also afforded me the opportunity of getting to know Joseph Bristow, whose interest in and support for my work have been steadfast, and without whose loans of ultra-rare, Wilde-related titles not held by the Clark collection (or, indeed, anywhere else) this book would not have been written. The Clark has become my second academic home, and it is with profuse thanks that I acknowledge the years of assistance that my work received from Bruce Whiteman, Gerald Cloud, Scott Jacobs, Patrick Keilty, Rebecca Fanning Marschall, Philip Palmer, and Nina Schneider. At University College, Oxford, I thank Elizabeth Adams for sharing discoveries and office space with my graduate student Michaela Posthumus and me as the Robert Ross Memorial Collection was being catalogued. At the Rosenbach Museum and Library in Philadelphia, I thank Elizabeth Fuller for exceeding every expectation with her assistance in getting me the materials I needed. At my own institution, I want heartily to thank colleagues at Rare Books and Special Collections, University of

British Columbia (UBC): Katherine Kalsbeek, Chelsea Shriver, Krisztina Laszlo, Felicia de la Parra, Jacky Lai, Vivian Yan, and Hiller Goodspeed. Libraries are fundamental to research in the humanities, and projects such as mine would be unimaginable without them and the amazing people who make such projects possible.

I have also benefited enormously from sharing work and ideas with colleagues both near and far from my home in Vancouver at conferences and academic gatherings over the years. In this inspiring company I place Aviva Briefel, Ellen Crowell, Colette Colligan, Bradley Deane, Petra Dierkes-Thrun, Jen Hill, Kristin Mahoney, Rebecca N. Mitchell, Daniel A. Novak, and Tiffany Werth. My research has also taken me to some fascinating non-academic research sites – namely, into the world of rare-book dealing and collecting on both sides of the Atlantic. For his extraordinary insight into book collecting and its history, I thank Mark Samuels Lasner, a sage among collectors, and for granting me access to the private archive of his London family firm, I thank Ed Maggs. Also in the United Kingdom, Timothy d'Arch Smith, Thomas Wright, and Bob Forrest have proven invaluable sources of arcane and essential information about Oscar Wilde's textual legacy.

This project has received institutional support from the University of California, Los Angeles, which took me to the Clark in the first place; from my home institution, the University of British Columbia, which supported a research assistant and a teaching leave; and from the Bibliographical Society of America, which supported a research trip to Oxford. I also want to thank Robert Langenfeld, editor of *English Literature in Transition, 1880–1920*, for permission to reprint portions of a 2011 article, which appear in chapter 4.

Closer to home, I want to thank my UBC colleagues Patricia Badir, Siân Echard, Kyle Frackman, Stephen Guy-Bray, Deanna Kreisel, Scott MacKenzie, Ira Nadel, Robert Rouse, and Sandra Tomc for their ideas and immensely helpful feedback on my work as various parts of this book were being written. My UBC graduate students Justin O'Hearn and Michaela Posthumus were consistently insightful and patient with me. My parents, Wendy and Gordon Mackie, have been an unflagging source of support throughout this book's lengthy gestation, and their good humour and curiosity about "Chan-Toonery" have meant a very great deal to me. My greatest debt of thanks, however, is to the indefatigably brilliant Vin Nardizzi. To say that this book would not have been possible without his encouragement and support is a massive understatement.

Lying, the telling of beautiful untrue things, is the proper aim of Art.

–Oscar Wilde

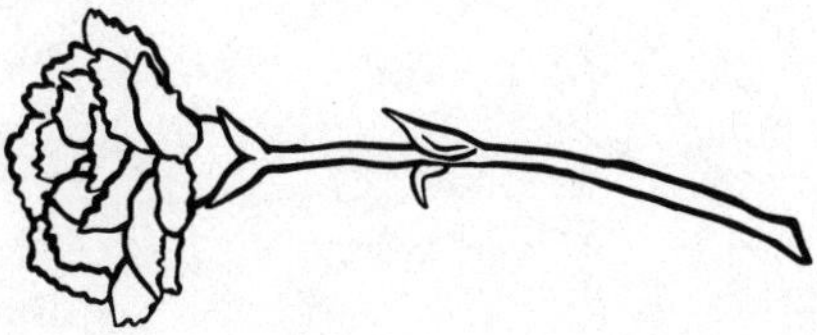

The Truth of Fakes

Executed on a scrap of a Sotheby's auction catalogue, a pencil sketch of a standing male figure in Renaissance dress, measuring about one inch by two inches, is as close, in material terms, to the true portrait of Mr W.H. that we may ever get (figure 1). In his own hand, the artist, Charles Ricketts, designates it "'Mr W.H.' drawn by C. Ricketts 22 Nov. 1912."[1] Otherwise known as Will or Willie Hughes, Mr W.H. is the imaginary Shakespearean boy-actor whose portrait – crucially, a forgery – is at the centre of Oscar Wilde's story "The Portrait of Mr. W.H." ([1889], 1921). As that portrait does in Wilde's story, this sketch records desire and loss. It is a pale substitute for a sumptuous painting in oil that Wilde had commissioned Ricketts to contrive in 1889, a reproduction of which was to serve as a frontispiece to a projected (but uncompleted) book version of Wilde's story about Shakespearean fandom. Lost in 1895, in the tumultuous wake of the Wilde trials, the Ricketts painting nonetheless endured in memory and legend, for Wilde's admirers, disciples, and fans tried to track it down. One such fan was Walter Ledger (1862–1931), a dedicated and assiduous collector of Wilde's writings during the first three decades of the twentieth century. In his methodical way Ledger contacted Ricketts in 1912 to inquire if the artist had any knowledge of the painting's fate, to which Ricketts tersely replied: "It is now 23 years ago that I painted Mr. W. H. for Oscar Wilde. I have no sketch of it & no photograph."[2] Despite his exasperation at Ledger's painstaking thoroughness, Ricketts was impelled to forge the artefact afresh, and Ledger felt that as part of Wilde's legacy this scrap of "Mr. W.H." – however meagre – merited preservation. The sketch seemed to have radiated enough aura for Ledger that he made it a precious keepsake, and it is for this reason that the sketch still exists today.

all charges on such re-sale shall be made good by the defaulters at this sale.

Gentlemen, who cannot attend this Sale, may have their Commissions faithfully executed by their humble Servants,

SOTHEBY, WILKINSON & HODGE,

13, *Wellington Street, Strand, London.*

Telegraphic Address: "Abinitio London." Telephone: 3852 Gerrard.

COMMISSIONS CANNOT UNDER ANY CIRCUMSTANCES BE ACCEPTED BY TELEPHONE.

"Mr W.H"
drawn by
C. Ricketts
22 Nov. 1912

233 F. Wheatley. The Cries of London, by T. G. Appleton, *signed proofs on india paper, the complete set, printed in colours* 13

J. A. McN. WHISTLER.

234 The Forge, and the Smithy, *lithographs*; and portrait of the

1 Charles Ricketts, "Mr. W.H.," 1912. William Andrews Clark Memorial Library, University of California, Los Angeles.

In pursuing the Ricketts painting, Ledger uncannily repeats, in part, the course of desire described in Wilde's tale of literary sleuthing and forgery. His actions seem to take Wilde's own depiction of Shakespearean enthusiasm as a model: Ledger and the bibliographer Christopher Millard (1872–1927) were followers of Wilde whose obsessive devotion to the writer's memory replicates the fascination and mystique exercised by Shakespeare over the characters in "The Portrait of Mr. W.H." But whereas the characters in Wilde's story channel, through a forged portrait, their passion for Mr W.H. into an ingenious explication of Shakespeare's sonnets to assert the existence of a young actor whom Shakespeare apparently adored, these men were passionate compilers of archives relating to Wilde's literary career and cultural afterlife. In both instances, one imagined and one real, the paradox of an original forgery – a portrait of Mr W.H. – enchants. Treasured by Ledger as if it were a relic, this elusive sketch of Mr W.H. by Ricketts thus exemplifies, in miniature, the larger circuits of Wildean fandom, forgery, and archive making that I explore throughout *Beautiful Untrue Things*.

For admirers and fans of Wilde like Ledger and Millard, such loving and careful acts of archival labour are expressions of devotion and enthusiasm. These men spent, for instance, more than a decade collecting and recording information about their literary hero for inclusion in the magisterial *Bibliography of Oscar Wilde* that Millard, under the pseudonym Stuart Mason, published in 1914. The primary fruit of their efforts, then, was the publication of reference books about Wilde, and these efforts – and the affiliations of the men who undertook them – are the subject of this book's next chapter. One of my central arguments is that the information made newly accessible in these books also enabled the labours of a more dubious set of Wilde fans who were operating in the 1920s in Dublin, London, New York, and Paris. Without the information recorded in them, these fans – "Dorian Hope," Hester Travers Smith, and Mrs Chan-Toon – would not have had the materials required to forge (in that term's most capacious, creative, and often criminal sense) novel myths about Wilde. In the bulk of *Beautiful Untrue Things* I elaborate the audacious, amusing, and sometimes desperate careers of these literary forgers. In their writings, impostures, scams, and dodges they forged, collectively, an extraordinary afterlife for Mr O.W.

Fandom, Forgery, and Authorship

After his death in Parisian exile and poverty in 1900, Oscar Wilde became the subject of legends created by diverse hands and different (and often competing) agendas.[3] To audiences that were nostalgic for the Victorian era, he could be a period piece, an emblem of frivolous Victoriana; to modernists, he might represent a defiant turn away from the nineteenth century's literary, social, and sexual constrictions; and still to others, Wilde became both the model and the martyr of a nascent homosexual identity.[4] His glamorous notoriety in life, which culminated in the dramatic collapse of his literary reputation during his three 1895 trials, allowed his followers and foes alike to project onto him whatever narrative they wished his memory to conjure. His posthumous twentieth-century devotees included ardent bibliophiles as well as multiple forgers who managed, with varying degrees of success, to exploit that notoriety in the commercial book market. "Their insurgence into what became an increasingly fictitious memory of Wilde," Joseph Bristow observes, "[makes] plain the degree to which his extraordinary legacy activated almost delusional, cultish fantasies."[5] These fantasies of intimacy with a dead author underwrote the production of a remarkable sequence of Wilde fakes – or, indeed, fake Wildes – that began to appear in both print and manuscript with increasing frequency in the 1920s. In effect, they prove to be the early modernist versions of a phenomenon that we would today call the cult of fandom. Throughout this study I show that, though undeniably exploitative, Wilde forgeries from the 1920s can also be productively, and more generously, understood as forms of fan fiction. Wilde, if he had still been alive, might even have appreciated some of this admiration.

In *Beautiful Untrue Things: Forging Oscar Wilde's Extraordinary Afterlife*, I uncover, analyse, and sometimes also play detective in an attempt to spotlight two forms of intersecting fandom: the bibliophilia for and the forgeries of Oscar Wilde that proliferated in the early twentieth century. In this study I elaborate several tangled narratives of literary desire, deceit, and loss about Wilde over a period of roughly thirty years in which he was alternately denigrated, memorialized, and forged, or made anew in books and manuscripts. The Wilde forgeries at the heart of this book are perhaps the most provocative illustrations of what Ellen Crowell has called the "intricate subcultures of [Wilde's] archival afterlife."[6] Like the thumb-nail sketch of Mr W.H. that the bibliophile Ledger treasured, the Wilde forgeries explored here are artefacts whose production, transmission, and claims to authenticity provide new insight into the rich and strange cultural afterlife of Oscar Wilde. But why, in the early decades of the twentieth century, did Oscar Wilde become the vehicle for the manifold textual fabrications of literary forgers?

Literary forgery has a long history that predates Wilde, and at its most basic level it can be described as creative work that engages in duplicitous representation(s) in material (or textual) form.[7] It is a practice that creates an illusion of authorial embodiment, wherein a text appears to be the creation of one hand, while in reality it belongs to another; in Harold Love's apt definition, a literary forgery is a "work composed with the intention to deceive and then promulgated under the name of another."[8] Forgeries are thus exercises in mystification, as Love further notes with a Wildean flourish: "Fakes are secretive: the real authors go to great pains to conceal their presence [...] the true fake is a creative achievement."[9] Such effort and labour are directed into the art of storytelling, for literary forgeries (printed books, manuscripts, and other ephemeral documents) are also biographical narratives; they tell stories about their putative author that are distinct from what is conveyed within their texts. Such stories tend to reinforce existing knowledge while also claiming to uncover new information. I do something similar in this study by bringing new information to light, for it represents the first serious scholarly assessment of Wilde fakes from the 1920s and the bibliophilic context without which they would not have flourished.

In all their varied formats, then, Wilde forgeries are material myths of authorship. Even if they are not authentic texts *by* Wilde, they are invariably texts *about* him. In these spurious narratives, as we shall see, extra-textual information about Wilde has a pivotal role in articulating a forgery's claims to authenticity. A forgery's strategic deployment of just this sort of information is labelled by K.K. Ruthven as an "authenticatory device."[10] One common example of an authenticatory device is a signature that upholds the illusion that the putative author's writing body has produced a particular text; another might be the revelation of biographical information external to the forged text itself in, for instance, a dedication or preface. Such paraliterary devices reinforce the deception proffered by the forgery by assisting in ascribing the forged text to the presumed author. Borrowing from Roland Barthes, for whom the representational illusion produced in realist fiction depends on a "reality effect," Ruthven argues that the illusion generated by the forger's strategic use of such extra-textual information might best be called an "authenticity effect."[11] In the archive of Wilde forgeries, the fact that Wilde wrote in a decadent, extravagant style, that he was a dandy and a homosexual, and that he was Irish, went to prison, and died in Paris will all be mobilized by forgers to produce this effect. Well-known information about Wilde's life and career, it turns out, afforded forgers ample opportunity for making texts under his name.

By such means, for Ruthven, "a literary forgery performs authenticity."[12] I elaborate the methodological implications of this phrasing over the course of this book. By jointly engaging book history and theatre studies I attend to the illusions and effects that the Wilde forgeries of the 1920s generated. Investigating a series of figures who inhabited Oscar Wilde's much-mythologized authorial persona – in forging him, they effectively wrote *as* Wilde – *Beautiful Untrue Things* therefore explores how literary forgery can also come into view as a form of performance art. Since, for Wilde, all art is "a mode of acting,"[13] it should not surprise us that forgers recruited his status as (arguably) the late-Victorian era's most successful dramatist to buttress and validate their own performances. Tellingly, the two figures about whom we have the most biographical information "acted" the part of Oscar Wilde by writing in the medium of drama, thereby reimagining a literary history that would otherwise have concluded with the sudden and memorable closing of Wilde's plays in London's West End following the scandal of his 1895 trials. In so doing, the spiritualist medium Hester Travers Smith (see chapter 3) and the forger Mrs Chan-Toon (see chapter 4) would seem to realize a desire for *more* of Wilde by expanding the bibliography of titles credited to him.

To forge Wilde by generating fakes attached to his name is not only an exercise in role-playing; it is also necessarily a form of imaginative appropriation and reinvention. In this light I consider the often-playful textual impostures analysed here as forms of fan fiction, which Karen Hellekson and Kristina Busse define as "the imaginative interpolations and extrapolations by fans of existing literary worlds."[14] Recent studies of fan fiction have begun to historicize a cultural phenomenon commonly thought to have originated with the productions of 1960s-era *Star Trek* enthusiasts, and *Beautiful Untrue Things* participates in that project. Scholars of the extraordinary fan culture that developed around Arthur Conan Doyle's detective Sherlock Holmes in the 1890s, for instance, have shown that fan fiction has firm late-Victorian roots.[15] (Arthur Conan Doyle will make a cameo appearance in chapter 3 as a witness in the curious case of Wilde's ghost.) As Daniel Cavicchi notes, "[w]hen most scholars outside of fan studies think about 'fandom' at all, they likely associate it with the consumption of science fiction television or moments in pop culture […], sensing that it has something to do with technology, the star system, consumption, and the complexity of self-formation and intimacy in the modern era."[16] The terms that Cavicchi rehearses here to articulate a "history of enthusiastic audiences" (the subtitle of his article) all pertain particularly well to Oscar Wilde, a figure often located at the vanguard of modern celebrity culture.[17] The reach of Oscar Wilde's posthumous fandom, as my chapters chart it, is vast indeed: by the 1920s, it takes in old and new worlds; it stretches from the metropole to the colonial outpost; and it even encompasses the great beyond.

In their status as fan fiction, the Wilde forgeries can also illuminate for us the Irish writer's position as an author in the literary canon. An "author's name," according to Michel Foucault, "is not simply an element of discourse […] it performs a certain role with regard to narrative discourse, assuring a classificatory function. Such a name permits one to group together a certain number of texts, define them, differentiate them from and contrast them to others."[18] For Foucault, the "author function" is central to any such process of classification, as it is keenly related to the power relations that cluster around matters of attribution. These relations, which involve matters of literary property and "the extent to which authors became subject to punishment,"[19] have a special resonance in Wilde's case, for the function exercised by the name Oscar Wilde was indelibly affected by two interrelated events that took place in 1895. First, Wilde was famously subject to state-sponsored punishment for what Foucault would call "transgressive discourses" when extracts of Wilde's own writings were submitted as evidence in a sequence of judicial proceedings that led to his imprisonment on charges of gross indecency. Second, Wilde's bankruptcy during the trials and the hasty sale of his literary property in their wake further marginalized the Irish writer by dispersing the books, manuscripts, letters, and records (and paintings) contained in his London house. After 1895 the classificatory power of the name Oscar Wilde proved simultaneously very strong and yet curiously weak: strong in so far as Wilde's sexual infamy was widespread;[20] weak in so far as his name became a negative space that could be occupied by a number of different hands, all performing and forging new versions of Wilde after the total collapse of his literary reputation.

As we shall see in the next chapter, Wilde's devoted bibliophiles worked tirelessly in the 1910s to police and reduce this negative space, to *strengthen* and delimit the classificatory power of the name Oscar Wilde. Since the function of the ostensible author in a literary forgery is to perform authenticity, where success requires the so-called author to operate as a source of cultural authority and literary value, chapter 1 thus also considers the dynamic situation in which that author had only a tenuous claim to such credentials in a period during which Wilde continued to be regarded with suspicion by the literary establishment. Tellingly, Wilde's name nonetheless became an even more unstable placeholder in the immediate aftermath of the collective efforts undertaken by Robert Ross (1869–1918), Ledger, and Millard to restore respectability to his literary reputation. We will glimpse this instability in chapters 2 and 3, in which the author of a forged text might be a loose set of individuals (for example, "Dorian Hope") or a set of collaborators, sometimes working together (for example, the spiritualists in communication with Wilde's ghost at Hester Travers Smith's seances) or in competition with one another (for example, the Soal brothers, who also claimed to communicate with Wilde's ghost). "Oscar Wilde" was thus a mask that many actor-writers could put on, with great effect.

The uncertain state of Wilde's place in British literary culture cannot account by itself for the appearance of multiple forgeries by multiple forgers who contrived pseudo-Wildean texts in a relatively concentrated period. These forgeries reached a critical mass in the 1920s once Wilde's books and manuscripts began to be sought after by collectors on the rare-book market. Major auction-sales of Wilde's manuscripts and first editions took place in 1895 (the Tite Street sale), 1905 and 1911 (the Glaenzer sales), 1920 (the Stetson sale), and 1928 (the Dulau sale), and the items dispersed in them constitute the bulk of today's Wilde archive. Despite the promising economic conditions afforded by the market, however, the profit motive among a disparate group of opportunistic eccentrics is also insufficient explanation for this sudden flourishing of Wilde fakes. So far as I know, none of the 1920s forgers made much money retailing artefacts and narratives to which they had attached Wilde's name.

Ironically enough, Wilde himself may well have endorsed the marginal and transgressive forms of literary production that passed under his name in the early twentieth century. The forgers took Wilde at his word as much as they followed his lead stylistically: located at the intersection of art and crime, forgery occupies a central position in Wilde's aesthetic philosophy and may well be the master Wildean metaphor for artistry and creativity.[21] Since Wilde's writings flamboyantly advocated multiple forms of artifice – including forgery – the forgers who annexed the name "Oscar Wilde" to their materials were emboldened to do so, as it were, on Wilde's own warrant. Neo-Wildean forgers cannily told (and sold) lies about the late-Victorian era's arch-liar on a commercial stage that Wilde himself had set, theoretically and imaginatively in his writings from the 1880s, and that had been recently, if still tentatively, spruced up by his rehabilitation in the literary establishment. On this stage – in the market of books – they retailed "beautiful untrue things."

I draw this phrase for the forger's craft from Wilde's 1889 dialogue "The Decay of Lying." In that text, Vivian sums up an entire aesthetic philosophy by asserting that the "final revelation is that Lying, the telling of beautiful untrue things, is the proper aim of Art."[22] Wilde articulated an aesthetic of deception and studied artifice in several works dating from the later 1880s; taken together, they mount a vigorous critique of purist views of artistic originality and creativity.[23] For example, in his promotion of lying as "the proper aim of Art," or of the "self-conscious and deliberate" character of "all fine imaginative work" in "The Critic as Artist,"[24] Wilde challenged the ideas about creative expression that he considered outmoded. In place of the familiar and influential Romantic paradigm of artistic originality captured by Percy Shelley's "profuse strains of unpremeditated art," we instead find

Wildean duplicity and theatricality.[25] In texts as generically diverse as the "Chatterton" notebook (c. 1886), the essay "Pen, Pencil, and Poison" (1889), and the story "The Portrait of Mr. W.H." ([1889], 1921), Wilde elaborated a theory of creative expression that condensed these ideas into an enthusiastic endorsement of forgery. Indeed, as Joseph Bristow and Rebecca N. Mitchell observe, "Wilde shows that all artistic creation is an act of forgery: an idea that animates nearly all his prose of the period."[26] Eschewing realism, with its dependence on fact, Wilde's critical and creative writing from the late 1880s celebrates illusion, myth, and lies. In a world where meritorious artists are mask-wearing liars, delighting themselves and their audiences by annexing and enacting different identities, the forger proves the ultimate artist.

Wilde theorized creative imposture by also identifying forgery as a *theatrical* art, and, as we shall see, the eccentric characters who forged in Wilde's name all displayed, in their different ways, a remarkable knack for theatricality. In a discussion of famous eighteenth-century forgers that highlights Thomas Chatterton, the unnamed narrator of "The Portrait of Mr. W.H." insists, for instance, that "his so-called forgeries were merely the result of an artistic desire for perfect representation; that we had no right to quarrel with an artist for the conditions under which he chooses to present his work; and that all Art being to a certain extent a mode of acting, an attempt to realize one's own personality on some imaginative plane out of reach of the trammelling accidents and limitations of real life, to censure an artist for a forgery was to confuse an ethical with an aesthetical problem."[27] Against models of creativity that privilege originality and the natural, Wilde claims for forgery the "Art" of performance; in its self-conscious artificiality, its attention to style, and its capacity to reshape the identities of its practitioners, forgery thus constitutes a "mode of acting" played out in defiance of "the trammelling accidents and limitations of real life." Understood as a means to achieve "perfect artistic representation," to forge was thus to enhance, dramatically, the creative possibilities of artifice; the verb *to forge*, after all, allows for a substantial degree of semantic slippage between "to make" and "to fake."[28] In specifically literary terms, the deceptions performed by the wearer of a forger's mask rework more conventional meanings of authorship. For Wilde, the purpose of art was thus not to create something original *ex nihilo* but instead to "realize one's own personality" by performing a persona or another self. By such logic, his forgers in the twentieth century simply staged a textual version of him.

Forgery and Desire in "The Portrait of Mr. W.H."

Fiction- and myth-making about a dead writer structure Wilde's most important and extended meditation on forgery, "The Portrait of Mr. W.H." In this story, the forged portrait of "Willie Hughes," an Elizabethan boy-actor who is the supposed dedicatee and "onlie begetter" of Shakespeare's sonnets,[29] paradoxically guarantees the genuineness of an outlandish literary speculation whose plausibility ultimately depends on the desire, transmitted from one man to another, for the theory to be real. As the story progresses, the theory about Willie Hughes is transmitted as if it were a form of contagion: to believe in Willie Hughes (and to experience the desire of wanting him to have been real) is to become infected with an obsessive, all-consuming, and possibly fatal disease. For Nicholas Frankel, "the value of forgery" in "The Portrait of Mr. W.H." inheres "in the *enthusiasm* it engenders, however briefly, for something – call it an idea or a set of associations – never previously incarnated in material form."[30] In Wilde's story, that enthusiasm undermines the categorical distinction between the genuine article and the material lie and articulates a Shakespearean fandom whose coordinates of desire, queerness, and loss set the pattern not only for the forgers' interventions into Wilde's afterlife but also for the homophile network of Wilde fans and bibliophiles that sought to recuperate his respectability in the 1910s. The story is thus a Wildean touchstone for the arguments and archives detailed in *Beautiful Untrue Things*.

"The Portrait of Mr. W.H." is, as scholars have noted, also a fictionalized performance of literary criticism. As Paul K. Saint-Amour observes, the story "*stages* analysis and theory in the theater of fiction."[31] Nicholas Frankel regards it as "really a work of critical theory conducted under the guise of fiction,"[32] and, for Jonathan Loesberg, the story comments on the "perverse" procedures (and possibilities) of literary interpretation itself.[33] In concert with these assessments, I further comprehend "The Portrait of Mr. W.H." as perhaps the best illustration of the dictum from "The Critic as Artist" that the province of the critic is "to deepen [art's] mystery, to raise around it, and round its maker, that mist of wonder which is dear to both gods and worshippers alike."[34] Unsurprisingly, then, the story eludes the stable interpretation that it provokes its reader to desire, just as the historical existence of Willie Hughes ultimately eludes the unnamed narrator, his friend Erskine, and Erskine's friend Cyril Graham. In elaborating such elusions, all the while defying conventional generic categories, "The Portrait of

Mr. W.H." employs a nested narrative structure, with a forgery located at its centre.

The paradox of "a forged portrait [that is] still a genuine artwork"[35] is not only at the core of Wilde's story; it also frames the story with a title. By naming a fictional material object in his text's title, Wilde indicates that the text is *about* that forged image, and so, like the novel *The Picture of Dorian Gray*, "The Portrait of Mr. W.H." can also be productively read as the story of an artwork. Unlike *Dorian Gray*, which opens in an artist's studio, "The Portrait of Mr. W.H." begins with a conversation about famous literary forgers, "a long discussion about Macpherson, Ireland, and Chatterton."[36] Recognizing these eighteenth-century forgers as "artists," the unnamed narrator and his friend Erskine agree, as if they were discussing literary matters at a salon, "that we had no right to quarrel with an artist for the conditions under which he chooses to present his work."[37]

On this non-judgmental note, "The Portrait of Mr. W.H." unfolds a tale about desire – or, specifically (and, at times, disorientingly), the communicable possibilities of a desire *for* desire. Bristow and Mitchell astutely label this emotion a "longing […] that can at last tire of its ambition to fabricate the truth."[38] A meditation on the vagaries of belief and "the status of proof itself,"[39] Wilde's tale recounts the circulation of the desire to believe in the veracity of a literary theory about the secret meanings of Shakespeare's sonnets. In this way, "The Portrait of Mr. W.H." also wishfully imputes homoerotic desire to Shakespeare. It seeks to uncover and to resolve the apparent mystery of *his* desire for Willie Hughes, or, as Erskine puts it, the "secret of Shakespeare's heart."[40] Seduced by a theory, Wilde's characters thus want a *biographical* speculation to achieve the status of fact, as the story recounts the cyclical fluctuations of their desire for Shakespeare to have been in love with a young man not merely in poetry but in real life. The stories that literary texts tell us, by such logic, are therefore stories about their authors, and desire and belief come close to being the same thing. For this story's Shakespearean sleuths, literature is crucially also biography, and what the sonnets promise is something beyond the literary: they reveal desirable information about Shakespeare's *life*. Willie Hughes is fascinating in so far as he confirms what these men want to believe about Shakespeare.

An inquiry into more than literary history, then, "The Portrait of Mr. W.H." proceeds as a conversation between characters who are as invested in the notion of proof as they are susceptible to the romance of mystery. Erskine shares with the unnamed narrator a conversation he once had with his friend Cyril Graham: "Who was that young man of Shakespeare's day," asks Cyril, the originator of the theory, "who, without being of noble birth or even of noble nature, was addressed by him in terms of such passionate adoration that we can but wonder at the strange worship, and are almost afraid to turn the key that unlocks the mystery of the poet's heart?"[41] According to Erskine, Cyril articulated his theory by "working purely by internal evidence,"[42] which he derived from the sonnets themselves. Initially sceptical, Erskine questions this method by protesting, "You start by assuming the existence of the very person whose existence is the thing to be proved."[43] But, for Cyril, Willie Hughes is "none other than the boy-actor for whom [Shakespeare] created Viola and Imogen, Juliet and Rosalind, Portia and Desdemona, and Cleopatra herself."[44] The secret inspiration for a series of female roles of escalating grandeur, Hughes's power of aesthetic enchantment (adduced from his abilities as an *actor*) renders him, for Cyril, "as real a person as Shakespeare."[45]

This attractive theory about Shakespeare's male muse, however, requires more than the proof derived from textual speculations and close literary interpretation. The "internal evidence" afforded by Shakespeare's texts proves insufficient to meet the evidentiary demands of historical fact when the discoverer of that fact (Cyril) wants to share it with someone else (Erskine). In order for it to be transmissible, the theory about Willie Hughes requires material evidence, captured in a concrete image. Such evidence appears in the (paradoxical) form of a forged portrait of the actor, which Aviva Briefel calls "an independently seductive object."[46] This artefact is contrived by Cyril, whom the story describes as "a young man who had a strange theory about a certain work of art [...] and committed a forgery in order to prove it."[47] Cyril forges a narrative about a famous author (Shakespeare) that adds to the allure of that author's art, and, in so doing, performs precisely the critical gesture of intensifying art's mystery and "mist of wonder" that Wilde champions in "The Critic as Artist." Cyril then commissions a forged painting – a symbol of art's power to invent a desired reality – to support that theory.

In the story within a story that Erskine narrates, Cyril wants so badly for his friend Erskine to believe in the existence of Willie Hughes that he hires an impoverished painter to fake "an authentic portrait of Mr. W.H. with his hand upon the dedicatory page of the Sonnets, [where] on the corner of the picture could be faintly seen the name of the young man himself [...] 'Master Will Hews.'"[48] Cyril then goes on to provide Erskine with a more mysterious origin for the painting: it has apparently been discovered in an old chest in a farmhouse in Warwickshire, "[d]rawing," as Briefel observes, "from the elaborate narratives of provenance used by forgers and dealers to validate the authenticity of artworks."[49] The painting looks to the unnamed narrator, when he first sees it in Erskine's house, like a Renaissance artwork: "It was a full-length portrait of a young man in late sixteenth-century costume, standing by a table, with his right hand resting on an open book. He seemed about seventeen years of age, and was of quite extraordinary personal beauty, though evidently somewhat effeminate. Indeed, had it not been for the dress and the closely cropped hair, one would have said that the face, with its dreamy, wistful eyes and its delicate scarlet lips, was the face of a girl. In manner, and especially in the treatment of the hands, the picture reminded one of François Clouet's later work."[50] Appearances are, of course, deceptive. In the back story that takes place long before the unnamed narrator sees the painting, the sceptical Erskine had (accidentally) discovered and exposed the "horrid lie" of Cyril's forgery, causing his distraught friend – "the youngest and the most splendid of all the martyrs of literature" – to commit suicide.[51] Erskine has retained the portrait, and he treasures it, as Cyril's "suicide lends a tragic grandeur to both the portrait and the theory."[52] In recounting Cyril's story to his unnamed friend, Erskine inadvertently manages to convince *him* of the theory and tells him, "[I am] very sorry indeed that I should have converted you to a thing in which I don't believe."[53]

Having absorbed the outline of the theory (and, just as importantly, Cyril's tragic-romantic enthusiasm for that theory) in the presence of the painting, the unnamed narrator proves a new convert. He enters into his own obsessive examination of the sonnets, arguing that "the moods and passions they mirrored were absolutely essential to Shakespeare's perfection as an artist writing for the Elizabethan stage."[54] He reads Willie Hughes into both Shakespeare's drama and the sonnets in ever-more elaborately homoerotic terms, although he stops short of speculating on the exact nature of their relationship, "not car[ing] to pry into the mystery of his sin or of the sin, if such it was, of the great poet who had so dearly loved him."[55] (Recalling a forger who, as Wilde says of Chatterton, seeks for "perfect representation" through crime, Shakespeare's aesthetic merit is guaranteed by his "sin.") The narrator's literary-historical research also leads him to speculate about the

"Dark Lady" of the sonnets as an erotic barrier between Shakespeare and the boy-actor. And he expounds, in the manner of "The Decay of Lying" and "The Critic as Artist," on the greater vitality (and truth) of art over life and on the paradoxically revelatory power of art's secrets and mysteries.

Speculative Shakespearean biography becomes the pivot point for the story's various discussions of homoerotic and homo-aesthetic desire. Eventually the narrator's studious immersion in Shakespeare leads him to uncover suggestive aspects of his own sexuality, of "the soul that hid within me, and had its mysterious passions of which I was kept in ignorance." "Strange," he muses, "that we know so little of ourselves and that our most intimate personality was concealed from us!"[56] Now that the revelatory beauty of "the essentially male culture of the English Renaissance"[57] has led him to a new understanding of his own "most intimate personality," he writes to Erskine, and "put[s] into the letter all [his] faith"[58] about Willie Hughes, only to discover that his own belief has been nullified in the process of writing it out. Articulating the "proofs" of the theory – narrativizing the desire encoded in the sonnets' verbal artistry – cancels the theory by draining it of lyric romance. The narrator then abandons Willie Hughes, wondering at last if he had "merely been influenced by the beauty of the forged portrait,"[59] but not before he learns, to his horror, that his friend Erskine, who has had possession of the portrait all this time, is reconverted to the theory by reading the unnamed narrator's letter.

For Erskine, newly energized, the theory's aesthetic beauty – tethered to the "romance" of the portrait – transcends all need for rational evidence, since "reason is dead against it."[60] "The only evidence for the existence of Willie Hughes," the exasperated narrator complains to Erskine, "is that picture in front of you, and the picture is a forgery."[61] Unable to corroborate the theory, Erskine soon dies. If a little corroboration, like sincerity in "The Critic as Artist," is a dangerous thing, then a great deal of it would seem absolutely fatal. Erskine leaves his friend a letter proclaiming his intention to die "by my own hand for Willie Hughes' sake," leading the narrator to assume that he, like Cyril before him, has "die[d] for a literary theory."[62] But this is not so. Erskine's "suicide" letter is itself a kind of forgery, designed specifically to rekindle the narrator's belief in the theory. It is a false representation, deliberately deceptive and misleading; rather than representing actual events (the intention to kill himself), the letter is a dramatic gesture designed to generate an aesthetic effect. Erskine, it turns out, was consumptive, not suicidal, a fact that nevertheless prompts the narrator to observe, "No man dies for what he knows to be true. Men die for what they want to be true, for what some terror in their hearts tells them is not true."[63] At story's end the unnamed narrator inherits the forged portrait from Erskine and displays it in his library to the admiration of his "artistic friends."[64] To them he omits to reveal the portrait's "true history" – in other words, its status as a forgery – and he finds that "when I look at it, I think there is really a good deal to be said for the Willie Hughes theory of Shakespeare's Sonnets."[65]

As this summary indicates, desire for the theory about Willie Hughes seems at once to be encapsulated within, and transmitted by, a forged object with an indefinable talismanic (and persuasive) power of its own. For Saint-Amour, "[i]n a sense Wilde's tale does nothing more than trace the portrait's production and circulation, calling special attention to the moments when it changes hands through inheritance."[66] The portrait passes between these men as a legacy, "intrusted," along with the theory, from one to another.[67] None of these men is related; it is as if the transmission of the theory has the capacity to generate homosocial bonds between them while at the same time sustaining a quasi-genealogical line that dictates the movement of desire and property. Erskine, in fact, calls the portrait "the only legacy I ever received in my life."[68] Each of the three men in the story believes the theory at one time, and each of them possesses the portrait at one time, although belief in the theory and possession of the portrait do not necessarily follow in lockstep. Belief, like possession, may be transient, but only the forged object endures.

In the world of "The Portrait of Mr. W.H.," if belief is haunted by doubt, then the materiality of the forged object – in other words, the faked *thing*, as opposed to the mere *idea* – is required to achieve the seductive purposes of persuasion. Cyril Graham, the instigator of the theory, initially has the portrait created to enhance his case for the existence of Willie Hughes – and to transmit his belief to a sceptical Erskine. But Cyril also planned to literalize the portrait's evidentiary function by turning writer and by publishing his theory along with the forged image. He aspired not only to convince his friend Erskine of the theory's veracity but also to persuade the general public of this theory through the medium of the book. Cyril's intention, as Erskine recounts it, was to enter the fray of Shakespearean scholarship by editing the sonnets, framing his argument for Mr W.H.'s part in the mythology of Shakespeare with an image that, as Erskine asserts, "it is quite clear

[…] that Shakespeare had […] in his possession."[69] In transforming the theory into a book, the two men "arranged that the picture should be etched or facsimiled, and placed as the frontispiece to Cyril's edition of the Sonnets."[70] Subject to mechanical reproduction, a copy of the forged painting would now be available to seduce all readers of Shakespeare who encountered the theory through Cyril's edition. The authority of this image rests on its mutually reinforcing relation to Shakespeare's text: the portrait of Willie Hughes illustrates the secret of the sonnets, while the sonnets are presented – "edited" – in order to corroborate the existence of Willie Hughes. The intentionally deceptive paratextual framing of Cyril's quasi-scholarly endeavour erases any distinction between fiction and fact. By promoting and extending Shakespearean mythology, Cyril's book project encapsulates his enthusiasm for Shakespeare – an enthusiasm that, far from being diminished, is considerably enhanced by the imaginary history represented by the portrait. Cyril's project also anticipates, as we shall see, Wilde's plans for *his* own book.

Picturing Mr W.H.: "An Authentic Clouet of the Highest *Artistic* Value"

One of Wilde's most durable maxims from "The Decay of Lying" is that life imitates art. The alluring portrait of Willie Hughes aptly illustrates this principle. Just as the ill-fated Cyril Graham never manages to publish his edition of Shakespeare's sonnets, Wilde was ultimately unable to follow through on his strikingly similar plan for publishing an expanded, book-length version of "The Portrait of Mr. W.H." Like much of Wilde's prose, this story was initially published in a periodical. It first appeared in the July 1889 issue of *Blackwood's Edinburgh Magazine*. Wilde, however, had bigger plans for his Shakespearean speculation and substantially elaborated the text.[71] He originally proposed "a dainty little volume" to William Blackwood in 1889,[72] but later transferred the book project to The Bodley Head (under the joint proprietorship of John Lane and Elkin Mathews) in 1893. This book was to be fitted with a frontispiece image of Willie Hughes by Charles Ricketts, who, with the exception of *Salome*, "designed and illustrated all of Wilde's books of the 1890s."[73] Under the title "The Incomparable and Ingenious History of Mr. W.H.,"[74] this project, though, was never completed. It was a casualty of the split in Mathews and Lane's business partnership and was derailed by the impact of the 1895 trials.[75] Even so, Cyril's proposal for an "etched or facsimiled […] frontispiece" is precisely what Wilde had in mind for the book-length publication of "The Portrait of Mr. W.H." when, in 1889, he commissioned Ricketts to create an original portrait of Mr W.H. in an antique style. Bristow and Mitchell have dubbed this painting "a forgery of a forgery."[76]

In *Oscar Wilde: Recollections* (1932) Ricketts tells of a visit from Wilde to the Vale, the house in Chelsea he shared with his artist partner Charles Shannon. Once there, Wilde told him:

> You are the man I have wanted; I wish you to paint a small Elizabethan picture – something in the manner of, shall we say, Clouet. I have written a narrative form of an essay on Shakespeare's sonnets, which I must read to you [...] My theory is quite revolutionary [...] I propose publishing this work in a delicate slim volume powdered with gold. Already I have been warned that the subject is most dangerous [...] When I have read my essay to you, I know you will be convinced and charmed. I have found from evidence in the Sonnets that Mr. W.H. was a young actor named Willie Hughes – is that not a charming name? Now, I need a portrait, which I describe, as a frontispiece. You will see a great deal depends upon this.[77]

This conversation – which in itself may be an invention masquerading as a memory – recapitulates the events of the story in the key of the biographical memoir. Wilde is Cyril Graham, enthusiastically acting the part of his own fictional character besotted with a theory, while Shakespeare remains a constant focus of fascination both within and without the fictional world of Wilde's story. Ricketts, for his part, is both Erskine and the artist who forges the portrait for Cyril. As the instigator of an elaborate literary game, Wilde wants Ricketts, the artist, to "forge" Mr W.H. and so bring into material existence the paradox of an original forgery. In so doing, Ricketts would thereby secure Wilde's mind-bending theoretical linkage of making and faking to an actual object. This "small Elizabethan picture," executed by a Victorian artist, would then be reproduced as the frontispiece to Wilde's planned book, bringing to life, outside of fiction, Cyril's design plan for his edition of Shakespeare's sonnets. In both instances the forged portrait emerges as a cipher for authorship. For, if the fictional portrait of Willie Hughes is about Shakespearean authorship, revealing, in Cyril's words, "the mystery of the poet's heart" that had prompted him to write the sonnets, then the Ricketts portrait organizes a Wildean notion of authorship that knowingly troubles the distinction between the real and the fake. Wilde's Shakespeare book, a "delicate slim volume powdered with gold," tells us more about Wilde (or what Ricketts recalls about Wilde) than it does about Shakespeare.

In Ricketts's telling, Wilde dramatically inhabited the role of an evangelist for the theory about Willie Hughes. Inspired by glamour rather than veracity, Wilde seduced his audiences with two highly theatrical readings: one of Shakespeare's sonnets, which was followed shortly thereafter by a reading of "Mr. W.H." at his London home. "If when he spoke of Shakespeare's verse, and paused to taste its beauties," Ricketts reminisces, somewhat rapturously, "I had been charmed, his rendering of prose pleased me even better. I have been told no one surpassed him as a reader of his plays and, where dialogue was concerned, diction and expression were alike varied and vivid. In passages of description there was a tendency to pause on certain words [...] There would even be a slight movement of the hand as if to arrest their sound."[78] Captivated by this performance, Ricketts was inspired to contrive the wished-for portrait. He recalls that "[w]ithin a fortnight I had painted the small portrait of Mr W.H. upon a decaying piece of oak and framed it in a fragment of worm-eaten moulding, which my friend Shannon pieced together."[79] Ricketts seems so enthused by the style and sweep of Wilde's "Portrait of Mr. W.H." that even this evocative description of his own painting echoes prose from Wilde's story about the forged portrait; the literary painting appears as "a small panel picture set in an old and somewhat tarnished Elizabethan frame."[80] Ricketts has thus forged a period piece.

With a view to the planned volume, Ricketts "made the [painting] a gift to Wilde, despite his perennial need for ready money."[81] (He was no profiteering art forger.) Wilde praised this artificially distressed "small portrait" by observing, "[I]t is not a forgery at all; it is an authentic Clouet of the highest *artistic* value. It is absurd of you and Shannon to try and take me in! As if I did not know the master's touch, or was no judge of frames!"[82] Wilde's commendation imputes to Ricketts his own conception of forgery's status as an aesthetic paradox, all the while teasing Ricketts in the process of praising him. What Wilde is saying, in effect, is that by offering him an "authentic Clouet," Ricketts and Shannon have failed at forging one. Ricketts finds himself in the impossible position of being too accomplished an artist to achieve the success of having created a forgery. In a world where deception is true artistry, authenticity becomes its degraded counterpart. Forgery and authenticity thus switch places, with Wilde playing the role of the connoisseur whose knowledge of "the master's touch" grants him the ability to detect an original – albeit one of the "highest *artistic* value" – masquerading as a fake.

That an actual portrait of Mr W.H. once existed might seem, at first glance, like a Wildean legend too good to be true. In a sense, it is. Ricketts's "authentic Clouet" disappeared with the dispersal of the contents of Wilde's home during his trials in 1895, where "the painting was sold for a guinea."[83] The catalogue for what has become known as the Tite Street sale gives the following description for lot number 125: "An old oil painting of Will Hewes, framed" (figure 2).[84] Though brief, this description manages to condense a fair amount of information about the object itself. The adjective "old," for instance, indicates the success of Ricketts's attempt to forge a Renaissance portrait "upon a decaying piece of oak": to the eyes of the catalogue's compiler in 1895, a picture painted in 1889 appears persuasively old enough. The name "Will Hewes," which imperfectly preserves the archaic spelling inscribed on Cyril's forged portrait, surprisingly identifies the subject without any reference to Wilde's story, as if Will Hew(e)s were indeed a plausible historical personage who could have been depicted in an old oil painting. The catalogue compiler has perhaps unwittingly accomplished what Cyril tries and fails to do in the story: to transform Willie Hughes into a real person. In the catalogue, as in Wilde's story, Willie Hughes nonetheless remains "a personality around whom a great deal of representation clusters – all of it false."[85]

Desperately Seeking Oscar

After the Tite Street sale, the loss of this Wilde relic provoked several attempts to locate and recover it, such as Ledger's inquiry of Ricketts that led the artist, in 1912, to sketch Mr W.H. for him. The pursuit of the portrait thus registers a fan-like fascination with a famous author among a group of men that is matched only by the commensurate fascination of Wilde's characters with Shakespeare. If the fictional portrait of Mr W.H. speaks to the "secrets" of Shakespeare's life, for Wilde devotees such as Richard Charles Jackson, Walter Ledger, and Christopher Millard, the Ricketts painting tells tales about Wilde's.

Although the painting of Willie Hughes is recorded in the Tite Street sale catalogue as merely another of Wilde's possessions, his portrait is not unconnected to one of the defining moments in the legend of Wilde's tragic downfall. By all accounts, the bankruptcy auction-sale of Wilde's household property that took place on 24 April 1895 was a

11

116 *A crayon drawing of a Nude Female at a Fountain,* attributed Whistler, framed
117 Two Arundel Society Publications, coloured prints
118 An oil painting, Study of a Head, by J. Carol Beckwith, exhibited, a ditto, Head—Jasmyn, a ditto, An Angel, by A. D. May, a ditto, Chinaman, by T. Wores
119 A Japanese picture, framed
120 An old oil painting, on panel, Group of Figures, ebony frame
121 A clever pen and ink sketch of Group of Figures signed and dated, and pencil sketch of a Figure, oak frames
122 An etching of a Lady, by Menpes after W. Graham Robertson, and a Manuscript Poem, by Keats, framed
123 A pencil sketch of a Lady, by Whistler, and 2 crayon full length figures, framed
124 A crayon drawing, The Editor of the Spirit Lamp at work by W. H. Rothingham, and a crayon Group, framed
125 An old oil painting of Will Hewes, framed
126 A water colour drawing, by H. O'Neill 1875, View of Cashel
127 An Etching proof, on Japanese paper, by J. Bastian Lapage, portrait of Sarah Bernhardt, and another portrait of same with autographs
128 A proof Etching, a portrait of Ellen Terry, and an engraving, La Cigale
129 Two photos of full length figures, framed, and a small Etching
130 A water colour drawing by H. O'Neil, View in county Monaghan, and another of Mountain Stream

2 Item number 125 in the Tite Street sale catalogue, 1895. Robert Ross Memorial Collection, University College, Oxford.

sad and chaotic affair animated by greed, prurient snooping, and homophobia. Many of Wilde's papers were simply stolen in what Wilde's first biographer, Robert Sherard, described as the "pillage of an unprotected house."[86] According to Thomas Wright, Wilde's house "was plundered by a frenzied crowd of curiosity hunters who had come in search of mementoes of the 'monster.'"[87] The crowd was not restricted to those hostile to Wilde, however. The curious also included sympathizers, such as Frederick Keppel, who attended the sale and explored the empty Wilde family house. He witnessed people "filling their pockets" with "papers which for the most part seemed to be mss. of Wilde's plays," and recorded that the "whole scene impressed me with deep melancholy [...] I could not but think what a terrible end to a home – a life perhaps – which had been so great a factor in spreading the gospel of beauty in our land."[88] Keppel's recourse to religious language is telling. In evoking Wilde's cultural impact through such language ("gospel"), Keppel draws on and reconfigures the myth-making that attended Wilde's entire career: Wilde was mocked as an "Apostle" who propagated a "gospel of intensity" in his lectures about aestheticism in the early 1880s, and, as we shall see in the next chapter, his figuration as a martyr was culturally pervasive.[89] For his part, Keppel sought mementoes or relics at the auction; he purchased several of Wilde's books.

A haul of a different kind was acquired by the eccentric collector Richard Charles Jackson, who "confessed to [Keppel] that he was among the crowd of depredation at Wilde's sale."[90] Jackson, who dressed sometimes as an Anglo-Catholic monk, styled himself "Brother à Becket," and was reputedly the inspiration for Walter Pater's *Marius the Epicurean*,[91] may not be an entirely reliable witness. Nevertheless, he recorded in 1897 his own memories of the Tite Street sale in a book he acquired there: Wilde's unique bound copy of the *Blackwood's* periodical version of "The Portrait of Mr. W.H.," which was accompanied by the 1889 letter to Wilde from William Blackwood accepting the story for publication. For Jackson, this book was not so sacred that he declined to write in it. The majority of his annotations are neatly presented in brown ink, although they are occasionally punctuated by outbursts of fervour in bright red, such as this exclamation, which could only emanate from the hands (and thoughts) of a fan: "This is Oscar Wilde's own copy."

Jackson bought a number of items at the sale, including the "beautiful antique Persian needlework carpet" from Wilde's study and what the *Manchester Weekly Times* dubbed "the chief curio offered for sale": a desk advertised in the catalogue (probably inaccurately) as having been Thomas Carlyle's.[92] As Rebecca N. Mitchell has shown, the desk's provenance was quickly disputed by the Carlyle family, leading one journalist to observe dryly that "the purchaser of a sensation has got very good value for his 14½ guineas. If it weren't the writing table of Mr. Thomas Carlyle, it was unquestionably the writing table of

Mr. Oscar Wilde."[93] Jackson reserved his greatest enthusiasm, however, for a relic he did not buy, apparently much to his regret – the painting itself. We can sense this enthusiasm's hold on him, more than two years after the Tite Street sale, when Jackson writes in the fly-leaf of Wilde's book about the links among Ricketts's "old oil painting," the tantalizing mystery of Mr W.H., and Wilde himself that continued to beguile him. On 8 October 1897, Jackson excitedly recorded his "mad" reaction to "The Portrait of Mr. W.H.":

> This is one of the most fascinating *brochures* which I have ever had the pleasure of reading – shall I be madman enough to interest myself in this "Willie Hews!" May I repeat "shall I," since to my eyes this identical portrait – this impudent forgery (as regards the painting is concerned), has been twice exhibited? [...] This portrait of "Mr. W.H." is lot no. 125 in the catalogue and is described as follows: "an oil painting Will Hewes, framed." This picture I saw at the sale, I also saw it at the shop of the bookseller who purchased it – and on the "morrow" of to-day I am hastening to Brompton to enquire all I can about its "fate," and present whereabouts.[94]

Gripped in real life by the enchantment of Mr W.H. (indistinguishable here from the emergent mystique of Oscar Wilde), Jackson hastened to trace the picture he neglected to obtain. He did not meet with success.

A few days later he visited the painting's purchaser, a dealer called Edwin Parsons. By his own account, Jackson pursued the portrait vigorously: "On visiting Mr. Parsons," he writes on the fly-leaf, and "after *thumping* the matter of this picture into him, he remembered the picture well – he bought it himself at the sale of Oscar Wilde and sold it also to a gentleman, who knew well what he purchased – that the said picture really *was* a genuine work of art, for the sum of five pounds; but he did not know *his* name nor remember him now."[95] In these two dated entries, Jackson transforms Wilde's "own copy" of "The Portrait of Mr. W.H." into a diary recording his pursuit of the painting. His life and Wilde's fiction merge in a single – and unique – book. Writing himself into the story (and yet narrating a new story at the same time) and amalgamating details of his day-to-day life into Wilde's personal volume, Jackson is as dazzled by the idea of Willie Hughes as are Cyril, Erskine, and the unnamed narrator in Wilde's story. In this anecdote the image of Willie Hughes, like Wilde himself, still has a capacity to engender fascination and to inspire the collecting of artefacts that emblematize that fascination. But for Jackson, however, the material instantiation of Willie Hughes – a kind of fetish object – functions as an adjunct to Wilde, not to Shakespeare. This picture exercises its magic in two ways; as an "impudent forgery" that is also "a genuine work of art," in Jackson's words, this unrecoverable vestige of Oscar Wilde shimmers between reality and fantasy. Sold to an anonymous "gentleman" and now lost to public view, the Ricketts portrait of Mr W.H. has become another Wilde legend.

Many years after Jackson's fleeting encounter with the portrait, its loss continued to inspire both longing and artistic production. It may have disappeared, but Wilde's most ardent fans certainly did not forget it. Christopher Millard, Wilde's bibliographer, and his collaborator Walter Ledger, the Wilde collector, sought to recover and preserve as much of Wilde's legacy as they could, as we shall see in the next chapter. Millard was an ingenious researcher, and he tried in 1911 to trace the painting by means of an annotated copy of the (by then extremely rare) Tite Street catalogue. He wrote to Ledger: "I bought a few weeks ago (at a rather tall price, I fear) a priced catalogue of the Tite Street Sale in 1895: by it I hope to trace the whereabouts of Ricketts's picture which was to illustrate 'Mr. W.H.'"[96] Like Jackson's earlier efforts, Millard's were clearly stymied, since the hunt would soon be carried on by Ledger using a new tactic: rather than pursuing the painting's purchaser, he went, as we have seen, back to its creator, Ricketts. It turns out that Ricketts had been keen to obtain the painting too, as he explained to Ledger: "It is now 23 years ago, that I painted Mr. W.H. for Oscar Wilde. I have no sketch of it & no photograph. I did not know that it had figured in the Sale; in fact I was told by a friend, who had undertaken to purchase it for me, that it did not turn up at the auction. This has been corroborated by my friend Robert Ross, who, independently, was on the look out for it […] I had imagined therefore that it had got lost or stolen, before, or during the sale, in which many low-class dealers and their men were present."[97]

Ricketts's version of the events of the sale differs from Jackson's (and the catalogue's) with regard to the painting, but his eagerness to recover it *for himself* suggests some competitive pique at Ledger's request for even a "sketch" or a "photograph" – for what would amount to a trace of a trace of Wilde. It is the Wilde association that persists for both Ricketts and Ledger in the letter's categories of artistic representation, which are listed in order of diminishing immediacy, from painting to sketch to photograph. Despite the passage of twenty-three years Ledger's curiosity about the painting's disappearance has the amazing capacity to spark Mr W.H.–related enthusiasm anew – this time, within the artist himself. Within a few days of this letter Ricketts had apparently softened towards Ledger and produced the tiny pencil drawing of "Mr. W.H." that we encountered at the opening of this book. Ricketts's sketch miniaturizes what Wilde labelled a "Clouet of the highest *artistic* value"; this is an appropriate format since Clouet was a Renaissance miniaturist. At Ledger's request, Ricketts forged Mr W.H. all over again, and his diminutive substitute for the lost painting encapsulates a larger narrative about Oscar Wilde and the "passionate adoration" and "strange worship" (as Cyril says of Shakespeare's feelings for Willie Hughes) that his literary legacy inspired among aficionados like Ledger.[98]

That logic of authorial association entranced Jackson, who thrilled to possess "Oscar Wilde's own copy" of "The Portrait of Mr. W.H." I have observed that Jackson's Wilde book functions as a diary, but it is also an archive, for it preserves not only Jackson's commentary on Wilde's text but also a letter (from Blackwood) and a pasted newspaper clipping recounting the publisher John Lane's disavowal of Wilde during the 1895 trials.[99] Among fans like Jackson, Keppel, Ledger, and Millard the circulation of Wildean relics comes to mirror the enthusiasm depicted in his writing, in which desired objects have the power to forge homosocial – and, as we shall see more explicitly in the next chapter, queer – communities. Writing about the forged portrait in "Mr. W.H.," Aviva Briefel notes that "transmission of the portrait from one individual to another [...] sutures the men into a tight group."[100] This observation could just as easily be made about the connections forged among the men who pursued the lost "authentic Clouet."

Preserved in the archival world of Wilde fandom shared by Ledger and Millard, the tiny sketch passed briefly into the public sphere after Millard's death in 1927. When it came onto the market at the Dulau & Co. auction of Wilde material in 1928, the sketch, "made for Millard when he was preparing his bibliography," was described in the auction catalogue as having been "intended to portray a rough idea of the *Portrait of Mr. W.H.*"[101] It sold for thirty shillings – an increase of nearly 50 per cent in price over what the "original" painting had achieved at the Tite Street sale in 1895. The inverse proportion between the increased value and the diminished scale of this trace of Wilde affords a perfect illustration of what Joseph Bristow has described as the "escalating material value attached to Wilde's legacy."[102] By the 1920s, collectors were willing to pay ever-higher prices for increasingly minimal material traces of Oscar Wilde.

Finally, we can regard the sketch of "Mr. W.H." (see figure 1) as the product of desire (transmitted from Millard and Ledger to Ricketts and shared between Ricketts and Ledger) for Mr W.H.'s tangibility, and thus for the material persistence of Oscar Wilde. What is new here, however, is that the nature of this desire could now be characterized as archival or memorial. Wilde's mythic Willie Hughes – to say nothing of Shakespeare – recedes from view, only to be subsumed into the larger legend of Wilde himself. Ricketts's 1912 sketch represents the posthumous manufacture of a piece of the Wilde legacy, in a manner that resembles the pattern that emerged in the 1920s as the Wilde forgeries began to circulate. In parallel with the story that "The Portrait of Mr. W.H." tells about Shakespeare, the Wilde forgeries discussed in the following chapters are biofictions: they tell elaborately theatrical stories – and lies – about Wilde's life and his writing; they are forged objects that someone *wants* to be true. Forgers and forgeries dramatize fictitious narratives about Wilde that can only be verified by a textual artefact (be it a book, a manuscript, or even an inscription) that can be as alluring as it is unreliable. As we shall see in the next chapter, it was to be the challenge of Wilde's posthumous admirers and champions to assess, and to separate, both the allure and the unreliability of their culture's representations of Oscar Wilde.

The Range of Chapters

Beautiful Untrue Things has four further chapters, three of which (chapters 2, 3, and 4) are case studies of specific episodes in the annals of Wilde forgery. In each of them a forger creates textual myths about Oscar Wilde; these are representations whose claims to authenticity (simultaneously biographical, epistemological, and commercial) are grounded in a sense of Wilde occupying a place at once central to, and yet marginal in, British literary culture. By tracing a history of the production and circulation of Wilde forgeries in the 1920s, I do not seek to authenticate Wilde "originals" or to construct a parallel canon of apocrypha,[103] but rather to illuminate the cultural work done by the rich signifying power of Wilde's name in the literary marketplace. We could designate this cultural work by the name of fan fiction, and one of this book's core arguments is that such fan fictions are forged upon a foundation of facts. The compilation and dissemination of such information by Wilde loyalists and bibliophiles, which I call *fan fact*, is the subject of chapter 1.

Despite their diverse circumstances Wilde forgers also maintained a consistent emphasis on Wilde's Irish identity. In the cases of the Irish-born Mrs Chan-Toon (née Mary Mabel Cosgrove) and Hester Travers Smith, for instance, claims of familial and national affiliation worked to consolidate and authenticate fictitious personal connections with the playwright. Such authenticatory manoeuvres disclose Oscar Wilde's literary and personal legacy as the site of a complex and layered form of textual desire for these forgers as well as for those obsessed with unmasking their forgeries. The most memorably aggressive and aggrieved member of the latter category would certainly be the bibliographer Christopher Millard, whose interventions into Wilde's archival afterlife crop up throughout this book and are explored in most detail in chapters 1 and 4. Shared by Wilde's posthumous defenders and forgers alike, this textual desire reveals these figures as players in an ongoing drama whose absent star they alternately impersonated, appropriated, and defended.

Each of the chapters in this book borrows its heading from a Wilde title – and then reforges it. Chapter 1, "The Importance of Being Authentic," considers the publishing activities undertaken by those loyal to Wilde's memory in the years immediately following his death in 1900. Wilde's close friend and literary executor Robert Ross, the bibliographer Christopher Millard, and the collector Walter Ledger responded to fraudulent representations of Wilde by articulating an official literary identity for the Irish writer. This tightly knit group of gay men employed editing, compiling, cataloguing, and publishing to counteract the pirated and misattributed Wilde titles that dominated the market in the first decade of the twentieth century. Laying in the process the scholarly and archival foundations for Wilde studies, these men aimed to establish a definitive canon cleansed of dubious texts that they felt misrepresented Wilde's authorial persona. They worked to rehabilitate Wilde by consolidating his textual corpus and pursued this task by making books together, such as Ross's fourteen-volume collected edition of Wilde's *Works* (1908) and Millard's *Bibliography of Oscar Wilde* (1914). This chapter thus traces the bibliographical history of Wilde books at the moment his canon was first being assembled. By emphasizing Wilde's genuine writings, the official canon excised the inauthentic intruders, which Ross designated "risky books" because they told stories that Wilde's partisans wanted to disavow.[104] Wilde forgeries, of course, were predicated on precisely the "risk" that Ross hoped to banish.

Chapter 2, "The Picture of Dorian Hope," concerns the Wilde forgeries – autograph plays, poems, letters, and other ephemera – that a shadowy figure known as Dorian (or Sebastian) Hope circulated on the rare-book market in 1921–2. Hope moved from New York to London and to Paris, peddling manuscript forgeries as he impersonated the French writers André Gide and Pierre Louÿs, both of whom had been friends of Wilde's. This forger's ostentatious pseudonym enacts a highly self-conscious mode of Wildean self-fashioning, and my analysis of the Dorian Hope forgeries emphasizes the queer coordinates of Wilde's authorial persona and legend. The unpublished manuscript poems and letters disseminated by Hope under Wilde's name, for instance, ingeniously exploit homoerotic codes in order to authenticate their representation of Wilde. Hope's surviving letters from the period offer a glimpse of a campy persona who performed aristocratic femininity by referring to himself, for example, as the "Dowager Empress of Iceland." Hope is by far the most mysterious and elusive figure whose Wildean literary performances I recover in this study. Despite scholarly speculation that Hope may have been Wilde's nephew Fabian Lloyd, who under the pseudonym Arthur Cravan claimed that Wilde was still alive in the 1910s, we can now prove that at least some of the Dorian Hope forgeries were contrived by an American poet called Brett Holland (1898–1934). That being said, I am less interested in establishing the forger's real name (if indeed "Dorian Hope" was a single person) than in investigating the acts of identity construction and manipulation articulated through the material lies that he (or they) invented about Wilde. In the case of Dorian Hope, theatrical personae, fictions, and lies prove more instructive than truths.

Chapter 3, "Pen, Pencil, and Planchette," examines the Wilde legends collaboratively fabricated by the spiritualist circle surrounding Hester Travers Smith (1868–1949), whose record of contact with Wilde's ghost, *Psychic Messages from Oscar Wilde*, appeared in 1924. Travers Smith was the daughter of the Victorian Shakespeare scholar Edward Dowden, who was acquainted with the Wilde family in nineteenth-century Dublin. *Psychic Messages* is a literary performance whose authenticatory manoeuvres, including the public intervention and support of Arthur Conan Doyle, anticipate, paradoxically, its denunciation as a hoax. Haunted by doubts of its own authenticity, the archive of spectral communications – of which *Psychic Messages* is only a portion – ingeniously literalizes the metaphor of the ghost-writer, one whose participation in literary production is concealed under another's name. Despite the sensation achieved by *Psychic Messages*, Travers Smith found less success with another document purportedly derived from contact with Wilde's ghost: an unpublished and unperformed three-act play entitled "Is It a Forgery?" This drama, recorded by planchette at Travers Smith's Ouija board, summons the style of *The Importance of Being Earnest*, the content of *The Picture of Dorian Gray*, and the plot elements of a lesser-known neo-Wildean novel, George Sylvester Viereck's *The House of the Vampire* (1907). The ghost play's title poses self-conscious questions about its dubious provenance and about the theatrical aspects of Travers Smith's enterprise. The return by "Wilde" to playwriting in the 1920s marks him as a revenant haunting modern British theatre, over which his dramatic style retained considerable influence.

Chapter 4, "The Devoted Fraud," explores the literary larcenies of the most successful of all Wilde forgers, the Cork native Mary Mabel Chan-Toon Wodehouse Pearse, née Cosgrove (b. 1873), otherwise known as Mrs Chan-Toon. In 1922 she persuaded Methuen to publish *For Love of the King: A Burmese Masque* as a Wilde play on the strength of her imaginary connection with its supposed author. Not only did she write it herself, but also, in forging Wilde, Mrs Chan-Toon audaciously recycled a title and plot that she had previously used for a short story published in 1900. A forger, impostor, and thief who was notorious in 1920s London and Paris for her theatrical attire, which included an opera cloak and a parrot constantly perched on her shoulder, Mrs Chan-Toon was also a prolific novelist; many of her writings are strongly marked by Wilde's influence. In forging a Wilde play suffused with an exoticism recalling *Salome* and Wilde's decadent phase, Mrs Chan-Toon engages in a cross-gendered literary imposture that is, crucially, also cross-cultural: *For Love of the King*'s setting and reliance on Burmese folklore link the play to her own writings on colonial life, such as the semi-autobiographical novel *A Marriage in Burmah* (1905). In this chapter I also show how biographical embroidery becomes an indispensable authenticatory technique for Mrs Chan-Toon, who once claimed – outrageously – to have been engaged to Wilde's brother Willie. A dedicatory letter published along with the play, explaining the provenance of *For Love of the King*, is a tour-de-force pastiche of Wilde's overwrought style, and its preface seeks to validate the play's attribution to Wilde by performing the voice of its putative author, who refers in homoerotic code to an aristocratic male lover. Despite the self-evidently commercial motivations underpinning Mrs Chan-Toon's impersonations, we might also construe her Wildean performances as fan-fictional homage to a literary idol.

My conclusion, "The Teacher of Fandom," introduces previously unexplored amateur forgeries of Wilde to illustrate the long history of forging his hand as an expression of desire for intimacy with the writer. In doing so, *Beautiful Untrue Things* also returns to where it began, by assessing the "fannish" and theatrical coordinates of the publisher Mitchell Kennerley's edition of *The Portrait of Mr. W.H.* (1921). The story of the recovery of that text's "lost manuscript," like the search for the lost Ricketts painting that begins this book, reinforces the recursive patterns of mystery and longing that the conjunction of Oscar Wilde and forgery continues to inspire.

Chapter One

The Importance of Being Authentic

Despite the seductive capacity of a forgery, such as the portrait of Mr W.H., to activate (if not to satisfy) aesthetic desires and fantasies, a duplicitous representation in art or literature remains tethered to its conceptual counterpart. In other words, forgery has no meaning without authenticity. There is no such thing as a fake without *at least the idea* of the real thing; both inhere in how we perceive authorship, the creative human presence behind the work. But what does the real thing look like when it emanates from Oscar Wilde, a writer who, as we have seen, not only championed the artistry of the unreal and the inauthentic but also was at times culturally marked as an impostor and a charlatan? Before we explore the Wilde forgeries that proliferated in print and in manuscript in the 1920s, we need to understand the unique state of affairs that made the mass of forgeries possible and perhaps even inevitable. This state of affairs had a momentous impact on the production and circulation in the 1900s and 1910s of texts bearing Wilde's name – not all of which were authored by him – before the mass of forgeries appeared. Such an understanding demands, in the first instance, a full accounting of the Wilde legend that flourished after his death in 1900, especially its rhetoric of martyrdom and sainthood. It also requires, in the second instance, an accounting of the dispersal and constitution, or reconstitution, of the Wilde archive, the hallmark of which was authorial authenticity. This chapter traces the bibliographical history of Wilde (and non-Wilde) books at the moment his canon was being assembled by a small group of gay men, and recovers their production of yet another Wilde legend, that of "real Oscar Wilde,"[1] to borrow a term from the biographer Robert Sherard. Before we encounter the fakes, we need to acquaint ourselves with the real thing.

In the first decade of the twentieth century the name Oscar Wilde was for many a byword for legend and scandal. It was indelibly associated with the 1895 trials' judicial finding of "gross indecency" and with the collapse of a stellar literary career into exile, poverty, and early death. According to the painter Walford Graham Robertson, "in the years that have passed since [Wilde's] death, the memory of the real Oscar Wilde has faded and has been replaced by a strange simulacrum, half invented by the curious, half dictated by the man himself."[2] Far from being forgotten by literary history, Wilde retained a powerful influence (albeit a contested one) over the early-twentieth-century imagination. His status as a legend – that "strange simulacrum" identified by Robertson – inheres in two indelible facets of his reputation: first, the sense that Wilde both illustrates and embodies the total merger of life with literature and was thus a player in his own drama; second, that he was *the* representative figure of an era in literary history. Wilde said as much of himself in *De Profundis* when he opined, "I awoke the imagination of my century so that it created myth and legend around me."[3] (This statement certainly proved a prophetic description of the *next* century as well.) His contemporary Richard Le Gallienne famously echoed this portrait of Wilde as a "symbolic figure" in his 1926 book *The Romantic '90s*. For Le Gallienne, since Wilde "summoned up so completely the various aspects and tendencies of his time, he has become its symbolic figure. He is, beyond comparison, the incarnation of the spirit of the '90s."[4] Le Gallienne's view was an influential contribution to what, by the 1920s, was the growing – but not always accurate – print record of Wilde's afterlife. In elaborating the records of this legacy, and their vulnerability to false representations such as forgery, I emphasize the supernatural resonances of the notion of an afterlife: like a revenant spirit, the early-twentieth-century Wilde was defined by damnation and redemption, by loss and recovery; he was conjured into being by defenders and detractors alike, and his legacy was more often met with strong feelings than with indifference. His was a memory, in sum, that inspired considerable partisanship, and throughout the 1900s and 1910s that partisanship (and the legends that informed it) contributed to the building, and the purging, of the Wilde archive.

In the years following the death of Wilde, his most vigorous defenders sought to revivify the writer's status by intervening materially into an afterlife that they tried to frame and, predictably, to control, but not always with full success. However, as subsequent chapters of *Beautiful Untrue Things* will show, a diverse and inventive suite of forgers could prove equally compelling keepers of Wilde's memory. The Wilde legend thus inspired intersecting forms of fandom, for it had the capacity to accommodate forgers' criminally imitative homage, on the one hand, and partisans' hyper-protective admiration, on the other. It is the hope (and challenge) of this book to reveal the surprising parallels between these two sets of Oscar Wilde aficionados, both of whom produced texts that had a material impact on Wilde's afterlife. This chapter attends to the first set, whose members included the bibliophiles Robert Ross, Christopher Millard, and Walter Ledger. The key difference between Ross's, Ledger's, and Millard's respective approaches to constructing and exhibiting the "real Oscar Wilde" to the world can best be described as one of tone, which might also index personal (queer) politics. This group of loyalists often worked as a collective, but their respective investments in Wilde and his literary legacy were nonetheless marked by their distinct personalities. Ross, the Establishment art critic, is persistently but cautiously defensive; Millard, the outspoken individualist, protests vocally and aggressively; and Ledger, the retiring suburban bachelor, shuns publicity altogether. In the vein of the original forgery at the centre of "The Portrait of Mr. W.H.," the legend of the "real Oscar Wilde" is forged by a collective homosocial enthusiasm shared by a trio of men.

Restorative Bibliography and "the Real Oscar Wilde"

This chapter focuses on the books crafted in the early 1900s by Wilde's self-designated guardians. Wilde's literary executor Robert Ross, Christopher Millard, and Walter Ledger all countered false representations of Wilde by articulating an authorized version of the writer: they insisted on the importance of being authentic. Their "real Oscar Wilde" would be a literary figure that was distinct, they hoped, from the scandalous biographical narratives to which he remained sutured. These Wilde partisans, according to Ellen Crowell, were "colourful individuals who supervised the flow of information about their beloved subject through the obsessive cataloguing, controlling, and concealing of a queer past."[5] Their endeavour to remake – better still, to reforge – Wilde through research and publishing can best be understood as a cluster of material interventions into Wilde's place in literary history. This is a process I call *restorative bibliography*. To rehabilitate Wilde they needed to restore an archive – a body of texts – that had been both literally and figuratively dispersed (along with Ricketts's portrait of Mr W.H.) at the chaotic auction of his literary property. With the common goal of recuperating Wilde's literary reputation from the formative and lasting damage of his 1895 trials, this cast of restorative bibliographers, in Jacques Derrida's terms, exerted "the power of consignation," which is paired with "the functions of unification, of identification, of classification": they "aim[ed] to coordinate a single corpus" by "*gathering together signs*" into a new Wilde archive.[6] They supervised a collaborative enterprise of preserving and listing books and writing others, correcting historical misperceptions, and above all deriving cultural respectability for Wilde from textual order (an established canon of texts) and writerly authenticity (verified authorship). Wilde's restorers thus saw literary history as revisable, not fixed; historical wrongs – such as Wilde's shaming and marginalization – could, with effort, be righted. The politics of their collective archival work were conservative by definition: they believed in undoing history's mistakes by restoring the influence and prestige of an older (literary) order in which Wilde held a place of respect. But theirs was also a queer conservatism that sought for a measure of respectability in disavowing the sexually scandalous; they insisted on a textual, as opposed to a sexual, register for apprehending Oscar Wilde. Such disavowals, as we shall see, did little to undermine the fact that they were also establishing a queer literary history – not unlike what Wilde himself had initiated in the Shakespearean speculations of "The Portrait of Mr. W.H." Among Ross, Millard, and Ledger, restorative bibliography demanded co-operation, scholarly commitment, and strong feelings of loyalty to Wilde's memory. It also, ironically, enabled their worst nightmare: an astonishing efflorescence of Wilde forgeries.

For this tightly knit group of gay men, the work of editing, compiling, cataloguing, and publishing Wilde's writings could be employed as a rebuke to what Ross dubbed "the demonstrations of knaves and fools."[7] The knaves and fools they wished to counter operated in print, and so print was the appropriate medium for their response. During the first decade of the twentieth century such "demonstrations" were most readily discernible in unauthorized Wilde publications – in other words, false and misleading representations of Wilde's authorship. These publications were not what we might call the "true forgeries" that we shall encounter in later chapters, but instead included pirated printings of Wilde's writings and disreputable apocrypha like the homoerotic tale *The Priest and the Acolyte*, which had been sensationally misattributed to Wilde following the trials.[8] Although piracies and misattributions do not conform to a narrow definition of literary forgery, which, as we have seen in Harold Love's formulation, is a "work composed with the intention to deceive and then promulgated under the name of another,"[9] they do, like forgeries, reorganize the coordinates of authorship along dubious and deceptive lines. In other words, they could produce similar *effects*. Such disruptive items had no place in the official story that Ross and his colleagues wanted to tell, and distinctions between piracies, misattributions, and forgeries mattered little to them. These unreliable texts were seen to be just as damaging to the textual authenticity of the "real Oscar Wilde." Laying the scholarly and archival foundations for Wilde studies, these men worked to rehabilitate Wilde by consolidating his body of work, and they pursued this task by making (and repudiating) books, thereby refashioning and repackaging the dead writer. Robert Ross, for instance, carefully edited and abridged the 1897 prison letter he called *De Profundis*, which met with considerable commercial success when he published it posthumously with Methuen in 1905. *De Profundis* was followed in 1908 by a massive edition of Wilde's writings, the *Collected Works*. This fourteen-volume project was made possible by Ledger and Millard's extensive bibliographical research into Wilde's literary career. It established previously unpublished texts as part of the Wilde canon and reintroduced texts that had fallen out of print. With these books in circulation, Ross and his colleagues hoped that the Wilde canon would be both complete and accurate, with the name of the author affixed to a recognized corpus of texts under the unassailably respectable Methuen imprint.

Wilde, however, was not just any author. His association with extra-literary legend and homosexual scandal rendered him uniquely vulnerable to a set of market conditions that fostered spurious texts published under his name. Christopher Millard suggestively termed the miasma of misunderstanding that surrounded Wilde "a vague fog of obscenity."[10] Clearing that fog was the challenge undertaken by these restorative bibliographers. During the Edwardian years and beyond, Ross and his allies were trying to purify a situation largely beyond their control. They had two big problems. The first was the dispersal of many of Wilde's manuscripts in 1895 at the Tite Street sale and during the associated looting of literary property housed there. The second was pirates. Almost everything Wilde had written had been pirated within a few years of his death by two publishers, Leonard Smithers in London and Charles Carrington in Paris,[11] both of whom issued numerous Wilde titles as so-called private printings in limited runs. In defiance of copyright, piracies masquerading as "private printings" effectively robbed the Wilde literary estate (of which Ross was executor) of income. Doubtful attributions, moreover, such as Latin and French erotic texts translated purportedly by "Sebastian Melmoth" (Wilde's post-prison alias) and issued by the flamboyant Carrington, traded on Wilde's reputation as a sexual outlaw.[12] In an ironic echo of the actions of the publishers, whom they saw as their opponents, under the management of Ross and his set the books *by* Oscar Wilde remained books *about* Oscar Wilde – although theirs was the Wilde they wanted the world to see. By foregrounding authentic Wilde texts, the official canon excluded the inauthentic ones – those that Ross called "risky books" because they told the wrong stories.[13] Nevertheless, as Joseph Bristow notes, "the more that disciples such as Ledger, Millard, and Ross tried to establish a firm bibliographical basis on which to appreciate Wilde's career, the more readily this legendary author became the object of peculiar fantasies, including their own."[14]

One of the major difficulties for these men, whom Ellen Crowell dubs "the gatekeepers of Wilde's posthumous legacy,"[15] was that, when Wilde died in 1900, most of his books had fallen out of print. (A few Wilde titles, such as *The Happy Prince* and *The Soul of Man*, remained in print with their authorized publishers despite the collapse of Wilde's reputation.) Their scarcity is suggested in a 1905 auction-sale catalogue of the collection of Richard Butler Glaenzer, which notes that "his books are sought by the collector and bibliographer at almost fabulous prices."[16] Despite its attenuated hyperbole ("almost fabulous"), this claim draws attention to the association of Wilde's books – his material traces – with fables and legends and with commercial value; it also points to the borders between truth and fiction, the believable and the unbelievable. When it came to many of the Wilde books then in circulation, acquiring information about what had been published, when, and by whom was crucial for Ross and his fellow "gatekeepers" to retake editorial and financial control of his literary legacy. By assessing the work of restorative bibliography undertaken by Wilde's posthumous champions, I explore the complex responses that such "risky books" provoked in the individuals whom the Glaenzer sale catalogue terms "the collector and bibliographer." I argue, moreover, that the work of curating, compiling, and collecting supervised by this coterie of Wilde admirers sought to remake literary history by transforming their private Wildean treasures into (bookish) public monuments. By means of books and a public memorial they effectively turned Wilde from reviled sexual outlaw to saint.

The Curator: Robert Ross

Writing to Wilde's son Vyvyan Holland in 1908, Robert Ross confessed that "[e]verything connected with your father has a sort of sacrosanct halo around it for me."[17] As Richard Kaye observes, "an exalted, sometimes semidisguised rhetoric of sainthood determined Wilde's twentieth-century afterlife."[18] Of course, this affiliation with martyrdom began with Wilde himself; it can be seen in his choice in 1897 of "Sebastian Melmoth" as an alias for his exile on the European continent, which combines the name of a favourite saint redolent with homoerotic associations and the surname of the hunted protagonist from his great-uncle Charles Maturin's 1820 gothic novel *Melmoth the Wanderer*. As Michèle Mendelssohn notes, such devotional rhetoric has only intensified over the years, for "today Wilde's sainthood is secure. He has become gay history's Christ figure."[19] That Wilde could be seen as saintly, however, could also be turned against his defenders, and a full understanding of Ross's confession requires us to acknowledge the jealous and competitive struggle over Wilde's memory between the literary executor and Lord Alfred "Bosie" Douglas, the lover for whose sake Wilde arguably went to prison. Although he was an outspoken homosexual apologist in his youth – the famous poetic line that Wilde defended in court about "the love that dare not speak its name" is Douglas's, not Wilde's – Douglas became increasingly homophobic and alienated from the circle of Wilde loyalists surrounding Ross after the death of the writer whom they both loved. By around 1910, Laura Lee records, "those who had been attracted to Bosie for his youthful idealism and his sexual boldness no longer related to him, and as their feelings about him changed, in many cases so did their memories. The further Bosie moved from the homosexual community, the more they were inclined to blame him for Wilde's downfall."[20] Ross and Douglas each felt betrayed by the other, and as Ross's restorative projects on Wilde's behalf progressed through the 1900s, Douglas went from devoted disciple of Wilde to aggressive antagonist of Ross, refusing to play the role of Judas that he felt Ross had scripted for him. Anxious to dissociate himself from Wilde's queer following, Douglas snidely referred to Ross and his associates as a "coterie of long-haired persons who weep at the mention of 'dear Oscar's' name and hold him up for a saint and martyr."[21]

Oscar Wilde had anointed Ross the caretaker of his legacy by naming him literary executor once he was released from prison, and, in presenting Wilde to the world after the writer's death, Ross had the challenge of rendering the "sacrosanct halo" of saintliness visible to the public at large and to promote it. Ross retained a deep personal investment in Wilde's memory throughout his life.[22] According to some accounts Ross had, in 1886 and at the age of seventeen, become Wilde's first male lover,[23] and he remained Wilde's closest friend and confidante, devotedly supporting him both emotionally and financially during and after the trials. The role of chief disciple was one that Ross crafted for himself, and he actively encouraged the narrative of his own steadfast loyalty – a position that became increasingly strident and controlling as his public battles with Alfred Douglas over Wilde's legacy intensified into the 1910s. A prominent art critic, man of letters, and gallerist – he was part owner of London's Carfax Art Gallery – Ross logically adopted a curatorial approach to the materials – the textual relics – that he termed "Oscar Wilde's literary remains."[24]

Not everything Wilde had written had been published at his death in 1900, and the longest and certainly the most significant of these "remains" was the letter that Ross published as *De Profundis* in 1905, following the advice of Methuen's E.V. Lucas. Although it was addressed to "Dear Bosie" (Alfred Douglas), Ross appointed himself as the letter's custodian and held on to it once Wilde was released from prison, perhaps out of fear that its harrowing denunciation of Douglas would lead its outraged addressee to destroy it. Douglas and Ross have left competing accounts of the letter's transmission, with Douglas insisting he never received the copy of the letter that Ross contended had been prepared for him, and in 1905 the world's first readers of *De Profundis* assumed that it had been addressed to Ross. Publishing the autobiographical prison letter that Wilde had originally called "Epistola: In Carcere et Vinculis" with Methuen gave Ross a perfect opportunity to launch his project of rebranding Wilde. Josephine Guy and Ian Small succinctly characterize this endeavour as "Ross's attempt in 1905 to rehabilitate Wilde's reputation with his carefully edited version of *De Profundis*."[25] Indeed, Ross wished to secure a better popular position for Wilde, but only on terms that he could control, and his editorial process counted censorship among its most urgent responsibilities. His construction of Wilde in *De Profundis* was accomplished by scrupulously selecting and arranging Wilde's own words and by providing the text with an editorial apparatus – a paratextual frame for a portrait of Wilde that the publication itself constructs in words. Ross's preface to *De Profundis* begins with an acknowledgment of his role, as he coyly allows that "for a long time considerable curiosity has been expressed about the manuscript of *De Profundis*, which was known to be in my possession."[26] According to this line of argument, the publication of *De Profundis* was a strategic, pre-emptive strike to satisfy the "considerable curiosity" of an audience that might otherwise be satisfied with Wildean representations not endorsed by Ross. This audience proved to be greater than that for any of Wilde's earlier books; in 1905 alone six editions of *De Profundis* were printed, and its sales were such that the profits allowed Ross to retire the Wilde estate's outstanding debts. For his part, Alfred Douglas "was unable to recognize in 1905 that De Profundis originated in a letter to himself."[27]

In the preface Ross clearly articulates the appropriate reception for the Wilde presented in its pages: a suffering and penitent figure, suitable for mass consumption. *De Profundis* inaugurated the myth of Wilde the martyr for a wide readership, and it continues to have an indelible influence on Wilde biography and criticism.[28] This is in no small measure due to Ross's curatorial work of framing, arranging, and expurgating a text that omits any overt reference to homosexuality. In view of the text's "uncertain reception," as Ross's preface to the 1908 edition notes with characteristic understatement, Ross personally undertook "the excision of certain passages,"[29] and indeed the published text of 1905 begins well into the letter, skipping over Wilde's bitter recollections of the troubled and passionate relationship with Alfred Douglas that led him to be imprisoned. *De Profundis* commences instead with a striking observation: "… Suffering is one very long moment. We cannot divide it by seasons. We can only record its moods, and chronicle their return. With us time itself does not progress. It revolves. It seems to circle round one centre of pain."[30] In prison, suffering overrides time itself, collapsing the rhythms of temporality into an undifferentiated cycle of pain, and the repeated pronouns *we* and *us* invite the reader to empathize with the authorial voice. On the page, though, the ellipsis that comes before this opening observation is as conspicuous as the sombre ideas it precedes; it makes visually apparent the fact that this testament is incomplete and that it has been edited and modified. In our first glimpse of *De Profundis*'s Wilde, speaking to us out of the depths of a prison cell, we also observe Ross as editor subtly – yet unmistakably – asserting his authority.

Ross's approach to the more ambitious project that culminated in the 1908 *Collected Works* was similar to his work on *De Profundis*, if considerably larger in scope. Kamran Ahmadgoli and Ian Small have named

Ross a "creative editor"[31] for his interventionist role in shaping Wilde's reception through editing and publishing in this format. For them, Ross was motivated by "an ambition to present [...] the least controversial figure of Wilde as possible."[32] His extensive editorial interventions into Wilde's texts had the cumulative effect, they note, of imposing "a sense of homogeneity and unity" onto Wilde's writings.[33] Ross's edition of the *Collected Works* effected an analogous transformation of Wilde's presence in the literary marketplace with a visually coherent sequence of identical volumes, finely bound with gilt decorations by Charles Ricketts, who had supplied binding designs for several Wilde titles as well as that elusive portrait of Mr W.H. Ricketts's part in rehabilitating Wilde was thus to assert the edition's aesthetic continuity with earlier books carrying Wilde's name. A materially distinguished set of books, the *Collected Works* did "justice to one of Wilde's central preoccupations"[34] – namely, that books under his name should be aesthetically beautiful objects. This set could also transform the unseemly chaos of piracies and misattributions, or what Christopher Millard called "horrid reprints,"[35] by the imposition of order and method. The result would be "an authoritative and collectable product, attractive to the bibliophile, and also partly intended to place [Wilde] firmly within a literary canon."[36] The autobiographical prison letter was incorporated into this official canon as volume XI of the *Collected Works*, along with several letters that Wilde had written to Ross from prison. The text with which Ross had shaped the myth of Wilde as a suffering martyr was in this manner admitted into the books of "the real Oscar Wilde."

As one might expect, the political and aesthetic agenda of the *Collected Works* was reflected in the high price for the set. It cost, in 1908, £8 2s. 6d., or the rough equivalent of £912 in 2018 funds.[37] By editing and publishing the *Collected Works*, Ross was not only promoting his vision of a "real Oscar Wilde" by putting out into the marketplace a critical mass of authentic texts, but also, in effect, building a sort of museum – a textual shrine – dedicated to Wilde, whose exhibits would be displayed in cases of handmade paper and fine bindings. Ross's editorial endeavours, moreover, derived their authority from a culturally prestigious framework – the collected edition of an author's works – that he hoped would secure posthumous cultural and economic capital for his friend.[38] And they did.

The *Collected Works* project also occasioned something of a splash. It was celebrated at a gala dinner held at London's Ritz hotel on 1 December 1908 in recognition of Ross's services as Wilde's literary executor.

Attended by over two hundred guests, the dinner marked the reunion of the surviving members of Wilde's circle, such as Ross, Max Beerbohm, and Ada Leverson, and the integration of new ones, such as Christopher Millard. (Although he was invited, Alfred Douglas declined to attend. It was Ross's show.) In his speech at that event Ross announced his receipt of a £2,000 donation to erect a monumental tomb for Wilde at Paris's Père Lachaise cemetery. The strikingly modernist design, a nude male sphinx described by its sculptor Jacob Epstein as "a flying demon-angel […] a symbolic work of combined simplicity and ornate decoration,"[39] would represent the culmination of all the efforts to recuperate and memorialize Wilde (figure 3). In this aim it has undoubtedly succeeded, since the tomb has become a shrine-like monument in the city of Wilde's exile and death. According to Ellen Crowell, it has "always, for better or worse, stood in as proxy for Wilde's physical body" and as a site for queer pilgrimage and mourning.[40] His admirers over the decades have expressed their veneration in a distinctive way; by leaving the impressions of lipstick kisses on the tomb, they have recorded their affection by marking the stone. But since 2012, no doubt because of an excess of such admiration, the tomb has been protected by a glass wall.

Like Wilde himself, however, the tomb generated its own controversies and scandals in its time, for as Crowell observes, "Epstein's sexed sphinx was read by both admirers and detractors alike as a limestone embodiment of the embattled Celt."[41] Once installed in 1912, the monument provoked the outrage of French authorities, who insisted that the winged figure's male genitalia be covered. Epstein refused, and a group of French artists, led by the writer Georges Bazile and supported by the avant-garde periodical *Action d'art*, issued a petition to the government in protest.[42] Although he had supported Epstein on principle and had written wittily in the *Pall Mall Gazette* that the provocative tomb's fate lay "in the lap of the gods, because that is precisely the part of the statue to which exception is taken,"[43] Ross nevertheless consented to placing on the monument "a large bronze plaque […] to cover the offending appendages,"[44] which was itself later removed in a protest orchestrated by the British occultist Aleister Crowley. Ross's acquiescence on this point is puzzling because he could have chosen an alternative design for the tomb that would have been more in keeping with his cautious approach in print to the queer politics of memorializing Wilde: a sculpture by Charles Ricketts entitled *Silence*. Lacking the demonstrably sexual challenge proffered by Epstein's design, Ricketts's *Silence*, "a

3 The tomb of Oscar Wilde. Courtesy of hasshe.com.

sculpture that seems to imply the viewer's participation in a shared secret history," according to Crowell, "advocates radical reserve as a posthumous protection against normative judgment."[45] This design thus more closely accords with the logic governing Ross's editorial practice. Whatever the reason for Ross's choice of Epstein over Ricketts – who was a member of his (and Wilde's) queer circle – the metallic fig-leaf affixed to the tomb represented a telling compromise, and it, too, recalled Ross's desire to cleanse Wilde of apparent sexual indecency in that other monument – a textual one – called Wilde's *Collected Works*.

For the Père Lachaise monument Ross chose an epitaph consistent with the image of Wilde as a suffering martyr. He extracted from *The Ballad of Reading Gaol* these lines: "And alien tears will fill for him / Pity's long-broken urn / For his mourners will be outcast men, / And outcasts always mourn."[46] By repurposing the lines that the poem applies to an executed murderer, Ross deftly extended the application of the social exclusion imagined in Wilde's poem to the wider public: to mourn for Wilde was to be in solidarity with society's outcasts. As he had done with *De Profundis*, whose opening passage (as edited by Ross) induced empathy for Wilde's suffering, and indeed with the entire *Collected Works*, Ross stage-managed Wilde's memory in his friend's own words at the Parisian tomb. And, for Ross, the tomb's meaning could not have been more personal. At his request, Epstein designed a special chamber at the base of the tomb to encase Ross's ashes, which were placed there in 1950. In death Ross could continue to proclaim his loyalty to Wilde as the writer's chief mourner. United with Wilde in death, he would also become a permanent (if silent) witness to the changing vicissitudes of his friend's place in history.

As editor of the *Collected Works* – of Wilde's textual body – Ross faced the common curatorial challenge of adjudicating between which items to include and which to exclude in exhibiting Wilde to the world. In compiling his edition of Wilde, Ross had not only to acquire copyrights or to arrange royalty agreements with diverse copyright holders but also, just as urgently, to ascertain the status and authenticity of all the various Wilde titles then in circulation. Ross was not universally hostile to everyone publishing Wilde, and he endorsed publications by Wilde loyalists. One such supporter was Arthur Lee Humphreys, manager of London's famous Hatchard's bookshop and a long-time friend of the Wilde family. Humphreys had collaborated with Constance Wilde on a compilation of extracts, entitled *Oscariana*, which was published in 1895 shortly before the trials. As the copyright owner of Wilde's essay "The Soul of Man under Socialism," Humphreys had taken the unusual step of keeping that text in print in multiple editions.[47] Ross approved of Humphreys's efforts to the extent that he contributed a preface praising the publisher's fidelity to Wilde's memory in Humphreys's 1912 edition of that title. According to Ross's "Superfluous Note of Explanation," after the writer's death "only one or two of Wilde's published dramas were to be found in London bookshops; some of the other works being surreptitiously sold in pirated editions. There was, however, one exception. The copyright of 'The Soul of Man' belonged to Mr. Arthur Humphreys, from whom copies could always be obtained."[48] The version of Wilde presented in Humphreys's *Soul of Man* – the principled champion of individualism – did not require extensive editorial intervention from Ross.[49]

More broadly, Ross and his collaborators were both meticulous and fretful in their curatorial practices, especially with regard to those texts "surreptitiously sold in pirated editions." Their joint task required fact-gathering bibliographical research to banish uncertainty; as Ross reminded Millard, "we don't want anything [in the *Collected Works*] that is not by Oscar himself,"[50] and they complained bitterly and publicly about the literary marketplace's version of Wilde that included titles "not by Oscar himself" such as a privately printed edition of *The Priest and the Acolyte*. As a consequence, their task also aimed to reinforce authorial purity; as Ross notes in his introduction to the edition's penultimate volume, *Reviews*, "I have decided [...] to include in the uniform edition of Wilde's work everything *that could be identified as genuine*."[51] Articulating the archival project's logic of authentication, this remark casts restorative bibliography as primarily a task of identifying, categorizing, and endorsing the "genuine."

Wilde's canon, of course, had been porous before the appearance of the *Collected Works* – a worrisome state of affairs for those who sought to assert the authenticity of certain texts to the exclusion of others. Writing to the *Times Literary Supplement* in 1907, Ross detailed the defensive motivation behind his editorial project: "I am fighting," he insists, "for Wilde's literary reputation, which is being [...] jeopardized by the attribution to him of spurious works."[52] Prior to the publication of the *Collected Works*, Ross found the public suggestions that he had received to include so-called less known works by Wilde in his forthcoming edition to be particularly galling because these helpful hints indicated the relatively successful infiltration of dubious texts into the amorphous Wilde canon. In reply to an article appearing in *The Sphere* in 1906, for instance, Ross wrote testily to its editor, Clement Shorter, protesting the persistent legend that Wilde had written *The Priest and the Acolyte*:

> In your delightful "causerie" of the week you kindly express a hope that the new edition of Mr. Oscar Wilde's works may contain some of the less known and privately printed (or may I say *pirated*) works, found for sale by some bookseller, and you mention among others *The Priest and the Acolyte* [...] No one with any knowledge of Wilde's peculiar style could imagine that he was the writer. It is the crude production of an undergraduate; and it is pornographic [...] I think you will agree with me that the ascription to him of worthless and obscene books is a posthumous punishment from which he should be released.[53]

The association of Wilde's name with pornography, even as a by-product of apparent ignorance and curiosity, such as Shorter's, was something that Ross, in his self-appointed role as defender of Wilde's precarious position in English letters, was unwilling to countenance. A February 1908 Methuen prospectus announcing the forthcoming *Collected Works* made Ross's editorial practice of exclusion very clear: "Purged of all nauseous apocrypha such as 'The Priest and the Acolyte,'" the document reads, "it will be seen in the new edition that [Wilde's] work gains by the ensemble; and that it may be regarded frankly and dispassionately without fear, shame, or disinfectant; or, indeed, apparatus of any kind."[54] With his imposing edition, Ross hoped, the "posthumous punishment" of Wilde – a different kind of prison sentence – would finally be commuted.

Litigation (or the threat of it) also remained as defining a feature of Wilde's literary afterlife as it had been at the disastrous climax of his career. After Wilde's death the former members of his circle became enmeshed in multiple courtroom clashes with Alfred Douglas over how the writer was to be remembered. Ellen Crowell aptly characterizes the situation as "vitriolic infighting."[55] Excluded from the Wilde narrative that Ross and his collaborators were carefully crafting, an increasingly conservative and paranoid Douglas believed himself to be the victim of a queer conspiracy led by Ross, whom he eventually dubbed the "High Priest of all the sodomites in London."[56] In Douglas's view, Ross's revival of Wilde's reputation had been accomplished at his expense, and he bitterly resented it: "[I]t was he," Douglas writes, "who was held up to the world as the faithful friend of Wilde [...] the noble disinterested friend, the pure, the holy person, in contrast to the wicked and depraved Alfred Douglas who had 'ruined' Oscar Wilde and 'betrayed' him."[57] Douglas did not attack Ross directly, however; in 1913 he sued Arthur Ransome, author of *Oscar Wilde: A Critical Study*, for libel. Ransome had hinted that Douglas, not Ross, was the true addressee of *De Profundis* with his obliquely damning description of a "letter [...] not addressed to Mr. Ross but to a man to whom Wilde felt that he owed some, at least, of the circumstances of his disgrace."[58] Ransome's book also revealed, without specifying details, that the letter's "rebuke" contained further uncomplimentary references to this unnamed "friend" who could be easily identified as Douglas by anyone possessing a passing familiarity with the Wilde case. Outraged at the *Critical Study*'s suggestion that he had deserted Wilde during the latter's 1897 sojourn in Naples (Ransome had written that Wilde's "friend, as soon as there was no money, left him"),[59] and yet fearful of being identified as homosexual, Douglas felt doubly attacked: from beyond the grave by Wilde and in the pages of a book that owed its existence to the Wilde archive assembled by Ross and his circle.

Ross's approach to the Wilde archive, as we have seen, was characterized by selective emphasis and suppression. The most spectacular instance of the latter, and most provoking to Douglas, was Ross's donation in 1909 of the *De Profundis* manuscript to the British Museum Library, to be sealed from public view for fifty years – and therefore safe from Douglas's interference. Ross retained a typewritten copy of the full letter for himself, and presumably he gave Ransome free access to this document.[60] Ransome recorded his gratitude by dedicating his critically even-handed book to Ross, and he thanked Walter Ledger "for much interesting information, and for the sight of many rare editions of Wilde's books that made possible the correction of several bibliographical errors into which I had fallen."[61] Accuracy, however, was not the primary point of dispute in the libel case *Douglas v. Ransome*. Ross subsidized the critic's legal costs in a sensational trial that became a proxy battle between Ross (who never appeared in the witness stand) and Douglas over how Wilde was to be remembered. The trial was punctuated by revelations that were humiliating for Douglas, for it included a public, courtroom reading of the full text of Wilde's prison letter. Ross, Millard, and those on their side "blamed Douglas for disloyalty to Wilde." But, as Laura Lee succinctly puts it, "greater society did not care about that. They blamed [Douglas] for having been Wilde's lover in the first place. That would be the real focus of the Ransome trial."[62] Ross controlled the records, and those records permitted his lawyers to rehearse facts in the courtroom about Wilde and Douglas's relationship to Douglas's disadvantage. Douglas lost the case in perhaps the most damaging way: although Ransome's book was deemed libellous, the evidence contained in the sealed *De Profundis* proved, when admitted as evidence, that the libels were true and therefore not subject to legal sanction. Eager, we can presume, to avoid further conflict, Ransome deleted the references to Douglas in subsequent editions of his *Critical Study*.

The pugnacious Douglas responded to this setback by taking to print, and he published the first of several autobiographies to retell the Wilde story from his point of view. *Oscar Wilde and Myself*, written in collaboration with T.W.H. Crosland, appeared in 1914. One of the most prominent sources of Douglas's indignation was Ross's control over the Wilde archive and that archive's capacity to generate further textual manifestations of what he labelled the Wilde myth: "[A]t the present moment," Douglas writes, "it is to the interest of everybody directly concerned that the Wilde myth should continue to exist. It is excellent for Wilde's publishers, excellent for the printing, paper, and bookbinding trades, and excellent for those critics and editors who are best known by their labours in connection to Wilde [...] It is also excellent for those depraved persons who take Wilde as their moral guide and who profess to believe [...] that the viciousness for which Wilde suffered imprisonment is a species of superior virtue."[63] Perhaps predictably, the Ransome case was followed by protracted legal wrangling throughout 1914 as the proxy battle over what Wilde had written became a direct fight between Ross, Douglas, and the latter's colleague Crosland as both Ross and Douglas employed "detectives to spy on one another."[64] These conflicts culminated in another libel action in 1914, into which an infuriated Douglas had goaded Ross. In an echo of the Wilde trials, Douglas produced evidence of Ross's homosexuality in court, and eventually Ross had to abandon the case. Unlike Wilde, however, the literary executor did not go to prison.

In the wake of this second trial Douglas continued to protest the power of the Wilde archive over his own reputation and the "myth" of Wilde's saintliness that archive could represent. He well understood (and especially resented) the institutionalization of that power in the donation of the *De Profundis* manuscript to the British Museum – a "consignation," to use Derrida's term, that effectively solidified Ross's authority over Wilde's place in literary history. In his 1929 memoir *The Autobiography of Lord Alfred Douglas*, Douglas reiterated his complaints about the custodianship of the *De Profundis* manuscript with the assertion that "the MS. now reposing in the British Museum quite plainly belongs to me, and I shall expect the custodians will now hand it over to me."[65] (They retained it.) In the clashes between Douglas and the representatives of the "Wilde myth" that he decried, the Wilde archive and so the question of whose version of "the real Oscar Wilde" would prevail were of central – and lasting– importance.

While Douglas was primarily concerned with his own reputation in his litigious irruptions into Wilde's afterlife, Ross was preoccupied with asserting literary property rights. Ross's anxiety over *dubia*, when combined with the desire to be comprehensive in compiling Wilde's texts, led him to the extraordinary step of threatening legal action against booksellers retailing Wilde piracies. By this method he hoped to quash any authorial ambiguities, thereby securing an unchallenged position for his collected edition and its "real Oscar Wilde." In July 1908 he issued a circular letter to the book trade, asserting his sole legal authority in matters related to Wilde's writings. In this memorandum, "re: Oscar Wilde Deceased," Ross issues this challenge:

> [M]y attention has been called to the very large number of unauthorised prints of the Author's Works being offered for sale in various parts of London [...] The sale of these unauthorised issues of Mr. Wilde's Works affects prejudicially the interest of the estate I represent [...] I am therefore issuing this circular to the many members of the book trade [...] as a caution that in the event of their being found from this time forward offering for sale or otherwise dealing in any unauthorised reprints of the late Mr. Wilde's Works, legal proceedings will at once be taken to prevent their doing so.[66]

Christopher Millard, as Ross's secretary and bibliographical sleuth for the *Collected Works*, was the individual responsible for calling his attention to the misconduct of certain booksellers, and it was Millard who wrote directly to individual booksellers, complaining of pirated editions and threatening to seize Wilde books of which he did not approve. He could wield hyperbole to intimidating effect, as one undated letter to a bookseller indicates: "As recently as 1910 a prosecution was undertaken in London which resulted in several persons being sentenced to heavy fines and long terms of imprisonment for conspiring to print, publish, and sell pirated copies of Oscar Wilde's works. I now therefore demand that you deliver up to me [...] all copies in your possession of any unauthorised editions of Oscar Wilde's works; failing which, legal proceedings will at once be instituted against you."[67] Ross made good on Millard's threats of such legal proceedings in 1914, when he brought a lawsuit against two booksellers in the court of Chancery for retailing Wilde piracies.[68] In the matter of "risky books," at least, the law could be marshalled to Wilde's benefit to disrupt the "conspiring" practices of wayward booksellers and publishers.

Millard's intimidation tactics were backed up by the voluminous knowledge he had derived from compiling and constantly revising lists of Wilde's publications. Ross's circular letter, for example, was supplemented by a substantial bibliography compiled by Millard under the pseudonym "Stuart Mason" that he employed in print when designating himself a Wilde expert. (For the private correspondence in which he threatened booksellers with goods seizure and imprisonment, he used his real name.) That particular bibliography terminated in a paragraph repudiating texts that purported to be authored or translated by Wilde, namely *The Priest and the Acolyte*, *The Satyricon of Petronius*, and *What Never Dies*. These titles, Millard notes, "were neither written, translated, nor edited by the late Mr. Oscar Wilde, and booksellers are earnestly requested to refrain from advertising them as such. Any one with a slender knowledge of the French, Latin, or English languages will be able to realize for himself that the Author of *Salomé*, who was a Demy (scholar) of Magdalen College, Oxford, and Greek Gold Medalist at Dublin, was incapable, even in his declining years, of the grammatical and grosser solecisms characterising these publications."[69] This defensive and elitist language illuminates both Millard's assumptions about Wilde and his investment in the rehabilitation-and-memorialization project. His scholarly Wilde is self-evidently a brilliant and accomplished writer who is the victim of public misperception. Such misperception, in Millard's (and Ross's) view, is the result of any of a variety of misrepresentations of Wilde's authorship (note the inclusiveness in banishing publications "neither written, translated, nor edited" by Wilde). The authenticity of the archive is of paramount importance to the success of restorative bibliography. Personally offended by market-driven misattributions on the dead writer's behalf, Millard resorts to citing academic credentials in order to bolster Wilde's precarious intellectual stature. But what is perhaps most striking here, and throughout Millard's extensive work on Wilde, is the desire to correct the record by rehearsing facts. Building a Wilde archive from an assemblage of facts would have the effect, Millard and Ross hoped, of driving out unwelcome fictions about Wilde, in effect replacing one narrative with another. It was to be one of the great ironies of Wilde's afterlife that his partisans worked to protect a writer devoted to the creation of beautiful untrue things by constructing an archival bastion of facts.

The Compiler: Christopher Millard

Christopher Millard was the primary conduit for many of the material components of Wilde's literary legacy, and as such he has wielded incalculable influence in shaping the archival underpinnings of Wilde studies. Millard's public part in the authentication of Oscar Wilde was multifarious, aggressively bookish, and characteristically aggrieved in its tone. It was also devoted and steadfast. Millard was an eccentric amateur scholar and book dealer who made little secret of his own homosexuality. According to A.J.A. Symons, in whom Millard inspired a fascination for the decadent writer Baron Corvo, "contrariety was perhaps his most consistent attribute," and he refused to submit to conventionality in any form, be it sexual, political, or otherwise.[70] Symons notes, for instance, that Millard was "an enthusiastic Jacobite, ostentatiously laying his white rose at King Charles the First's feet every year, and [he] acknowledged Prince Rupert of Bavaria as his rightful sovereign; in later years, he became an ardent socialist, [and] wore flaming ties."[71] Even the pen name "Stuart Mason" that publicly identified Millard as a Wilde expert represented an amalgam of his varied affiliations, combining a loyalty to the Stuarts with an affinity for structured (and secretive) all-male sociability.

Millard's lifelong interest in Wilde, whom he never met, can be traced to a letter he wrote to *Reynolds' Newspaper* in 1895, protesting Wilde's conviction for gross indecency – a charge for which he too was twice imprisoned later in his life.[72] Except for that early letter, which decries the fact that "because this man has dared to choose *another form* of satisfying his natural passions the law steps in,"[73] Millard's advocacy for Wilde was not explicitly articulated in terms that critiqued institutionalized homophobia. It is perhaps unsurprising, then, that Millard's unfinished biographical sketches, "Oscar Wilde: A Chronological Biography" (1905) and "Oscar Wilde's Life and Literary Career" (1911), barely mention the trials and Wilde's prison sentence.[74] Rather, his protest was almost exclusively registered in bookish activities that Nicholas Frankel has called "gathering the fragments."[75] He constructed an archive in order to systematize the chaos of Wilde's contested literary legacy, and excelled in tracking down and making lists of anything and everything associated with Wilde. He was particularly good at ferreting out overlooked poems and journalistic pieces published in periodicals. He collected scarce editions, translations, manuscripts, photographs, and ephemera. His veneration of Wilde is discernible among the sundry photographs and cartoons assembled as saintly relics for an incomplete and unpublished project – a "visual narrative," in Daniel Novak's phrase – that he called his "Iconography of Oscar Wilde."[76] This work, along with the two unfinished biographies of his hero, registers the scale of his ambition and obsession, as well as their limitations.

Millard's archival devotion to Wilde extended to the compilation of a vast collection of periodical cuttings (it runs to fifty-six volumes) now held at the William Andrews Clark Memorial Library, University of California, Los Angeles (UCLA). This collection of "Wildeana Clippings" captured nearly every printed reference to Wilde, in multiple languages, between the years 1909 and 1927. (After Millard's death this repository was sold at an auction, whose sale catalogue described it as a "monumental and exhaustive collection, absolutely unique of its kind, and impossible to replace. It was [...] supplemented by the ardent and unparalleled research of its compiler, [and includes] everything that could even be remotely construed as a reference to Wilde.")[77] Millard even collected living people who had been part of Wilde's circle. Arguably his biggest coup in Wilde collecting came in affiliating himself with Robert Ross, and his employment as Ross's secretary gave him some influence over Ross's collected edition of Wilde, several volumes of which he copy-edited. A vocal expert on Wilde's writings, as we have already observed, he certainly exercised that influence as the often-belligerent, litigious enforcer of Ross's authority over Wilde copyrights.

Millard staked his own curatorial authority over matters related to Wilde on a substantive corpus of publications, all of which can be understood as instances of restorative bibliography. His expertise, in other words, was generative, and between 1905 and 1920 he issued thirteen Wilde-related books under the pseudonym "Stuart Mason." The six-hundred-page *Bibliography of Oscar Wilde* (1914), on which he worked intermittently for a decade, is packed with information unavailable elsewhere and remains a monument to his zealous aspirations for what restorative bibliography could achieve. In a preface Millard records his own surprise at the project's scale, noting that "when, more than ten years ago, the collecting of Oscar Wilde's books was begun [...] with a view to compiling a bibliography, it was with little idea that the task would prove so onerous."[78] The *Bibliography* assembled and printed in one place more information about Wilde's career, his publications, and his literary reputation than had ever been previously compiled. More than a century after its release, it remains a standard reference work. Stuart Mason's magnum opus more than lives up to Walter Ledger's hope that a comprehensive Wilde bibliography would mark the "logical terminus" to the *Collected Works*.[79] That continuity is palpable even in the *Bibliography*'s binding, whose gilt-stamped designs by Ricketts emphasize its status as an extension of the *Collected Works*.

As a book dealer, Millard made a meagre living buying and selling Wilde items (Walter Ledger was a dependable customer), and his sales to collectors like William Andrews Clark Jr of Los Angeles, which form the basis of the Wilde collection at UCLA's Clark Library, were crucial for establishing an institutional archive whose components had been widely dispersed.[80] As Frankel aptly observes, "the present-day character of the Wilde archives at UCLA's Clark Library owes much to Millard's own collections, some of which were simply absorbed directly into the Clark's collections."[81] Indeed, in the formation of the Wilde archive at the Clark Library the synergistic relationship between Millard's scholarship and bookselling, on the one hand, and Clark's collecting, on the other, has yet to be fully explored. It was Millard, for instance, who drew his frequent customer into the inner circle of Wilde-fan sociability. When, in 1922, the American collector issued the first privately printed instalment of a catalogue called *Wilde and Wildeiana* that detailed his growing collection, he sent a copy to Millard. Ever the bibliographer, Millard replied with a lengthy letter that included five typed pages of mixed praise and critique in the form of "comments on the book's contents."[82] Along with his comments Millard enclosed a book that had belonged to Robert Ross, and he also supplied Clark with the London address of Wilde's son Vyvyan Holland.[83] With these exchanges of books and information, Millard was inviting the collector into a community of Wilde admirers whose members were affiliated, in large measure, by their archival custodianship of Wilde's memory. In doing so, the impecunious Millard also subtly underlined that Clark's wealth was no match for his connections, and Clark's initiation into this network of Wilde loyalists depended on his act of gatekeeping.

In his role as compiler and retailer of Wilde's literary effects, Millard was an unapologetic completist, despite the fact that some of his own books and projects remain unfinished. He champions the generative effects of the completist method in the pages of his *Bibliography*, where he observes that "it is only by publishing matter which has already been collected that it is possible to procure fresh material and to correct existing mistakes."[84] According to A.J.A. Symons, Millard, while living in a tiny bungalow in the 1920s, "was a great man for files and cases, and could put his hand at a moment on any scrap or book, despite the seeming disorder of his shelves and floor."[85] His home quarters thus come into view as an archival repository; it is easy to imagine him writing in such a workspace, literally surrounded by Wildeana. His first Wilde book, for instance, which is a translation of André Gide's *Oscar Wilde: A Study* (1905), contains an extensive bibliography. He also contributed bibliographies (sometimes anonymously) to other books about Wilde, such as Robert Sherard's *Life of Oscar Wilde* (1906) and Ross's *Collected Works* (1908).[86] Millard's talent for identifying uncollected periodical publications is showcased in his *Bibliography of the Poems of Oscar Wilde* (1907), on which he collaborated with Walter Ledger. In 1920 he issued a catalogue that assembled over 140 editions and translations of *The Picture of Dorian Gray*. He was unfazed by Aldous Huxley's attack in the *London Mercury* expressing "irritation [...] that people should be so stupid as to collect books because they are rare and not worth reading. One wonders, for instance, if human labour and ingenuity might not be extended in a more profitable undertaking than the compilation of a catalogue of about one hundred and fifty editions of *The Picture of Dorian Gray*."[87] In Frankel's words, "bibliography was for [Millard] a way of rationalizing or articulating his interests,"[88] a scholarly (and therefore respectable) method for channelling his passionate enthusiasm for all things Wildean.

Millard thus created works of reference about Wilde by collecting, arranging, and rehearsing facts – and, just as importantly, by packaging and repeating this information in the books he published. In addition to bibliographies, the Wilde archive that he assembled and shepherded into print included translations (e.g., Gide's *Study*), extracts (*The Oscar Wilde Calendar*), editions of previously unpublished material (*Impressions of America, by Oscar Wilde*), court records (*Oscar Wilde: Three Times Tried*), and literary-historical compendia, such as *Oscar Wilde: Art & Morality*. With this latter title, which came out in two editions, in 1908 and 1912 respectively, Millard rehearsed the entire controversy that had surrounded *The Picture of Dorian Gray*, which ranged from the early hostile reviews of the novel and Wilde's replies, to its appearance as evidence in Wilde's first trial and beyond. In so doing, Millard assembled in one volume a mini-archive of documents pertaining to the reception and publication history of what remained "the most disparaged and discredited of Wilde's works."[89] Perhaps most telling, however, are the first two words of the book's title (Wilde's name), which announce its subject to be Wilde himself just as much as the terms that organized the controversy surrounding his novel.

The subtitle of the (enlarged) second edition of *Oscar Wilde: Art & Morality*, "A Record of the Discussion Which Followed the Publication of 'Dorian Gray,'" makes Millard's archival impetus clear. This "record," assembled by Millard, serves primarily to remediate and authenticate and to separate facts from lore in the case of an undoubtedly "risky book," the copyright for which was still owned by the Parisian publisher Charles Carrington, who was much loathed by Millard. ("To Hell with Carrington," he exclaimed in a characteristic letter from 1905.)[90] *Art & Morality* is an obsessively inclusive volume, for, in addition to reprinting the reviews of *Dorian Gray* and Wilde's acrimonious correspondence with the editors of newspapers that had attacked it, it offers a meticulous chronology of the novel's publication history, multiple illustrations (including facsimiles of manuscripts and printed title pages), a list of textual variants between editions, a sixty-page bibliography, and copious footnotes throughout. No space is wasted in this volume's devotion to advancing Wilde's cause, either; otherwise blank pages are decorated with Wilde quotations. For Millard, apparently everything about *Dorian Gray* is worth preserving in a coordinated barrage of information whose combined characteristics of apparent orderliness and overwhelming detail endeavour to stabilize the status of both the novel and its author. Ironically, however, the unruly, hoarding quality of Millard's Wilde publications reveals not so much their desired effect – order and stability – as the less-than-entirely-successful *effort* to produce them.

Millard pursued this strategy again in *Oscar Wilde: Three Times Tried*, which is his 1912 accounting of the Wilde trials. With this large and imposing volume (running to nearly five hundred pages) Millard seeks once again to set the record straight and to battle the sensationalizing misrepresentations of his hero, such as the Carrington-published *Trial of Oscar Wilde: From the Shorthand Reports* (1906). He tackles the trials directly, not so much to critique the injustice of their ultimate verdict, as he had done in 1895, but rather with a view to correcting misperceptions about Wilde. As he notes in the volume's preface, since "the books [Wilde] wrote are now being opened afresh [...] it is essential that they come before us for literary judgment free from anything useless and external."[91] He conjures an archive of facts whose "footnotes and appendix contain information which is now made public for the first time"[92] in order to counter the Wildean lore that he imagines to be in the public's mind. Knowing well that the trials turned on the revelation of sexual information, however, Millard is just as much a defensive editor as is Ross. Although he professes to present court testimony "as fully as possible," such information can only be relayed through an editorial filter, "with due regard to discretion."[93] Even more striking for a man who was relatively open about his own homosexuality is the unusual caution he took to insulate himself from the lingering contamination represented by the trial – or perhaps from the threat of litigation on the part of Alfred Douglas. Uniquely among Millard's Wilde books, *Three Times Tried* was published anonymously, without the Stuart Mason pseudonym.

It is worth noting here that Millard's (or rather, Stuart Mason's) defensive and public hoarding of Wilde material could backfire by appearing excessive and ridiculous, as Huxley's critique of the collection of myriad *Dorian Gray* editions suggests. Although he privately supported Millard with encouragement and employment, even Robert Ross could be dismissive of "Stuart Mason's" books. Indeed, Ross's public endorsement of Millard's scholarship was a decidedly mixed blessing. When asked, as Wilde's literary executor and thus as the acknowledged guardian of the writer's legacy, to write an introductory preamble to Millard's *Bibliography* (a task he could hardly decline), Ross articulated his reluctance by disparaging Millard's scholarly style. His "Introductory Note" to the 1914 *Bibliography* seems more unfriendly than not, and he begins by distancing himself from the project:

> The author of this astonishing and ingenious compilation has asked me to write an introduction, not because he imagines I know anything about bibliography, but because he wishes for the *imprimatur* of Wilde's Literary Executor. [...] I cannot pretend to have read this book through; but I can affirm that in turning over the proofs for ten minutes I have learned more about Wilde's writings than Wilde himself ever knew [...] I acquired more information than I shall be able to make use of in a lifetime. [...] To those versed in the science of bibliography, Mr. Stuart Mason's labours require no praise or commendation from me. But I want to assure those, such as myself, who are entirely ignorant of enthusiasm for fourteenth editions or of the aesthetic excitement over a misprint of twenty years ago, that there is an enormous amount of diverting reading under these heavy-looking headings and that Mr. Stuart Mason's book is not nearly so dull as it looks.[94]

There is more than a hint here of disharmony among the loyal keepers of Wilde's memory, as Ross seems to be recoiling from Millard's attachment to Wilde or, more precisely, from Millard's enthusiasm and its data-driven expression – a combination (it would seem) of emotional over-investment and stultifying pedantry. However much Ross's own efforts on Wilde's behalf may have depended on Millard's work, here Millard appears to have wasted his (and Ross's) time with a project (almost) not worth undertaking. For Ross, there remains something "risky" in Millard's labour-intensive attachment to his subject, a private enthusiasm that loses credibility in being shared so publicly and so extensively in print. Nevertheless, the *Bibliography of Oscar Wilde* stands as the fullest expression of Millard's recruitment and deployment of Wildean information to establish not only his subject's authenticity but also, and just as crucially, his authority over it. This is a book whose design, we recall, makes it a companion to Ross's *Collected Works*.

After Ross's death in 1918, Millard had the field largely to himself. His proprietary approach to the expert archival knowledge exemplified by the *Bibliography* can be glimpsed in his responses to others' subsequent forays into Wildean restorative bibliography. Millard, as we have seen, invited the Los Angeles collector Clark into his world of bookish Wilde fandom, but his doing so did not preclude a tinge of possessive jealousy. He must have felt some degree of pique at the notion that Clark's sumptuously produced *Wilde and Wildeiana* catalogues could compete with his books. In a 1922 letter to Clark, thanking him for a gift of the first volume of that catalogue, Vyvyan Holland records Millard's grudging approval of Clark's role in preserving the Wilde archive by noting that the "best testimonial [that the catalogue] has had is undoubtedly that it has excited the envy and unwilling admiration of Mr. Millard, who seldom admits that anyone but himself knows anything about his subject!"[95] Even if Millard did not physically own it all, he felt that the Wilde archive and the knowledge that it represented – a paper proxy for the dead writer himself – were unquestionably his property.

The Collector: Walter Ledger

Despite the ostensibly informative character of Millard's Wildean scholarship, Ross's critique of the extraneous effort discerned in Millard's methods keys us into the affective register of surplus emotion that underlies (or exceeds) it. That affective register (and its bookish expression) defined the Wilde-centric friendship between Millard and Walter Ledger, a collector whose bibliophilia was animated by hoarding and sentimentality. An eccentric bachelor who broadcast his enthusiasm for boating by costuming himself as "an old-fashioned Jack Tar, with open neck and a blue-and-white sailor collar and bell-bottom trousers" (figure 4),[96] Ledger devotedly collected everything he could obtain with Wilde's name on it: every edition of Wilde's books, including every translation into languages other than English; every periodical piece; every substantive engagement with Wilde's writings in the press; and every auction-sale catalogue. Thanking Ledger in the preface to the *Bibliography*, Millard observed that "his collection of Wilde is almost without an omission and certainly unrivalled."[97] Unlike Millard, who, beginning in 1920, bought and sold Wilde material to support himself, Ledger had the means to accumulate Wilde materials over the course of more than three decades of collecting. Ledger's private repository of Wildeana was the master archive that made Millard's bibliographic

4 Walter Ledger, 1913. Robert Ross Memorial Collection, University College, Oxford.

publications possible, and its material aggregation of texts, praised by Millard, Ross, and Arthur Ransome, represented his indispensable contribution to the collaborative project of restorative bibliography.

Among Millard, Ross, and Ledger, Wilde and his textual afterlife thus figure as vehicles of affective exchange, a channel for a friendship that, as we have seen, could, at times, become strained. If Wilde was understood as a saintly figure for this circle of gay men, he represented a "conception of sainthood as not so much exemplary as communal," in the words of Richard A. Kaye.[98] For them, in other words, Wilde was instrumental in community formation, and reverence for his memory not only brought them together but also sutured them to each other for many years. Ledger registered his admiration for Wilde in the collecting work of many decades; that work led to the formation of a substantial archive that he donated to the University of Oxford in Robert Ross's name at his (Ledger's) death in 1931. Called the Robert Ross Memorial Collection, the archive – comprising books, periodicals, press clippings, scrapbooks, ephemera, bibliographical notes, correspondence, and marked-up auction catalogues – is itself a tribute to an intimacy with Wilde that was shared among Ross, Millard, and Ledger, who archived, in a self-effacing manner, his own part in an authenticatory project of canon building.

With characteristic thoroughness Ledger documented his entire correspondence with Millard, which he preserved in five large albums covering 1904 to 1927. Although extensive, the conversation is almost entirely one-sided, since it mainly comprises Millard's half of the two men's twenty-three-year correspondence.[99] Millard and Ledger wrote almost exclusively about Wilde; however, their correspondence is remarkable not only for the detailed enthusiasm with which they shared bibliographical information about obscure publication venues, publishers, prices, print runs, and the like, but also because it never features discussions of the *content* of Wilde's writing. To give a sense of the tenor of the correspondence, I quote at length from a representative 1905 letter from Millard to Ledger that records a moment when the two men were consumed with accumulating facts and locating sources:

> Many thanks for your letter. I enclose [a] list of the "World" contributions. They are all new to me and I feel lucky in having got hold of them. I have no doubt there are others yet to be found. Ross says he thinks "The Birthday of the Infanta" came out in French & English in *Le Figaro Illustré*, but I can get no confirmation of this from the office in Paris or in London. Ross also says that "Lord Arthur Savile" came out in *The Court & Society Review* (as also "Harlot's House") but I can find no trace of such a paper in the Bodleian or Brit[ish] Museum Catalogue. O[scar] W[ilde] referred in his trial to a letter he wrote to the *Scots Observer* in reply to a criticism on "Dorian Gray," but the paper is defunct and I cannot get a trace of it. I have the exact date etc. of all the *Pall Mall Gazette* articles. Have you a copy of "English Poetesses" from the *Queen*? If so, lend me yours and I can make a typed copy and return it. [...] I have Carrington's prospectuses of "The Duchess of P[adua]" and the "Trial" but have seen neither book yet. To Hell with Carrington. He has brought out *Intentions* in French too.[100]

It is hard to imagine two more devoted Wilde fans, and yet Ledger and Millard never analyse the writer's work; they do not commit themselves to either praise or critique. Preoccupied with the accumulation of bibliographical information, their correspondence is unconcerned with aesthetic or critical matters. Conversing in titles, Wilde's bibliographers do not engage in the very "literary judgment" for which Millard wished to clear the way by publishing *Three Times Tried*. Millard took the value of Wilde's writings for granted, as did Ledger, and I speculate that they understood their relation to Wilde's texts to be following a model of librarianship as opposed to one of literary criticism. A basic shared assumption about Wilde's literary value underwrote their work and energized their friendship. The burden of Millard's many books on Wilde was to communicate that value to the world.

Although Ledger, to whom Millard dedicated the 1906 Stuart Mason volume *Impressions of America* as a "pledge of friendship,"[101] shared with Millard an enthusiasm for Oscar Wilde, he was decidedly more cautious about its public expression – at least in England. Early in their collaboration Ledger also wrote to publishers about questions of Wilde's authorship, but he adopted a more diplomatic tone than did Millard. He wrote, for instance, to the Paris publisher P.V. Stock in 1905, alerting him to the presence of three apocryphal (and possibly forged) stories in a collection of Wilde's short fiction that Stock had published in French translation. More pleading than threatening, Ledger says of the stories ("The Orange Peel," "Old Bishop's," and "Ego te Absolvo"): "[J]e n'ai aucune hésitation de vous assurer ma conviction qu'elles n'ont jamais été écrites par Wilde. Je ne puis m'empécher de vous supplier instantanément de les supprimer, et de refaire votre livre." (I have no hesitation in assuring you that Wilde never wrote them. I must also beseech you to suppress them instantly, and to reissue your volume.)[102] Stock had been so cautious about publishing these stories that he had issued a disclaimer along with his edition of Wilde's stories: "Nous les traduisons ici bien que l'authenticité nous en paraisse éminement suspecte." (We translate them here in the full awareness of their eminently doubtful authenticity.)[103] Alert to the "eminently doubtful authenticity" of other representations of Wilde published from Paris, Ledger was equally concerned to share with Stock the danger that Charles Carrington represented to the Wilde archive. He writes: "Je crains que M. Carrington a publié plusieurs oeuvres apocryphe de Wilde – des traductions qu'il n'a jamais faite." (I'm afraid that Mr. Carrington has published several works of Wilde apocrypha – translations that he never did.)[104] Ledger's powers of persuasion were clearly effective because Stock, although he continued to publish Wilde translations, did not include the offending and "eminently doubtful" texts in any of his subsequent volumes. In his own formal and tactful way, and especially in the French language so greatly loved by his literary hero, Ledger could also make an impact on the book trade's representation of Wilde.

Although it was he, and not Millard, who began the project that culminated in the *Bibliography*,[105] his collecting-driven research led to only one publication: a sixteen-page bibliography of *Salomé* (1909) that listed the play's translation into thirteen languages.[106] Ledger's punctiliousness about Wilde exceeded even Millard's, as Millard makes clear when commenting on some papyrophilic research that Ledger had shared with him: "Your bibliographical matter is, of course, much more fully carried out than mine, but it seems to me questionable whether such minute details as to the colour of paper etc., are of such sufficient interest as to repay the extra trouble [of including them in the *Bibliography*.]"[107] (Such "minute details" about paper stock, as we shall see in the next chapter, would undo a Wilde forger.) It is unlikely, however, that Ledger's withdrawal from the co-authorship of the Wilde bibliography he and Millard had contemplated was prompted by such mild criticisms among friends. Sexual legislation continued to have a sustained impact on Wilde's legacy; only now it influenced the lives of Wilde's ardent followers. In 1906 Millard was arrested, tried, and imprisoned for three months on a charge of gross indecency. Fearing the contamination of public association with Millard's homosexuality – even when shielded from Millard's legal identity by the "Stuart Mason" pseudonym – Ledger retreated from the publishing project to his insulated world of private collecting. (Ross, for his part, stood resolutely by Millard regardless of the bibliographer's legal troubles.) Ledger remained a silent partner in their scholarly venture, and a valued one, as Millard made clear in a 1906 letter about the authorship of the bibliography. "I do not think," Millard states, "I can ever do it independently of you and it would hardly be fair to publish it under my name alone, though I fully understand, of course, that you do not wish your name to appear in collaboration with mine after what has occurred."[108] Despite Ledger's retreat into the figurative closet of his library, their friendship continued unabated until Millard's death in 1927.

Ledger's Wildean devotions were therefore largely private. In addition to collecting, he augmented the archive with artefacts of his fandom by crafting his own keepsake treasures: he transcribed and decorated Wilde texts, which he sometimes shared with Millard and Ross. For example, in 1907 Ledger painstakingly traced Wilde's handwritten alterations and corrections to the manuscript of *The Duchess of Padua* that Ross owned, on delicate paper that he then preserved. He catalogued his effort by appending a note explaining precisely what he had done: "the alterations and corrections shewn on the thin paper pages in this volume, were traced by me from Oscar Wilde's The Duchess of Padua, he property of Mr. Robert Ross. Walter E. Ledger. Wimbledon 13 June 1907."[109] Creating and annotating his own Wilde manuscripts, Ledger amplified his voluminous archive of printed materials by writing out Wilde's words with his own hand. He also wrote out a keepsake version of Wilde's early play *Vera* and presented it to Ross. Telling Ledger he would treasure it, Ross nonetheless identified an irony in Ledger's fandom and wittily expressed his appreciation for Ledger's being simultaneously a Wilde loyalist *and* a copyist, by adding, "[Y]our powers of forgery are almost unholy."[110] In uncanny anticipation of the very forgers about whom he and Millard were to complain bitterly in the 1920s, Ledger acts here as if he were Oscar Wilde, writing (or rather copying) *as* Wilde, his manuscript mimicry a literally handmade act of homage. Like Millard, he seems to have prioritized the figure of the author over that author's actual literary creations, and indeed, by tracing out "unholy" forgeries, he was able to imaginatively *become* Wilde the writer.

As we shall see in subsequent chapters, the parallels between Ledger's sentimental archive and the archive of manuscript forgeries generated by such figures as Dorian Hope are both striking and provocative. In both instances imitation functions as a form of fantasy authorial embodiment. The critical difference between Ledger's Wilde manuscripts and the 1920s forgeries obtains mainly in the absence of any intention to deceive on Ledger's part, to say nothing of their sequestration from commerce. Despite his "powers of forgery," Ledger was not looking to misrepresent Wilde's authorship in the hope of financial gain, which was unquestionably a salient motivation for the 1920s Wilde forgers. Ledger copied Wilde's words for an intimate circle of fellow fans. Written for private circulation, and not for the literary marketplace, Ledger's neo-Wildean texts secure intimately tactile – handwritten – bonds. Traced by Ledger, the archive of Wilde's memory transcends the "fabulous prices" of the manuscript as commodity that was described in the 1905 Glaenzer sale catalogue, its value inhering instead in the status of a precious, and private, gift.

Protesting *The Priest and the Acolyte*

By way of concluding this chapter's overview of the authenticatory function performed by the assembling of the Wilde archive in the early twentieth century, I turn to a more specific illustration of the simultaneously protective and assertive character of restorative bibliography as practised by Christopher Millard. As I observed at the beginning of this chapter, the authenticatory activities of Wildean restorative bibliography included publishing, archiving, and settling scores publicly. Millard's bold effort to neutralize the misattributed story *The Priest and the Acolyte* brings together all of these activities in one publishing endeavour. Although Ross had certainly been offended by the ascription to Wilde of *The Priest and the Acolyte* because of that text's sexual content, it was Millard who took up the fight over what Ross called "the crude production of an undergraduate" with the most fervour. He took the unusual step of republishing the story in 1907, adding it to the growing list of books on Wilde by "Stuart Mason." In doing so, Millard characteristically tried to have it both ways. He tried to burnish Wilde's reputation by repudiating a "crude production," while at the same time he kept the topic of same-sex desire (even if disavowed) in circulation. Close attention to this peculiar undertaking illuminates the tenor of Millard's investment in guarding Wilde's posthumous reputation, for it set the pattern for his approach to exposing forgeries for the next two decades.

The book that Millard brought out with London's Lotus Press is fully entitled *The Priest and the Acolyte: With an Introductory Protest by Stuart Mason*, and its substantial preface indignantly counters the anonymous story's attribution to Wilde. According to Millard, "so many copies of 'The Priest and the Acolyte' have been sold by unscrupulous publishers and booksellers under the implication that it is the work of Oscar Wilde that it has been thought good to issue this edition with the object of putting an end, once and for all, to the possibility of purchasers being misled as to the authorship."[111] The matter-of-fact language that frames his "Introductory Protest" obscures the full strangeness of the story's republication. Robert Ross termed it a "repulsive little book," although he allowed that Millard's "preface is quite admirable."[112] Under his Stuart Mason pseudonym, Millard sought publicly to settle a question of authorship that probably mattered more to him than to putative "purchasers being misled." (It is nonetheless amusing to imagine the feisty Millard as a sort of consumer advocate for Wilde collectors.) The impersonal language of altruism and accuracy ("it has been thought good") authorizes a personal investment; Millard is setting the record straight, "once and for all." Rather than let an unexceptional short story wither into insignificance, he brings it back into circulation in order to exonerate Wilde in the only way he can – by combatting gossip with fact. As we have seen before, the Wilde he conjures is Wilde the writer, scholar, and saint, rather than the symbol of sexual infamy. Indeed, in his unpublished sketch "Oscar Wilde: A Chronological Biography" he notes: "It would scarcely be necessary to mention that the story of 'The Priest and the Acolyte' […] was written by an Oxford undergraduate, but that it has since been reprinted and offered for sale under Mr. Wilde's name by pornographic booksellers and other lewd fellows of the baser sort."[113] Millard, in effect, wants to neutralize the linkage between Wilde's name and "lewdness," and yet what is most striking about this particular recuperative publishing venture is the limitation it places on the power of naming. Writing under the cover of a pseudonym himself, Millard will not (or cannot) name the "pornographic booksellers and other lewd fellows," nor does he name the story's real author.

Millard's argument against Wilde's authorship in the "Introductory Protest" derives largely from the homoerotic story's role in testimony at Wilde's first trial, which is a subject upon which Millard was still making himself an expert. (His 1912 volume *Oscar Wilde: Three Times Tried*, we recall, was to be the most comprehensive account of the trials to date.) Lawyers at the trials alleged Wilde's relation to the story on the basis of association, namely the contiguity of *The Priest and the Acolyte* (signed, with suggestive anonymity, "X") with Wilde's provocative "Phrases and Philosophies for the Use of the Young" in the single-issue Oxford magazine *The Chameleon* (1894). *The Chameleon* had a decidedly homoerotic flavour, for it also featured the Alfred Douglas poem "Two Loves," a defence of same-sex passion that concludes with the famous line "I am the love that dare not speak its name" – a phrase that Wilde memorably and eloquently defended in court. During the trials the logic of the writer's legal opponents was simple: if he contributed one piece to the magazine and defended another, then he certainly knew about and probably approved of the unsigned story.[114] The trials did not name Wilde as the story's author, however. Despite his marked hostility to the writer, in the courtroom the lawyer Edward Carson is clear in *not* attributing the story to Wilde: "I am not in the slightest degree accusing you of having published it," he told Wilde as the writer sat in the witness box.[115] Nevertheless, Carson was keen in this moment to exploit any possibility of inferring guilt by association. In recounting the passages of courtroom testimony in the substantive introduction to his edition of the story, Millard is interested in breaking a chain of association pieced together in the courtroom, and secured in the literary marketplace by "unscrupulous publishers and booksellers" who issued the story under Wilde's name for the first time in 1905.[116] The story was not authentic Wilde, and Millard was keenly aware of the legal impact of authorial attribution or misattribution.

Millard's "Introductory Protest" thus attempts in 1907 to detach Wilde from literature labelled "immoral" by the court,[117] and by extension to erode the association between Wilde and deviant sexuality, a linkage made most spectacularly by the introduction of *The Picture of Dorian Gray* into evidence during the trials as a "sodomitical book."[118] Although Wilde may have been guilty of "gross indecency" according to the law (a detail that the "Protest" fails to mention), Millard takes it upon himself, in revisiting the 1895 courtroom drama, to prove Wilde innocent in the matter of literary attribution. To Millard, the non-author of *The Priest and the Acolyte* is the victim of injustice: "It was not fair," Millard writes, "to judge a man's conduct by his books, but the Prosecution had gone much further than that, and had sought to judge Wilde by books he did not write, and by a story which he had repudiated as horrible and disgusting. Public opinion had been excited [...] by the quotation in Court of passages of literature for which he was not responsible."[119] "With that story Wilde had nothing whatever to do," he insists, "and to impute to him anything in it was quite absurd."[120]

However completist he may have been with regard to bibliographical matters, Millard was rather more selective in his presentation of Wilde's literary opinions. Wilde often said inconvenient things that could make the job of a loyalist like Millard more difficult. He cites Wilde's courtroom pronouncement that the story was a "violat[ion of] every artistic canon of beauty," which "filled [him] with disgust,"[121] but omits to mention the writer's private assessment (from a letter about which Millard, who handled hundreds of Wilde's letters, may have known) that "it has interesting qualities, and is at moments poisonous: which is something."[122] Recalling Dorian Gray's having been "poisoned by a book," the epithet *poisonous* is certainly an apposite term for a story that, as an unintended parody of *Romeo and Juliet*, ends with a tableau of the priest and his adolescent acolyte expiring from the combined effects of poison and forbidden love. According to Timothy d'Arch Smith, the story "may perhaps be considered the first piece of English fiction to echo the firmly-placed French syndrome of the 'naughty' priest."[123]

So what was Millard's thinking when he republished an unquestionably "risky book" whose queer subject matter could appear to strengthen the association of Wilde's name with deviant sexuality? The material character of Millard's extensive interventions into Wilde's textual afterlife provides one answer. If the Wilde legend could be shaped by "risky" authorial misrepresentations – piracies, misattributions, and forgeries – it could also be manipulated by books that legitimized Wilde, the writer. Although Millard's extensive Wilde-publishing efforts were varied, in the main they repackaged existing material by or about Wilde. As he did in his correspondence with Walter Ledger, Millard in his books circled paratextually around Wilde's writing, embroidering the edges of his martyred hero's canon. His version of *The Priest and the Acolyte* is unique among his publications, however, in being about a work emphatically *not* by Wilde. (And yet, ironically, that text's unstated authorship is precisely the reason behind its republication.) By republishing it in "protest," Millard is asserting control over a rogue text – containing and reframing it so that an otherwise damaging text can be repurposed to serve the ends of restorative bibliography. By attempting to neutralize the extra-literary court narrative linking Wilde to *The Priest and the Acolyte*, Millard is deprogramming a reader's perception of Wilde as its author. In so doing, he recalls an analogous form of control asserted by Ross in the *Collected Works*. He insists that Wilde ought to be understood and appreciated in terms of books as opposed to sexual deviance, his place in literary history secured by legitimate, recognized texts. And he closes his "Protest" by doing precisely this, concluding that his purpose was to "dissociate the name of the author of 'Salomé' and 'Lady Windermere's Fan'" from a sentimental story about pederastic doom.[124]

Tellingly, however, unconventional sexuality never disappears from Millard's thoughts. By taking control over, and indeed disciplining a rogue text, Christopher Millard's "Protest" replicates the breathless language of Victorian flagellation pornography. For example, he describes the story's real author (whom he does not name but whom he knows to be John Francis Bloxam, an Oxford contemporary of Alfred Douglas's who edited *The Chameleon*, and later became a priest), as "an insufficiently birched schoolboy."[125] By this logic, his "Protest" also performs a punishment: the punishment of a text that he presumably desires to extend to the punishment of an unnamed person at that point still living. Justice for Wilde – his release from what Ross had called "posthumous punishment" – could only be achieved, it would seem, by what amounted to an act of literary retribution.

My discussion of Ross, Ledger, and Millard's complex relation to Wilde has frequently returned to the religious metaphors that the writer who dubbed himself "the Infamous St Oscar of Oxford, Poet and Martyr"[126] so strongly admired. These metaphors can also afford us insight into Millard's special investment in Bloxam's story, as much as he loathed that story. Millard, as this book's subsequent chapters will show, was himself both Wilde's priest *and* his acolyte over the course of the 1920s: the spiritual guardian committed to scholastic labour, loyalty, and punishment (if necessary), on the one hand, and the devoted follower, on the other. Wilde's writings were his sacred texts. And just as much as he struggled to detach Wilde from forgery and other false representations, he was dedicated to forging his hero in another sense, by creatively remaking him in the world of books.

Chapter Two

The Picture of Dorian Hope

In April 1921 the Dublin bookseller William Figgis received an unsolicited letter carrying the signature of the French writer André Gide. Gide, who had known Oscar Wilde and had published a book about him, offered to sell Figgis some Wilde manuscripts "which were in his possession."[1] In a subsequent letter in October, Figgis's correspondent offers to sell the manuscript of *The Importance of Being Earnest*, describing it as "the complete manuscript, in perfect condition, written in ink and with numerous corrections throughout." "It seems to me," Gide continues, "that it should bring a good price, remembering that, by critics among Wilde's contemporaries, it was generally characterized as his *chef-d'oeuvre*."[2] Intrigued by the prospect, Figgis entered into further correspondence. A few days later, a similar offer, to sell the manuscript of Wilde's *Salomé*, arrived at the London bookselling firm Maggs Brothers, only this time the alleged sender was Pierre Louÿs, the dedicatee of the play's French version.[3] The offers to the two firms then escalated rapidly, with both French authors proposing to sell numerous manuscripts in nearly every genre in which Wilde wrote: plays, short fiction, criticism and journalism, poetry, and personal letters. The authoritative provenance of these items attracted both firms, and they pursued what appeared to be fortuitous business opportunities. In both instances, however, Figgis and Maggs were the victims of elaborate frauds, and the manuscripts turned out to be forgeries – all apparently contrived by Dorian Hope.

Of all the eccentric characters that created material lies about Oscar Wilde in the early twentieth century, Dorian Hope has remained the most obscure – until now. He comes into view by means of anecdotes, legends, and scattered journalistic accounts, and his persona is always relayed via role-playing and impersonation. And although my analysis of Dorian Hope's multifarious archive suggests that the Wilde manuscript forgeries offered to Figgis and Maggs were more likely produced by a group rather than an individual, we can nevertheless assert that the writerly mask of "Dorian Hope" is the invention of a roguish American poet who was born with the name Brett Holland (1898–1934). The queer-identified son of a bourgeois family from Gastonia, North Carolina, Holland was a literary adventurer who patterned his escapades after the example of Oscar Wilde. Like Wilde, he staged a spectacular debut in New York. On the other side of the Atlantic, however, Holland (and probably others) employed the name "Dorian Hope" to different purposes. The purpose of this chapter is thus not simply to establish the identity of the forger (or forgers) who used the alias "Dorian Hope," although the story of the various attempts to do so, and on which I also touch, is fascinating in itself.[4] Instead, I am more interested in how the Dorian Hope forgeries constituted an intervention into Wilde's cultural afterlife. I argue that the impersonations and outrageous textual performances that define the Dorian Hope archive constitute a form of neo-Wildean myth-making – a creative endeavour strongly recalling the Shakespearean myth-making undertaken by the fictional literary enthusiasts in "The Portrait of Mr. W.H." In that story the theory about Willie Hughes emerges most powerfully as the imaginative construction of a group of like-minded men – a beautiful untrue thing that, however briefly and precariously, sustains a bardolatrous community of Shakespeare fans. Similarly inspired by Wilde's memory, the Paris-based community that employed the name "Dorian Hope" (and of which Brett Holland was a part) forged texts that contributed to a literary idol's legacy.

It would be naive, of course, to diminish the fact that the Dorian Hope forgeries were criminal deceptions. They were certainly exploitative and undertaken in the expectation of financial gain. The letter from Gide to Figgis, for example, states that the manuscript of Wilde's play "should bring a good price." Even so, mere profiteering seems insufficient in accounting for the richness and strangeness of the Dorian Hope forgeries – to say nothing of the effort (and financial outlay) required to produce them and to sustain the fraud. In embellishing, embroidering, and extending existing narratives about Wilde, Dorian Hope was also a fan of Wilde's. Fandom is not a new phenomenon, and recent work in audience and reception theory points to a lengthy history for the enthusiasm described by the term. Daniel Cavicchi, for instance, historicizes fandom by associating it with the nineteenth-century rise of mass culture and defines it as a matter of "people forming intimate relationships with media stars through their consumption."[5] It should come as no surprise that Oscar Wilde, an early "media star" and one of the progenitors of celebrity culture, should become the focus of such attention. With the history of fandom in mind, we can comprehend the 1920s Wilde forgeries in a way that is markedly different from how the representatives of Figgis and Maggs, as well as Christopher Millard, Robert Ross, and Walter Ledger, did. Many of them are forms of fan fiction – and Brett Holland, as we shall see, was nothing if not an enthusiastic Oscar Wilde fan.

The archival practices of contemporary fan fiction also provide helpful models for conceptualizing the Dorian Hope forgeries. Although frequently undertaken collaboratively and exchanged online in our contemporary moment, fan fiction, for Abigail Derecho, constitutes, at a more basic level, what Jacques Derrida has called an "archontic" literature:

> A literature that is archontic is a literature composed of texts that are archival in nature and that are impelled by the same archontic principle: the tendency toward enlargement and accretion that all archives possess. Archontic texts are not delimited properties with definite borders that can be transgressed. So all texts that build on a previously existing text are not lesser than the source text, and they do not violate the boundaries of the source text; rather, they only add to that text's archive, becoming part of the archive and expanding it.[6]

By generating "continuations" that serve as narrative expansions of Wilde's legend, his forger-fans build their own Wilde archives out of existing source material, both biographic and bibliographical.[7] They expand the archive of information about his life and manufacture additional details about his writings, even occasionally adding "new" texts. In their breadth and diversity, Dorian Hope's forgeries and impostures thus tap into and thematize Wilde's well-known celebration of romanticized mystery. Kin to Lady Alroy in Wilde's "The Sphinx without a Secret," a story that was forged twice in this period, Dorian Hope created mysteries that transformed readers, clients, and victims into unwitting detectives. It is with a spirit of respect for both sides of Dorian Hope's textual interventions – that is, for mystification as much as for detection – that I have pieced together these archival traces to offer a composite sketch: the picture of Dorian Hope.

As had the piracies and misattributions explored in the previous chapter, the Dorian Hope forgeries had the effect of queering the

Wilde archive, in the sense of rendering it strange and uncertain. Such uncertainties were, as we have seen, countered by Wilde's advocates, including Robert Ross and Christopher Millard, both of whom sought after Wilde's death to purify the Wilde canon of dubious texts. (For a time Millard was even taken in by Dorian Hope's contrivances.) Dorian Hope also queered the Wilde archive in another way. In correspondence, using period slang and innuendo, he marked himself as sexually queer. Newspaper reports of Brett Holland's activities also categorize Dorian Hope in this way, as when a *Washington Times* article winkingly observed that Holland/Hope was remembered in that city for contributing a "'dash of lavender' [to] Twentieth Street NW, where Bret [sic] tried unsuccessfully to start a second Greenwich Village."[8] The penetration of Hope's documents into the Wilde archive, then, could work to undermine the project of making Wilde respectable again, which perhaps accounts for the doggedness with which Millard would pursue Dorian Hope.

This chapter showcases three views of Dorian Hope. First, it explores his initial emergence in New York in 1920, where that name attached itself to a volume of plagiarized poetry, a minor scandal, and a bizarre correspondence. Second, it investigates Dorian Hope's spectacular appearance in Paris in 1922. And, third, it traces his eventual misidentification (by Millard and others) with Wilde's nephew by marriage, the proto-Dadaist poet and boxer Arthur Cravan, who was born Fabian Lloyd. In so doing, this chapter attends closely to the style and content of the Dorian Hope manuscript forgeries and establishes their sources in printed books. For varied though these artefacts are, they bear witness to an extraordinary investment of creative labour and research into generating beautiful untrue things in the name of Oscar Wilde.

Pearls and Pomegranates from a "Faded Auntie": Dorian Hope in New York, 1920

The ostentatious pseudonym "Dorian Hope" is itself a miniature masterpiece of neo-Wildean myth-making. "Dorian" comes, of course, from Dorian Gray, while "Hope," as Wilde's son Vyvyan Holland attests, would appear to derive from Adrian Hope, a relative of Constance Wilde's by marriage (and a London neighbour of the Wildes) who "was one of the family trustees" and became the legal guardian of Oscar Wilde's two sons after their father's imprisonment.[9] The alias itself – the forger's *nom de contrefaçon* – thus amalgamates a famous fictional character with biographical fact and demonstrates a kind of insider's knowledge of Wilde's world. As we shall see in subsequent chapters, this pattern of slyly blending fact with fiction also typifies other forgers' Wildean interventions.

Although hundreds of forged pages of Wilde manuscripts have come to be associated with the name Dorian Hope (most of these now reside in archival collections at either William Andrews Clark Memorial Library at UCLA, or with Maggs Brothers Ltd in London), Dorian Hope made his debut not as a forger but rather as an eccentric plagiarist-poet with strongly Wildean antecedents. In 1920 the New York publisher Putnam issued a slender volume of poems under the name Dorian Hope with the decadent-sounding title *Pearls and Pomegranates*. The title alludes to Wilde's fairy tale "The Nightingale and the Rose," in which the martyr-like Nightingale muses, "Surely love is a wonderful thing. It is more precious than emeralds and dearer than fine opals. Pearls and pomegranates cannot buy it, nor is it set forth in the market-place."[10] At the end of the story, however, the Nightingale's sacrifice proves hopeless, as materialism triumphs over love, which, "is always telling one of the things that are not going to happen, and making one believe things that are not true."[11]

In Hope's book of verses, the Wilde references continue into the dedication. Offered to the American poet Florence Earle Coates (1850–1927), "A Slight Tribute to Her Distinction as an Artist / Her Nobility as a Friend" reprises almost verbatim Wilde's dedication of the play *An Ideal Husband* (published in 1899) to the writer Frank Harris: "To Frank Harris[:] A slight tribute to his power and distinction as an artist[;] his chivalry and nobility as a friend." The dedication probably encodes a pun on the "Hope" moniker because Coates's conservative and sentimental poetry frequently extolled the spiritual virtues of hope. It is also ironic and mischievous, as her anti-modernist views were diametrically opposed to Wilde's. She inveighed, for instance, against literary "novelty" and "morbidity" in a 1916 interview with the *New York Times Magazine*, whose strident title – "Godlessness Mars Most Contemporary Poetry" – would have elicited a chuckle from Wilde.[12] Under his given names (the link to "Holland," which Constance Wilde employed to assume a new identity for herself and her sons Cyril and Vyvyan after the scandal of her husband's trial and imprisonment, is one of history's unintended ironies), Brett Holland was actually acquainted with Coates. In a 1921 interview with the *New York Evening World*, she explained his alias: she reports that "she knew Holland [...] and said he had assumed the name of Dorian Hope because of his admiration for

Oscar Wilde's character Dorian Grey [sic]."[13] Beyond the dedication, the rest of the volume's contents, some fifty-six short lyric poems, were all written, it turns out, by poets other than Dorian Hope. In its entirety, *Pearls and Pomegranates* is an amalgam of several forms of unoriginality: quotation, allusion, and out-and-out plagiarism.

Although the poems comprising *Pearls and Pomegranates* are derivative, unlike the volume's title and dedication, their source is not Wilde. According to an unsigned 1921 *New York Times* article exposing the plagiarism, the poems were "filched" by Bret Holland, who posed as a Putnam employee and paid for their publication.[14] Holland had been publishing verse in newspapers since at least 1918,[15] but under his own name; representing *Pearls and Pomegranates* as the work of "Dorian Hope" marked a new phase in his creative output. The extent of the plagiarism in *Pearls and Pomegranates* was revealed when the poet Miriam Vedder recognized several of her own poems in the volume, including one that had already appeared under her name in the *Wellesley Review*, along with some by her recently deceased friend Augustin Lardy. She complained to the publishers, who promptly withdrew the book from the market.

According to the *New York Times*, the sequence of events leading to the volume's publication is dubious. "Bret Holland," representing Putnam's, had met with Lardy's mother and had "assured her that he would arrange for the publication of her son's poems."[16] In securing the poems for publication, Holland apparently did not realize that the stack of manuscripts he received from her also contained multiple pieces by another writer, Miriam Vedder.[17] Once collected into *Pearls and Pomegranates*, the poems came off the presses as the ostensible work of a single author, "filched" from both the dead and the living. By the time the imposture was discovered in 1921, however, Dorian Hope had fled to Europe, beginning a pattern of successive disappearances – or, rather, exits from the stage of Wildean performance.

From London, Holland/Hope audaciously replied to the scandal, which encompassed not only plagiarism, but also forged letters and unpaid bills, once word of multiple accusations in the press reached him. In doing so, he channelled the style of Oscar Wilde. Casting himself as a misunderstood artist (in bohemian – and convenient – European expatriation), Hope railed against tawdry journalistic intrusions into his affairs. In a lengthy letter to his hometown newspaper, *The Gastonia Gazette*, he admits that "during those rose-coloured months" in New York, he

> did numberless things – some of which were creditable; I wrote some of my best sonnets and made some of my worst enemies. And some of which were necessarily other than creditable, because I lived to the fullest, as one should do everything that one does."

Nonetheless, Dorian Hope – again, sounding very much like Wilde – affirmed that his "place is and always will be with Art, and with the disciples of Art.[18] Closing out this lengthy and self-justifying reply with the signature "Dorian Hope," Holland challenged his critics to "remember these facts and leave my name serenely to the immortality that it deserves." He here claims a mystique informed by Wilde's example: Wilde had warned the hostile critics of *The Picture of Dorian Gray* "to leave my book, I beg you, to the immortality that it deserves."[19] Adapting Wilde's phrase, Dorian Hope has altered the object of this desired "immortality": his creation is not so much a "book" but a *name*.

I strongly doubt that Dorian Hope's main concern in the publication of *Pearls and Pomegranates* was the literary content of the volume or, for that matter, the five hundred dollars it cost him to publish seven hundred copies. Rather, *Pearls and Pomegranates* represents publishing as performance art. Enclosed by the Wildean paratexts of its title and dedication, the book itself from this vantage is pure spectacle – an art piece that conjures into being a Poet. Herbert S. Gorman, who reviewed the volume for the *New York Times Book Review* prior to the plagiarism's discovery, noticed as much when he observed that the paratextual framing of *Pearls and Pomegranates* generates more interest than do its poetic contents. "Imagine," Gorman muses, "what memories the title of the book and the name of the author provoked! Dorian Gray and Lawrence Hope [*sic*] and […] all the poetical appanage of those Saffron Nineties! But when one gets into the pomegranate it is a sad fact that but few pearls are to be found." Gorman detects the flavour of a stunt in the volume, and not only in the poems themselves. He assures his readers that Dorian Hope can only be a pseudonym because "Miss Hope […] is, of course, a woman."[20]

Gorman's review presciently captures the cross-gendered coordinates of Dorian Hope's self-presentation as a poet, as we shall see in Hope's private correspondence and in some of the surviving records of Brett Holland's early life. It also registers the overwrought 1890s mood that Hope was trying to evoke. What this very brief reception history of *Pearls and Pomegranates* most succinctly records, I think, is how Dorian Hope's performance of authorship pays homage to Wilde's own endorsement of "annexation" as a creative mode. "It is only the unimaginative who ever invent," Wilde maintained. "The true artist is known by the use of what he annexes, and he annexes everything."[21] If a volume of poetry published under the name Dorian Hope affords its compiler the opportunity to stage authorship, then it does so by using the poems of others as props. And in a further conceptual nod to Wilde's privileging of form over content, the plagiarized words of Vedder and Lardy – the scaffolding of authorship – represent mere content subordinated to the supremacy of form. Less important than the mutually reinforcing paratexts of title, author name, and dedication that wittily frame the material book as performance art, the poems pad Dorian Hope's project of producing a "book" and himself as an "author" (figure 5). In conjuring Dorian Hope, the poems may be negligible, but inhabiting the role of a poet is everything.

Indeed, the creation of "Dorian Hope" would appear to be the culmination of Brett Holland's larger project of cultivating and broadcasting a personality. Although he began to fashion himself as a poet by publishing verse in newspapers, he had also engaged in other kinds of performances, which involved gender nonconformity, petty larceny, or both, long before he adopted the Dorian Hope persona. Holland was remarkably mobile, too: before establishing himself in New York, he appears to have attracted attention in numerous cities across the United States, including Baltimore, Wilmington, Charleston (West Virginia), Indianapolis, and Washington, DC. In all of these places he had a durable appetite for publicity – and notoriety. In 1916, for instance, Holland is mentioned in news reports as a drag performer of considerable skill. Working as a product demonstrator in a shop window in Wilmington, Delaware, Holland "attracted much attention. He is considered one of the best women impersonators in the country."[22] In 1917 he was arrested in Indianapolis for ordering and then not paying for women's clothing acquired through the mail. When, according to this news bulletin, he "dressed in female attire [he] had a distinctly feminine appearance," and he flaunted "the acquaintance he had with the furbelows which naturally belong to femininity."[23] By 1919, after a stint in the navy, Holland began entertaining members of the military in Washington, DC with his "character impressions."[24] These youthful adventures assume a more coherent shape with the emergence, in New York, of the Dorian Hope persona.

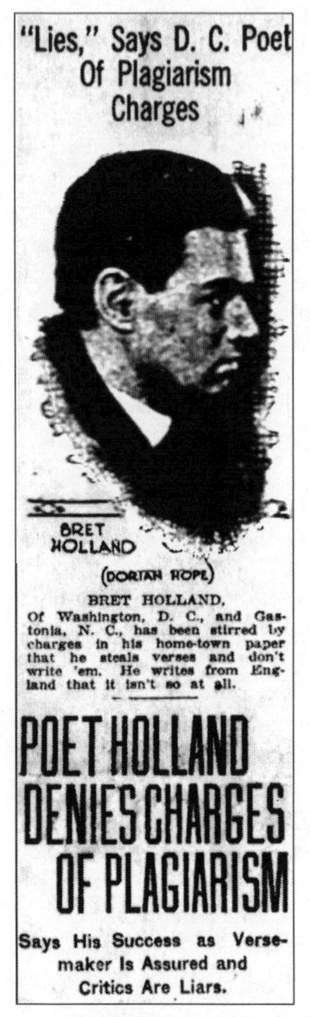
"Lies," Says D. C. Poet Of Plagiarism Charges

BRET HOLLAND (DORIAN HOPE)

BRET HOLLAND,
Of Washington, D. C., and Gastonia, N. C., has been stirred by charges in his home-town paper that he steals verses and don't write 'em. He writes from England that it isn't so at all.

POET HOLLAND DENIES CHARGES OF PLAGIARISM

Says His Success as Versemaker Is Assured and Critics Are Liars.

5 A picture of Dorian Hope, *Washington Times*, 24 August 1921, 1.

By 1920, as we have seen, Holland had moved to New York, and beyond the covers of *Pearls and Pomegranates* or the offices of Putnam's, the name Dorian Hope lent itself to further identity-construction projects that align with, and amplify, the gender nonconformity of Holland's earlier extravaganzas. The most illuminating source of information about Dorian Hope before the emergence of the Wilde forgeries comes not from journalistic publicity, but rather from his own private correspondence. As a self-proclaimed poet, Dorian Hope lived in a series of New York hotels in 1920. Just as Hope/Holland had paid for the publication of a book of poems, in this second appearance Hope was so invested in the accoutrements of the role of "Dorian Hope" that he had that name printed on visiting cards and had a supply made of monogrammed letterhead stationery. He employed the latter in a sequence of often-outrageous letters addressed to Philadelphia clergyman Herbert Boyce Satcher. From March to September 1920 Hope adopted an emphatically queer and campy persona, even styling himself in one of these missives the "Dowager Empress of Iceland."[25] Although these letters make no reference to either *Pearls and Pomegranates* or Oscar Wilde, the camp aristocratic femininity they display has a Wildean antecedent, for this "Dowager Empress" and "faded auntie" is, like Dorian Gray himself, apparently anxious about aging, and in several others letter he/she calls herself an "antique." (Unlike *Pearls and Pomegranates*, the Satcher letters display no affectations of nostalgia for the 1890s.) By September 1920, however, Hope had departed "the suburbs of old-maidenhood," apparently having sailed for England, leaving in his wake an ocean-liner postcard sent from Southampton and signed "Queen Mary." Seen from New York, our first view of Hope concludes with a departure, securing for himself a self-regarding mystique with the punning proclamation "I *hope* you are as happy as I am."[26] Happy or not, Satcher never heard from this queenly Dorian again.

In their mobilization of camp, theatrical effeminacy, and coded (and not-so-coded) homoeroticism, these letters are revealing documents in the history of queer sensibility and style. For instance, the term *auntie*, as used by Hope, was by 1920 already a familiar code word for effeminacy and sexual deviance. According to Eve Kosofsky Sedgwick, "'aunt,' 'auntie,' or the French 'tante' were recognized throughout the nineteenth century, and are still widely recognized, as terms for [...] 'a passive sodomist' or [...] for any man who displays a queenly demeanor."[27] The recipient of these missives, Herbert Boyce Satcher, was an Episcopalian clergyman in Philadelphia, a book collector, and a bibliographer of church music. He was also a closeted gay man[28] who served as an audience to Dorian Hope's epistolary performances. No mere spectator, Satcher also proved adept at reading Hope's queer codes, for he labelled his correspondent "an obvious homosexual."[29] Communicating in queer argot, Hope would have been taking for granted Satcher's ability to interpret the range of queer meanings in his letters. George Chauncey, the historian of early-twentieth-century gay New

York, observes in his discussion of "camp culture" that "the very fact that [gay men] could use a common code emphasized their membership in a group to whose codes they alone were 'wise,' and became a sign by which they distinguish themselves from outsiders."[30] The ironic deployment of female pronouns was just such a common code, and Hope, who had a background in cross-gender impersonation and performance, relied on it heavily.

A scholarly man, Satcher not only maintained this queer archive of letters for forty years after Hope's disappearance but also wrote a brief memoir of his encounter with Hope, which is now preserved at UCLA's Clark Library. (As a matter of fact, the institutionalization of the Wilde archive at the Clark prompted Satcher's recollections, for he only recorded his memories of the encounter after reading about Dorian Hope in a book collectors' journal, and later by corresponding with the Clark librarian of the day, Lawrence C. Powell). "The Dorian Hope Story," according to Satcher, "turned out to be a fascinating story of intrigue, subterfuge, chicanery, and criminal manipulation."[31] In this document Satcher recounts that he first met the peculiar individual whom he called a "vagrant poet" – then going by the name of James M. Hayes – in Philadelphia in 1919. They had initially been introduced by Satcher's friend Harold J. Sweeney, a clergyman from Elizabeth, New Jersey. Sweeney was deeply impressed by the thoroughly bohemian Hayes/Hope, describing this "poet friend" to Satcher as a "real genius," despite being a "physical and moral wreck" and "a moral bankrupt." "To know him or meet him," said Sweeney, "is like knowing Poe or Maupassant or Verlaine or Musset or Whitman or Swinburne."[32] When they parted, Hayes/Hope expressed his unambiguous interest in developing further intimacy. According to Satcher, he "slipped into my hand a visiting card on which the name 'Mr. Dorian Hope' was engraved. He said I should use the name in any communication with him [...] his appearance, as I remember, was not dapper, but rather derelict, with a velour hat drawn down close to his eyes."[33] The acquaintance was renewed by letter, and the correspondence between the two lasted for six months. (I can find no record of Brett Holland using the alias James M. Hayes, but the bohemianism, poetry, and queer affect, not to mention the frequent relocations, do strongly recall Holland's various irruptions into public view.)

Although only the Hope side of the correspondence – consisting of seven letters and one postcard – survives, it is nonetheless remarkable for the verbal portrait it paints of a highly stylized persona that is instantly recognizable as queer. In one of the earlier missives Hope (invoking the royal *we*) provides a neo-Wildean rubric (along with Dickinsonian dashes) for interpreting his highly theatrical rhetorical flourishes. "Don't take me too seriously," he tells Satcher in the "Dowager Empress of Iceland" letter, "but of course there is always an element of reality beneath our exaggerations."[34] Wayne Koestenbaum's concept "divaspeak" aptly captures this persona's "exaggerated" mode of expression. "Divas," Koestenbaum writes, "aren't afraid to praise themselves. Divas talk like Oscar Wilde. Or Oscar Wilde talked like a diva [...] Divaspeak helps the diva steal the show and then, with a rhetorical flourish, assert that the show was her property all along." One of the characteristic features of this linguistic mode, he continues, is "its sublime lack of respect for the truth."[35] For Hope, stylized unseriousness and camp insincerity become their own form of truth – a "reality" that recalls the performative play that *The Picture of Dorian Gray* calls "a method by which we can multiply our personalities."[36] Coming from Dorian Hope, this warning not to take him too seriously is also a promise, since Hope's "reality" is the diva's plane of existence; it inheres in the transmission and amplification of pure flamboyance.

Punctuated with hyperbolic, cross-gendered references to aging, Hope's letters also express desire for youthful male beauty. Sometimes Hope casts his crone self as an asexual, fluttery spinster, whereas at other moments he (or she) is decidedly more sexually assertive. The old-lady allusions seem designed at least partly to tease the spinsterish bachelor Satcher (who was, however, only thirty at the time); at one point Hope goads Satcher for mailing him a letter from "Cranford" – perhaps a nod to that imaginary town populated by elderly ladies in Elizabeth Gaskell's novel. A sequence of "boy" references, for their part, pushes the letters' flirtatious envelope rather further in the direction of scandalizing their reader. In the "Dowager Empress" letter, for example, Hope delights in mingling the sacred and the profane with a recollection of cruising in Satcher's church. He admits to Satcher, "I am envying you your dinner engagement made in my hearing – the companionship of the juvenile who occupied the seat behind me during services," and goes on to reminisce about "that angel faced boy of whose profile I became ardently enamoured, in an abstract, artistic way." This passage combines Uranian boy-love with Wilde's own taste for the homoerotic appreciation of "profiles."[37] That these verbal sallies apparently met with Satcher's disapproval is registered in the following letter – addressed formally to "Mr. Satcher," whereas the previous one had been more intimately addressed to "Satcher." In this subsequent missive Hope writes with mock contrition, "I am happy to know that *circumspect* is the essential qualification admitting me to the ambrosial hours of my desire – I pledge to fulfill all requirements asked of me, and to substitute my vice of verbosity with the stupidity of silence – "[38]

Hope did not stay silent for long, and his verbosity returned in an extravagantly outspoken letter in which he invited Satcher to visit him (figure 6):

> Dear Reverend,
> I am happy to have this note from you [...] I am destined to be in New York for another month, except for the week ends. You might dash your self over and visit me – I will be very happy to have you. The *Naked Boy* sounds like music from on high to the faded pink of my antique ears, but the Atlantic fleet is here for two weeks and sailors have been *entertaining* me magnificently – Tonight I have one with me – here watching me write these notes – He resembles an archangel, slightly damaged!
>
> Your friend,
> DH.[39]

Here, churchy camp is another of Hope's keynotes, in the references to "music from on high" and fallen archangels, and it registers how he likely saw Satcher: as a repressed inhabitant of what Dominic Janes has termed the "ecclesiastical closet."[40] On the basis of the letters Satcher's status as a clergyman seems to have contributed largely to Hope's interest in him, and it is with reference to Satcher's religious calling that Hope becomes most flirtatious. Contemplating an unrealized visit from Satcher – whom he addresses as "Saint Peter" – Hope tells him, "[I]f I know when you are coming, I will instruct the people here [i.e., at his hotel] that any one with [a] Roman Collar must be admitted – the clerical collar is becoming and I hope you will wear it when I see you – "[41] If he expected to prompt Satcher into a confidence or an indiscretion that he could use for blackmail, neither seems to have happened; Satcher was far too guarded to take Hope's bait. He declined to play the priest to Hope's acolyte.

Although Wilde himself became a distinctly British cultural icon, it was in New York that he staged his mass-cultural debut, for that city witnessed not only the beginning of the 1882 North American lecture tour but also the performance of his first play, *Vera; or, the Nihilists.*[42]

SAN RAFAEL
65-67 WEST 45TH STREET
NEW YORK

Dear Reverend—
I am happy to have this
note from you – My cries
of Friday prove to be false
alarms for I am destined
to be in New York for another
month, except for week end –
You might dash your self
over and visit me – I will
be very happy to have you.
The Naked Boy sounds
like music from on high
to the faded pink of my
antique ears, but the
Atlantic fleet is here for

SAN RAFAEL
65-67 WEST 45TH STREET
NEW YORK

two weeks and sailors
have been entertaining
me magnificently —
Tonight I have one with
me – here now watching
me write these notes –
He resembles an archangel
slightly damaged!

Your friend
D H

6 A letter from Dorian Hope to Herbert Boyce Satcher, 1920. William Andrews Clark Memorial Library, University of California, Los Angeles.

Whether or not Dorian Hope was following Wilde's example of inaugurating a career from New York, Satcher seems to have assumed that his correspondent was British. In "The Dorian Hope Story" Satcher remarks that the final postcard – signed "Queen Mary" – "was postmarked Southampton on his return to England" (figure 7),[43] thereby implying, with the notion of a "return," a British origin for Dorian Hope. And yet Hope was eager to display his familiarity with American culture in his correspondence. If the accuracy of Satcher's memoir can be relied upon, the two only spoke in person once, and although Satcher records nothing about the sound of Hope's voice, it is not hard to imagine Dorian Hope speaking with a feigned accent, regardless of his actual nationality. In one of several letters that threatens a visit, Hope drops some conspicuously American names: "When you deem it to my temperamental advantage, dispatch your lonely antique and she will be over at the specified time appearing Madonna-like in a hat of crushed strawberry effect, the shawl left her through Hetty Green's will, and the late Lydia Pinkham's pink tights – "[44] This drag performance in costumes that had been inherited from a notorious miser known as the "Witch of Wall Street" (Green) and the inventor of patent remedies for menopausal discomfort (Pinkham) probably never took place, but it does reinforce Hope's campy affinity for the imagery of moneyed, elderly femininity – here, however, in the key of American business success as opposed to "Dowager Empress" European royalty. As was Wilde's own celebrity, the fame (or notoriety) of these two women was a product of the English-speaking world's commodified mass culture.[45] As Hope's pursuers on the other side of the Atlantic wished to do, Satcher wanted to establish a nationality along with a singular identity for Dorian Hope. Even so, references to these capitalist mavens offer no reliable hint to Hope's actual nationality; they would be accessible to any anglophone inhabitant of New York City.

Satcher apparently never heard from Hope again and only revisited the 1920 correspondence upon reading about Dorian Hope's connection to the Wilde forgeries in the *American Book Collector*, an activity that prompted him to turn amateur sleuth. In reviewing the correspondence after forty years, Satcher noticed a "marked resemblance of the writing in my Dorian Hope letters to that [...] in the supposedly forged letters and manuscripts"[46] reproduced by Dudley Edwards in a 1957 article for that journal. Throughout the correspondence Hope's handwriting appears remarkably like Wilde's. To anyone acquainted with Wilde's hand, the resemblance is unmistakably striking. I am no handwriting

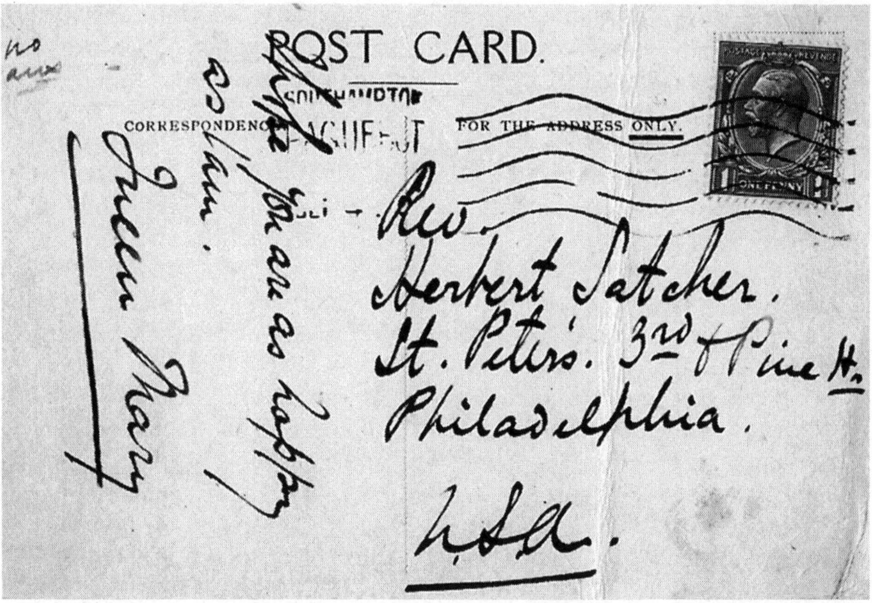

7 Dorian Hope's "Queen Mary" postcard, 1920. William Andrews Clark Memorial Library, University of California, Los Angeles.

expert and would describe that resemblance as more of a stylistic approximation than an exact imitation, but it is recognizably similar to Wilde's distinctive hand in the languid, rounded shapes of individual letters and entire words. The similarity in the handwriting confirmed for Satcher, as it did for Edwards, the unity of one iteration of Dorian Hope (the queer New York poet) with another (the Paris-based Wilde forger whom we met in this chapter's opening pages).

His curiosity piqued, Satcher set off on his own "Wilde Goose Chase," to borrow the title of Edwards's article. His inquiries about Dorian Hope led him to discover two volumes of religious poetry by a Roman Catholic "priest-poet" actually named James M. Hayes, who had published a poem entitled "The Burning Bush," which Hope had shared with Satcher years earlier and claimed as his own at their first meeting. Hayes's poems, according to Satcher, were "definitely religious, and shot through with Roman Catholic piety."[47] Hayes was a nuns' chaplain in Washington, DC; perhaps he, too, had encountered Brett Holland, alias Dorian Hope? At any rate, Satcher concluded that this poet's name was merely another one of the false identities annexed by Hope, since the "James M. Hayes of the poems was definitely not the 'James M. Hayes' Sweeney and I knew."[48] By the time of Satcher's investigations, however, this lead had turned a literal dead end, for the real Hayes had since died.

In "The Dorian Hope Story" Satcher labels the Dorian Hope forgeries an "ironical postscript to the Oscar Wilde tragedy," and he concludes the account of his sleuthing with an affirmation of the Arthur Cravan-Fabian Lloyd theory of Dorian Hope's identity. Although the mystery of Dorian Hope had led him to pursue a trail of empirical evidence, to consult experts and public records, the investigation he recounts in his "Dorian Hope Story" ultimately adheres to the narrative logic of family scandal and tragedy. Under this logic Dorian Hope can be identified and classified by the defining feature of the Wilde myth, the criminalized spectacle of homosexuality. Focusing on Fabian Lloyd's father, Otho Lloyd, who was Constance Wilde's brother, Satcher underscores patriarchal intergenerational shame in drawing out the irony of Hope's queerness. "The brother-in-law who was so shocked at Oscar Wilde's behaviour that he could not endure the prospect of his nephews [Cyril and Vyvyan Holland] even bearing the name of their father," he writes, "could not have foreseen at this stage that his own son would turn out to be what he had so militantly condemned in Wilde, and with the added stigma of forgery, and the attempt to capitalize on Wilde's genius twenty years after this death."[49] The underlying assumption in Satcher's "Dorian Hope story" is thus that the "exaggerations" of his correspondent's letters disclose a queer truth: the identity of a forger who, as an "obvious homosexual" and as Oscar Wilde's nephew by marriage, came equipped with a queer pedigree. But that very "obviousness" is just as comprehensible as role-playing by someone who was well enough informed about queer subcultural modes of expression and capable of dramatizing them effectively. Dorian Hope's obvious queerness, in other words, is also legible as the expedient manoeuvring of a con artist trying to authenticate a forged persona. As a closeted clergyman, Satcher would have been vulnerable to Hope's importunings, but he seems not to have been the easy mark that Hope took him for. Instead, Satcher proves an invaluable witness in the case of Dorian Hope.

Pearls, pomegranates, and Herbert Boyce Satcher behind him, Hope's eventual departure for England on the Queen Mary marks a reassessment of his New York plans.[50] In short order, he embarked on yet another deception and reinvented himself with another Wildean alias.

By 7 October 1920, a man calling himself *Sebastian* Hope was living in London and writing to Alfred Douglas.[51] When Hope contacted him, Douglas was the editor of a right-wing journal called *Plain English* and anxious as ever to protect his reputation from imputations of homosexuality. Although his extremely litigious life continued to be dominated by the legacy of his relationship with Wilde, as we observed in the previous chapter, he seems not to have noticed that this "Sebastian" Hope (the new name alluding to Wilde's alias Sebastian Melmoth and/or to the gay male icon St Sebastian) may have been on something of a fishing expedition. Hope had at this point fastened himself onto another clerical personage, the Catholic bishop of London, Ontario (then residing at the Jermyn Court Hotel in London, England) through whom he received two letters from Douglas. Christopher Millard asserted in 1924 that these letters were themselves forgeries – that they had been written by Hope, not Douglas.[52] If they are fakes, then the forger would have had the capacity to produce a forged British postmark on the envelope enclosing the first one, itself an impressive feat; at the same time, the possible status of these Alfred Douglas letters as forgeries does nothing to diminish their role in marking Hope's imaginative interventions into Wilde's afterlife.

I am, however, relatively confident of the Douglas letters' authenticity and in the identity of Dorian with Sebastian Hope because the details of Sebastian's London movements so strongly recall Dorian's New York ones. Both Hopes rely on contacts with churchmen, take up temporary residences in big-city hotels, and traffic in poetry. A zealous Catholic and an acknowledged expert in the sonnet form, Douglas declined Hope's submission of a sonnet to his journal, telling his correspondent with some asperity: "if you had read the 'Note' at the end of my collected Poems you would have known my views about sonnets."[53] Those views are nothing if not self-congratulatory, and in that "Note" Douglas remarks that the sonnet "has always been my favourite instrument of expression in poetry and [...] I may safely say that no other English poet with the exception of Rossetti [...] has devoted so much laborious work to it."[54] I doubt, however, that Hope had sincere ambitions to publish original poetry; he did not in New York. Practising on Douglas's vanity, Hope had given Douglas the opportunity to pronounce on poetic form.

Once Douglas had asserted his own importance, he was inclined to be generous towards Sebastian Hope – precisely the position that Hope was manipulating him to adopt. I suspect what Hope was really after was information about Wilde's final years in Paris. Researching the Wilde legend by going to one of its main sources, Hope seems to have been cautious with his early inquiries: a question about "pre-war 5 franc notes" produced only an admission from Douglas that (as Hope would have known) he himself had "lived in Paris altogether from about 1897 to 1902."[55] Many of Wilde's final letters, written from Paris to various correspondents, include requests for money. Hope, perhaps with as-yet-unwritten forgeries in mind, may have been attempting to solicit some period-appropriate detail from Douglas. The "5 franc notes," moreover, may represent an error on Hope's part because the expatriate Wilde invariably requested funds from his correspondents in pounds sterling. Hope still had more to learn.

The two surviving Alfred Douglas letters to Sebastian Hope, respectively dated 7 and 9 October 1920, show that Hope was working with some panache to cultivate Douglas's friendship. They do not indicate precisely what he was up to. What they do appear to demonstrate is a rather rapid increase in intimacy, moving in the space of two days from a literary rejection to a social invitation. Contemplated social visits had been a hallmark of the Satcher correspondence, with Dorian Hope threatening Satcher with his campy sociability, but this time the recipient of Hope's attention makes the invitations. Hope appears sufficiently charming that Douglas wanted to extend their acquaintance despite the "inadmissible" condition of his sonnet. Douglas's second letter to Sebastian Hope speaks to just how charming Hope could be, as he asks him, rather spontaneously, to join a trip to Brighton, where he was going "to have tea [...] at the Convent of the Sacred Heart with two little girls (aged 8 & 12) who are at school there. Why not come down to Brighton too?"[56] In anticipation of a homoerotically charged proposition uncannily similar to that depicted in T.S. Eliot's *The Waste Land* (1922), Douglas breezily continues, "I have ordered a room at the Metropole Hotel. So if you come down we can spend a couple of days together."[57] We can only speculate on what information (if any) Hope eventually gleaned from Douglas, but the acquaintance was maintained into the next year, for Douglas inscribed a first-edition copy of *The Rossiad,* his verse satire attacking Robert Ross, to Sebastian Hope in February 1921 – unless, of course, that inscription is another of Hope's forgeries.[58] Hope's brief connection with Douglas soured when, impersonating an editor at Douglas's journal, Hope briefly repeated the role of shady editor that he had played (formerly as Brett Holland) at Putnam's in New York. Douglas got wind of this scam and in March

1921 issued the following "Warning" to his readers: "It has come to our knowledge that a certain person hailing from America who goes by the name of Sebastian (or Dorian) Hope has represented that he is the assistant editor of *Plain English*. The gentleman in question has not, and never has had, any connection at all with this paper. We would be greatly obliged if any one of our readers who may have received any communication from Mr. Hope purporting to emanate from *Plain English* would supply us with details in confidence."[59]

Douglas's warning, strictly speaking, is not wholly accurate; Hope had tried to publish a poem in the journal the year before. More importantly, it establishes two important pieces of the Dorian Hope puzzle: first, it links Sebastian with Dorian Hope; and, second, it records that Hope had indeed emanated from "America" (note, however, Douglas's caution in declining to assign Hope a definite nationality). Whether Douglas succeeded in tracking his quarry, or even in uncovering further "details in confidence" about him remains unknown, for by the spring of 1921 Hope had moved on to other projects, leaving Douglas and *Plain English* behind him. He had also relocated to Paris.

A "Well Turned-Out Youth" in a "Magnificent Fur-Lined Overcoat": Dorian Hope in Paris, 1921–2

On the very day that William Figgis received his first Parisian letter from "André Gide" – 5 April 1921 – the plagiarism of *Pearls and Pomegranates* was exposed in the *New York Times*. By then, however, Dorian Hope's New York days were well over. The circumstances surrounding the production and circulation of the forgeries sold to Figgis and Maggs Brothers are both murky and complex, and the available information is incomplete. Before I explore the forgeries themselves in detail, it will be helpful to go over their emergence in the market for rare books and manuscripts in order to speculate more definitively as to how (and why) they were produced.[60] Since William Figgis was the more extensively involved, kept the best records, and even wrote "sensational reminiscences" on the subject, his archive provides the clearest path towards reconstructing as much as possible the Wildean representations undertaken by Dorian Hope in Paris.[61]

As we have seen, both firms (Hodges Figgis in Dublin and Maggs Brothers in London) were impressed with the provenance of the Wilde manuscripts offered to them from Paris. Accordingly, they made purchases from both "André Gide" and "Pierre Louÿs." Relatively soon after these early transactions, however, "doubts began to creep in concerning the authenticity of these MSS"[62] at Maggs Brothers, the purchasers of *Salomé*, and they set about scrutinizing the documents they had acquired. They determined that the paper used in the putative *Salomé* manuscript was not only American in origin but also produced after 1915 by a paper manufacturer in Massachusetts – a physical impossibility for a manuscript known to have been written in Paris in 1891–2. They then determined that the Paris address used by "Pierre Louÿs," 11 rue Scribe, was the Paris American Express office. ("André Gide," it later turned out, had also been using this address.) Likely sensing the imposture's imminent detection, "Pierre Louÿs" had ceased contact with Maggs Brothers by June 1921, and on 1 July the firm wrote to the real Louÿs, confirming that someone had been using his name in order to sell dubious Wilde manuscripts: "It is evident therefore that some one has been personating you and offering for sale in your name manuscripts alleged to be in the autograph of Oscar Wilde."[63] No further manuscripts were offered to or purchased by Maggs, and to this day the firm retains its archive of Wilde fakes.

The masquerade persisted, however, as William Figgis's entanglement with "André Gide" grew in complexity. Figgis purchased numerous Wilde manuscripts from "Gide" and went on to sell some of them to dealers and collectors. An October 1921 letter describes some of the titles possessed by "Gide," in the casual, yet professional tone that Figgis's Paris correspondent adopted throughout their period of contact, all the while displaying ample bibliographical knowledge of Wilde's varied publications: "There are eight personal letters, very substantial and characteristic ones, though not lengthy. Some fragmentary pages of the *SPHINX*, manuscripts of several sonnets, a review of 'Mr. Swinburne's Poems & Ballads', Third Series. (Appeared in the Pall Mall Gazette. June 27, 1889.), and a story called *The Sphinx Without A Secret*. I have, too, a first edition of *Dorian Gray*, in French, (Savine 1895), copy with elaborate presentation autograph inscription in English and signed in full."[64]

Figgis's correspondent was encouraged by the £130 that the dealer paid for these items, and a later letter increased the stakes of their transactions with a more ambitious list of texts: "There are the complete manuscript of the immortal *Ballad of Reading Gaol*, *A Woman of No Importance*, *Lord Arthur Savile's Crime*, *The Nightingale and the Rose*, *The Decay of Lying*, and two letters of the greatest possible interest [...] To dwell on descriptions of the other pieces would be to emphasize the obvious.

They are all well preserved and complete, conforming to Methuen's published texts to which you may easily refer."[65]

Up to this point, Figgis's Paris correspondent had assiduously cultivated his target by enhancing his claims to reliability. He had, for example, built trust by purchasing books from Figgis and scrupulously paying for them, thereby establishing what seemed to be a conventional business relationship with some modest transactions. He brazenly cashed cheques made out to "André Gide," and so Figgis had no reason to doubt that he was dealing with the real Gide. (In later transactions "Gide" requested that money be wired to his "secretary," "Monsieur D. Hope.")[66] "Gide" also had a talent for name-dropping, demonstrating his familiarity with members of Wilde's circle. Robert Ross, for one, is mentioned many times as a source of his wares. Ross had died in 1918 and so could not be called upon to dispute any claims made by "Gide." Figgis's correspondent sometimes maintained that with regard to certain manuscripts he was acting as a go-between for another seller, the estate of the recently deceased French writer Octave Mirbeau. Mirbeau had defended Wilde in the French press after the trials, so a connection between the two would seem plausible. Such consignments were not an unusual practice in the rare-book trade and could go some way to accounting for why numerous manuscripts were being made available by a single vendor. Having displayed such bona fides, "Gide" floated an exclusive arrangement with Figgis: "as you have an entrée in to the market," he assured the dealer, "I do not want to take the matter up with anyone until I have written you."[67] And he seemed helpfully well informed about the state of that market, as many of the manuscripts he had for sale were acquired "when anything bearing Wilde's name was not worth a hapenny on the other side of the channel."[68] Keeping up with changing times and markets, "Gide" obligingly suggests that "you will probably see your way to convert these [i.e., a new set of manuscripts on offer], along with the others you have, into a profitable sum in dollars. Wilde's popularity in America is astounding and as you wrote me some time ago, all the money is now in America."[69] A bookseller's challenge in marketing Wilde, it seems, could be easily surmounted by going to (not just following) the money.

Despite these displays of a swindler's perspicacity, some of the merchandise proffered by Figgis's correspondent also puzzled the bookseller. There was, for example, some confusion caused by erroneous dates on certain Wilde letters. "Gide" explained away these forgers' errors by affirming, "I hate to think of my letter to you having embodied any inaccurate information. I need hardly say how unintentional it was. As regards the [Wilde] letters, it is not a matter of such deep concern; we all confuse dates and, as you will have them right away, the question will soon have done with."[70] Further difficulties emerged for the Dublin dealer when two manuscripts, "The Tomb of Keats" (an early journalistic piece) and "The Disciple" (a prose poem), which he had sold to the London firm Davis & Orioli, were "returned [...] as doubtful."[71] Acting throughout in good faith, Figgis began to make some discreet inquiries of his own. By December 1921 he was in touch with Maggs Brothers, who, upon examining some of Figgis's "Gide" manuscripts, averred that all the Wilde manuscripts coming from Paris were forgeries:

> Similar manuscripts, very carefully done to represent the originals, with corrections, directions to printer etc. also some fragmentary pieces, have been offered for sale both in London and in Paris (from the latter address the vendor improperly used the name of a famous French author); they have likewise been offered for sale to a well-known New York dealer – All these manuscripts upon close inspection were declared to be forgeries, and subsequent events confirmed this. The handwriting and general appearance of both lots of manuscripts display characteristic similarities, so much so as to make us believe they eminate [*sic*] from the same pen.[72]

Intrigued and suspicious, Figgis took a bold step. He turned detective and went to Paris. Through a bookselling colleague there, C. Frederic Harrison of Brentano's, he made contact with the actual Gide. According to Harrison, the real Gide spoke "very bad English" – unlike the source of the Wilde manuscripts – and found the entire business "all very mees-tee-reeus."[73] Resenting his name being used in what increasingly appeared to be an elaborate fraud, Gide determined to help Figgis and Harrison, and together they set up what amounted to a sting operation.

It was in Paris, in January 1922, that William Figgis met a man calling himself Dorian Hope. Having written to arrange a meeting with "Gide," Figgis found himself delayed on his journey to France by bad weather. By the time he got to Paris, he had missed his appointment but was met at his hotel by a curious personage whom he had not expected – "one Dorian Hope." This is Figgis's description of the figure he met:

> He was dressed like a Russian Count with [a] magnificent fur-lined overcoat; a plausible well turned-out youth of about 25. He represented

> himself as secretary to Andre Gide who, he said, was unavoidably absent, in Italy. He had given him messages of great distress at missing my visit and so on. I had a long chat with this emissary and did my best to catch him out in the conversation but indeed I found him well acquainted with the position and with all that had transpired between "Andre Gide" and me. I have since felt more or less convinced that he was the prime mover in the whole business.[74]

For his meeting with Figgis, Hope had costumed himself in an approximation of the striking fur-trimmed coat that Wilde – himself a mere "youth" of twenty-seven at that point – had worn upon his arrival in New York in 1882. (Paris in January must have been so cold that this Dorian Hope needed rather more robust outerwear than the velour hat that Satcher's correspondent had memorably worn in Philadelphia in 1919.) The photographer Napoleon Sarony, whose images "often created as much as they recorded celebrity status," produced a series of widely circulated photographs of Wilde wearing this coat, making it just as famous as its wearer (figure 8).[75] By likening Hope to a "Russian Count," though, Figgis seems not to have picked up on the visual citation of Wilde's much-photographed "fur coat." Nonetheless, his description of Hope's attire brings the most iconic image of Wildean dandyism immediately to mind.

That fur coat had been one of Wilde's most prized possessions, so much so that he thought – and wrote – about it in prison. He was so horrified to learn that it had been converted into ready cash by his impecunious brother during his (Oscar's) imprisonment that he could not bring himself to name Willie Wilde (or his wife, Lily) in a letter from prison to Robert Ross bemoaning the loss of his property: "I would take it as a great favour if More [Adey] would write to the people who pawned or sold my fur coat since my imprisonment, and ask them from me whether they would be kind enough to state where it was sold or pawned as I am anxious to trace it, and if possible get it back. I had it for twelve years, it was all over America with me, it was at all my first nights, it knows me perfectly, and I really want it."[76] Was Dorian Hope displaying the New York poet's mischievous sense of humour by stage-managing the reappearance of the famed coat, or was he living out a sartorial fantasy by costuming himself *as* Wilde? Although it is impossible to judge the seriousness (or otherwise) of the gesture, his spectacular outfit clearly made an impression on Figgis. It also reveals the degree of his investment in Wildean fantasies, for this performance,

8 “Oscar Wilde.” Photograph by Napoleon Sarony, New York, 1882. William Andrews Clark Memorial Library, University of California, Los Angeles.

unlike those of "Gide," was now corporeal. Hope's textual imposture had, for a moment, become physical embodiment, and Figgis's description of a "well turned-out youth of about 25" meshes well with what we know about Brett Holland, who would have been 24 at the time. After this appearance Hope becomes much more conspicuous in the "Gide" correspondence, although he remains just offstage and never writes to Figgis under that name. "Gide" always refers to Hope in the third person as a "friend" or "secretary." Hope's Wildean appearance, moreover, is amplified by a description that sounds like wish-fulfilment, for, according to "Gide," "[i]t pleases me to hear how charming you found young Mr. Hope. He has an astounding popularity everywhere, always in demand, always found extraordinary in his conversation."[77] This account could easily depict the social successes of a young Oscar Wilde on his North American tour, luxuriating in that celebrated fur coat.

Having met Dorian Hope and the real Gide in Paris, Figgis returned to Ireland. An indignant Gide related to Figgis that he had gone to the police "to give a detailed account of the forgery of which you are the victim," and strongly advised the bookseller to press charges.[78] Figgis, meanwhile, asked his Paris correspondent to send "an affidavit declaring his bona fide"[79] along with a fresh batch of manuscripts that had been offered. Now that the real Gide was aware of the impersonation, Hope would be running an even graver legal risk in consenting to this plan. "This I knew he could not do," Figgis recalled, "without further dangerous and incriminating forgery."[80] The audacious "Gide" nonetheless sent him more materials, but at this point the swindle began to deteriorate. Figgis kept what he had and declined to pay, openly expressing "doubtfulness" about the manuscripts. He wanted another guarantor who could vouch for them. "Gide" replied with a telling choice: Pierre Louÿs. "Immediately after your letter asking for one signature in addition to my own came, I wrote for that of Pierre Louys: surely no single name would be more satisfactory than that of him who corrected the proofs of Salomé, contributed generously to its composition in its final draft, and him to whom Wilde dedicated the drama when it was published?"[81] Such assurances were accompanied by increasingly desperate demands for money, which may also explain why the Paris correspondent began moving around, from Amsterdam to Brussels to London. His final, frustrated letter (dated 27 April 1922) threatens Figgis with unnamed (likely non-existent) competition in the book trade: "I have arranged to sell the mss. here in London," he writes, "[and] have found a purchaser who will pay me what I have paid and a considerable profit besides, and I expect you to return the mss. at once."[82] This Figgis did not do. Instead he pursued a new line of inquiry. He began corresponding with Christopher Millard. Surprisingly, Millard – at first – believed the Wilde manuscripts from Paris to be the real deal.

Millard was not only the leading Wilde expert; he was also a well-connected rare-book dealer, and he was quite excited about the lucrative possibilities afforded by what he called "literary property of very considerable value."[83] For example, he offered several items then held by Figgis to his wealthiest client, the Los Angeles collector and keen Wilde fan William Andrews Clark Jr.[84] Throughout the spring of 1922 Millard's generally astute commercial judgment came up against his intense personal interest in Wilde. Although Figgis warned him that "we are not in a position to guarantee that they are genuine,"[85] Millard pursued the manuscripts with avidity. It appears that he badly *wanted* them to be the real thing, so much so that he came up with convoluted explanations for inconsistencies in the dating of certain letters, such as "Wilde's" apparent use of the French Revolutionary calendar, dated from 1789. For Millard, the main difficulty in finalizing a purchase remained that Dorian Hope had (once again) disappeared and so could not be paid for the documents that were still in Figgis's possession; this situation caused enough of a delay for Millard to rethink his original position on the manuscripts and, as Figgis put it, to "further probe their genuineness."[86]

Millard did just that, and by July, after a devastatingly momentous meeting at Maggs Brothers, he issued a humiliating retreat. He explains it in a letter to Figgis:

> This letter is more painful for me to write than it will be for you to read. Maggs showed me to-day all his Wilde documents and correspondence about them and I was suddenly convinced that I had been deceived and that all the Dorian Hope manuscripts are forgeries [...] I see now in a flash all the forger's blunders which I tried to explain away – the letters dated from a London club after Wilde's arrest, the letter to Octave Mirbeau dated from Paris while Wilde was still in Naples, the question of the same paper being used for "The Nightingale and the Rose" in 1887 as for "The Ballad of Reading Gaol" ten years later. Yet so convinced was I of the genuineness of all these letters and manuscripts that I found explanations that satisfied me. But Maggs' things are without any possible doubt forged: they all

> come from the same source as yours, and I cannot any longer pretend that I think yours are genuine.
>
> This man who called himself Sebastian Hope to Maggs and Dorian Hope to you must be an extraordinarily clever person and his slips are hard to explain. Most difficult of all to explain is the blunder he made in putting all these things on the market at the same time. I verily believe that if he had been content to offer one here and one there, he would have never been detected.[87]

Millard, as we saw in the previous chapter, was a punctilious bibliographer who prized exactitude and completeness in everything related to Wilde. From his perspective the organizing principle behind the Dorian Hope forgeries was error. The forger's errors, on the one hand, are illuminating in so far as they reveal the manuscripts' spuriosity by contradicting trivial but externally verifiable facts (such as Wilde's whereabouts on a particular date). On the other hand, a commercial "blunder" – we could call it a forger's error in strategy – proves mystifying. The greed (or penury?) evidenced by flooding the market with multiple Wilde manuscripts "at the same time," Millard suggests, has led inexorably to Dorian Hope's detection. Had he been less ambitious or more "content" with a con of smaller scope, he might have gotten away with it.

Millard's comments about "slips" and "blunders" provide a helpful structure for looking more closely at the Dorian Hope forgeries themselves. When surveying the patterns and characteristic features displayed by the mass of "Oscar Wilde" material emanating from Dorian Hope, I am struck by not only what Dorian Hope got wrong but also what he got *right*. Despite the errors identified by Millard as "clumsy," the very scale of these forgeries could impress even him, as he admitted in a contrite letter to Clark rescinding an offer of manuscripts he now knew to be forged: "I have occasionally seen a forged letter or a faked inscription in a book of Wilde's, and have condemned it; but I did not think it would be possible to forge successfully a long manuscript."[88] In the aggregate the Dorian Hope forgeries display an almost encyclopaedic level of expertise about Wilde's life and career that, ironically enough, mirrors Millard's own. Analysing the forgeries without the burden of Millard's professional or commercial stake in Wilde's writings can help us learn a great deal about how, and perhaps even why, they were contrived in the first place.

Surveying the Forgeries: Dorian Hope's Archive(s)

In order to discuss the Dorian Hope forgeries in more detail, we need first to return to New York in 1920, and to the month of April, to be precise, which occupies a curious gap in Dorian Hope's correspondence with Herbert Boyce Satcher. On 23 April the Anderson Galleries held a sale by auction of the Oscar Wilde collection of John B. Stetson Jr. The Stetson sale was a major event among literary auctions, and it is very tempting to imagine Brett Holland, who once claimed to be a book dealer "always able to speculate on rare editions and rare MSS," in attendance.[89] It also had a formative impact on the shaping of the Wilde archive, forgeries included. The auction catalogue's introduction does not exaggerate when it announces that the sale represents "the greatest Collection of the Works of Oscar Wilde that has ever been formed. Indeed, it is unlikely that such a complete and important collection of manuscripts and books by and relating to a single author has ever before been brought together."[90] The sale, consisting of 423 lots, realized US$46,870 in two sessions.[91] It proved beyond any doubt that Wilde's literary legacy had value – especially in the market for rare books and manuscripts. More specifically, it affirmed that there was a robust market of American collectors for Wilde, as "André Gide" would later remind William Figgis. The *New York Times* on the next day drew attention to the prices reached by many items and named two main buyers: legendary Philadelphia dealer Dr A.S.W. Rosenbach, "the principal purchaser at the sale"; and New York dealer Gabriel Wells.[92] But if the sale itself represented a treasure-trove of Wilde material, assembled first by Stetson and then dispersed to dealers, collectors, and institutions, then its catalogue proves a treasure-trove of *information*. Matthew J. Bruccoli observes that under the management of Mitchell Kennerley (1878–1950; also the publisher, in 1921, of the expanded "Mr. W.H.") the catalogues of Anderson Galleries were compendia bristling with data. Into the 1920s, as their

> descriptions gradually became fuller [...] facsimiles of the major items became obligatory features of the Anderson Galleries' catalogues. Arthur Hooley, Kennerley's versatile man of letters, compiled many of the literary catalogues and took pains to make them readable [...] The Anderson catalogues not only provided bibliographical descriptions but also explained the importance of the items [and] depending on the value of the items, book descriptions could be quite elaborate [...] The Anderson maintained

a reference library and a staff of cataloguers whose work required considerable research.[93]

As an archive that easily lends itself to data mining, the Stetson sale catalogue would thus be a boon to anyone conducting research on Wilde, his writing, his world, and the commercial value of his work – whatever their objective might be. And the Dorian Hope forgeries are nothing if not the products of significant research.

The materials on offer at the Stetson sale were diverse and wide ranging. They represented every stage of Wilde's career as a writer, from his first publication right up until the end of his life. According to the catalogue's introduction, they comprise nothing less than a "library": "There are original manuscripts, many of them complete, of nearly all of the writings of Oscar Wilde; first editions and presentation copies of all his published works; long series of autograph letters to the men and women intimately identified with his life; letters to him from well-known men and women of the period, and a long series of books relating to his life and works. It is at once a collector's and a student's library and contains the material for a detailed history of the life and times of Oscar Wilde that has yet to be written."[94]

The Wilde legend ("a detailed history of [his] life and times") was palpable – and accessible – within the catalogue's seventy-three pages. Among them we find minutely detailed descriptions of manuscripts that offer insight – some of it necessarily speculative – into Wilde's writing process, in addition to bibliographical particulars related to the transmission of those texts into print. For example, the description of lot 83 – the typescript of "A Good Woman" (later retitled *Lady Windermere's Fan*) – indicates that "the author has corrected [the play's four acts] very extensively, by deleting and adding. The manuscript varies in many instances from the printed version, whole passages being left out, and in some instances, passages deleted in the present copy have been re-instated in the printed text."[95] In describing lot 96, the manuscript of the long poem *The Sphinx* (figure 9), the catalogue compiler indicates that this "collection of stanzas written by Wilde for his poem 'The Sphinx' exhibits in a marked degree his efforts to obtain the most striking and effective rhythmical production. On several sheets he has marked words in rhyme, apparently for the purpose of using them later as his composition progressed."[96] Such descriptions offer prospective buyers a sense of a work's textual stemma: they indicate, for instance, how the manuscript differs from (or matches) the final, printed text;

MANUSCRIPT OF "A GOOD WOMAN"
("LADY WINDERMERE'S FAN")

450.– 83. LADY WINDERMERE'S FAN. Typewritten Manuscript of "A Good Woman" (afterward's altered to "Lady Windermere's Fan"). The Four Acts complete. 4 vols, 4to, wrappers, preserved in a full crimson levant morocco solander case. [1892]

The separate Acts have been bound up for convenience in revising, and the author has corrected them very extensively, by deleting and adding. This manuscript varies in many instances from the printed version, whole passages being left out, and in some instances, passages deleted in the present copy have been re-instated in the printed text.

PRESENTATION COPY TO LORD ALFRED DOUGLAS

300.– 84. LADY WINDERMERE'S FAN. A Play about a Good Woman. Small 4to, original buckram gilt, uncut, in full olive levant morocco solander case.
London: Elkin Mathews and John Lane, 1893

FIRST EDITION. AUTOGRAPH PRESENTATION COPY FROM OSCAR WILDE TO LORD ALFRED DOUGLAS, with inscription on fly-leaf: *"For Alfred Bruce Douglas from the author. London, Nov. '93."*
ONE OF FIFTY COPIES ON LARGE PAPER.

AUTOGRAPH PRESENTATION COPY TO MARCEL SCHWOB

275.– 85. LADY WINDERMERE'S FAN. A Play about a Good Woman. 8vo, original cloth, ornaments in gold on sides, uncut.
London: Elkin Mathews and John Lane, 1893

FIRST EDITION. AUTOGRAPH PRESENTATION COPY FROM OSCAR WILDE TO MARCEL SCHWOB, with inscription on fly-leaf: *"To my friend Marcel Schwob, in sincere admiration and regard. Oscar Wilde, '94."*
[SEE ILLUSTRATION]

25.– 86. LADY WINDERMERE'S FAN. A Play about a Good Woman. 8vo, original cloth, ornaments in gold on sides, uncut.
London: Elkin Mathews and John Lane, 1893

FIRST EDITION. Laid down on inside of front cover, is a copy of the Play Bill of the initial performance of this Play, at the St. James's Theatre on Feb. 20, 1892.

20.– 87. LADY WINDERMERE'S FAN. A Play about a Good Woman. 8vo, original cloth, ornaments in gold on sides, uncut.
London: Elkin Mathews and John Lane, 1893

FIRST EDITION.

15.– 88. LADY WINDERMERE'S FAN. A Play in Four Acts. 12mo, original wrappers, preserved in a half green morocco slip-case. [New York, 1893]

This acting edition was probably prepared for the production of this play at Palmer's Theatre, New York City, in February, 1893.

2.– 89. LADY WINDERMERE'S FACHER. Das Drama eines guten Weibes. Ins Deutsche übertragen von Isidore Leo Pavia und Herman Freiherrn von Teschenberg. 8vo, half maroon levant morocco, gilt top, uncut, original wrappers bound in.
FIRST GERMAN EDITION. Leipzig, 1902

18

In a dim corner of my room,
For longer than my fancy thinks,
A beautiful and silent Sphinx
Has watched me through the dusky gloom.

Come forth my lovely seneschal,
and rub your head against my desk,
Come forth ~~thou~~ you exquisite Grotesque,
Half woman, and half animal.

Come forth my lovely languorous Sphinx,
and put your paws upon my knee,
and let me stroke your ears, and see
Your body spotted like the Lynx.

Ten thousand weary centuries
are thine, while I have hardly seen
Some twenty summers cast their green
For autumn's gaudy liveries.

O tell me, were you standing by
when Isis to Osiris knelt,
and did you see the Egyptian melt
Her union for Antony

And did you talk with Thoth, and did
You hear poor roaming Io weep,
and did you know the Kings that sleep
within the mighty pyramid.

[NUMBER 96]

9 Facsimile of *The Sphinx* in the Stetson sale catalogue, 1920. Author's own collection.

the kinds of interventions Wilde made at various points in the writing process; and, in the case of *The Sphinx*, they record his capacity for verbal experimentation. Rather than polished, finished productions, these are working documents that, like the manuscript of "The Soul of Man under Socialism," which "has been profusely corrected by Wilde, evidencing the thought given by him to this subject,"[97] bear witness to literary labour undertaken over time. That Dr Rosenbach paid US$1,450 for this draft of *The Sphinx* proves that a "collection of stanzas" in Wilde's autograph could command a significant price.[98]

The Stetson sale catalogue constructs an audience of Wilde "students" and "collectors" seeking privileged access to the writer's mind via the artefacts offered for sale. What might its detailed descriptions tell a would-be forger? In short, a great deal. For one thing, they confirm that Wilde wrote in drafts, correcting and revising as he went along.[99] This procedure has considerable implications for someone contriving forgeries because it means that it is perfectly plausible for several authentic manuscript versions of a particular text, representing different stages in its author's conception of the work, to exist simultaneously. If we allow ourselves to think as forgers, then this feature of Wilde's writing process is immensely fortuitous. The movement of one authentic manuscript version of a particular text through an auction house – like *The Sphinx* at the Stetson sale – does not make the appearance on the market of another manuscript version of the same text, possibly representing an earlier, later, partial, or discarded draft, particularly suspicious. There can thus be multiple "authentic" versions of one text. There would be no immediately apparent contradiction – no crisis in the perception of authenticity – between the lengthy *Sphinx* manuscript described previously and the incomplete manuscript consisting of two leaves on low-quality paper ("Some fragmentary pages of the *SPHINX*") that William Figgis acquired from "Gide" in 1921. Such a situation had to be very reassuring for forgers, and it is one of the reasons I am convinced that the Stetson sale catalogue served Dorian Hope as a forgery-generating archive.

A forger contriving manuscripts of known titles has to be careful, of course, in selecting which texts to forge. Although there is some overlap between the titles that appeared in the Stetson sale and those that emerged from Paris in 1921–2, it is not extensive, and when such overlap exists, it actually tends to work in the forger's favour. The corrected typescript of *A Woman of No Importance*, for instance, was auctioned in New York in 1920, whereas Dorian Hope sold William Figgis a lengthy,

168-page handwritten manuscript in 1921: the title is the same, but the Stetson typescript and the Hope manuscript appear to represent different stages in the play's composition and transmission. At the very least, the catalogue could inform a forger about which Wilde titles had emerged into the New York saleroom, and which ones had not. Forgers could also glean plenty of information from the Stetson catalogue about the physical characteristics of Wilde manuscripts. For one thing, the catalogue is rich in facsimile illustrations of Wilde's highly distinctive handwriting. There are eleven of these facsimiles, each taking up an entire catalogue page. They constitute the catalogue's only illustrations and represent a variety of occasions for writing. They include different literary genres, from poems to plays to prose works; private letters; and inscriptions in printed books. All of these images could have been used as templates for an enterprising forger. An "extraordinarily clever person," to use Millard's term for Dorian Hope, could learn not only how to copy Wilde's hand but also a fair amount of supplementary information about how he put ink to paper: his characteristic methods of inscribing presentation copies of his books; his approach to the spacing of words on the page of a manuscript, and how this differed depending on the genre of the text; his extravagant tendency to maximize his use of paper by committing relatively few words to a single page; and his partiality for writing in notebooks. It is nonetheless telling that the catalogue is otherwise silent on the particularities of paper, for it is precisely this sort of "blunder" – the American paper produced after 1915 and used for the forged *Salomé* manuscript – that led Maggs Brothers to conclude that their Wilde manuscripts from "Pierre Louÿs" were forgeries.

The Stetson sale catalogue was not the only printed reference point for Wilde's handwriting. Indeed, Dorian Hope (or a group of forgers working under that name) could have made use of over a dozen sources printed before 1921 that contained facsimiles of Wilde's hand. Millard's 1914 *Bibliography*, for instance, is packed with facsimiles, as is Robert Sherard's 1916 biography *The Real Oscar Wilde*. (Sherard's book even includes the facsimile of a poem dedicated to Wilde by Pierre Louÿs, in Louÿs's handwriting.) Judging from the sheer volume of information available in these reference works (and I include the Stetson sale catalogue in that category), I propose that Dorian Hope worked from previously published sources. With multiple examples of Wilde's hand available in books, he had no need to acquire genuine (and expensive) manuscripts to serve as models from which to copy. Moreover, if the Dorian Hope manuscripts derive from *printed* texts, they reverse the conventional process of textual transmission from a handwritten-manuscript stage (its status provisional with regard to authorial intention) to a finished and final work in print. Here, the facsimile autograph ironically precedes and serves as a pattern for the (forged) handwritten manuscript when the forger generates a "unique" manuscript by carefully imitating the handwriting illustrating the pages of a printed book.

In point of fact, this is the case with many of the Dorian Hope forgeries that appear to derive from printed books. The forged *Earnest* manuscript – the hook that caught William Figgis in 1921 in the first place – is telling in this connection. It is equipped with a superscribed dedication on the first leaf: "To Robert Baldwin Ross. In appreciation & in affection. O.W."[100] (As we have seen with the rehashing of *An Ideal Husband*'s dedication in *Pearls and Pomegranates,* Dorian Hope took careful notice of Wildean dedications.) This wording on the forged *Earnest* manuscript closely approximates the dedication that first appeared in the play's 1899 first edition: "To Robert Baldwin Ross[:] In appreciation. In affection." Wilde revised the play for publication after he was released from prison, and, as Nicholas Frankel observes, "some of the play's most memorable lines date from this time."[101] But the appearance of the dedication to Ross on a *manuscript* implies that the dedication was coeval with the writing of the play itself. Wilde's dedication of the play to Ross in print was a testament to his friend's loyalty to him in the tumultuous years *after* he had gone to prison, shortly after the play's 1895 theatrical premiere. By including the dedication on the first leaf of the forged manuscript, Dorian Hope demonstrates ignorance of this fact in erroneously conflating two different periods in the play's textual history.[102] This is a classic case of self-defeating authenticatory excess; in trying to include too many details to enhance a manuscript's plausibility, the forger can also unwittingly give the game away.

A comparison of the forged manuscript of *The Sphinx* that Figgis bought in 1921 and the poem's appearance in multiple facsimiles can help us to grasp better Dorian Hope's reliance on print sources. Wilde's ultra-decadent poem was first published in 1894, and, although its origins "are clouded in myth,"[103] its recent editors affirm that Wilde had been working on it as early as his student days at Oxford and continued to work on it in Paris in 1883.[104] It is by far his most facsimiled poem, and I would hazard that this unique situation obtained because many different manuscripts of the poem, with textual variations, were in circulation in the early twentieth century. Facsimiles of parts of the poem appear in Millard's *Bibliography of the Poems of*

Oscar Wilde (1907), in the authorized 1909 American edition of Wilde's *Poems*, in a 1911 Sotheby's auction catalogue, in Millard's *Bibliography of Oscar Wilde* (1914), and in Sherard's *Real Oscar Wilde* (1916), as well as the Stetson sale catalogue (1920). The Millard (1914) and Sherard facsimiles, which are identical, reinforce the observation about rhyming word sequences made in the Stetson sale catalogue's description of the poem. Along with some amusing doodles, for instance, Wilde has grouped together "stiff / hieroglyph / hippogriff / glyph" on one part of the page in those facsimiles, and "oreichalch / catafalque / talc" on another part.[105] The facsimile in the Stetson sale catalogue, however, shows an entirely different aspect of Wilde's work on the poem in a sequence of finished quatrains. Despite some degree of duplication, then, taken together these sources could give forgers a lot of material to work with.

Let us examine in precise detail the ways in which the authorized poem and the forgery stack up against one another, to have a better sense of how a forger might have navigated among these materials. The poem's first edition (1894) renders the opening stanza – printed entirely in capital letters – into two long lines of eight syllables:

> IN A DIM CORNER OF MY ROOM FOR LONGER THAN MY FANCY THINKS
> A BEAUTIFUL AND SILENT SPHINX HAS WATCHED ME THROUGH THE SHIFTING GLOOM.[106]

In Robert Ross's authorized collected edition of 1908, however, these elongated lines were returned to a (presumably earlier) quatrain format:

> In a dim corner of my room for longer than
> My fancy thinks
> A beautiful and silent Sphinx has watched
> Me through the shifting gloom.[107]

This stanza conspicuously avoids placing rhymed words at the end of each line. If we jump ahead to the manuscript facsimile in the Stetson sale catalogue, we can see precisely how much, to borrow two words from the opening stanza, the poem's verbal "gloom" has "shifted." And we do not need to consult an original Wilde manuscript to accomplish this. The words reproduced in the 1920 catalogue from an earlier, undated manuscript are close but not identical to those in the two published versions, and they appear in the catalogue facsimile in a quite different – and more traditional – arrangement, in an iambic tetrameter quatrain with an *abba* rhyme scheme:

In a dim corner of my room,
For longer than my fancy thinks,
A beautiful and silent Sphynx
Has watched me
through [from]
the dusky gloom.[108]

For its part, the fragmentary Dorian Hope forgery includes two versions of the poem's opening quatrain, with some unrelated words (however appropriate to sphinxes) thrown in to enhance the illusion of a fragmentary draft:

In a dim corner of my room
For longer than my fancy thinks
~~When fancy dreams & silent thinks~~
A beautiful & ~~silver~~ silent Sphinx
Has guarded well the captive gloom

~~Omniscient~~
With somnolent solemnity
In a dim corner of my room
For longer than my fancy thinks
A beautiful & silent Sphinx
Has watched me through the
Shifting gloom.[109]

The only differences in phrasing between the second Dorian Hope stanza and the 1908 version in Ross's edition are the ampersand and the layout of the verse. From manuscript to print, the shape of the lines changes, of course, and although Dorian Hope was quick to assure Figgis that the *texts* of his Wilde manuscripts could be verified by the Ross edition and "conform[ed] to Methuen's published texts to which you may easily refer," here in the second Dorian Hope stanza we find conformity with the word order found in the Stetson sale catalogue, amplified by the substitution of the (authorized) adjective "shifting" (likely from Ross's edition) for the Stetson facsimile's "dusky."

By placing two versions of the same stanza in a sequence in this manuscript, Dorian Hope thus offers up an imaginary progression from a rejected draft (with crossed out lines and an invented "captive gloom") to a more finished one whose words nearly exactly match those to be found in the sale catalogue and (however differently arranged) in Robert Ross's Methuen edition. In producing this particular document, the forger, I speculate, worked from (at least) two sources: a printed text of the poem, probably from Ross's Methuen edition of Wilde's *Collected Works;* and a facsimile reprint of the manuscript, probably the one in the Stetson sale catalogue. The result is nothing less than a newly forged textual history for *The Sphinx.*

In total, the forgery of *The Sphinx* reproduces the first two and the last of the poem's stanzas over two leaves. The forger has omitted the long middle of the poem, whose printed text runs to 176 lines. In comparison to the massive length of some of the other Dorian Hope forgeries, such an omission could appear rather lazy. But we need to remember that in this instance the forger was contriving a fragmentary and necessarily incomplete document; he sought to generate the illusion of a neglected draft whose value to a collector inhered precisely in its provisional state. More broadly, Dorian Hope seems to have put a great deal of effort into contriving *different types* of Wilde forgeries, and therefore subtly different kinds of deception. Literary manuscripts of familiar texts have been painstakingly copied out in the knowledge that there is a printed text against which the manuscript could be compared. The imaginative labour and studied craft in these cases work to fabricate alternate textual histories for known works with corrections, additions, and excisions that Wilde himself never made *but could have.* Such interventions indicate a playful and yet loving attitude towards Wilde's texts, for, in making such revisions, the forger is writing *as* Wilde, "correcting" the text as the writer was known to have done. The extended (and likely tedious) process of a manuscript forgery's contrivance is thus also a period of imaginary self-transformation, for in those moments the forger is pretending to *be* Wilde. In order to make these documents convincing (and even Millard was convinced for a while), a forger has to know the real thing very well indeed, and the familiar literary text is a platform – a stage, if you will – for (self-)invention. By copying out his writings, Dorian Hope gets to inhabit the role of Oscar Wilde, if only temporarily.

Forging personal letters is, by contrast, quite a different matter.[110] Literary manuscripts, as we have seen, can exist in multiple and non–mutually exclusive formats, but there is generally only a single authentic copy of a letter, and so no reliable printed guideline for a forger to follow (or embellish). A number of Wilde's letters, representing different aspects of his life and career, had appeared in print before the emergence of the Dorian Hope forgeries, but, unlike the literary texts compiled in Robert Ross's edition of Wilde's *Collected Works*, these would not necessarily have provided a forger with templates for duplication. Letters are sites of an interpersonal exchange between two individuals, and to forge a letter Dorian Hope would need to know more significant personal details about Wilde's life: the identities of his correspondents and his relationships to them, what kinds of things he wrote to them about, and the manner in which he wrote. Within those parameters the forger has to meet the challenge of making up entirely new material that could pass muster. The vital difference between forging literary manuscripts and personal letters, then, is that in contriving letters the imaginative platform is not Wilde's writing but his life, and the forger is called upon to exercise imagination without the kind of safety net afforded by a well-known manuscript and its printed simulacrum. (The monetary rewards, however, could be immense. A group of twenty-five genuine letters from Wilde to Alfred Douglas fetched US$7,900 at the Stetson sale.)[111] If there is a greater risk of detection in contriving a personal letter, it should come as no surprise that it was among the fake Wilde letters that Millard, with his expert knowledge of Wilde's biography, came to smell a rat.

Forged Wilde letters had been in circulation since at least 1911, and Millard, true to form, publicly exposed them. Writing to *Publishers' Circular* under his Stuart Mason pseudonym, Millard had warned members of the book trade about "holograph letters purporting to have been written by Oscar Wilde during the last few years of his life," some of which he found to be "sufficiently skilful to deceive anyone except an expert."[112] These forgeries could be detected, Millard asserted, by attending to a small but significant error in the renderings of Wilde's post-prison address in Paris: certain letters had him living not in the rue des Beaux Arts but in the *avenue* des Beaux Arts. Ten years later, the errors in the forged Wilde letters associated with Dorian Hope were equally vulnerable to such scrutiny; even so, they could also be elaborately and impressively inventive. In these letters "Wilde" is seen to be writing to some of the most intimate associates of his last years: Alfred Douglas, Robert Ross, and the publisher Leonard Smithers. These items authenticate themselves by drawing together the defining coordinates of the

Wilde legend: they employ a decadent style and refer, vaguely but plausibly, to homosexual lovers. Where possible, however, they *improve* that legend: Wilde's Parisian exile loses its misery and squalor and instead comes into focus as a state of romanticized, world-weary wisdom.

Such letters can be decidedly playful, like this example addressed to "Robbie" (Robert Ross) that Maggs Brothers acquired from "Pierre Louÿs" in the spring of 1921:

> My dear Robbie:
> It was good of you to write me so many nice letters. I want to believe every word you write but when I compare your actions with your words I can only say & think – alas! – I know that you are perfectly sincere & if you could only live up to the beautiful things you say & write – I would be very happy. I have been very much on the go since I came here & have met some very interesting types of people. I enclose this extract from a letter, which places the word "finis" to the history of a romance in which the leading figure was what the Sphinx would call a dashing French army officer.
>
> "The gray shadows are beginning to mantle the western hills. A golden sheen of sunlight hovers in the wide court just outside my window, but as the sun descends nearer the far western rim of the world, so goes the coloured light. The stars soon will break through the southern sky like myriads of saffron daisies. It seems strange how I became so madly infatuated by your personality. I was a savage before you tamed me. Today I have about ten francs left. Please send me fifty francs." And thus all romances end. The moral is "look out for your bank account."
>
> Send me letters often, but remember when you are writing that someone will read the letter – or try to read it. Your handwriting becomes more & more like the hieroglyphs on the sandstone obelisks.
>
> Yours ever
> Oscar[113]

It is not difficult to imagine the forger behind this letter taking pleasure in concocting such a distinctly Wildean fantasy. He gets to cram in so much: a male object of desire (a "dashing French army officer"); a decadent description of "coloured light" and "saffron daisies"; and even two "Sphinx" references – one to Wilde's friend Ada Leverson, whom he nicknamed "Sphinx," and another to the poem that rhymed hieroglyphs and obelisks. This letter imagines Leverson, the novelist who was one of Wilde's most stalwart allies, as an intimate confidante as the two of them trade stories with "Robbie" about attractive men. Although dashing army officers were not at all Wilde's type, here an illusory tryst is recounted in a pastiche of Wilde's prose poetry, complete with the forger's slyly winking moral about a financial swindle. If this is the version of Wilde that the forger thinks a collector might be after, then he is more than happy to supply it.

Another letter, addressed to Alfred "Bosie" Douglas, opens up imaginary vistas into the performance history of *The Importance of Being Earnest*, a play that is forever entangled with the narrative of Wilde's downfall. *The Importance of Being Earnest* premiered on 14 February 1895; Wilde's name was removed from the programme and the play's advertising after his arrest on 5 April, following the collapse of the first (libel) trial; and it closed on 8 May. The "Bosie" letter is dated only "Tuesday 23rd" and, since it refers to the termination of the play's theatrical run, such a date would have to represent an early month in 1895. The only possibility for this imaginary Tuesday would be 23 April, when Wilde was in and out of the Bow Street police court, awaiting his second trial that would begin on 26 April. He was therefore in no position to be hosting any "party" like the one mentioned in the letter:

> My dear Bosie:
> Your letter just came: *The Importance of Being Earnest* is playing two weeks longer & of course we can have the party. I am willing to see that Hodges boy again only for your sake. He is common & thoroughly unfit as a companion with whom one could afford to be seen *in public!*
>
> I will be in the office all afternoon & hope you will look me up there around four or five o'clock.
>
> Yours
> Oscar[114]

The forger of this letter displays uneven knowledge about the theatrical disruption occasioned by the scandal of the trials. On the one hand, "two weeks" after 23 April fits with the play's actual closing on 8 May, but, on the other hand, during this tumultuous month Wilde spent much of his time in court – and not an "office." This letter also reimagines

Wilde and Douglas's connections with working-class male prostitutes or "renters." Indeed, it was his public connections to such "boys" (and his concurrent desire to shield Douglas) that arguably sealed Wilde's doom in court in 1895. Unlike in real life, the "Oscar" of this letter is more circumspect about his companions, but he articulates his caution in terms of an awareness of a danger that he could only have possessed *after* Edward Carson's brutal questioning at the Queensberry libel trial about his transgressively cross-class associations – namely the risk he ran by being seen "in public" with "common & thoroughly unfit" young male "companions." In summarizing his case against Wilde during that trial, Edward Carson had asked, with devastating understatement, "Has Mr. Wilde been unable to find more suitable companions [...] in youths of his own class?"[115] In this document the forger's knowledge about Wilde is thus as conspicuous as the "blunders" Millard identified. And it is crucially a knowledge that the trials have crystallized.

A third forged letter does something uniquely outrageous, even for Dorian Hope: it actualizes the ambition of Herbert Boyce Satcher's New York correspondent and names Dorian Hope as a poet. Picking up a theme seen throughout the Hope-Satcher correspondence (the opportunity for music that a poem provides), this letter, also addressed to "Bosie," is accompanied by a sixteen-line lyric poem entitled "If Thou Wilt Be," to which is affixed an addendum ("By Dorian Hope & not Oscar Wilde") and an injunction ("See note") that compels the reader to return to the "Bosie" letter. The two forged documents are a package deal that mutually reinforce one another. In yet another fantasy inversion of textual transmission, here the copyist is Oscar Wilde, and the writer of original verse is Dorian Hope. The letter runs as follows:

> Bosie:
> I have copied the verses by Dorian Hope that I was telling Miss Wren about. She thinks of setting them to music & I will be happy to see it done. The author is really the Dorian Gray of my book.
>
> Oscar
> June. 26. '94. 16 Tite St.[116]

In a baffling transposition of the real and the fake, the poet Dorian Hope acquires further authentication by being named as the inspiration for the character of Dorian Gray. As a result, Dorian Hope receives a (self-) promotion: not only is he acquainted with Wilde, and the subject of an intimate discussion between "Oscar" and "Bosie," but also that acquaintance has had a momentous impact on literary history. Like Dorian Gray and his portrait, the representation and the real thing change places, and a new order of precedence emerges. Dorian Hope is cast as a historically *real* person – "really the Dorian Gray of my book" – whereas Dorian Gray, already "real" and known to literary and legal history, is the belated and secondary representation of someone who never actually existed.

A puzzle, or, better yet, a sphinx-like riddle, this letter could be regarded as a precursor to contemporary, internet-based fan fiction, and its production expands the forger-fan's archive in both a material and an imaginative sense by fabricating (and retailing) a new origin story for Wilde's novel. But unlike fan fictions that seek to extend and continue familiar narratives and to imagine new scenarios with beloved characters, here, in Dorian Hope's Wildean invention (or intervention) the fiction reimagines the circuits of influence among author, reader, and literary character. It dwells particularly on the ironies that, when imagined through forgery and fandom, these circuits of desire and creative activity generate. Hope not only is eager to take credit for the original poem "If Thou Wilt Be," but also stages some anxiety (in the underlined postscript "By Dorian Hope & not Oscar Wilde") that his literary property may be confused with Wilde's (figure 10). In a manner of speaking, such confusion is precisely what he has been attempting to create all along by annexing Wilde's name to his textual fabrications. Here, however, Hope asserts a claim to originality – but within the framework of a forgery.

A Study in Purple

Oscar Wilde's distinctive handwriting, which Walter Ledger described as "Greek-like,"[117] often (but not always) rendered the letter *a* as a Greek alpha, α. Forgeries, however, very rarely replicate this feature of his script, which can at times resemble a plus sign. Genuine Wilde manuscripts also frequently render a lower-case letter *e* as a small cursive capital, and, unlike the alpha (which forgers tend to overlook), this feature is frequently overdone in the forgeries. Wilde's characteristic graphological *inconsistency* can thus make forging his handwriting quite a challenge. Wilde wrote either in black or brown ink or in pencil, and sometimes in both; a single manuscript in ink could contain corrections and additions in pencil, or the other way around. Purple ink, however, was not generally part of his repertoire.[118] More than thirty years after the Dorian Hope forgeries had been circulated, Wilde's son

If thou wilt be.

If thou wilt be the falling dew
And fall on me alway,
Then I will be the white, white rose
On yonder thorny spray.
If thou wilt be the white, white rose
On yonder thorny spray.
Then I will be the honey-bee
And kiss thee all the day.
If thou wilt be the honey-bee
And kiss me all the day.
Then I will be in yonder heaven
The star of brightest ray.
If thou wilt be in yonder heaven
The star of brightest ray.
Then I will be the dawn & we
will meet at break of day.

The rose.

By Dorian Hope
& not
Oscar Wilde

10 "If Thou Wilt Be," by Dorian Hope, c. 1921. Courtesy of Maggs Bros. Ltd, London.

Vyvyan Holland affirmed: "my father never wrote in purple ink."[119] Wilde did correct some early manuscripts in purple *pencil*, and several typescript versions of his lecture "Art and the Handicraftsman" witness corrections and additions in purple pencil (but not ink).[120] Taking a cue, perhaps, from the real Pierre Louÿs, who frequently used purple ink, Dorian Hope goes beyond mere corrections in coloured pencil; he writes out entire manuscripts in purple ink.

Although it is easy to imagine Wilde employing such a rare and decadent colour, it is perhaps even easier to imagine that forgers engrossed in Wildean myth-making would have wanted him to have done so. A number (but not all) of Dorian Hope's forgeries of Wilde make lavish use of purple ink, a practice that produces a more aesthetically arresting object than an authentic Wilde manuscript. (One forgery acquired by Figgis, the article "Mr. Swinburne's Poems & Ballads (3rd Series)," takes decadent colouring to an extreme: it uses purple *paper*.)[121] The lengthy manuscript of "Lord Arthur Savile's Crime," which was sold to Figgis, uses one colour to authenticate the other by beginning in black and switching to purple ink part-way through.[122] Purple ink has also been used in this manuscript for corrections, and, as Dudley Edwards has observed, the uncorrected text *without* purple interpolations "fails to make sense," suggesting that the corrections and the main text, though appearing in different colours of ink, were written out at the same time.[123] In other words, if the corrections are integral to the linear flow of the narrative, then they are not "corrections" to an existing text at all; they are forgeries denoting fake compositional timelines. The forgery of "The Young King," which was sold to Maggs Brothers, reverses this apparent prioritizing of one writing medium for composition and another for corrections, as the main text is written out in purple ink, and the corrections appear in pencil. In both cases, however, the forger is trying to generate the illusion of a manuscript's creative gestation over time. Under this (imaginary) scenario, after working on a story, and setting that writing aside, the writer has returned to these documents to replace old ideas with new ones. He has crossed out words, substituting preferred alternatives, and has amplified underdeveloped passages. The different writing media serve to enhance a fantasy timeline for the composition of these stories.

If the purple ink unites the two batches of forged manuscripts, which are separated only by their transmission to different dealers, and we can conclude – as both Millard and Maggs did – that they emanated from the same source, then we can also learn much about that source by considering them together. There are far more manuscripts, and of different kinds, in the "Gide" batch acquired by Figgis than in the "Louÿs" batch acquired by Maggs because the forger dealt with Maggs Brothers for a much briefer time period. The initial offers of Wilde manuscripts, we recall, were made to both firms in April 1921. By June 1921 Maggs Brothers had confirmed that the French *Salomé* manuscript was a forgery because it had been written on American paper made after 1915. Faced with such damning evidence, "Louÿs" withdrew, and under the name of "Gide" the forger dealt only with Figgis. The most clumsily executed forgeries are with the "Louÿs" group; altogether, the forgeries improved – they became more plausible – after the "Louÿs"-Maggs connection had been severed. I suspect that this is because more people became involved in the production of Wilde forgeries after the initial round of impostures. My broadest speculation about the forger's identity is that "Dorian Hope" in Paris was probably several people, working together. In that case "Dorian Hope" names not only an individual forger, such as Brett Holland, but rather an entire neo-Wildean workshop of forgers. By tracing Dorian Hope in 1920s Paris, we come into contact with a possibly unique artistic milieu in that creatively fertile time and place: the forgers' *atelier*. Although I can easily picture Brett Holland, a singular instigator with a strong personality like Satcher's "auntie" Dorian, coordinating these efforts and costuming himself to meet William Figgis, the very unevenness of the forgeries in the aggregate argues strongly against a single person's being responsible for all of them, even in the event that one individual may have been managing the operation's correspondence by impersonating Gide to Figgis and Louÿs to Maggs. But, then again, even Gide and Louÿs may have been impersonated by different forgers.

Looking carefully at how the Dorian Hope forgeries deploy their primary authenticatory devices – namely, information about Wilde and his circle – reveals how often they display inconsistent levels of knowledge. Such inconsistencies might obtain within a single forged document, as we have seen in the "Bosie" letter about the 1895 production of *The Importance of Being Earnest*. The forgers began their enterprise with big-name items – the plays *Earnest* and *Salomé*. As the con progressed, and as their research into and knowledge of Wilde increased, they introduced more generic variety into their offerings. Greater variety, however, brought with it a larger scope for error. Perhaps the forgers' biggest mistake (and an indication that their operations were imperfectly coordinated) was that both batches of forgeries contained manuscripts of the short story "The Sphinx without a Secret." The "Louÿs" document, acquired by Maggs Brothers, approximates a fair copy; written in purple ink, it contains almost no corrections. The "Gide" version, also in purple ink, consists of twenty leaves detached from a ruled notebook. It is a much more elaborate affair. Filled with corrections and interpolations, it is clearly meant to be interpreted as a working draft.[124] But why offer the *same* text (albeit in non-identical formats) to both purchasers? One answer could be, again, that different people produced the respective forgeries and that forger A was simply unaware that forger B was also copying out "The Sphinx without a Secret." (That Parisian forgery atelier was likely a very busy place.) In both cases, moreover, the forger appears to demonstrate an incriminating level of ignorance about the publication history of the story. The forged manuscripts carry the final title under which the story was published when it was collected in *Lord Arthur Savile's Crime & Other Stories* in 1891, but upon its initial periodical publication in 1887 the story appeared in *The World* as "Lady Alroy." Yet the fake fair copy that carries the final title is signed "Oscar Wilde" and dated "1887," implying the forger's keen awareness of the story's publication history.[125] Instead of enhancing a forgery's credibility, such contradictory details undermine it. So what is going on? What happens if we read these mistakes as *deliberate*?

It is tempting to read a playful hint into what Millard might call a forger's slip or blunder. By inviting scrutiny, the apparent mistake of twice circulating "The Sphinx without a Secret" produces a confession on the forgers' part, interwoven with a subtle and elegant reading of Wilde's short story. In the story itself, the beautiful Lady Alroy exudes an "indefinable atmosphere of mystery" that excites in the besotted Gerald Murchison's "most ardent curiosity."[126] She employs aliases and false identities; she appears in disguise, "deeply veiled"; and she rents rooms so that she can be observed sneaking in and stealing away. She makes an art of engineering mystery for its own sake, and the narrator concludes, "Lady Alroy was simply a woman with a mania for mystery [...] imagining she was a heroine."[127] Notwithstanding the obvious anagram of *royal* in *Alroy*, the story's "secret" is the absence of one. There is no content here, only form – an atmosphere of intrigue with no real cause. "The Sphinx without a Secret" is thus an anti-detective story, and its self-cancelling mystery gently satirizes the genre fiction that made the career of Wilde's contemporary Arthur Conan Doyle; his first Sherlock Holmes story, "A Study in Scarlet," had also appeared in 1887. Conspicuously emphasizing this particular Wilde text by offering it twice (and perhaps assuming eventual discovery), the forger(s) could be allegorizing his (or their) own practice. Lady Alroy's "secret" does not exist; instead, it is a beautiful untrue thing. Is Dorian Hope just another sphinx without a secret?

That story concludes with Murchison musing, "I wonder," but, if we set wonderment – which is certainly one of Dorian Hope's objectives – aside for the moment, we find that there is still quite a lot to learn from the forgeries' more easily detectable mistakes. The Maggs forgeries are notable for subtle, yet demonstrable, errors in detail. One letter (in purple ink) to "Robbie" is dated "Sept. 23rd '95," when Wilde was in prison and forbidden from writing letters to anyone. This error in chronology is surprising because the "Robbie" letter from September 1895 also signals, revealingly, the literary and market-related categories of information that would matter to a forger. Elaborating on the theme of Wilde in financial difficulties that is found in a number of forged letters, its writer proposes selling Wilde's "Arnold & Pater volumes" to Bernard Quaritch. In doing so, the forger indicates both an awareness of two of Wilde's major philosophical influences and a familiarity with the London rare-book world by naming a prestigious bookselling firm that was *not* approached by Dorian Hope. And this letter to "Robbie" is not the only time that Dorian Hope made this very blunder in timing. A note appended to a forged manuscript of the homoerotic poem "In the Forest" (a genuine Wilde text) reads "Written under compulsion at Paris. July, 1896. O.W.," which is another impossible date because Wilde was then not in Paris but, again, in prison.[128]

Other factual mistakes in further forged letters are as straightforwardly identified. In one letter, for example, "Louÿs" offers Maggs Brothers the manuscript of Wilde's story "The Young King," adding the apparently helpful (albeit erroneous) bibliographical detail that it was "one of four stories published by Methuen & Co, as a 'House of Pomegranates.'"[129] Although "The Young King" appears in that short-story collection, Wilde did not originally publish *A House of Pomegranates* with Methuen but with Osgood, McIlvaine, the publishers of *Lord Arthur Savile's Crime & Other Stories*. The forger probably had the (posthumous) Methuen edition of Wilde's *Collected Works* to hand – we recall that a letter from "Gide" to Figgis touted the conformity of his Wilde manuscripts to "Methuen's published texts" – but he is confusing and conflating two distinct periods in the publication history of "The Young King." Here, as in the letter to "Robbie," we can observe that despite its best efforts the forger's letter falls victim to the tensions between its factual errors and its authenticatory devices. Indeed, in the "Young King" ("Methuen") example, a clumsily handled authenticatory device can turn into an error.

William Figgis's "Gide" forgeries, for their part, engage authenticatory devices that are just as daring, though less vulnerable to externally verifiable facts. One such example is the intricately monogrammed "OW" writing paper (a substantial investment in stationery on the part of the forger) that is used for "Wilde's" letters – written in purple ink, naturally – to Octave Mirbeau. "André Gide," as we recall, wrote to Figgis in fluid, idiomatic English. The real Gide's command of the English language was far weaker, as Figgis's colleague C. Frederic Harrison reported. In contrast, the "Pierre Louÿs" letters to Maggs Brothers exhibit some grammatical errors that one might associate, at first glance, with a Frenchman's imperfect grasp of the English language – precisely the impression that the forger wished to produce. But when Maggs Brothers submitted one of their "Pierre Louÿs" letters to the real Louÿs for examination, the author annotated the ungrammatical contrivance "throughout the manuscript of which I have addressed to you": "ce n'est pas un français qui a écrit ça" (a Frenchman did not write this).[130] To the real Louÿs this was not the error of a francophone trying to write in English; rather, it was the error of an anglophone forger impersonating a francophone.

While the putative Frenchness of the sources of the Wilde forgeries counts as a failing authenticatory device, even more enlightening slips can be detected in the culturally and monetarily specific English words used by the forgers. "Gide," as we recall, had flaunted his familiarity with the market for Wilde by referring to a recent past when Wilde manuscripts had not been worth even a "hapenny" in Britain, and he spelled out the vernacular term for the halfpenny coin. After Figgis met Dorian Hope in Paris, moreover, "Gide" sought payment for his wares in "cheques," as when he instructed Figgis to "send your cheque at the earliest possible moment. My friend, Mr. D. Hope [...] will be here in town and will undertake the settlement for me."[131] He uses this word several times in the correspondence and always with that spelling. (Cash would have been so much simpler!) "Louÿs," however, prefers the typically American spelling *check* in writing to Maggs: "The manuscript will follow in a day or two [...] and I will be grateful to have your acknowledgment and your check as soon as you decide to keep it."[132] If neither was French, was "Gide" British, and "Louÿs"

American? This apparent inconsistency would make more sense if we imagined different people, possibly at different times, involved in the respective impersonations of Gide and Louÿs. The reliance on the Paris American Express office for correspondence, the use of paper manufactured in Massachusetts for the *Salomé* forgery, and the confidence about the US market for Wilde all argue strongly for Dorian Hope's American origins. And yet Herbert Boyce Satcher, who met a man calling himself "Dorian Hope" in the United States, assumed his correspondent to be British. So too did the real André Gide: his pride still injured by the impersonation, with the help of the French judicial system he located a "Mr. Hope (Dorian Sebastian)" in London in 1922. Writing to Figgis, Gide provided the Dublin dealer with this Hope's address, adding that he had "been in England for 3 months," and "in case the man is an Englishman [...] extradition [to France] would not be possible."[133] Gide's sleuthing had turned up what is possibly the single most valuable, and overlooked, clue linking Brett Holland to Dorian Hope: the address that he cites in that letter, "24 Earls Court Gardens, London S.W. 5"[134] is identical to the address Brett Holland openly provided to his hometown newspaper, *The Gastonia Gazette*, when he wrote to that publication in high dudgeon to defend his activities as Dorian Hope in New York. And yet that clue seems to have been abandoned: Gide assumes that a London address meant British nationality. When news of the Wilde forgeries reached the New York press, Dorian Hope was described not only as a "dilettante poet," but also as an "English dandy."[135] Appropriating identities and nationalities was nothing new to Holland, however. As a youthful female impersonator, he had claimed to be a native of Bordeaux, France; presenting Dorian Hope to the world as "an English dandy" would seem well within his range.[136] English or not, Dorian Hope was (or rather *were*) an anglophone expatriate presence in Paris in the early 1920s, chasing the ghost of his (or their) literary idol in the city of Wilde's exile and death.

Aside from relatively modest payments received from Figgis and Maggs, Dorian Hope seems not to have made much money from the great Oscar Wilde caper of 1921–2. Figgis records, for example, that he paid "André Gide" a grand total of £138 for two batches of manuscripts.[137] Although this is a substantial sum, it is a far cry from the newsworthy prices realized at the Stetson sale in 1920.[138] The time, effort, and outlay that palpably contributed to the forgeries do not seem to have produced a particularly impressive return on investment. This failure to profit complicates a reductively commercial explanation for the forgeries and brings into even greater relief a deep investment in Wilde that exceeds the petty mistakes of those forgeries. It strongly signals a fannish desire to contribute to the Wilde legend by producing "new" relics of a venerated martyr. If we understand these forgeries as at least partly motivated by a desire to participate in myth-making, then it is also possible that a whole community of Wilde forger-fans, with "Dorian Hope" as its collective pseudonym, may have been operating in Paris in the early 1920s. This is not to diminish the larcenous ingenuity of Brett Holland, for if we ask whether the Dorian Hope apparelled in a Wildean fur coat to meet Figgis in January 1922 could be the same person who wrote campy letters referring to himself as a "lonely antique" in New York during the spring and summer of 1920, then the answer is almost definitely yes. That said, the archival evidence of the forgeries themselves points to Dorian (or Sebastian) Hope as a cipher rather than a person; he may well be a placeholder for several individuals (including the New York *Pearls and Pomegranates* plagiarist) who fashioned neo-Wildean personae and artefacts. "Dorian Hope" would thus name a counter-community of rogue fans in Paris challenging the work of Wilde's partisans on the other side of the Channel who hoped to preserve his reputation by exposing and denouncing spurious Wilde texts.

Figgis did not pursue the mystery of Dorian Hope to the extent of initiating a prosecution, probably much to Gide's disappointment. His cheques cashed in Paris, he was left with the manuscripts, which, he recorded, "were parcelled up and consigned to an ancient press reserved for blighted expectations."[139] Christopher Millard, however, continued to look into the matter, even after issuing the humiliating admission that Dorian Hope had duped him. Millard clearly took this personally, and over the summer of 1922 he spared no effort in tracking down a culprit. He found one in Arthur Cravan, whose eccentric activities he had been documenting since at least 1914.[140] A mere two weeks after his reversal over the forgeries Millard wrote to Figgis to announce his new theory:

> I strongly suspect that the man Hope is Fabian Lloyd, a son of Otho Lloyd who is the brother of Mrs. Oscar Wilde. Before the war Fabian Lloyd under the pen-name of Arthur Cravan ran a little magazine called "Maintenant" and one of his stunts was a story that Wilde had recently visited him in Paris and that he was not dead. An American newspaper in November 1913 described him as a 'gigantic athlete who is practicing the professions

> of poet and prize fighter in Paris' and his age is given as 23 years which would make him about 33 now. Fabian in his story of Wilde being still alive declared that in Wilde's empty coffin was buried an unpublished manuscript called 'Amen: A Comedy? A Tragedy' which shows that ten years ago this Fabian Lloyd was tampering with the subject of 'manuscripts.'[141]

Millard's suspicion only hardened into certainty after this epiphany. In a 1924 letter that he sent to New York publisher and gallerist Mitchell Kennerley – whose auction house had been the site of the Stetson sale in 1920 – Millard underlined this hardening when he declared, emphatically, "The forger is FABIAN LLOYD."[142]

Such is the weight of Millard's testimony on Wildean matters that the names Arthur Cravan and Fabian Lloyd have been linked to Dorian Hope's ever since. Vyvyan Holland also endorsed the theory that Dorian Hope was his "first cousin," effectively granting Millard's speculation the status of fact.[143] The Fabian Lloyd-Arthur Cravan theory is particularly appealing for two reasons: first, it introduces another plausibly outlandish figure to the Dorian Hope story, and, second, it tidily contains a disparate archive of forgeries under the heading of an individual perpetrator. Cravan's strange investment in Wilde mythologizing, his family connection, and his movements between Paris and New York furnished Millard with the evidence he needed to name a singular candidate for the role of "Dorian Hope." The problem with this linkage is that Millard's evidence for identifying Dorian Hope with Cravan is circumstantial at best. And despite Millard's meticulous research and record-keeping, this initial identification also reflects the bibliographer's unawareness of the American newspaper coverage that had mocked Brett Holland's poetical career as Dorian Hope. The naming of Cravan as Hope is more the result of Millard's need to assign an identity to the forger who had "tampered" with the literary remains of his idol than the result of a sustained investigation, such as the more technical one to which he submitted the Dorian Hope manuscripts. But this surprisingly persistent theory, which for decades has been replicated in scholarship and library catalogues, has never been seriously challenged in Wilde studies, despite the fact that Arthur Cravan had disappeared off the coast of Mexico in 1918.[144] Although his body was never recovered, Cravan was presumed dead long before Dorian Hope ever began publishing in New York and before the Wilde forgeries emerged from Paris. But perhaps, like the venerated uncle he claimed had faked his own death, Cravan too could come back from the grave.

"I Am Sebastian Melmoth": Arthur Cravan and "Oscar Wilde Is Alive!"

Arthur Cravan, poet and pugilist, was an outrageous character in his own right with an emphatically Wildean flair for self-promotion. He was born Fabian Avenarius Lloyd in Lausanne, Switzerland, in 1887, the son of Otho and Nellie Lloyd, and thus was Constance Wilde's nephew. He cultivated notoriety by combining the unlikely professions of heavy-weight boxer and avant-garde *littérateur* and adopted an ambitiously combative approach to both (figure 11). Most memorably, perhaps, he created the identity "Arthur Cravan" and lived an itinerant bohemian life. After a rollicking stint in Berlin, he landed in Paris in 1909, where from 1912 to 1915 he wrote poetry and published a confrontational, proto-Dadaist magazine called *Maintenant* ("Now"); one of the targets of his mockery was André Gide. With Wilde's gift for spectacle he emulated his uncle by delivering lectures in outlandish clothes; one 1914 newspaper report describes a "Futurist Lecture" given by Cravan in Paris in which "the nephew of Oscar Wilde [...] a clean-shaven, tall young man, appeared on the stage dressed in black trousers and dancing pumps, with a white flannel shirt open at the throat. He was girdled with a scarlet sash [and] began his 'lecture' by firing a pistol several times."[145] He later sparred with the exiled American heavyweight champion Jack Johnson in Barcelona, was arrested for indecent exposure at the opening of an art exhibition in New York (where he also met the modernist poet Mina Loy, whom he later married), and fled to Mexico to avoid conscription by the United States in the First World War. His turbulent life "of invented personae, double identities and successful disguises"[146] unfolded in a sequence of well-timed disappearances. As the subtitle of a recent graphic novel about Cravan attests, he was indeed the "mystery man of the twentieth century."[147]

In October 1913 Cravan published an article entitled "OSCAR WILDE EST VIVANT!" in *Maintenant* (figure 12). The magazine provided Cravan, its putative editor, a platform for his literary provocations and permitted him to stage diverse creative personae under multiple pseudonyms. "A confection of poetry, essay, polemic, and scandal, *Maintenant* was entirely written and published by Cravan," observes Charles Nicholl.[148] The magazine also demonstrated a sustained interest in the uncle by marriage whom Cravan had never met. Under the pseudonym "W. Cooper," he published a two-part series of "documents inédits sur Oscar Wilde" (unpublished items about Oscar Wilde) in the magazine's

11 Arthur Cravan in boxing gear, c. 1916. Courtesy of Wikimedia Commons.

April 1912 and July 1913 issues that dealt with Wilde's appearance and manner.[149] By asserting Wilde's continued existence, however implausibly, Cravan accommodates his uncle to the new century he never saw, "forging" him in 1913 in the sense of making new myths about him. The claim from Paris that Wilde was alive had not gone unnoticed by the writer's stalwart defenders. Robert Sherard, the Wilde biographer, reports that Cravan's "story was much quoted at the time, and [it] evoked a number of quite unnecessary refutations."[150] The *New York Times* even reported on the story. Despite this (bad) press, in 1917 a modernist little magazine in New York called *The Soil: A Magazine of Art* published a translation of Cravan's article under the title "Oscar Wilde Is Alive!" in two separate, illustrated parts. The story of Wilde's undeath just would not die.

"Oscar Wilde Is Alive!" begins as a kind of disjointed and trance-like surrealist dream that unfolds over an evening of heavy drinking. In this biofiction Cravan, who proclaims his true identity as Wilde's nephew, Fabian Lloyd, describes a nocturnal visit that he received in Paris on

Numéro Spécial

2e ANNÉE Nº 3 Octobre-Novembre 1913

MAINTENANT

REVUE LITTÉRAIRE

DIRECTEUR : Arthur Cravan

PARIS — 67, Rue Saint-Jacques, 67 — PARIS

à partir du 15 octobre :

29, Avenue de l'Observatoire, 29

Le Numéro : 50 Centimes

SOMMAIRE

Oscar Wilde est vivant ! par Arthur Cravan

Deux Portraits inédits d'Oscar Wilde par E. Lajeunesse

OSCAR WILDE EST VIVANT !

C'était la nuit du vingt-trois mars dix-neuf cent treize. Et si je vais donner des détails minutieux sur l'état d'âme que j'avais en cette soirée de fin d'hiver, c'est que

12 *Maintenant*, 1913. Rare Books and Special Collections, University of British Columbia.

23 March 1913 from an aged, white-bearded figure who dramatically reveals, "I am Sebastian Melmoth." Melmoth is cryptic: he admits to dying but never reveals the secret of his return from death. Like a child anxious for parental approval, Cravan, whom Melmoth affectionately calls "dear Fabian," shows his uncle his "literary review" and even proposes different ventures to benefit both of their careers: "I shall ask you for one of your books, which I will publish as a posthumous work; but, if you prefer, I [can] become your impresario; I [shall] immediately sign you a contract for a tour of lectures in the music halls."[151] Although Melmoth becomes "more and more amused" by this plan to capitalize on his mystique, he does not sign on. Instead, he leaves a drunken Cravan with the avuncular parting words "you are a terrible boy."[152]

The April 1917 translation of Cravan's story opens with an "Announcement" that declares, in a disembodied editorial voice, "None of the documents on Oscar Wilde appearing in this issue have ever been published before [...] It was due to the kindness of Mr. Arthur Cravan, Oscar Wilde's nephew, that we were fortunate enough to secure them."[153] More a fantasy dossier than an article claiming to represent real events, the miniature archive of Cravanesque myth-making assembled in *The Soil* includes reprinted Wilde letters; "unpublished" images of him; "Some Stray Sayings"; lengthy checklists of information, detailing his personal appearance ("Big frame, but well-proportioned [...] inclined always to corpulence");[154] and, perhaps strangest of all, an inventory of the items contained in his house, and their arrangement. This last item, which resembles set designs for a stage play, is attributed to Cravan's father, "Wilde's brother-in-law."[155] Cravan's approach in this publication may thus be comprehended as that of an "impresario," and staging an insider's knowledge of Wilde's world enables him to capture some of the reflected glory of his avant-garde precursor. It is no coincidence that the first part of the story of Wilde's return is followed in *The Soil* by a mock interview with Cravan, "Arthur Cravan vs. Jack Johnson," which extolls the nephew's boxing prowess and expresses Cravan's admiration for his celebrated Barcelona opponent. As had *Maintenant* before it, *The Soil* affords Cravan the chance to generate his own mystique via the pre-existing mythology of Wilde.

The stunt narratives "OSCAR WILDE EST VIVANT!" and "Oscar Wilde Is Alive!" certainly – and famously – associated Arthur Cravan (or Fabian Lloyd) with Wildean hoaxes – in two languages. But was he also Dorian Hope? The articles persuaded Millard and Holland that the two men were the same, and Cravan seems to be the type of person who could turn forger. He was an outrageous character of internationally recognized eccentricity. He was a poet. He rebelled against authorities of all kinds. He concocted identities. He had lived in Paris and New York and had caused mayhem in both cities. He was Wilde's nephew by marriage, and one could easily imagine that the family connection gave him privileged access to information and materials about Wilde (though it did not). The central tenet of the supposition that Cravan is Hope is that, if all these things are true, then who else *could* be Dorian Hope? But the ineradicable problem with this theory remains that it requires a man who died in 1918 to be alive into the 1920s. And, for that matter, this theory also fails to consider the queer coordinates of the Dorian Hope persona that define Brett Holland far more readily than they do Arthur Cravan. It is not that Arthur Cravan's history of womanizing heterosexuality disqualifies him from performing a sexual identity that was not his. Rather, it is that in Cravan's Wilde myth-making we find not a whiff of Dorian Hope's characteristic strategy, his employment of queerness as a device to authenticate a multiplicity of neo-Wildean representations. Cravan's Wildean biofictions, by contrast, are more homo-indifferent than homoerotic.[156]

The archival record establishes that Dorian Hope was particularly active as a literary provocateur and Wilde mythologizer in New York and Paris. Yet these are precisely the two *worst* places for Cravan to have gone if he wanted to fake his 1918 death and re-emerge, unrecognized, with a new identity by 1920. He had made himself conspicuous in both cities in the 1910s, as indeed he did everywhere he went. In a biographical sketch on Cravan, Charles Nicholl makes this point in his assessment of the "sightings" of Dorian Hope. For Nicholl, "Hope's presence in Paris in the early 1920s seems to argue against [Cravan's] being him: Cravan had been a well-known figure there a few years previously. It is one of the problems of these supposed sightings: the settings are unimaginative – a creaky ghost in predictable haunts. A glimpse of him in Tahiti or Tashkent would fit the bill rather better."[157] Arthur Cravan's real end likely held almost as much romantic exoticism as these glimpses because he was probably either drowned at sea or murdered by pirates on the west coast of Mexico near Puerto Angel, where he was last seen. He had hatched a typically far-fetched plan to sail around Cape Horn to meet his wife, Mina Loy, in Buenos Aires but never arrived. (Loy was pregnant at the time and, in 1919, bore a daughter whom she named Fabienne, after Fabian Lloyd.) "Physically huge but strangely weightless," Nicholl observes, "Fabian Lloyd lived a life of indefinition – aliases, disguises, blurrings of fact and fantasy. He was a kind of illusionist, his greatest feat the creation of 'Arthur Cravan,' his last trick the classic one of vanishing."[158] But on this occasion he probably never re-materialized.

Even if Arthur Cravan and Dorian Hope – ingenious rogues both – were not identical, they did share one thing in common: an abiding interest in Oscar Wilde that was so intensive that they enlarged his literary legacy with fresh legends, outlandish fantasies, and textual fabrications. "Wilde wanted to kill people who imitated him," Cravan asserts in "Oscar Wilde Is Alive!" "[B]ut he at last understood, and said one day to a lady, the mother of the celebrated poet, Arthur Cravan: 'I understand; it [imitation] is admiration.'"[159] From New York and Philadelphia in 1920 to Paris and London in 1922, Dorian Hope may be a moving target, but he – or, more likely, *they* – can also be considered a prism through which such collective admiration was gloriously refracted.

Chapter Three

Pen, Pencil, and Planchette

For all of his bombast, Arthur Cravan was not the first person to proclaim Oscar Wilde's survival in the New York press. The eccentric German-American writer George Sylvester Viereck (1884–1962) made a similarly spectacular assertion in 1905, a mere five years after Wilde's death.[1] Viereck's coyly entitled article for the New York journal *The Critic*, "Is Oscar Wilde Living or Dead?," claimed that Wilde was then living incognito in New York City. Excited to be relaying a piece of juicy gossip (albeit one of his own invention), Viereck embraced the outlandish theatricality of the public announcement. "I am aware," he concedes, "that what I shall say has all the thrill of the melodrama."[2] Highly attuned to the status of his information as "rumor" and "conjecture" and to the tension between these categories and those of fact and fiction, Viereck nonetheless assumed the role of detective, and pieced together "a chain of circumstantial evidence" to announce Wilde's literal comeback following the publication in 1905 of *De Profundis*.[3] Viereck's Wilde is both a martyr for art and a kind of sinister mastermind, biding his time in secret: "And would it not be quite in accordance with his character," Viereck asks rhetorically, "to carry to the last point of consistency the Christ pose, blasphemous perhaps, which he adopted especially in his last book 'De Profundis,' and from his tomb to roll the stone and rise from the dead?"[4] In a scenario that is gothic and biblical by turns, Wilde is undead and unredeemed, and Viereck – as someone who has weighed the evidence concerning Wilde's resurrection – comes into focus as an apostle who believes.

A couple of years later Viereck's fannish discipleship of Wilde took a distinctly supernatural turn. In 1907 he published a homoerotic novel called *The House of the Vampire*, a text that borrows from both *The*

Importance of Being Earnest and *The Picture of Dorian Gray*. Its characters include, for example, two best friends named "Ernest" and "Jack" and a vampiric writer and villain, Reginald Clarke, who recalls Dorian's tutor in decadence, Lord Henry Wotton, and indeed Wilde himself. But for all his self-making as a writer attempting to bring Wilde back to life – at least imaginatively – so as to vivify his own literary career, Viereck's contributions to Wilde's afterlife in the 1900s were, as we saw in the previous chapter, surpassed in both ornateness and strangeness by those of Arthur Cravan in the 1910s. And these, in turn, were outdone in the next decade by another neo-Wildean publishing spectacle that is the subject of this chapter: the mediumistic writings collected and edited by Hester Travers Smith and published in book form as *Psychic Messages from Oscar Wilde* (1924).

Haunting the spiritualist seance rooms and Ouija boards of the 1920s, this version of Wilde was not merely undead; he made up for over two decades of silence by becoming hyper-communicative. Through the mediums Travers Smith and Geraldine Cummins, the spirit of Wilde took up the Ouija board's planchette and even "wrote" a three-act play with a title – "Is It a Forgery?" – that slyly nods towards "The Portrait of Mr. W.H." The culmination of several months of ghostly transmissions in 1923 and 1924, the "new" play provocatively stages the fraught questions of imposture and authenticity that *Psychic Messages* had already broached, and its title encapsulates the aura of deliberate mystery as well as the evidentiary manoeuvres that we have observed in other manifestations of Wilde forgery, such as the manuscripts contrived under the name of Dorian Hope. In taking on the role of the ghost's amanuenses, Travers Smith and Cummins forged, I argue, a phantom drama under the name of Wilde's ghost that was also possibly indebted to Viereck's novel. We could label this play a form of fan fiction *avant la lettre*.

Oscar Wilde was himself fascinated by the paranormal, although he is not known ever to have attended a seance – in life, that is. Curiosity did draw the writer to a meeting of the spiritualist Society for Psychical Research in 1885,[5] and, more generally, as John Stokes observes, "[p]remonitions, prophecies, and strange coincidences are [...] a constant thread in Wilde's work."[6] Supernatural happenings structure several of his stories, such as "The Canterville Ghost" (1887), which amusingly brings together questions of authenticity, imitation, and supernatural fakery. In that story the ghoul haunting a Tudor country house, Canterville Chase, is vexed by his inability to inspire fear in the house's new

American owners, the confidently materialist Otis family. The ghost performs the roles of dead characters, such as "Dumb Daniel, or the Suicide's Skeleton," and "Martin the Maniac, or the Masked Mystery," in order to scare away the family, but they all prove ineffectual.[7] He is outdone by the gravest of ghostly insults when the mischievous Otis twins not only manage to scare him with their own fake ghost but also declare *him* to be a spectral forgery. The ghost is horrified to discover that what appeared to be a "grisly phantom" is only a dummy, complete with a placard that spells out his humiliation in no uncertain terms. In a neat Wildean inversion of the real and the fake, the Otises pronounce their faux ghost – in equally phony Elizabethan orthography – "Ye Onlie True and Originale Spook." As for the actual ghost, their placard advises, "Beware of Ye Imitationes. All Others are Counterfeite."[8] In this ghost story the scepticism represented by the avowed forgery – the fake ghost – is enough to undermine the spectral authority of the real thing.

Not ghosts but psychic divination is at issue in another Wilde tale from this period, "Lord Arthur Savile's Crime" (1887), in which a visit to a palm-reader produces a terrifying prophecy of murder that proves inexorable. Wilde had visited several palmists and had his palm read by "Cheiro," the astrologer and "society palmist," in 1893. "Cheiro" (the name stems from *chiromancy*, or palmistry) dramatically predicted Wilde's downfall, telling the writer that his right hand was "that of a king who will send himself into exile."[9] The palmist recalled a later meeting with the exiled Wilde in Paris in 1900, in which Wilde related to him that seeing him "brought the dead past out of its grave."[10] André Gide had tried to do something similar, in fact, according to Wilde's biographer Robert Sherard. At a seance held at Gide's house in 1905, Sherard reports, "Wilde's wraith was evoked from the Yonder-Land." The spirit was not particularly communicative or specific, however, as it opined that life beyond the grave consisted only of "a chaotic confusion of fluid nebulosities."[11]

This phrase from the spirit's speech could readily be repurposed to describe the claims and counter-claims made by the Wilde ghost's channelling mediums and automatic writers in the 1920s. This chapter tracks such claims and counter-claims across the haunted (and confused) corners of Wilde's afterlife, from Viereck's fictionalizing contributions to his legend, to Travers Smith's spirit writings and Wilde's irruption into spiritualist print culture – where the discussions and debates about his return to eloquence were extensive – to the ghostly resumption of his dramatic career, having written, posthumously, "Is It a Forgery?" In the spiritualist press Wilde's ghostly messages were known as the "Oscar Wilde scripts," and this resonant term *scripts* conveys at once both the theatricality of their transmissions and the materiality of their transcription. Over the course of this chapter we shall observe the participants in the affairs of Wilde's ghost publicizing, scrutinizing, debating, and probing these scripts for evidence of authenticity and imposture. Were the scripts, in fact, forgeries? The concepts of literary forgery and textual appropriation thus organize (or haunt) all of these neo-Wildean representations.

One figure who passed judgement on the "Oscar Wilde scripts" was Arthur Conan Doyle, who had known Wilde and who vigorously endorsed Travers Smith's *Psychic Messages* as evidence of the discarnate survival in print of his old acquaintance.[12] To my mind, the story about the channelling of Wilde's ghost in the 1920s, which is only partly captured in *Psychic Messages*, shares compelling affinities with the genre in which Doyle's consulting detective Sherlock Holmes excelled. Cluttered with clues afforded by the ghost's distinctive personality and style, the story of Oscar Wilde's ghostly return resembles neither one of Viereck's gothic tales, nor, for that matter, one of the quasi-scientific case studies admired by serious spiritualists such as Doyle and the Society for Psychical Research. Its ironies, in point of fact, align it with the structures of Wilde's own short fictions, for the history of this ghost is a detective tale in which the detectives investigate a case of forgery that they may, in fact, have themselves perpetrated. At heart and in practice, as we have seen, Wilde's fans – both the forgers and the bibliographers who aimed to expose their biofictional performances as fakes – were all, in their separate ways, detectives. What distinguishes this cast of supernatural detectives from those studied so far, however, is the way that they squabbled with one another in the spiritualist press over the ghost's scripts. In my analysis of these pugnacious communications it becomes clear that these spiritualist factions were struggling to assert who had control over the most reliable record of contact with "Ye Onlie True and Originale Spook."

George Sylvester Viereck's Undead Wilde

George Sylvester Viereck was obsessed with Oscar Wilde, and he leveraged professions of admiration for the Irish writer to promote his own career. In a 1907 interview with the *New York Times* that followed the publication of his first book, for instance, he grandly declared that his "three best friends" – the "three personalities that have meant the most to him" – were "Christ, Napoleon, and Oscar Wilde."[13] According to Viereck's biographer, "there had been, perhaps, no greater influence on his life" than Wilde,[14] and his fervently neo-decadent early writings are heavily marked by Wilde's influence. As Christopher Millard had done, Viereck also sought vicarious contact with his hero by associating with former members of Wilde's circle. In New York he cultivated the literary friendship of the poet Richard Le Gallienne. But perhaps his greatest social coup in this connection was the decades' long correspondence that he maintained with Alfred Douglas, whom he met in 1901 at the age of seventeen. With Douglas's approval, Viereck planned to publish a German translation of "The Ballad of Reading Gaol," which he also intended to dedicate to Wilde's former lover.[15]

Although Viereck modelled the style of his political rebelliousness on the author of "The Soul of Man under Socialism," the content of their respective views diverged widely. Wilde's left-wing politics left Viereck unmoved. The self-proclaimed illegitimate grandson of Kaiser Wilhelm I was a lifelong propagandist for German expansion; he eventually turned to fascism.[16] From 1914 to 1917, before the entry of the United States into the First World War, he edited and published a pro-German propaganda magazine, *The Fatherland*. He was also one of the first English-speaking journalists to interview Adolf Hitler (in 1923), and during the Second World War he was imprisoned in the United States for his pro-Nazi activities. Despite Viereck's continued attachment to Wilde and even Douglas's repudiation of Wilde, their political views would come to coincide over the years; in one 1936 letter, for instance, Douglas confided to Viereck that he was "quite on the side of Hitler."[17] Politics aside, Wilde's legacy nonetheless continued to haunt both their lives.

The impact of Wilde on Viereck's writing is perhaps most notable in *The House of the Vampire* (1907). The novel tells a relatively straightforward gothic tale indebted to *The Picture of Dorian Gray*. Moreover, it is replete with neo-Wildean *aperçus*. For instance, the observation that "all genuine art is autobiography. It is not, however, necessarily a revelation of the artist's actual self, but of a myriad of potential selves" remixes Lord Henry Wotton's comments in *Dorian Gray* about art and self-development.[18] But *The House of the Vampire* is not a novel about magic portraits; instead, it explores the dynamics of influence between an older and a younger man. It recounts the tragic story of a young writer, Ernest Fielding, who becomes the protégé of Reginald Clarke, a figure modelled on Lord Henry or Wilde himself, who "was still remembered in New York drawing-rooms as the man who had brought perfection to the art of talking. Even to dine with him was a liberal education."[19] Although he is not technically undead, Clarke proves a sort of psychic vampire in the novel. He drains creative energy, inspiration, and even entire literary texts from his victims – particularly the young men he invites to live with him in his luxurious Manhattan apartment, the "house" of the book's title. This is exactly what he does to Ernest, who had mentally composed a play in the vein of *Salome*, "The Princess with the Yellow Veil." Clarke psychically plagiarizes this play, which the novel describes as "heavy, perfumed, Oriental – interwoven with bits of gruesome tenderness," and at the very moment that Ernest, furtively reading his own words in Clarke's manuscript, realizes that this mental theft has occurred, he feels "as if an icy hand had gripped his heart."[20] That "icy hand" image is an unmistakable allusion to Dorian Gray, who, when he acknowledges the inevitability of aging, "felt as if a hand of ice had been laid upon his heart."[21]

This allusion keys us into the novel's status as an extended commentary on creativity and originality. Indeed, by absorbing and representing material drawn from Wilde, Viereck practises what his own charismatic villain comes to preach as a theory of art. As a writer, Viereck is something of a vampire himself in relation to Wilde's texts. Although the relationship between Reginald Clarke and Ernest Fielding is patterned on the one between Lord Henry Wotton and Dorian Gray, Clarke's vampirism reverses the polarity of Lord Henry's influence. Where Lord Henry suggestively imposes his personality upon Dorian, poisoning his soul with a malign influence, Clarke is instead one "of those unoriginal, great absorptive minds who [...] are born to rob and rule" and who commit "intellectual burglaries."[22] When Ernest confronts him, Clarke denies that his artistic practice constitutes theft and articulates a self-justifying theory reminiscent of Wilde's own championing of creative annexation: "I absorb. I appropriate. That is the most any artist can say for himself."[23] As Paul K. Saint-Amour rightly observes, the novel is a parable of intellectual property, a "thriller [that] celebrates plagiarism as a form of spiritual vampirism."[24] *The House of the Vampire*'s spookiest moments occur when it depicts such absorption: the vampire Clarke steals into the sleeping Ernest's room to probe his brain for ideas, with "long, tapering fingers that every night were groping in the windings of his brain. It was a well-formed, manicured hand that seemed to reach under his skull, carefully feeling its way through the myriad convolutions where thought resides."[25] Despite this viscerally gruesome encounter, the novel declines to name Clarke definitively as a plagiarist. When Ernest discovers another manuscript with his words written out in Clarke's hand, he (implausibly) admits, "[T]his was indeed authentic literature, there could be no doubt about it."[26]

In the stylized pastiche of Wilde's own idiom, *The House of the Vampire* thus articulates a supernatural reworking of theories drawn from "The Decay of Lying" and "The Critic as Artist." "Creation," Clarke tells Ernest, "is a divine prerogative. Re-creation, infinitely more wonderful than mere calling into existence, is the prerogative of the poet. Shakespeare took his colours from many palettes. That is why he is so great, and why his work is incredibly greater than he."[27] By means of Reginald Clarke, Viereck absorbs and reprocesses the very intellectual territory of Wilde's anti-Romantic view of creativity, which was surveyed in my introduction. Even so, it would be mistaken to label *The House of the Vampire* an uncritical endorsement of the villainous Clarke's "unoriginal" compositional practice; Viereck's approach – and, for that matter, the attitude behind his assimilation of Wilde – is far more ambiguous than that. After all, Reginald Clarke is denounced by Ernest as a "thief" and a "vampire," as an "embezzler of the mind," and as "utterly vile and rapacious, a hypocrite and a parasite."[28] The novel's bizarre climax crystallizes this ambiguity. As the entirety of Ernest's mind suffers "an irresistible suction," Reginald Clarke's physical body dissipates in a decadent nimbus of "blue, crimson, and violet" sparks, leaving behind something that "was all brain ... only brain ... a tremendous brain-machine ... infinitely complex ... infinitely strong."[29] Ernest, for his part, is defeated; drained and sapped by Clarke, the vampire's victim becomes "a dull and brutish thing, hideously transformed, without a vestige of mind."[30] Original or otherwise, Clarke's artistic practice leads in the end away from creation towards utter destruction.

As a neo-Wildean allegory this ending could also be read as an elaboration of a better-known vampire tale from the previous decade, Bram Stoker's *Dracula* (1897). Exploring Wilde's impact on the development of vampire mythology, Talia Schaffer traces the fictional framing of Stoker's bloodthirsty Count to Stoker's own repressed sexuality and (more pertinent to this discussion) to his youthful literary and personal competition with Wilde. She observes that "Wilde is a vampire who stalks the margins of Stoker's texts [...] and the vampire is famously hard to kill."[31] The character of Dracula, she further remarks, "is Wilde-as-threat, a complex cultural construction not to be confused with the historical individual Oscar Wilde. Dracula represents the ghoulishly inflated vision produced by Wilde's prosecutors; the corrupting, evil, secretive, manipulative, magnetic devourer of innocent boys."[32] In light of the plot details of *The House of the Vampire*, we could say that Schaffer could just as easily be describing Viereck's Reginald Clarke and his hideous effect on Ernest's mind.

Although Viereck wrote novels and is remembered mainly as a journalist and a political propagandist, he first launched himself into literary life as a poet. Much of his work during this early phase of his career featured exotic and homoerotic themes. For instance, his first volume of poetry, *Nineveh, and Other Poems* (1907), includes a lyric on Shakespeare's "Mr. W.H.," a "strange boy whose golden head / With blossoms of unending song / Was garlanded."[33] Despite his far-right politics, Viereck remained a champion of sexual freedom, maintaining a friendship with Magnus Hirschfeld, the German sexologist and homophile advocate whom Viereck dubbed the "Einstein of sex" and whose Berlin institute was to fall victim to the Nazis.[34] In Viereck's poetry Wilde proves a ghostly presence – sometimes quite literally. Viereck's 1912 volume of poems, *The Candle and the Flame*, contains "A Ballad of Montmartre," which stages the meeting of the ghosts of Wilde and the German poet Heinrich Heine:

> Within the graveyard of Montmartre
> Where wreath on wreath is piled,
> Where Paris huddles to her breast
> Her genius like a child,
> The ghost of Heinrich Heine met
> The ghost of Oscar Wilde. (lines 1–6)[35]

Having glided across Paris from his recently completed tomb at Père Lachaise cemetery for a phantom-to-phantom chat, Wilde's ghost remains a victim of homophobia and ignorance – as Wilde was in life. But, crucially, the ghost is also unrepentant. He projects great dignity in his forthright dissidence. "A Ballad of Montmartre" elaborates the legend of Wilde the queer martyr, who rejects the pseudo-scientific judgments of sexological texts such as Richard von Krafft-Ebing's *Psychopathia Sexualis*. As he tells his fellow-ghost,

Cite not Krafft-Ebing, nor his host
Of lepers in my aid,
I was sufficient as God's flowers
And everything He made;
Yea, with the harvest of my song
I face Him unafraid. (lines 37–42)[36]

This articulate spirit also returns from the grave to comment on a posthumous reputation defined by animosity and homophobic misunderstanding. In Viereck's poetic imagining, the definitive Wilde text in this connection is, of course, "The Portrait of Mr. W.H.": "I hear the din thereof / When with sharp knife and argument / They pierce my soul above, / Because I drew from Shakespeare's heart / The secret of his love" ("A Ballad of Montmartre," lines 32–6).[37] Although "[c]racked seemed and thin the golden voice" (line 45), this spectral Wilde nonetheless proves a robust figure of resistance to sexual philistinism.

Despite being diminished by death – "the worm to none is kind" – Viereck's ghost of Oscar Wilde is conspicuously perceptive, communicative, and opinionated (line 46). He is aware of and sensitive to his posthumous literary reputation, "the scorn of knave and fool" (line 28), meaning that even as a ghost he is fully capable of apprehending what the world of the living thinks and says about him. Beyond the pages of Viereck's poems, however, the Irish writer maintained his silence towards the living for a few more years – that is until he emerged in a burst of prolixity at a London seance held by Hester Travers Smith on 8 June 1923. At this and further seances Wilde's ghost continued to discuss the vagaries of his reputation, and, more intriguingly, he even became a playwright once again. Or was it all, to repurpose the title of Travers Smith's three-act play, an elaborate forgery?

Writing Wilde's Ghost

In a flurry of notices that appeared in several London papers during the final days of July 1923, Oscar Wilde's ghost made a dramatic entrance into the public consciousness. An unsigned article in the 30 July 1923 issue of the *London Daily Mail* called "A Queer Story of Spiritualism" sketches the general scenario behind the delivery and reception of these spirit messages.[38] It provides several representative passages of Wilde's apparently immortal wit, asking at its outset, "Is it Oscar Wilde's handwriting? Is it Oscar Wilde's style?" These phantom bon mots went on to provoke "quite a sensation" in both the mainstream and the spiritualist presses and were eventually collected in Hester Travers Smith's *Psychic Messages from Oscar Wilde*.[39] The *Daily Mail*'s questions, however, will haunt the story of Wilde's ghost as it is told by those who participated in – or merely commented on – the drama of the seance table. By stressing the scrutiny of "Oscar Wilde's" handwriting and literary style, the *Daily Mail* aligns spirit messages with a common method for detecting literary forgeries.

In what is probably the most quoted passage of all the "Oscar Wilde scripts," the spirit playfully informs the medium: "Being dead is the most boring experience in life. That is if one excepts being married or dining with a schoolmaster. Do you doubt my identity? I am not surprised because sometimes I doubt it myself. I might retaliate by doubting yours."[40] All doubt aside, the ghost certainly moved with impressive celerity from initial contact with the living (on 8 June) to a form of materialization in print (by the end of July). If we were to consider the "queer story" in the *Daily Mail* to be a publicity stunt, a marketing strategy to generate advance buzz for subsequent spectral transmissions, then it was an unqualified success. According to Hester Travers Smith's biographer, Edmund Bentley, "the Wilde case gave her work a recognition which never diminished," and through the 1920s she acquired "a clientele second to none throughout the country."[41] In Simone Natale's terms, Travers Smith turned "the celebrity status of [a] spirit author" like Wilde to her distinct advantage, for "the profitability of spirit writings was ensured by the fact that the spirit had been a famous writer in life."[42]

Oscar Wilde's ghost attracted enough attention to afford his self-described editor (Travers Smith) a measure of transatlantic fame. An American edition of *Psychic Messages* came out in 1926 with a more sensational title that tethered the moral ambiguity of Wilde's reputation to his place in the afterlife. It was called *Oscar Wilde from Purgatory*.[43] The medium's Wildean encounter even inspired an opportunistic imitation in the United States: *The Ghost Epigrams of Oscar Wilde* was published in New York in 1928, and its contents were ostensibly compiled by a pseudonymous and all too aptly named figure, "Lazar."[44] While a few of these "ghost epigrams," such as "All works of art are the autobiographies of liars," sound plausibly Wildean, others betray their fraudulence by reproducing the vernacular speech of 1920s America ("virtue carries its own reward and a mighty sad consolation," and "Bachelors are the bootleggers of love").[45] Throughout the English-speaking world, it seems, Wilde had too much to say to stay dead.

Exemplifying what Helen Sword has termed "necrobibliography" – her neologism for the books written by the dead – Travers Smith's Wilde messages are constituted by and mediated through the culture (or "occulture") of the 1920s. The mass bereavements that resulted from the Great War are often recruited to account for spiritualism's wide popularity in the 1920s, as the survivors of the war sought solace through occult contact with loved ones who had died.[46] Despite spiritualism's popularity, mediums were also often viewed with suspicion as possible fakers, a stance that persisted to define spiritualism's popular image into later decades. Noël Coward's *Blithe Spirit* (1941), for instance, both confirms and up-ends such an image: it stages the amusing hijinks that ensue when a medium who is expected to prove "a real professional charlatan" and "a complete fake" nonetheless witnesses the materialization of two ghosts who refuse to stay dead.[47]

In Sword's words, the 1920s were a decade that "saw an unprecedented boom in otherworldly messages and spirit communication"[48] from dead male writers who engaged in conversation with several professional female mediums. Travers Smith, who had reverted to her maiden name, Dowden, by the latter part of the decade, counted luminaries such as Francis Bacon and William Shakespeare among her spirit contacts. A representative figure in the post–Great War spiritualist heyday, Travers Smith, for Sword, is one of "the best-known female mediums of the modernist era [who] either came from literary backgrounds or undertook literary careers quite separate from their mediumistic vocations."[49] Hester Travers Smith was quite literally a *ghost writer*. By such logic, according to Sword, "a medium such as Hester Dowden becomes a ghostwriter in two senses: ostensibly allowing ghosts to write through her, she in fact writes through them."[50] Mediumship thus provided Travers Smith an entrance into the literary world, albeit one that came to be marked by charges of fraudulence, misrepresentation, and even forgery – charges that, moreover, neither she nor her partisans could ever quite manage to neutralize.

The contours of Travers Smith's biography bear out Sword's thesis. The daughter of the eminent Shakespeare scholar and Trinity College (Dublin) professor Edward Dowden, Travers Smith had grown up in a cultured and privileged world not unlike Oscar Wilde's own. Although they never met – in life – their backgrounds as artistic Irish expatriates are remarkably similar. In Dublin the Dowdens were acquainted with Lady Jane Wilde (Oscar's mother), and in later years Edward Dowden supported a petition to grant "Speranza" (her pen name) a civil list pension. Hester married a doctor (the profession of Wilde's father), but their marriage broke down during the First World War. She was granted a divorce in 1922, by which time she had installed herself and her daughter in Chelsea, the very London neighbourhood that Oscar Wilde had inhabited a generation earlier. After working as a freelance journalist, she established her career as a professional medium and psychic investigator. She maintained a cordially distant relationship with spiritualist officialdom but gained the endorsement of Sir William Barrett (the founder of the pre-eminent spiritualist organization the Society for Psychical Research), who lent his imprimatur to her books *Voices from the Void* (1919) and *Psychic Messages from Oscar Wilde* (1924). According to her biographer, as a psychic investigator "her mind remained always extremely cautious [...] she was always on the look-out for fragments of her subconscious mind suddenly coming to the surface, and taking the place of a discarnate who purported to write through her hand."[51] Such disavowals stage self-scrutiny as a means of enhancing the credibility of the medium's claims. They were also reiterated features of her alleged contact with Wilde, about whose *Poems* (1881) her father had once presciently remarked that "want of sincerity, and of original power of thought and feeling will condemn him to be only a phantasm."[52]

As this remark uncannily anticipates, modes of Wildean authorship tacitly structure Travers Smith's spiritualist writings about Wilde's ghost. Indeed, her book and the periodical controversies that surround it recapitulate the very questions of influence, mediation, and deception that characterize Wilde's own critique of originality. In the context of the ghost's messages, Elisha Cohn has described this critique as Wilde's "play of imitation": "For by presenting Wilde's ghost messages for publication," Cohn observes, "[Hester] Dowden foregrounded the notion that original authorship is deeply mediated, while at the same time insisting that this truly was Wilde's spirit, as if authorship were an unconscious and inter-subjective process of imitation. Dowden's writings do not seek to establish Wilde's identity, but rather the ghost's."[53] For Travers Smith, then, *this* ghost's writing is both authentic (it emanates from a real ghost and is therefore not a form of forgery) *and* structurally collaborative (the ghost only "writes" through living people). It is, as Cohn says, an "imitative collective process."[54] But, as the controversy about these messages unfolds, this process will prove to be more collective (and, for that matter, imitative) than Cohn and Sword have contended.

Originality, of course, is not the only conceptual pillar of modern authorship challenged by spectral texts. So too is the idea of intellectual property. To whom do Wilde's "psychic messages" belong, anyway? As Sword details, such messages map onto the territory of literary larceny in tangible legal terms: "mediumistic appropriations of literary identities can have very real and concrete consequences for those institutions charged with protecting the property rights of authors and the integrity of their work. For instance, copyright law [...] has little to say about the legal status of literary texts supposedly authored in the spirit world."[55] During her period of contact with the spirit, Travers Smith always carefully presented herself as the "editor" of Wilde's messages and never as their author. She claimed only to have arranged and curated the ghost's *communiqués* for her readers. (And in this role she served as a paranormal counterpart to Robert Ross, Walter Ledger, and Christopher Millard, whose respective efforts in curating the writer's afterlife were explored in chapter 1.) Travers Smith thus figures herself as the ghost's editor, but we could also usefully regard her as a participant in highly theatrical events, as a kind of impresario. Her seances featured an elaborate set-up, prescribed roles for participants working together, and audiences of varying kinds. Like dramatic spectacles, they required both the collaboration of the spiritualist performers on the one hand and the observation of the witnessing audience on the other. According to Simone Natale, both "spiritualist performances at séances" and "publications [by dead authors] were based on a successful combination of claims of authenticity and the pursuit of entertainment."[56] They "provide a further link between spiritualism's print and performance cultures."[57] A term for the textual link between print and performance is, of course, the ghost's *scripts*.

Wilde's purported messages to Travers Smith thus glimpse a moment in which literary fabrications and phantoms meet, because, as we have seen, they literalize the metaphor of the ghost-writer, a figure whose participation in literary co-production is artfully concealed under another's name. They also complicate this figure for authorship, for Hester Travers Smith was seldom alone when contacted by Wilde's ghost in her secluded Chelsea drawing room. The psychic messages themselves occupy less than half of the text of a volume otherwise dominated by its considerable authenticatory architecture. Just as much, if not more, attention is given to detailing how the messages were received; identifying and giving the credentials of those who were present at the sessions; rehearsing the methods employed to record the messages; and classifying the forms of analysis to which they were subjected, including graphological comparisons, complete with facsimile illustrations comparing Wilde's handwriting to the automatic writing taken down during the seances. The ghost, it turns out, had a knack for reproducing Wilde's handwriting that is only rivalled by Dorian Hope.

Psychic Messages describes two methods by which Wilde's ghost communicated with Travers Smith. Each method required the medium to work collaboratively with other humans (or non-humans), and so each had what we might call its own particular casting requirements. The first method of ghostly contact was automatic writing, a process whereby the hand of an "automatist," in this case a certain "Mr. V." who "wrote in a state of semi-coma," rapidly produced a script while in physical contact with the channelling medium.[58] Mr V. was the *nom de spiritisme* of Samuel Soal, an energetic psychic researcher who produced all the Wildean automatic script writings published by Travers Smith. (He also produced other Wildean messages with different mediums, as we shall soon see.) Throughout the seance the medium also maintained contact with an entity known as her "control" – a reliable spirit who would regularly act as a discarnate intermediary between the living world and the "communicator" spirit. Travers Smith's control or "spirit guide" was a 2,000-year-old Egyptian known as "Johannes."[59] The second, and generally more laborious, method of contact was by Ouija board, a technique that did not require the presence of Mr V. Travers Smith had considerable expertise in this method, to the extent that she included helpful "Hints to Experimenters at the Ouija-Table" in her first book, *Voices from the Void*.[60] During these sittings Travers Smith was joined by her frequent collaborator and fellow medium, the novelist and sometime playwright Geraldine Cummins. Cummins acted as a "recorder" and wrote down what the moving planchette spelled out on the surface of a Ouija board marked with letters and numbers. In such sessions the medium questioned the garrulous ghost, giving him the opportunity to opine on a number of topics while his views were recorded.

Three topics stand out among all of the spirit's messages. First, like Viereck's ghost of Wilde, the spirit is amply aware of what is going on in the here and now, especially when it comes to modernist literary matters. He holds rather low opinions of contemporary writers, and in fact he proves to be a somewhat shady shade; when he was asked to pronounce on the Sitwells, for example, Travers Smith records that "the criticism communicated by Oscar Wilde was considered too malicious to be published."[61] Second, the one-time *bon vivant* complains bitterly about the gloom and loneliness of his discarnate existence as a phantom whose mind has survived intact. And, third, he petulantly rehearses his pained awareness of his status as "social leper" and a "criminal."[62]

The ghost adopts an oracular, sage-like tone to evoke his existence in the spirit world, and when he speaks of his ghost-life – "this condition into which the Almighty has found it His pleasure to confine me" – he resembles Wilde writing about prison in *De Profundis*.[63] That introspective prison memoir, which chronicles Wilde's spiritual purification by suffering, provides an imaginative template for his ghost's thoughts about the afterlife, as this pastiche of *De Profundis* makes clear: "I wither here in the twilight, but I know that I shall rise from it again in ecstasy. That thought is given to us to help us endure ... The human spirit must pierce to the innermost retreats of good and evil before its consummation is complete. I suffer here because my term is long, and yet I have the power of knowledge – knowledge, such as all the justice that has tortured the world since it was born, cannot attain to."[64] As John Stokes wryly points out, Travers Smith's "most recognizable control is *De Profundis*."[65] The ghost further echoes *De Profundis* by dwelling on the material and reputational cataclysm brought on by the trials. Indeed, he seems at one point to refer directly to the dispersal of his literary property at the time of the Tite Street sale in 1895: "I had lost everything except my genius. All the precious things that I had gathered about me in my Chelsea home and that had become almost a part of my personality were scattered to the winds or lost or passed into careless and alien hands. The very children of my imagination were thought unworthy to live, and a lady whom I had trusted and who in the days of my pride had often called me her friend deliberately destroyed a manuscript of mine. As the man was tainted so must his work be tainted also."[66] This little tale of lost manuscripts, though never repeated by the ghost, is a tantalizing one; it is precisely the sort of information that Dorian Hope (or Mrs Chan-Toon) would have found useful. Oscillating between amusing quips that recalibrate famous witticisms ("I have nothing to declare except my genius" is recast in terms of loss) and biting commentary, Wilde the revenant thus reinforces the characteristic features of his posthumous reputation: he has suffered immensely for his own crimes against society but remains a uniquely quotable personality. The hallmark of Wilde's ghostly identity is its consistency with his legend, and, according to Travers Smith, this ghost is "certainly less changed by the 'process of dying' than any other ghost I have come across so far."[67]

Oscar Wilde's ghost also offers numerous details about his life, which, in her role as editor, Travers Smith is consistently anxious to point out that she could never have known. For example, she disclaims subconscious knowledge of Wilde's biography by professing to contrast what she does know about him with what she (supposedly) does not or cannot know. "[W]hen I asked the address at which Sir William and Lady Wilde lived in Dublin, which I knew, the reply to my question was that it could not be recalled; but the Tite Street address [in London] which I did not know, was given."[68] In offering such careful disclaimers, Travers Smith underlines the tension in spiritualist discourse between authenticity and fraudulence by returning to matters of proof and doubt. In doing so, she calls into question her own capacity for deception by turning to the language of theatre: "What I doubt," Travers Smith writes, "is, that as definite an entity as the Oscar Wilde of these scripts can be *dramatized* by Mr. V. or myself."[69] She is simply too inept an actor, she assures her readers, to be acting – and therefore she must be telling the definite truth about the ghost. But as readers of these psychic messages, can we be so certain that Travers Smith's acting abilities are not eclipsed by her talents for scriptwriting?

Hester Travers Smith and Geraldine Cummins both published articles in the *Occult Review* on the Oscar Wilde scripts that detailed their investigations and findings. Travers Smith's "The Return of Oscar Wilde" appeared in two parts, in August and September 1923 (they were later collected and amplified in *Psychic Messages*), and Cummins kept public interest alive by bringing out "The Strange Case of Oscar Wilde" in February 1924.[70] Tellingly, both titles have the particular flavour of Sherlock Holmes stories. This gesture to detective fiction is not all that surprising, considering Arthur Conan Doyle's extensive and personal participation in this "strange case." An avowed spiritualist, Doyle was by the 1920s deeply devoted to propagating spiritualist and other paranormal causes. His enthusiasm was equalled by his credulity, however, as he famously endorsed the faked photographs of the so-called Cottingley fairies in the *Strand Magazine* in 1920 – that is, in the very venue in which his supremely rationalist detective Holmes had made so many memorable pronouncements on logic and the deductive method.[71] The great detective's creator was, alas, spectacularly unskilled at detecting forgeries.

Having read what he called Travers Smith's "wonderful" first article in the *Occult Review*, Doyle wrote to the medium directly. He had spent years making the case for spiritualism, and the return of Oscar Wilde seemed miraculously to furnish the support that his work required. As we have seen with Brett Holland and the Dorian Hope forger-fans, Wilde's memory had the power to activate and to satisfy literary desires. "I think," Doyle writes, "the Wilde messages are the most final evidence of continued personality that we have." He continues, with mounting eagerness: "One could at a pinch imitate style, but one could not imitate the great mind behind the style. It is to me quite final [...] If you are in contact you might mention me to him – I knew him – and tell him that if he would honour me by coming through my wife who is an excellent automatic writer, there are some things which I should wish to say."[72] Although Wilde did not honour him (or his wife) with a visit, Doyle kept up his involvement with what, in a later letter, he called Travers Smith's "epoch-making" discoveries.[73] He reviewed *Psychic Messages* when it came out, for instance, and lent the full weight of his support to her project, defending her book from the repeated public criticisms of Mr V.'s brother, C.W. Soal, to which we will turn in the next section. Doyle's argument, which he detailed in an assessment of the case in his final book, *The Edge of the Unknown* (1930), was that the scripts must be considered authentic evidence of ghostly existence because they captured Wilde's unique personality – or, as he put it in his first letter to Travers Smith, "the great mind behind the style." Messages that appeared to him "most characteristic of Wilde's personality and literary style" were "not merely adequate Wilde" (and possibly forged) but "exquisite Wilde" (and therefore authentic).[74] Adducing evidence on the basis of "personality," "style," and individualizing characteristics and details, Doyle adapts the methods of his own detective. In the words of Elana Gomel, Doyle's analyses "derive identity from stylistic performance."[75] Like Sherlock Holmes, Doyle summons concrete proof from intangible impressions.

For Doyle, then, the spirit's reproduction of the recognizable style and personality of the living Wilde corroborates the claims made by the medium. But it also does more; it trounces all assertions to the contrary. Writing to the *Occult Review* in 1924, Doyle channels Holmes when he methodically organizes his reasoning:

> When I consider the various corroborations in this case of Oscar Wilde:
>
> 1. The reproduction of his light style.
> 2. The reproduction of his heavy style.
> 3. The reproduction of character.
> 4. The recollection of incidents, some of them quite obscure, in his own life.

5. The reproduction of his handwriting.
6. And (not least in my eyes) the similarity of the conditions which he describes upon the other side with those which our psychic knowledge would assign to such a man, I consider the case a very powerful one indeed.[76]

As articulated by Doyle, the weight of evidence leads to a conclusion so overwhelming that one might even call it elementary: this ghost is the real deal.

Ironically, the most powerful form of proof offered in *Psychic Messages* for the identity of a ghostly Wilde is material, for graphology is recruited to the spiritualist cause and cited as corroborating evidence. Although it only rates as number five on Doyle's checklist, the issue of ghostly handwriting was a vital feature of the public presentation of the spirit messages; the early *Occult Review* articles display facsimile comparisons between the automatist's conscious hand and his trance-induced ghost writing, along with comparisons between the writing of the living Wilde and that of the dead Wilde (figure 13). In *Psychic Messages* Travers Smith similarly presents her readers with a series of handwriting facsimiles; the hands reproduced are hers, Mr V.'s, a genuine example of Wilde's, and one of the "second Oscar Wilde script" that was taken down in Mr V.'s automatic writing (figure 14).[77] As we might expect, the channelled handwriting uncannily resembles that of the living Wilde, which appears for convenient comparison on a facing page. "Neither Mr. V. nor I had ever seen Wilde's writing so far as we could remember," she notes. "When he was gone it struck me that it would be interesting to compare the script with a fac-simile, if I could find one. I was singularly fortunate, for at the Chelsea Book Club, not only did I see a fac-simile of Wilde's writing, but an autograph letter of his happened to be there for sale. I was amazed; the handwriting seemed similar, allowing for the fact that our script was written with a heavy pencil and the autograph letter, probably, with a steel pen."[78] Travers Smith does not record whether she purchased the letter, but, as we shall see, Mr V. certainly had access to other examples of Wilde's handwriting. In any event, by staging her own amazement at the graphological comparisons presented in her book, Travers Smith masterfully guides her readers towards a clear-cut "yes" as an answer to the authenticatory questions that opened the article in the *Daily Mail* in 1923: "Is it Oscar Wilde's handwriting? Is it Oscar Wilde's style?"

after another, and rejects them in turn. The spirit hypothesis he rejects because, as he says, " everything seems to prove that the intelligence is a function of the brain " ; and he will admit no brain other than the physical one. " The lucidity of some mediums," he says, " is amazing, but lucidity is not survival. Survival implies the continuance of personal consciousness. Frederick Myers lived on the earth. He was himself and no other, with tastes, thoughts and an intelligence which made him a definite personality, very different from all others. But when Mrs. Verrall's hand writes, ' I am Myers,' or Mrs. Piper's voice says, ' I am Myers,' it is useless to try and find vague or even exact analogies between Mrs. Verrall's and Mrs. Piper's Myers and the real Myers as known on earth." " I do not," he says, " share the robust faith of Mr. Hubert Wales, who writes that ' spirits have bodies which, though imperceptible to our senses, are solid to them as ours are to us.' "

DOUBTING THOMAS.

Surely this is just where the value of such communications as those which I publish in the present issue, purporting to emanate from Oscar Wilde, is made manifest. In these the real man as he was on earth seems to speak to us again, and to be asked to identify the communications, even without the name of the communicator being given, would be the easiest thing possible to anyone who had any acquaintance with the writings and characteristics of the alleged communicator. What more can be asked? What more conclusive answer could be given to Professor Richet's doubts? Not only this, but the signature of Oscar Wilde itself repro-

EVIDENTIAL VALUE OF THE " WILDE " SCRIPT.

Pity Oscar Wilde
Believe me
your sincere friend
Oscar Wilde

duces the style and character of Wilde's own handwriting (unfamiliar, be it remembered, to the transmitters of the mes-

13 Facsimile of automatic writing from the *Occult Review*, 1923. Author's own collection.

FAC-SIMILE, SECOND OSCAR WILDE SCRIPT.

14 Handwriting facsimiles in *Psychic Messages from Oscar Wilde*, 1924. Author's own collection.

The Strange Case of the Brothers Soal

After the publication of the first few Wilde scripts, a new set of his spirit messages, entirely unconnected with Hester Travers Smith, appeared in the *Occult Review*. Mr V. (Samuel Soal) had continued to record Wilde's posthumous observations, and with the help of new and different mediums. He and Travers Smith had fallen out, and Soal lost no time in informing the medium that he did not need her help to contact the ghost. "I shall go on producing 'Wilde' scripts with as many mediumistic persons as I can get to co-operate and I think the net results should be a very interesting contribution to abnormal psychology," he huffed.[79] In "A New Message from Oscar Wilde," published in November 1923, his brother, C.W. Soal, makes clear that these Soal brothers wanted to apply their own investigative procedures, which C.W. Soal calls "the important task of verification," to the revenant Wilde.[80] Their independent inquiries, which Travers Smith did not incorporate into her book, and which included a lengthy article in the *Quarterly Transactions of the British College of Psychic Science*[81] and an acrimonious public correspondence in the *Occult Review* with Geraldine Cummins, come closest to acknowledging – again, in the key of investigation and analysis – the fictive nature of the entire spiritualist proceeding. In their earliest iterations, at least, I read the Soal interventions less as allegations of calculated duplicity (though they might appear this way to a non-spiritualist) and more as naively competitive attempts to undermine Travers Smith's authority as a medium and psychic investigator. Although C.W. Soal was careful not to attack Travers Smith directly, his *Psychic Science* article nonetheless proposed that the Wilde channelled by Helen MacGregor (another medium), in conjunction with his brother, was simply superior to Travers Smith's Wilde. Unlike the productions of Travers Smith's shabby spook, their newer scripts "have an energy and a flow which seems lacking in some of the earlier ones. Here Wilde is getting into his swing."[82]

Contradictory assertions about how much – or how little – of Wilde Mr V. had read constitute the core of C.W. Soal's contribution to the controversy. Mr V. apparently knew relatively little of Wilde's writings and less about Wilde's biography. In the *Daily Mail* piece that announced Wilde's irruption into spiritualist circles, for instance, Mr V. is represented as "little interested in literature." Moreover, he "really knows little about Oscar Wilde. He says he does not remember seeing a facsimile of Wilde's writing, unless [he] has picked up a book containing it on a bookstall at some time or other."[83] The logical corollary to this statement, much emphasized by Travers Smith and Cummins, is that such ignorance renders Mr V. (and, by extension, the medium herself) immune to accusations of fraud; in the absence of knowledge about Wilde, he could not have been capable of representing that knowledge as an emanation from the ghost. Being both ignorant and not guilty, Mr V. is thus innocent in two senses because forgery would require both knowledge and intent. Assessing the "evidential value" of the scripts, Mr V.'s brother modulates such claims with the admission that Mr V. may have been better informed than had previously been acknowledged:

> Since the production of the first script Mr. V. has, with the exception of the newspaper comments and Mr. Lawrence [*sic*] Housman's new book *Echo de Paris*, carefully abstained from reading any literature bearing on the personality of Oscar Wilde. Previous to these experiments, Mr. V. had read Methuen's Shilling Edition of *De Profundis*, [...] *Dorian Gray*, [...] and *Selected Poems*. None of these books are in his library, but were lent to him by a friend, and Mr. V. tells me he did not read any of them more than once. He said, moreover, that Wilde's style did not particularly impress him [...] Wilde's writings he once stigmatized as "frothy stuff."[84]

And yet such "frothy stuff," which Mr V. read before the seances, provides an imaginative model for the ghost's messages. Laurence Housman's book is a telling item on Mr V.'s reading list, for it was an important addition to the growing bibliography of memorials that sustained the Wilde legend in the 1920s. In *Echo de Paris* (1923), which is a fictionalized reconstruction of an extended conversation that took place in 1899, Housman writes *as* Wilde and inhabits the Irish writer's style with considerable charm. Unlike Travers Smith's ghost, his Wilde is an overtly biofictional character, and Housman asks his readers only to *imagine* what the spiritualists wish more definitively to prove. Comparing the seance scripts to Housman's book (to the disadvantage of the former), London's *Daily Sketch* asked, "[W]hy do the Spiritualists worry about getting messages from an apparently weary Oscar Wilde while we have Laurence Housman still with us? Mr. Housman can do it much better to judge from the sparkle in his new book 'Echo de Paris.'"[85] Housman writes that in Parisian exile Wilde's "life had already become a tomb. And it is as a '*monologue d'outre tombe*' that I recall his conversation that day."[86] The conceit that Wilde could speak "from beyond the grave" constituted much of the book's appeal, so much so that the dust-jacket blurb on the American edition described the experience of reading *Echo de Paris* this way:

> As if Oscar Wilde lived again –
> As if you talked with him – and
> heard that magic conversationalist,
> the fame of whose talk has become
> legendary –[87]

Albeit in a more sensational register, this promotional copy neatly captures the efforts of Travers Smith and Cummins. And, according to C.W. Soal, the book acted as a direct inspiration to his brother's trance-induced reproduction of "that magic conversationalist."

In his 1924 *Psychic Science* article C.W. Soal even more decisively cast doubt on the authenticity of the Wilde-ghost scripts. In that critique, which is extensively illustrated with handwriting facsimiles, Soal makes a surprising concession to scepticism; he asserts that his brother's automatic scripts, which bear a passing resemblance to Wilde's hand, must be considered forms of "imitation." Over several seance sessions, according to Soal, his brother's "Wilde" hand developed with practice, and "there had been a real improvement in the imitation as we pass from the earlier to the later scripts. As one who has known Mr. V.'s own handwriting for years [...] I can say without hesitation that the first O.W. script [...] is simply Mr. V.'s handwriting slightly disguised."[88] "Wilde's calligraphy is the easiest in the world to imitate," he further observes, "and it may well be by this time that Mr. V.'s subconscious mind has mastered a tolerable imitation which it can reproduce without much effort."[89] An admission that denies its status as such, this discussion, which exemplifies what Helen Sword calls "popular spiritualism," "embraces rather than eschews paradox."[90] After producing some thoroughgoing analyses of Wilde's literary style, Soal goes on to assert that "the best guarantee I can give the public of my brother's conscious honesty is the fact that he has insisted on my publishing these results of my investigations."[91] "Conscious honesty" is a telling phrase in an article that puts a great deal of pressure on the effect of unconscious influence in imagining various scenarios whereby Samuel Soal (Mr V.) could have passively absorbed, and so unwittingly reproduced, both Wilde's style and facts about his life. (His having done so would indicate that his own reading, and not a ghostly intelligence, was behind the Wilde scripts.) In effect, C.W. Soal maintains that, even if Mr V.'s scripts should be considered imitations, his brother is not consciously responsible for any deception.

By comparing the handwriting, and the style of the ghost's apothegms, with Wilde's own and by assessing what Mr V. knew about Wilde, C.W. Soal undertakes a massive amount of research, and his reading reminds me of nothing so much as the archive that informed the Dorian Hope forgeries. Handwriting, literary style, and biographical knowledge are all matters that a literary forger would have to master, and Soal attends to them carefully. He analyses Wilde closely and finds the writer to be an inveterate self-plagiarist and verbal recycler. By this logic, according to Soal, such practices on the part of the psychic investigators would therefore receive Wildean authorization, and, had "one of these [repeated] phrases or a variation of them appeared in our script, it is almost certain that some critic would have cried 'Plagiarism!' Whereas, in reality, we should simply have been reproducing something that is entirely characteristic in our author."[92] Soal finds theoretical Wildean justifications for the aesthetics of deception handy, as well, when he avers that one way of reading the scripts produced by his brother is "simply to regard them as literary productions." In so doing, he channels the arguments in favour of creative deception and insincerity in "The Decay of Lying" and "The Critic as Artist":

> For in order to produce good work the artist need not be sincere in his relations to the larger issues of life, or in his allegiance to the moral verities [...] but only to be faithful to the mood that he is seeking to interpret. No true artist ever really means what he says; he is too entirely occupied in trying to say what he means. The literary artist is sincere when he has achieved a perfect correspondence between form and feeling, the mood and the means of expression. He is insincere insofar as he has failed in this. Nothing more and nothing less is required of him.[93]

Soal wants to have it both ways: to clear his brother of any potential charges of "Plagiarism!" (or outright forgery) and to maintain that, in the case of Wilde at least, "literary" deception may be entirely appropriate where "sincerity" is irrelevant to art.

In his role as an investigator, C.W. Soal plumes himself on his scepticism and impartiality (as does Travers Smith). But, unlike spiritualism's famed champion, his capacity for belief has its limits, and he is unwilling to be seen "going so far as Sir Arthur Conan Doyle."[94] And yet, as Doyle had done, he and his brother play detective. They consistently employ what might be termed a Sherlockian method to analyse their Wilde scripts. Working to distinguish between what the medium and/or the automatist may have known and the information presented in these new scripts, they seek, by the process of elimination, to infer that previously unknown information could only have come from a ghost. In so doing, they implicitly follow Sherlock Holmes's most famous investigative precept. Examining an apparently impossible locked-room murder in *The Sign of Four* (1890), Holmes tells Watson: "How often have I said to you that when you have eliminated the impossible, whatever remains, *however improbable*, must be the truth?"[95] According to this logic as applied by C.W. Soal, though it may seem improbable, the existence of Wilde's ghost is the only remaining hypothesis once "the impossible" – conscious deception by Soal's brother – has been eliminated. Soal's laborious authenticatory manoeuvres are, in their way, as theatrical as the seances themselves, for they *stage* scepticism, investigation, and scrutiny. In the pages of *Psychic Science* Soal is both sleuth and actor as he performs the role of ghost detective.

After airing his views in *Psychic Science*, C.W. Soal further sought to bolster his credibility as a psychic investigator by attacking and undermining Travers Smith's associate Geraldine Cummins. He does so in March 1924, in direct response to the *Occult Review* article published by Cummins in February, shortly before the appearance in print of *Psychic*

Messages from Oscar Wilde. In "The Strange Case of Oscar Wilde" she had offered her *Occult Review* readers a selection of anecdotes received from the spirit Wilde that, apparently, she and Travers Smith could not possibly have known, such as a story from Wilde's childhood about an Irish priest called Father Prideaux Fox. Cummins reaffirms that "the handwriting in the script is a strong link in the chain of evidence [...] One long message was written at a speed of nearly 800 words in an hour. Is it possible to forge at such a rate?"[96] I especially want to highlight the telling verb she employs here, *forge*, since this moment marks its first appearance in the print record of the Wilde scripts. The charge of forgery had long been haunting the Wilde-script controversy, and once it emerged into print, its effects could not be contained.

C.W. Soal answers the provocative question of whether it would be "possible to forge at such a rate" with withering effectiveness. He demolishes Cummins's arguments, noting that research in existing books could have supplied the unknown childhood details: "it was not necessary to go to Ireland or indeed any further than the appendix of Thurston Hopkins' *Oscar Wilde*, or to Stuart Mason's *Bibliography of Oscar Wilde*, since either of these works contain all the details relating to Father Fox which were communicated at the sitting." "I have," he continues, "traced every one of the supposed 'Memories' to their probable sources in biographies and other books of reference."[97] Cummins's question also provokes Soal to revisit the controversy over the ghost's handwriting: "In her article Miss Cummins asks, 'Is it possible to forge Wilde's handwriting at a speed of 800 words per hour?' I answer emphatically 'Yes.' I have recently experimented in reproducing blindfold, memorized but previously unpracticed passages in imitation of Wilde's handwriting [...] Previous to these attempts I have practiced Wilde's calligraphy for about half an hour daily for five or six days. Wilde's habit of separating letters makes his handwriting peculiarly easy to imitate."[98] In describing these "experiments," he confirms that one could indeed "forge Wilde's handwriting at a speed of 800 words per hour," but stops just short of accusing Cummins and Travers Smith of forgery and does not seem to be doing his brother's reputation any favours, either. (We might also pause for a moment to contemplate the utter bizarrerie of the timed forgery experiments that Soal describes, complete with blindfold and memorized passages of text.) So what, ultimately, is at issue in this squabble among spiritualists?

In order to answer that question better, we should return to the 1924 *Occult Review* article by Cummins, which amplifies advance publicity for *Psychic Messages* with an escalation in the spiritualists' claims about the ghost's writing. In addition to mentioning that the "communicator" is by "turns arrogant, charming, bitter, ironical, and extremely courteous," Cummins announces that the ghost has moved beyond epigrams and anecdotes and has returned to the genre that secured his greatest fame. Oscar Wilde's ghost has begun writing a *play*: "He is at present communicating a play with clever intrigue in the Wilde style of the nineties. He writes and rewrites his dialogue and becomes furiously impatient if interrupted, or if his ideas are not instantly understood. We have asked him to modernize the play in treatment and manner, so that it might have a more popular appeal. But this he seems quite unable to do; he continues to treat it in the Wilde manner."[99]

By this point, Mr V. was no longer involved in automatic writing experiments with Travers Smith; he and his brother had moved on to working with other mediums. Cummins and Travers Smith now undertook spectral contact with "Wilde" exclusively by Ouija board (the second method of communication outlined in *Psychic Messages*), without the participation of the Soals. At stake in this controversy, it seems to me, are allegations of forgery (as crime and in evidentiary terms) and the existence of the discarnate survival of spirits. Additionally, the news items suggest a struggle for control of the putative ghost's "writing" and implicitly pit the two methods of ghost-writing (automatic writing and Ouija board) against one another, with proponents of each technique alleging proprietorship of the ghost's literary output. The matter of copyright thus becomes particularly vexed when multiple living individuals lay claim to the writing of one ghost. Indeed, in a 1927 dispute with another psychic investigator, Frederick Bligh Bond (who, incidentally, had also been present at some of Travers Smith's Wilde sittings), Cummins herself came to play a definitive role in establishing copyright over spirit messages in Britain. In the copyright case of *Cummins v. Bond*, the court ruled that, "since it had no jurisdiction over the afterlife, Cummins was the sole author because it was she who held the pen."[100] This judgment came too late, however, for Soal to assert such rights on his brother's behalf in the case of the Wilde scripts.

Somewhat ingeniously (if unconvincingly), C.W. Soal resolves the matter of the ownership of Wilde's ghostly transmissions by figuring an increase in the ghost population. According to the communications received by a new medium, Helen MacGregor, and written out by Samuel Soal (Mr V.) in September 1923, the Wilde of Travers Smith's seances could be considered merely a ghostly doppelgänger:

QUESTION: "How is it you are able to communicate through Mrs. Travers Smith, if, as you say, you are imprisoned in my brain?"
ANSWER (OSCAR WILDE): "That is most probably another part of myself, a poor fellow-unfortunate who suffers even as I suffer."
QUESTION: "What do you mean? Surely there are not two Oscar Wildes?"
ANSWER (OSCAR WILDE): "Does that cause you to wonder? Yes, it really is so. Quite possibly our name is legion."[101]

Competing with their spiritualist rivals, the Soals assert that their Wilde (to say nothing of their Wilde script) is simply superior to Travers Smith and Cummins's "poor" and "unfortunate" one. With an irony that Wilde himself would have loved, originality – or better yet, uniqueness – apparently matters less than aesthetic merit.

Despite such volleys, C.W. Soal was bested, according to Cummins, by sustained literary production in the form of a new play "in the Wilde style of the nineties." No mere conversationalist, the Wilde who communicated via planchette at Travers Smith's table managed to produce a document that the two collaborators provisionally entitled "The Extraordinary Play." Plugging the play in the *Occult Review*, Cummins quotes some of its pithy lines that prove quite appropriate to the controversy at hand (the speech prefixes appertain to unnamed characters):

S—— Do you believe in the supernatural, sir, may I ask?
R—— I do not even believe in the natural, Strang. Belief is the refuge of those who are too dull to imagine.[102]

According to Cummins, the "extraordinary" play provides the best evidence yet for the existence of ghosts. Better still, she claims that it outdoes Samuel Soal's (Mr V.'s) automatic writing. Her ghost, after all, is engaged in a vastly more prestigious literary endeavour. "The three-act play," she writes, "which is being communicated through the ouija board, from what purports to be Oscar Wilde, is to my mind more convincing as evidence of the survival of a very remarkable personality than any of the previous automatic scripts received."[103] This new script is thus an original, and not a forgery, because its method of transmission is truly "more convincing."

As for C.W. Soal and his brother, they have been outdone, and, as Cummins observes with some icy satisfaction, Soal's "exhaustive analysis of the *smaller portion* of this curious case in *Psychic Science* is extremely interesting and instructive."[104] But the controversy just would not die. In the very next issue of the *Occult Review* Soal

intensified his charge of fraud against Cummins by repeatedly highlighting the concept of forgery. According to Soal, "only by studying what could be forged normally can we gain any estimate of what can be forged unconsciously."[105] Consciously committed or not, *forgery* is now a fully operative term in the controversy over the Wilde scripts, and, having issued that spiritualist insult, C.W. Soal retired from the fray. Samuel Soal (Mr V.), however, took up the cause shortly thereafter, writing in 1926 for the first time about his own part in the case. Although he has nothing to say about his brother's critique, he follows its line of argument implicitly. Rather than confessing to forgery, he claims simply to be investigating a paranormal occurrence, and he succeeds "in tracing many passages in these scripts to their probable origins" in printed materials that were "undoubtedly in my possession at the time of the sitting."[106] Intriguingly, Samuel Soal expands upon this near-retraction a few years later in an entry that he composed on "Spiritualism" for *A Dictionary of the Occult* (1935). Disavowing his role in the transcription of Wilde's spirit messages, he even discredits Mr V., his pseudonymous former self. In a voice distanced from Mr V.'s he writes:

> We need not linger over those alleged communications from dead authors which claim to reproduce their peculiar literary styles and habits of thought. Such were the spirit "messages" which purported to come from Oscar Wilde in 1923. In the first place it is extremely difficult to prove that such automatic writings are genuine and not essays deliberately composed and memorized, then afterwards reproduced in the séance-room. It would be fairly easy for any competent writer to produce a few pages of Oscar Wilde and also to write a few short impressionistic essays in Wilde's decorative manner [...] And even if these messages are genuine automatic scripts the imitation of the style and handwriting of the dead author proves very little. It is certain that the automatist "Mr. V." had read several of Wilde's books and he may have seen a specimen of the handwriting of the dead author in a facsimile in the Comtesse de Brémont's *Oscar Wilde* – a book prominently displayed in the bookstalls about the year 1915.[107]

According to this line of argument, the ghost's having been a famous author whose writing has been "prominently displayed" taints the psychic experiment, and so what Soal's brother had once called "conscious honesty" no longer seems to matter much. What this entry registers most powerfully, however, is the impact of the Wilde scripts on the practice of spiritualism itself, for even at a distance of more than a

decade Samuel Soal wants both to bury *and* to resurrect the controversy in a definitive publication on the occult.

The Ghost in the Audience

The question of ghostly consciousness and perception turns out to be as critical as the honest (or dishonest) consciousness of the living to this strange case of Wilde's supernatural communications. In the series of questions quoted from the Soal and MacGregor seance the ghost is described as being "imprisoned" in the brain of the medium, presumably making use of her eyes to visualize the world of the living. An analogous, albeit more free-spirited, form of spectral mental possession is also the manner in which Wilde's ghost, according to Travers Smith, accesses the minds of contemporary authors. In response to Travers Smith's questions about the ghost's (extensive) *reading*, her phantom interlocutor reveals: "I will go on and tell you how I have wandered into the minds of the moderns, as you are pleased to call them. It is a rather entertaining process. I watch for my opportunity, and when the propitious moment comes I leap in to their minds and gather rapidly these impressions, which are largely collective."[108] Having entered the mind of John Galsworthy, for instance, the ghost unexpectedly names him his "successor, in a sense."[109] Borrowed eyes afford Wilde's ghost the means to experience new literary work and to revisit his own. It is by this method that the ghost could accompany Travers Smith to a 1923 revival of *The Importance of Being Earnest*, where, according to Cummins, "he has been able to use Mrs. Travers Smith's eyes in order to see the play."[110] This process of inter-psychic mental access recalls the technique of Viereck's vampire Reginald Clarke, who probes the brains of his victims, searching for literary property to purloin. By contrast, Travers Smith's Wilde is a much more benign entity, inquisitively tagging along to a show – like one of her Pekinese lap-dogs smuggled into the theatre.

A real theatrical production furnishes the back-drop for this extraordinary scene of play-going. Staged at London's Haymarket Theatre, this revival of *The Importance of Being Earnest* was directed by Allan Aynesworth (the original Algernon, in the first 1895 production), with costumes updated to reflect the fashions of the 1920s. Hester Travers Smith attended a performance in December 1923, accompanied by her ghost. Alert to the value of maintaining a steady flow of publicity, she offered an account of this spiritualist field trip to the London *Sunday Express*, which was later reprinted as an appendix to *Psychic Messages*.

(That newspaper's editor, James Douglas, was fascinated with spiritualism and had corresponded extensively with Doyle about the Wilde scripts.) Unsurprisingly, the often-scathing spirit adopts a critical tone towards the production. This artist *is* a critic; he takes a proprietary view not only of the whole play but also of the performances of individual actors – "his" characters – suggesting that they "remodel their work a little, in deference to the author's wishes."[111] This "smartened" and modernized production has been transposed into a time from which the ghost feels estranged, and he tells the medium: "I do not wish to cavil at the present age, but the Haymarket company and its producer must forgive me if I am surprised rather than enchanted by what they have accomplished."[112] Although he admits to being behind the times – "a shade démodé" – he nonetheless views the Haymarket production as a "complete misapprehension of my play."[113]

These observations establish the revenant Wilde as a figure firmly fixed in the past, the representative of a bygone Victorianism. Having returned from the dead to write again, he makes it quite clear that he does not want his new play to appear too modern. He prefers to maintain, in Geraldine Cummins's phrase, "the Wilde manner." That very tension between past and present comes to animate the play that the ghost has been writing; when asked if he will go on with the composition of his "new play" after witnessing a performance of his old one, the ghost is tantalizingly guarded, allowing only that "it is certain it will be written, and in a manner different from my poor little 'Earnest.'"[114] From one perspective, this prophecy proved to be only half right because the new play eschewed "difference" from *Earnest* for highly recognizable stylistic and thematic borrowings; so indebted is the new play to its predecessor that the first scene of its second act takes place in the foyer of a theatre during a performance of *Earnest*. (The very scene of Travers Smith's visit to the theatre thus comes to figure in the play that the ghost purportedly writes through her.) From another perspective, since Wilde had not (so far as I know) previously attempted playwriting by Ouija board, this statement is an accurate description of the "extraordinary" means by which the new play was apparently composed. Just as importantly, it establishes the 1923 Haymarket production of *Earnest* as a model against which the ghost – and the mediums through whom he writes – will compare the new drama. Much like other publicity-seeking ghostly *communiqués* shepherded into print by Travers Smith and Cummins, the ghost's review of a contemporary production generates publicity by whetting public appetite for a spectacular materialization of what, on a metaphysical plane, spiritualism itself craved: a dramatic meeting between the past and the present.[115]

The Extraordinary Play: *Is* It a Forgery?

For all the controversy and publicity it stirred up, to say nothing of the success it contributed to Travers Smith's career as a medium, *Psychic Messages from Oscar Wilde* amounts to a mere prologue to the later and less well-documented communications that Travers Smith received from the spirit Wilde. As with the psychic messages, but more explicitly, the question of forgery also organizes these later and decidedly more dramatic *communiqués*. According to Travers Smith, the drama initially called "The Extraordinary Play" was retitled "Is It a Forgery?" (phrased as a question) at the suggestion of the ghost himself, and its composition was completed by 31 July 1924. In a 1928 article on the spirit play's origins, Travers Smith recalls that a fellow spiritualist, Gertrude Kingston, objected to the original title and thought fit to tell the ghost as much during a seance. "This is a very bad name for the play," Kingston informed the ghost. "Can't you think of something better?" A famous stage actress and one of the few female theatre managers at that time, Gertrude Kingston (1862–1937) was more than qualified to offer such a critique, and the ghost deferred to her professional expertise. In his reply the ghost instructed her, "Call the play *Is it a Forgery?* and say the author himself is debating the question."[116] This "question" of the play's status definitely had an impact on its fate, for despite Kingston's plans to produce it, it was never performed, let alone published, and it survives only in a hand-corrected typescript held at UCLA's Clark Library.[117] In this format the play is prefaced by a lengthy "foreword" composed by Geraldine Cummins for inclusion in a projected, revised edition of *Psychic Messages* that would include the play; this edition never materialized. Like the manuscript of the play, the typed prefatory paratext contains many handwritten corrections, at once indicating the sustained effort and the larger designs that the mediums had for this collaboration between the worlds of the living and the dead. Unfortunately for their theatrical ambitions, "Is It a Forgery?" was destined to remain a phantom production, unseen by the world – but certainly not for lack of trying.

Travers Smith and Cummins shopped the play around, boldly reaching out to several influential theatre professionals, including the actor-managers George Grossmith and Gerald du Maurier. Edmund Bentley records that "the play was sent to Sir Gerald du Maurier, and interested him, but he finally decided not to produce it. Probably its psychic nature scared him."[118] The son of Wilde's contemporary, the satirist George du Maurier, Gerald du Maurier managed Wyndham's Theatre in London's Charing Cross Road. It appears that at some point the idea for a production of the ghost play was transferred to the New (now Noël Coward) Theatre in St Martin's Lane, which is situated directly behind Wyndham's. The only potential producer untroubled by the "psychic nature" of the play was Gertrude Kingston, who had secured the ghost's personal blessing to mount a production during a 1925 seance. When asked by Kingston for advice about the correct dramaturgical approach needed for such an unconventional show, the ghost equivocated about the play's status: "Secure the goodwill of your public by saying that it is supposed that this play is a forgery, but that as it has come to light it may amuse the public as a parody of Wilde."[119] Whether parody or forgery, the ghost confides, "it has undoubtedly overstepped the limits I confined myself within when I was still alive."[120] Despite this evasiveness about the play's authenticity, the ghost had no reservations about the necessity of promoting the drama. When asked by Kingston, "Shall I publish this?," the ghost replied, "Pray do, dear Gertrude. Publicity is the soul of success."[121]

It was the medium herself, however, who pursued "the soul of success" in print, and, as she had done with the earlier messages, Travers Smith turned again to the periodical press for publicity. A spring 1928 staging of "Is It a Forgery?" seems at one point to have been in the offing, and Travers Smith advertised a prospective theatrical production in the pages of *The Graphic*: "As matters stand at the moment of writing, we have arranged to produce at the New Theatre, on March 27 [1928] *Is it a Forgery?* which purports to have been written by the discarnate spirit of Oscar Wilde through my mediumship."[122] This planned production under Gertrude Kingston's management did not take place, however, for on that date the New Theatre was occupied by a play called *The Wrecker* (described as a three-act "train mystery") that ran from December 1927 to April 1928.[123] It is difficult to say whether Travers Smith was misrepresenting the arrangements for the play's production, whether the New Theatre's owners withdrew their support, or whether she quarrelled with Kingston. Kingston's memoirs only record that "the play […] was never produced, for reasons into which I do not need to enter here."[124] In any case, it is likely that "Is It a Forgery?" on the West End stage, at the New Theatre or not, would have been a train wreck of an altogether different kind.

The most likely explanation for the play's false starts is that legal complexities intervened. In a letter dated 1 March 1928 to Wilde's son Vyvyan Holland, Gertrude Kingston breezily asks if Holland "may have read of the play 'Is it a Forgery?' [that] I am intending to produce which is in rehearsal."[125] Holland clearly had heard of the play, and as administrator of the Wilde literary estate he was evidently not impressed. Kingston's missive registers her surprise at receiving a stern warning from the estate's lawyers stating that "the production is calculated to bring contempt and ridicule on [Wilde's] name & reputation."[126] Although Kingston professes ignorance about the administration of the Wilde estate, her letter strongly hints at her suspicion of Vyvyan Holland's intervention to thwart the production of the ghost play. "I hope you know enough of my work," she writes, "to recognize that I should be as respectful of your father's literary genius as you would be."[127] However respectful she may have been, Holland was not about to permit a dubious new drama – especially one whose very title foregrounded its probable fraudulence – into the closed canon of his father's writings. Following the pattern set by Ross and Millard, he sought to protect Wilde's legacy by purging it of forgeries, including those purporting to be written by a ghost. Rebuffed by Holland, Gertrude Kingston moved on to other projects, and the ghost's would-be producer recorded her pique at this rejection in her memoirs: "Wilde or no Wilde, a subconscious or merely clever imitation, the theme of the play was striking and no one need have been ashamed of it."[128]

Just as Travers Smith had familial associations with Wilde himself, so too did she and Geraldine Cummins have links to his theatrical world. It makes some sense, then, that they would try to mount a play by him. Indeed, Travers Smith's son-in-law, the Irish playwright and theatre producer Lennox Robinson, mounted another revival of *The Importance of Being Earnest* at Dublin's Abbey Theatre in 1926. For Robinson, Wilde's comedy ought to be seen as an unapologetic artefact of its time and thus did not readily lend itself to "the brilliant idea of presenting it in 'modern dress.'"[129] In voicing such an opinion, he firmly concurred with the views expounded by the playwriting ghost about the earlier revival of *Earnest* at London's Haymarket. Geraldine Cummins, herself a playwright, remained a stalwart promoter of the spirit play. Unfazed by the abortive attempts to mount a West End production in 1928, she tried years later to have it published and met only with further rejection. In declining her proposed book, publisher Andrew Dakers told Cummins: "It was curious how I found much of Wilde's communication very convincing as having the hallmark of his wit and epigrammatic style, but that the play itself seemed quite otherwise. It does not strike me as being up to his standard."[130] Lennox Robinson himself agreed, telling Cummins: "I've read the 'Oscar Wilde' play, of course it is interesting but I don't think it's much good. The first two acts are imitation Oscar but there isn't a really brilliant epigram, everything is derivative, curiously the third act which is Maeterlinck is much more interesting [...] Of course I'd love the play to go on and be a success but I can't feel very enthusiastic about it."[131] The mediums' varied experiences with the theatrical and publishing worlds tell us that, by the mid-1920s (and certainly by the late 1940s, when Cummins was pitching the play as part of a new edition of *Psychic Messages*), Wilde occupied a decidedly fixed place in the dramatic repertory, and, from the perspective of London's culture industries, the ghost play – "scary" or not – simply was not marketable.

Although it is uneven, the play represents one of the most fascinating scripts about Wilde's afterlife, and it reads like a cleverly wrought piece of fan fiction. As fan fictions do, it seeks to expand on a writer's existing imaginative world. "Is It a Forgery?" also rewards insider knowledge about (and fannish connections to) Wilde's milieu. The revised title that the ghost allegedly suggested to Gertrude Kingston, for example, is a nearly exact quotation from "The Portrait of Mr. W.H." In so labelling the play, this ghostly emanation draws readers back into a nexus of existing Wilde texts, as the earlier psychic messages had done. In that story, we recall, the unnamed narrator asks his friend Erskine about the status of the putative portrait of Shakespeare's beloved Willie Hughes. "But is it a forgery?" he asks, only to receive the reply, "Of course it is."[132] Recalling *The Picture of Dorian Gray*, the play also contains an enchanted portrait in an artist's studio, although the *legitimacy* of the artwork is never called into question in the play (in contradistinction to the forged Willie Hughes portrait in "The Portrait of Mr. W.H."), which leaves the referent for the title's ambiguous "It" extremely suggestive. Equipped with an interrogative title that is also a Wilde quotation, the play thus thematizes the very questions of critical inquiry and possible fraudulence that define the spiritualist project.

Despite the ambiguity foregrounded by the ghost's chosen title for his new script, Cummins's foreword insists that the play is not a forgery but rather a collective effort whose human participants were decidedly subordinate to the whims of the imperious ghost. This arrangement caused some practical difficulties at the Ouija board. At one point a Miss Marion Dawson was tasked with recording the communications of the spirit Wilde, which turned out to be a rather vexing process, as Cummins puts it: "The communicator [i.e., the spirit Wilde] found creative work under such circumstances extremely difficult at first. Again and again he lost his temper and waxed bitterly sarcastic at the expense of the recorder. 'He made me so angry there were times when I could have killed him,' said Miss Dawson to me. There were certainly times when I too sympathised with her murderous designs upon a ghost."[133] Despite such annoyances (is it possible to murder a ghost?), Cummins's account of the composition of the play is replete with the same authenticatory manoeuvres that were made in *Psychic Messages*, which had only recently appeared in print. For example, the medium is repeatedly represented as having little acquaintance with Wilde's work, aside from having read a couple of plays and *De Profundis*. Wilde's ghost, for his part, is highly concerned with asserting ownership of *his* creative work, and he chastises the medium for any attempts at collaborative correction:

> When the play was typed and Mrs. Dowden [Travers Smith] was able to read it through she altered the dialogue in a few places. The alterations were of a trifling character, numbering twelve in all. In a subsequent sitting Wilde noted every alteration when I read the script aloud to him. In each case the traveller [planchette] was pushed about with great violence. I was sensible to a very real emotion. "That is not my work" came with angry exclamation; and we were severely taken to task to daring to alter his dialogue. It was either rewritten by him or put back into its original form. The play is therefore given to the public in the exact shape in which it was communicated.[134]

Cummins's explanation renounces writerly collaboration (to say nothing of duplicity) by having the ghost stake a claim to literary property that is tantamount to copyright.

In terms of its artistic merits, the ghost play proves to be a fannish pastiche of Wildean society comedy and *Dorian Gray* spookiness. It undeniably demonstrates considerable knowledge of Wilde's writing and his characteristic style. "In the first two acts of the play," Travers Smith recalls, "Wilde is reminiscent of his old self."[135] The central character in "Is It a Forgery?" is an artist by the name of Gerald Barens, whose studio is visited by several quasi-Wildean characters in the first act. At tea he entertains the lorgnette-wielding, Bracknellian Lady Bertram and her eminently marriageable daughter Beatrice, a rather knowing ingénue who functions as an amalgam of *Earnest*'s Gwendolen Fairfax and Cecily Cardew. Her marriage to Gerald is all but assured if he would only go through the motions of making it official by proposing. There is also plenty of epigrammatic dialogue, and some of it certainly echoes Wilde's "old self," as in Lady Bertram's observation that "[g]ossip is the exclusive property of the lower classes. Scandal is good form; it may be talked in any drawing-room."[136] Despite such debts to *Earnest*, this light society comedy is also mixed with menacing intrigue drawn from *Dorian Gray*. Gerald, who appears distinctly unwell, has completed a painting – which remains mysteriously veiled – and he resists all demands to show it. Then a very cryptic character named John Franklin appears, fascinating Beatrice, who, though she does not realize it yet, has considerable psychic abilities. Franklin, it turns out, is somehow sapping Gerald of vitality, and he is recognized by Mrs Garvin,[137] the play's worldly woman with a past, as her old lover Cyril L'Estrange; L'Estrange has been dead for twenty years. Franklin is an undead entity – a "resurrection" – who has returned from "the land of naked souls"[138] and has "compelled" Gerald to paint an enchanted portrait of him, and the painting has transferred Gerald's drained life force to the undead revenant. This plot arc (a variant of the plot of *Dorian Gray*) has a distinctly fan-fictional flavour. Perhaps a better title for the play would have been *The Picture of Dorian Gray with Vampires*.

The play further indulges its fannish side with L'Estrange's first name; Cyril was the name of Wilde's eldest son, who had died in the Great War. As in *Dorian Gray*, art and life continually trade places. Franklin/L'Estrange, for instance, knowingly declines to attend the second act's offstage performance of *Earnest*: "because I am living in drama at the present. That is why I do not want to see the play."[139] As a character from the past, moreover, he has taken Lennox Robinson's advice about the inadmissibility of modern dress to performances of *Earnest*; he prefers to wear "such old fashioned clothes."[140] At the studio at the end of the second act, Franklin/L'Estrange reveals all, including the portrait of himself as a younger man. Having transferred Gerald's life energy to himself by means of the portrait, the undead Franklin/L'Estrange informs the assembled characters, "I have come back from the land that lies beyond the grave."[141] At this point Gerald, who is near death, melodramatically names him a "Vampire." (Here the play amalgamates Viereck's *House of the Vampire*, which also features a dandy vampire who absorbs an artist's life essence.) Franklin/L'Estrange admits to Gerald, "I sucked your life to give me life," but in doing so he explains that he has returned to carry his former lover Mrs Garvin back with him to the spirit world. "You played your part," he off-handedly responds to Gerald's accusation of vampirism.[142] Like the figure of Reginald Clarke in Viereck's *House of the Vampire*, Franklin/L'Estrange is an aesthete who has "lived for beauty," and he justifies his vampirism as simply a practical necessity.[143]

The third act, which is set in "the realms of the unseen," according to the foreword, changes the tone (and setting) of the play completely. Even so, it manages to bridge the divide between Wildean decadence and theatrical modernism: the stage directions call for a "set as Gordon Craig," a celebrated modernist theatre practitioner, "would set it."[144] Musing about such designs, Wilde's ghost strikes a decadent tone: "Rich thoughts come to me for this act. It must be brilliant as the hall of a sultan's palace, a blaze of colour and light beyond what is usual, and I shall surprise the audience by this aspect of our side which has never been suggested to them before. It shall be a great hall, and through it are passing the shades who have come over borne by their guides … It must be more terrible and exciting than *Salome*."[145] Despite this and some similarly decadent flourishes, there is little else here that recalls Wilde. (Lennox Robinson identified a better analogue in Maeterlinck.) Instead, the ghost play's third act gives us a tour of the shadowy realm of the spirit world and what happens to "traveller souls" there. Mrs Garvin has successfully been "called" away from her physical life by Franklin/L'Estrange to this desolate place to begin her journey towards enlightenment. Gerald and Beatrice are reunited as "brother and sister" souls (not as bride and groom) at the play's end, and the curtain descends on a beautiful and mysterious netherworld that I would consider to be the fulfilment of a spiritualist's desire for precisely how the great beyond *should* appear. "Your body is a husk that you left behind when your soul had come to ripeness," Franklin/L'Estrange tells one of his fellow phantom "Travellers" in the spirit realm. "Your world is gone, space is gone, time is gone … Time is eternity."[146]

This play tells us much more about its real artificer(s) than it does about its putative author, and it seems to fulfil a desire for literary expression mediated (here most literally) through the creation of a new myth about Oscar Wilde. For my purposes, at least, "Is It a Forgery?" is the product of an era in which the forging of new Wilde legends made possible the fulfilment of writerly aspirations, and it belongs, as Joseph Bristow and Rebecca N. Mitchell say of *Psychic Messages*, "to a broader cultural wish to reanimate his spirit."[147] It is also an artefact, in my estimation, whose contents amply answer in the affirmative the question posed by its title.

Chapter Four

The Devoted Fraud

One of the most peculiar moments in *Psychic Messages from Oscar Wilde* (1924) comes near the beginning of the book when Wilde's ghost names a certain Mrs Chan-Toon. In one of the earliest Wilde scripts taken down by Mr V.'s automatic writing, the ghost deflects questions about himself by suggesting other avenues of inquiry into his status as the real ghost of Oscar Wilde. "Do not degrade me into giving you facts," he querulously tells the seance participants. "Enquire about Mrs. Chan Toon. I had the honour of her acquaintance some years ago" (see figure 14).[1] Curious about either Oscar Wilde or spiritualism (or both), Hester Travers Smith's readers could be forgiven for finding this outburst puzzling, for it introduces a decidedly exotic and unfamiliar source for "facts" about Wilde's ghostly return. In another record of communications received at a different sitting, Mrs Chan-Toon's name surfaces again. "Tell us about Mrs. Chan Toon," asks the medium. "I will not tell you anything about her," the ghost replies, "for I want you to make enquiries about the lady. She was a perfect specimen, fit for the satin lining of a jewel-case; and if she is still alive she could tell you much that would throw a light on my life as she knew it."[2] Mrs Chan-Toon is figured here as an elegant mystery and an object fit for a detective's pursuit; however, though the ghost apparently desires the medium to "make enquiries" about this "perfect specimen," the only clues he provides come in the form of cryptic hints. Mrs Chan-Toon comes into focus in *Psychic Messages* as a corroborating witness, as someone who can apparently produce first-hand biographical information about Wilde. So just who is this Mrs Chan-Toon? And what does she know?

This chapter takes up the ghost's challenge and makes enquiries about the lady in question. It does not seem that Hester Travers Smith or her collaborators played sleuth and followed Mrs Chan-Toon's trail; if they did, neither their published psychic scripts nor the ghost play "Is It a Forgery?" records any further information about her. But the book *Psychic Messages from Oscar Wilde* does contain an incredible material trace of Mrs Chan-Toon: a facsimile of her name appears in an example of Mr V.'s automatic writing, against which, of course, readers are invited to compare Wilde's actual hand. This is as close, I propose, that Mrs Chan-Toon ever got to Oscar Wilde, for so far as I know they never met in the flesh. They seem to encounter one another only on the page, in reminiscences as fabricated as Mr V.'s Wilde scripts would prove to be. Perhaps the spiritualists sitting around the seance table eyed Mrs Chan-Toon as a potential threat or as competition in the business of forgery. For Mrs Chan-Toon – properly Mary Mabel Agnes Chan-Toon Wodehouse Pearse (née Cosgrove) – was not only the most brazen but also the most successful of all the 1920s Wilde forgers. Although she was unmasked in 1925, the year after the publication of *Psychic Messages from Oscar Wilde*, her devoted fraudulence continued well into the next decade.

As a champion of lying in art, Wilde was, as we saw previously, a theorist – and something of a practitioner – of aesthetic imposture. But he is surely the only such advocate who posthumously became the subject (or the object) of numerous literary forgeries. Furthermore, the multiplicity of Wilde forgeries is matched by the variety of forms of deceptive writing they exemplify. This book has investigated a series of dubious interveners in Wilde's posthumous literary legacy who each produced different types of material lies about Wilde. We could consider all these false representations as distinct forms of forgery, from deliberate misattributions to Wilde of books that he did not write (published by Charles Carrington and Leonard Smithers), to autograph manuscripts purporting to be his work (contrived by Dorian Hope), to self-reflexively doubtful claims of contact with his discarnate spirit (recorded by Hester Travers Smith and Geraldine Cummins). Uniquely among this cast of what Robert Ross would call "knaves," Mrs Chan-Toon achieved the literary forger's holy grail: she forged an entire book. She persuaded more than one publishing house to issue a "Burmese masque" called *For Love of the King* ([1921], 1922) under Wilde's name, which the indefatigable Wilde bibliographer Christopher Millard denounced in 1925 as "one of the most remarkable literary forgeries of recent years."[3] She is thus the only forger to add a title to the list of Wilde's works under the imprint of his authorized publisher, Methuen. She invented both texts and rumours and (for a few years, at least) transformed them into facts. She was a liar on a scale Oscar Wilde would have admired, for no other Wilde forger came as close as she did to perfecting a beautiful untrue thing in the name of her literary idol. In this capacity she also had the potential to destabilize the project of authentication undertaken by Ross, Millard, and Ledger to secure Wilde's canonical status in English letters.

Over the course of my research for this book I have discovered that Mrs Chan-Toon wore many masks both in and out of print.[4] Ostentatiously eccentric, she was renowned for appearing in a long black cloak with her constant companion, a parrot named Co-co, perched on her shoulder. Indeed, Mrs Chan-Toon's personae, which included "Mabel Cosgrove" (her maiden name), "Mimosa" (a pen name), "Mrs. Wodehouse Pearse" (her second married name), and "Princess Orloff" (one of her socially aspirational impostures), bear witness to Wilde's own view that identity is best apprehended as a multiplication of personalities, to paraphrase Gilbert in "The Critic as Artist."[5] Even so, I shall refer to the forger of *For Love of the King* as "Mrs. Chan-Toon" for three reasons.[6] First, this was, for a time, her legal married name, and it was under the surname of her Burmese first husband that she sought to associate herself with the memory of Oscar Wilde. Second, it was under this name that she achieved a modest reputation as a writer of novels, short stories, and folkloric reportages – mainly on Burmese themes – between 1903 and 1914, a span constituting the most prolific phase of her (legitimate) writing career. Finally, it was as Mrs Chan-Toon that she became a literary criminal and impostor of no small daring and skill; she was, as Wilde said of Thomas Griffiths Wainewright (the subject of "Pen, Pencil, and Poison"), "a forger of no mean or ordinary capabilities."[7] As we shall see, Mrs Chan-Toon was both a careful and a crafty reader of Wilde, so much so that her self-fashioning in the public sphere of print took shape along neo-Wildean lines. Although her Wilde forgeries were unquestionably engineered in the hope of sorely needed financial gain, Mrs Chan-Toon was also the ultimate Wilde fan, and those forgeries were the work of a most devoted fraud.

This chapter details Mrs Chan-Toon's self-invention as a novelist, swindler, forger, and spy.[8] First, it analyses the publication history of *For Love of the King*, elaborating not only the play's appeal to those readers in the early 1920s who regarded it as a relic of Wildean decadence, but also its troubling impact on the Wilde canon. Second, it considers the two prefatory paratexts that authenticate the forged play, both of which create a fictional (or fan-fictional) provenance in which Mrs Chan-Toon boldly inserts herself into the story of Wilde's life. This well-researched fraud ingeniously mingles biographical facts and fabrications in order to establish a false textual genealogy for the play that casts the forger as Wilde's muse and confidante; instead of the fan being inspired by Wilde, she imagines Wilde, the playwright, being inspired by *her*. In this mythical relationship between writers, Wilde emerges as the object of Chan-Toon's textual desire, and her forgery of Wilde becomes the fulfilment of an ambition unsatisfied by her own literary career. Third, the chapter engages the plot of this "fairy play," showing that, although it represents a masterful pastiche of Wilde's decadent style, its Burmese themes align it far more closely with Chan-Toon's own writings. These themes give Chan-Toon's game away, keying us into her spectacular attempt to inhabit, extend, embellish, and forge a legend of Oscar Wilde. Fourth, it explores the emblematic function of Mrs Chan-Toon's parrot, Co-co, whose image was captured in a 1926 news report about her conviction for a theft that was unrelated to the Wilde forgery (figure 15). Since parrots are noted for their exoticism as well as their capacity for verbal mimicry, Co-co could signify both Mrs Chan-Toon's first husband, an exemplary colonial mimic man, and her persona as a forger. Configured in tandem, the post-colonial and print cultural resonances of the parrot perched on Chan-Toon's shoulder can help articulate a new way to understand literary forgery and its hybridizing impact on the emerging canonicity of a figure as fraught as Oscar Wilde. Fifth, and finally, it surveys an archive of previously unknown and unpublished neo-Wildean contrivances that Chan-Toon promulgated in the 1930s, well after she had been found out to be a literary fraud. Turning from drama to memoir, she forged fantastical links between Wilde, her first husband, and George Bernard Shaw.

The Publication (and Litigation) History of *For Love of the King*

In October 1921 the British periodical *Hutchinson's Magazine* published a "Remarkable Literary Discovery: New Unpublished Work by Oscar Wilde." This discovery was the play *For Love of the King*, a "Burmese Masque" that was ostensibly composed in 1894 at the height of Wilde's success as a West End dramatist. Its having remained unknown and unpublished was explained in a document prefacing the play-text: a dedicatory letter signed with Wilde's name and addressed to Mrs Chan-Toon,

15 Mrs Chan-Toon with Co-co, 1926. William Andrews Clark Memorial Library, University of California, Los Angeles.

the Irish-born wife of a celebrated Burmese barrister (known simply as Chan-Toon or Mr Chan-Toon) who had studied law in late-Victorian London and was later appointed to the judicial bench in Rangoon.[9] Mrs Chan-Toon claimed to have been a close friend of Wilde's, and the play, according to this letter, had been intended as a personal gift to her.

It would not, of course, have been the first posthumous appearance of a text by Wilde; Mitchell Kennerley's expanded edition of *The Portrait of Mr. W.H.* had just been published in 1921 in New York. Similarly, the Stetson sale in 1920 had brought to light manuscripts of previously unpublished Wildean texts.[10] But, unlike the publication of a familiar title from a manuscript "lost to the world" and newly rediscovered, as *The Portrait of Mr. W.H.* (1921) was,[11] the "discovery" of *For Love of the King* represented something quite different. It was a hitherto unknown, unpublished, and therefore completely *new* Wilde title. And it was a *play* – the very genre for which Wilde was most famous. Whereas Hester Travers Smith and Geraldine Cummins's ghost play "Is It a Forgery?" purported to come from beyond the grave, Chan-Toon's "Burmese Masque" was apparently resurrected from the literary graveyard. But from whose graveyard had the play been exhumed? *For Love of the King*, as we shall see, has an outrageous back story. Amazingly, Mrs Chan-Toon had already published a short story with this exact title, under a cloak of anonymity, in 1900 (it was accredited to "The Author of *Told on the Pagoda*," which is an even earlier publication of hers that had appeared under the pseudonym "Mimosa").[12] In a feat of brazenness the devoted fraud *plagiarized herself* in order to forge Wilde. This back story has been completely overlooked by Wilde bibliographers, then and now. The play's provenance in Mrs Chan-Toon's own portfolio eluded even the literary forensics that accompanied the dramatic legal wrangling between Christopher Millard and the publishing firm Methuen over the forgery's exposure.

Prior to that dispute, *For Love of the King* was initially accepted as a genuine Wildean text. It was published in two periodicals (the British *Hutchinson's* and the American *Century Magazine*, which included lavish illustrations) and was then issued in 1922 in book form by Methuen as a supplement to Robert Ross's edition of Wilde's *Collected Works*. More a dramatic scenario than a fully realized play, *For Love of the King* is an orientalist fairy tale filled with royalty, palaces, peacocks, concealed identities, and magical transformations. Its luxuriant exoticism recalls the mood of Wilde's own decadent writings, such as the symbolist drama *Salome* (an inspiration for the ghost-writer of "Is It a Forgery?") and the long poem *The Sphinx* (that Dorian Hope had forged). *For Love of the King* also suggests Wilde's sumptuously written short fiction, or, as Edmund Gosse put it in his review of the play, "one of those gilded and perfumed apologues […] in *A House of Pomegranates*."[13] What Gosse and all subsequent commentators on the play failed to apprehend was its origin in a short story published in the periodical *The Idler* two decades before, during the early phases of Mrs Chan-Toon's literary career. "For Love of the King" (1900) is not identical to *For Love of the King* ([1921], 1922), but the contours of the plot, which involves the transformation of a beautiful young woman into a bird and the sacrifice of her life to save a Burmese monarch, are the same. In adapting her own text and transforming it into a (temporarily) plausible Wilde original,

Mrs Chan-Toon worked to enhance the stylistic and generic markers of Wilde's authorship: she intensified the decadent mood of the story and made it into a play.

To readers unfamiliar with Mrs Chan-Toon's obscure short story, *For Love of the King* would seem at first glance like an example of Wilde's work, if a somewhat embarrassing one. Although he accepted it for publication, E.V. Lucas, publisher's reader for Methuen, privately described it as "awful tosh."[14] Far from ensuring the play's swift exposure as a forgery, the awkwardness and ineptitude that Lucas deplored paradoxically ensured its acceptance as genuine; it appeared to be precisely the sort of thing that Wilde *would not* have wanted published, making it all the easier for most of the editors and publishers with whom Mrs Chan-Toon negotiated to affirm its authenticity. One of the play's earliest publishers was not entirely convinced, however, and an editorial note in the *Century Magazine* offered the following disclaimer: "In the instance of the discovery of so interesting an unpublished manuscript, there is always the possibility that some may question its authenticity. We can only say that the manuscript has come into our hands from Mrs Chan-Toon through a trustworthy intermediary. It will, in any event, be diverting to watch the critics discuss the question of its genuineness."[15] The *Century*'s observation proved to be prescient because the play received renewed interest from the British press in 1925, after Millard had denounced it as a forgery. When Millard was investigating the play and Mrs Chan-Toon's role in its transmission, he canvassed various publishing firms that Mrs Chan-Toon had approached. C.S. Evans, one of the directors at William Heinemann, recalled in 1925: "I believe I was the first publisher in London to whom Mrs Chan-Toon brought the proposal. She came in to see me one day unannounced, and was one of the most amazing figures I have ever seen in the course of a varied life. She was dressed in a black cloak and bore upon her shoulder a live parrot, attached by a string to one of her buttons. I felt at the time perfectly certain that the authenticity of the play was, to say the least of it, difficult to sustain, and refused to have anything to do with it."[16]

Despite such nagging doubts about its authenticity and such "diverting" scenarios featuring Mrs Chan-Toon and Co-co, the newly published play, as Gosse's critique intimates, attracted the censure of reviewers hostile to Wilde's decadent period. As an example of "his last literary phase," according to an anonymous *Times Literary Supplement* critic, "it shows Wilde sensuously gloating (as he gloated in *Salomé*) over the lust of the eye – and the nose."[17] "The best thing about the book is the binding," sniffed London's *Evening Standard*.[18] Such reviews, moreover, damned it by faintly praising stylistic extravagances that were, by the 1920s, decidedly old-fashioned. In view of its slight literary merit, Gosse drew attention to the play's intriguing provenance, conveniently supplied by the letter dedicating the play to Mrs Chan-Toon. He described this letter as "the best thing in the book; as a sample of Oscar Wilde's preposterous prose it well deserved preservation."[19] I am tempted to agree with Gosse's assessment, for although Wilde never wrote that letter, it is certainly worthy of preservation as a minor masterpiece of the forger's art.

A curiosity to bibliographers and book collectors (and, it would appear, to other Wilde devotees such as the spiritualist community surrounding Hester Travers Smith), *For Love of the King* was published as a book in an edition of one thousand copies in 1922 (figure 16); it was reprinted only once, the next year. An undated American edition published by Putnam (the firm that had fallen victim to Dorian Hope in 1920) followed in 1923. Within three years of the play's release in volume form Christopher Millard had denounced it as a forgery and accused Mrs Chan-Toon of perpetrating a gross literary fraud. Millard's obsession with exposing the forgery was triggered by Mrs Chan-Toon herself – or more precisely, by her persistent forging of texts in Wilde's name. In June 1925 she approached Millard with some forged Wilde letters for sale. He rejected them and was infuriated by Mrs Chan-Toon's pronouncements that she was the possessor of an unknown archive of Wilde manuscripts. (Since the "Burmese" play had been accepted as Wilde's, she could easily claim to be the owner of more unpublished Wilde manuscripts. The trick had worked once, so she tried it again.) But, as we have seen, Millard had long established himself as the ultimate Wilde archivist, and he did not take well to competing claims for that title.

In July 1925 Mrs Chan-Toon gave two self-promoting interviews to the gossip columnist "Mr. London" (Hannen Swaffer) of the *Daily Graphic*. Mrs Chan-Toon had memories of Wilde and the 1890s to share. She authenticated her connection to Wilde with a sly reference to *For Love of the King*, and both interviews hinted at further Wilde items in her possession: "'He wrote a play for me as a wedding present, *For Love of the King*,'" she told the columnist, "'but I had to sell it later' [...] From time to time he gave her little poems and other pieces of his work. 'These will be very valuable one day,' he would say."[20] The *Daily Graphic* went so far as to print one of these "little poems," a piece of

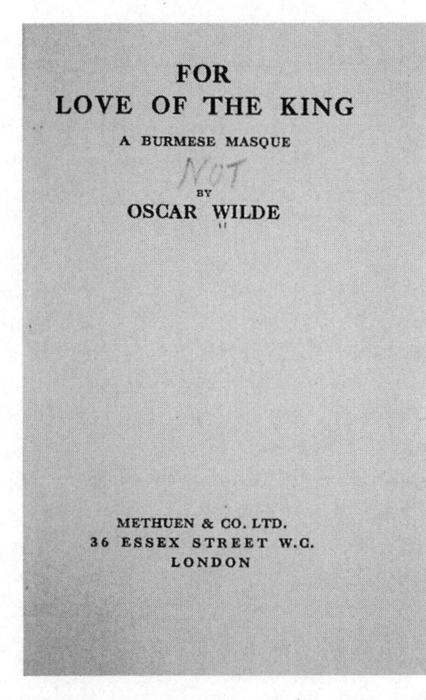
FOR
LOVE OF THE KING
A BURMESE MASQUE
NOT
BY
OSCAR WILDE
METHUEN & CO. LTD.
36 ESSEX STREET W.C.
LONDON

16 Title page of Christopher Millard's copy of *For Love of the King*. William Andrews Clark Memorial Library, University of California, Los Angeles.

faux juvenilia called "Opportunity" that Wilde had apparently written at the age of eighteen and gifted to his friend. Millard dismissed it as "doggerel verse,"[21] but, even so, it probably represents Chan-Toon's final successfully published Wilde forgery.

By making repeated reference to the commercial value of Wilde manuscripts while retailing invented memories of her connection with Wilde, Mrs Chan-Toon stage-managed the *Daily Graphic* interviews to advertise her archive of forgeries. She purported to recollect: "After our talk he sat down and wrote these verses and gave them to me, as he gave me many others in later years, when he would accompany the gift with the remark, 'keep these, they may be valuable some day.' Wilde knew he was a genius."[22] Mrs Chan-Toon's grandest claim was that she was writing a memoir of her time with Wilde, based on her private cache of Wildean documents. (This ambitious project never came to fruition, even though Mrs Chan-Toon had already, in 1924, advertised the imminent publication of a book called *Oscar Wilde as I Knew Him*.)[23] "Mr. London" reported that Mrs Chan-Toon's putative archive indicated that a large number of unknown Wilde materials had yet to be unearthed. "There are a good many of Oscar Wilde's letters and even poems drifting around which have never been published," the column observed. "Some of them are in the possession of Mrs. Chan-Toon, wife of the barrister whose uncle was King of Burma, for she knew Wilde and his family during his lifetime. She has now written a book containing much fresh matter and some new stories about that star of the 'naughty 'nineties,' and it will be published in the autumn."[24] This scenario is a forger's fantasy, but for Millard the threat to Wilde's legacy and reputation represented by this potential escalation in the scale of Mrs Chan-Toon's interventions (a whole fake biography!) was simply too much to bear. He went on the attack.

Millard's zeal in denouncing the play and its publishers ultimately led to a libel suit, filed against him by Methuen. Millard wrote a flurry of letters to newspaper editors, which he collected and published along with some of his own sleuthing correspondence in a pamphlet that detailed his pursuit of Mrs Chan-Toon.[25] In his capacity as an antiquarian book dealer, he also offered the play for sale in one of his catalogues in order to afford himself the opportunity of decrying the forgery – a strategy that strongly recalls his protest publication of *The Priest and the Acolyte* in 1907. Further still, he had an eye-catching poster printed to advertise his "Sensational Charge of Literary Forgery," which he intended to have carried throughout London's streets on sandwich boards (figure 17). For its part, Methuen understandably objected to his persistent public statements that accused the publishing house of having "foisted" a forgery by "an unscrupulous woman" on "an unsuspecting public."[26] Although Millard (unsurprisingly) welcomed the trial, which took place in 1926, as an opportunity to expose Mrs Chan-Toon in the most public of venues, unfortunately for him the case did not turn on the authenticity of the play but instead on his maligning of the reputation of a respected publishing firm. Much to Millard's disappointment, Mrs Chan-Toon was unavailable for cross-examination in the courtroom; she was in prison serving an unrelated six-month sentence for theft.[27] Nonetheless, the trial achieved his ambition of exposing the forgery, and he noted afterward that "until the case came into court no paper would mention Mrs Chan Toon's forgeries; whereas now she has been exposed under both her names in practically every newspaper in the country."[28]

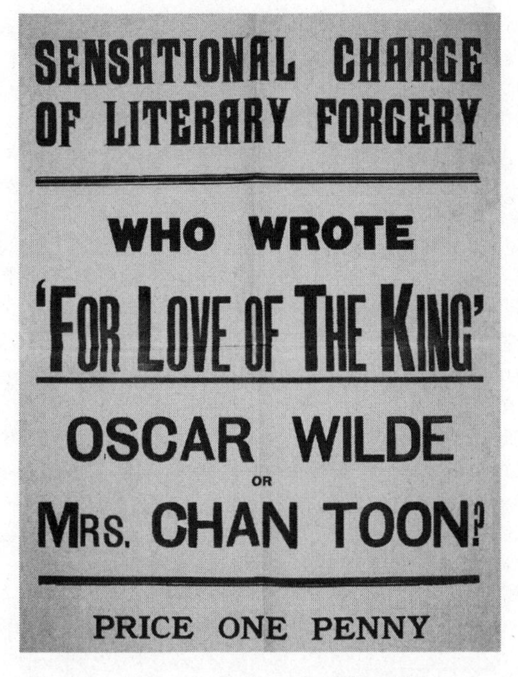
SENSATIONAL CHARGE OF LITERARY FORGERY

WHO WROTE

'FOR LOVE OF THE KING'

OSCAR WILDE

OR

MRS. CHAN TOON?

PRICE ONE PENNY

17 "Sensational Charge of Literary Forgery," 1925. William Andrews Clark Memorial Library, University of California, Los Angeles.

Once Millard lost the trial, *For Love of the King* was quickly forgotten. It has been almost entirely ignored by literary criticism.[29] The scholarly neglect accorded to the play can be best explained by two factors: a lack of aesthetic merit, on the one hand, and, on the other, its nebulous literary status as a forged artefact. Regardless of the play's aesthetic merits and authorship, *For Love of the King* rewards further attention because it dramatizes the central feature of Wilde's cultural afterlife, namely the performance of an authorial identity derived as much from popular legend as from literature. Certainly unperformable as a play, *For Love of the King* nonetheless engages in its own kind of high artifice and performance. As do many of the other Wilde forgeries examined by this book, *For Love of the King* supplies characteristic elements of Wilde's legend – exoticism, stylistic affectation, and suggestive hints of homosexuality – as authenticatory devices, in K.K. Ruthven's sense of the phrase. The literary performance of *For Love of the King* ultimately fails, of course, because its illusion of authenticity cannot be sustained.

The Paratexts

The Methuen edition of *For Love of the King* begins with two prefatory documents, an unsigned "Introductory Note" by E.V. Lucas and a dedicatory letter credited to "Oscar Wilde," whose presence serves to authenticate the play that follows. The documents that introduce the play vary between editions and between periodical and book versions, although every version contains the dedicatory letter, addressed to Mrs Chan-Toon. For example, the *Hutchinson's* periodical version is introduced by an unsigned preface entitled "A Remarkable Literary Discovery," which includes details about Mrs Chan-Toon and the play's provenance that are not supplied in the Methuen edition. Similarly, the Putnam (American) edition contains a promotional blurb on its dust jacket claiming that "Burmah, the whole Orient in fact, fired Wilde's imagination with its glamor," a phrase absent from any other edition.[30] These documents are the book's paratexts, in the sense articulated by Gérard Genette: they occupy a liminal, mediating zone between the reader and the play-text and, in so doing, condition the reader's experience of the play.[31] They are thus ideally placed to operate as authenticatory devices. The "function of paratextual features," according to Ruthven, "is to indicate exactly what sort of book confronts us, and thus prevent misreadings that arise from misidentification."[32] Of course, a particular sort of misreading is exactly what the paratexts to *For Love of the King* are cleverly designed to produce. The provenance supplied by the play's paratexts, which "explains its origin,"[33] engages the active deception of the reader in order to secure the identification of Mrs Chan-Toon's forged text as a previously unpublished play by Oscar Wilde. The paratextual "Introductory Note" and dedicatory letter accomplish this feat by affording the volume a rhetoric of authenticity grounded in biography: they embroider a legend of Oscar Wilde by positioning *For Love of the King* – and the supposed connection between Wilde and Mrs Chan-Toon – as forgotten and newly "rediscovered." Previously unknown details about Wilde's private life are thus made available for public consumption. A private friendship and the private "fairy play" "written just for [her] own amusement"[34] are "now made public" for the first time.[35] A public gesture thus authenticates a private one.

The first paratextual document to the Methuen edition, the "Introductory Note," provides biographical details about Mrs Chan-Toon that deftly mingle fact with fiction. "Mrs. Chan Toon," the note explains, "before her marriage to Mr. Chan Toon, a Burmese gentleman, nephew of the King of Burma and a barrister of the Middle Temple, was Miss Mabel Cosgrove, the daughter of Mr. Ernest Cosgrove of Lancaster Gate, a friend of Sir William and Lady Wilde, and herself brought up with Oscar and his brother Willie."[36] Here Mrs Chan-Toon has adroitly woven herself into the genealogical fabric of Wilde's biography. If we are to judge by the success of the autobiographical *De Profundis*, not to mention the Wilde biographies and epistolary memoirs that proliferated during the interwar period – which furnished both the Dorian Hope forgers and fake psychics such as Mr V. with so much helpful information – it was Wilde's life, as much as his writing, that appealed to early-twentieth-century buyers of books carrying his name. But the personal connection between Wilde and Mabel Cosgrove is pure fantasy. There is no evidence that she ever met Wilde. She was indeed born in Ireland, and she did marry Mr Chan-Toon, a Burmese barrister who was an authority on jurisprudence and Buddhist law.[37] She was, however, born in 1873 (and in Cork, not Dublin), some nineteen years after Oscar Wilde, and thus was definitely not "brought up" with the Wilde brothers.[38] The *Hutchinson's Magazine* preface includes the more outrageous claim, absent from the Methuen edition, that she was engaged to and later jilted by Oscar Wilde's elder brother, Willie: "Mabel, a girl of striking beauty, was a great favourite of Lady Wilde's [...] Her engagement to marry Willie Wilde had been announced when the poet's brother met Mrs. Frank Leslie, whom he afterwards married."[39] (Willie Wilde married the American journalist Miriam Leslie in 1891, many years after Lady Wilde had given up hosting Dublin salons.) The sometime Mabel Cosgrove thus appears as a Wilde family member *manquée*.

The names alluded to in the "Introductory Note" as witnesses to her friendship with the Wildes are well chosen. Mrs Chan-Toon knows enough about Wilde's life, his family, and his associates to connect herself convincingly with them; it matters much that, when she first approached publishers with the play in 1921, all the salient members of this group, including Lady Wilde, her son Willie, and even Miriam Leslie, were conveniently dead. With no one from the Wilde clan to dispute her claims, her story proved tantalizingly plausible. It must have persuaded E.V. Lucas, who, despite his private doubts as to the play's aesthetic merits, wrote the unsigned introductory note, giving the bogus biographical narrative supplied by Mrs Chan-Toon the authoritative imprimatur of Methuen.

In articulating the forger's narcissistic wish-fulfilment, wherein a middle-aged woman who was formerly a "girl of striking beauty" desires to have been "a great favourite of Lady Wilde's," the "Introductory Note" proves, as Wilde put it in "The Portrait of Mr. W.H.," an "attempt to realize one's own personality on some imaginative plane out of reach of the trammelling accidents and limitations of real life."[40] In this note there are also traces of careful, even crafty, research that support such a fantasy. It mentions Robert Ross (who had died in 1918), for instance, in his capacity as Wilde's literary executor and editor. In a manner designed to enhance Mrs Chan-Toon's claim to the role of a friend whose personal loyalty to Wilde's memory was above base commercial motivations, she shrewdly inserts herself into the narrative (explored in chapter 1) of Wilde's literary authentication and canonization as well. "For a long while," the note tells us, "Mrs. Chan Toon, who after her husband's death became Mrs. Woodhouse-Pearse [*sic*], refused to permit the masque to be printed. The late Robert Ross wanted to include it in an edition of Wilde's works, but he could not obtain its owner's consent."[41] This little detail constructs a narrative of textual desire that casts Mrs Chan-Toon as a loyal friend who withstood the appeals of Wilde's posthumous bibliographers, editors, and publishers, by withholding the play. But she has now had a change of heart and has decided to share with the world her token of friendship with Wilde. The best way to memorialize Wilde, it seems on the basis of this note, is to submit – though only after "a long while" – to the persistent entreaties of profiteering publishers.

For Methuen – as for Putnam, whose dust jacket for the play advertises the publisher's fifteen-volume list of "The Works of Oscar Wilde" – publishing the play had the added virtue of supplementing Ross's edition of Wilde's *Collected Works*, because without *For Love of the King*, that edition – fourteen years old by the time the forged play appeared in book form in 1922 – would suddenly appear deficient. The imminent appearance of the Methuen edition elicited an observation by the *Liverpool Daily Courier* that "collectors of Wilde's work who thought they had a complete set will have a surprise when they hear that a new play by Wilde is to be published by Messrs. Methuen."[42] The forgery's boldest claim is therefore that its "remarkable discovery," to use the terms provided by *Hutchinson's Magazine*, completes the Wilde canon. Even so, the critic for the *Times Literary Supplement* mused, "[W]e cannot help wondering whether Wilde would have cared to see this pretty compliment to a lady out among his collected works."[43] The posthumous canonization of Wilde, a register of the success enjoyed by Robert Ross and his colleagues, has transformed an ostensibly ephemeral document – a "pretty compliment" or a "wedding present" – into a valuable commodity in the literary marketplace. What Wilde would have wanted, of course, is beside the point; the posthumous process of canon formation erases his volition. But had his ghost been able (or willing) to comment, it would surely have appreciated the irony of a situation in which Wilde's rehabilitation actually facilitated the production and dissemination of a forgery.

By extending and elaborating the narrative set forth in the "Introductory Note," the second paratextual document – a dedicatory letter, signed "Oscar Wilde" and dated 27 November 1894 – overlays fact with fiction. The date, a few months prior to the 1895 trials that led to Wilde's imprisonment, seems plausible, even attractive in its proximity to the defining event of the Wilde legend: the spectacular courtroom debut of the homosexual as an embodied form of identity. The historical record, however, leaves little room for the play's composition. During late November 1894 Wilde was busy negotiating the terms for a collection of aphorisms entitled *Oscariana*. He was also preoccupied with the casting and rehearsals for his new play *An Ideal Husband*.[44] Nevertheless, the Wilde of this dedicatory letter has the time to thank "dear Mrs. Chan Toon" for her gift of a book of Burmese tales entitled *Told on the Pagoda*. After her 1893 marriage to Mr Chan-Toon, the future forger lived for a period in Burma. Under the pseudonym "Mimosa," she published (in 1895) this beautifully designed book of folkloric fairy tales, parables, and naturalistic sketches, illustrated with contemporary photographs of Burmese people, landscapes, and architecture. Inspired by these "Tales of Burmah" and by "long and luminous talks with your distinguished husband [...] when I was meditating writing a novel as beautiful and as intricate as a Persian praying-rug," Mrs Chan-Toon's friend Oscar reciprocates her literary gift with "a fairy play entitled 'For Love of the King,' just for your own amusement."[45] The personal connection between the writers is once again figured as familial, and at one remove from Wilde himself, but, whereas Mrs Chan-Toon had previously associated herself directly with Oscar Wilde's mother and brother, here the connection is forged via her "distinguished" (and also long-deceased) first husband.[46]

Once Mrs Chan-Toon's link to Wilde has been firmly established both personally and bibliographically, the letter deploys a new strategy. It drops broad hints about Wilde's homosexuality, thereby confirming the play's veracity by alluding to a concealed truth about Wilde that was well known to posthumous readers. The sharing of secrets in the private correspondence cements the imaginary relationship. In Wilde's voice, the letter reveals an acquaintance with "a perfectly wonderful person ... who has irradiated the present with sinuous suggestion: a Swedish Baron, Athenian in mind, and Oriental in morals. His society is a series of revelations ... "[47] The decadent male homosexual is densely encoded here in a sequence of common late-Victorian tropes. This man is an aristocrat, whose intellect is described by an affinity for "Greek" things,[48] and whose "Oriental morals" recall the associations of languid, exotic corruption that often figured in Victorian orientalist and homoerotic discourses.[49] The confidential tone with which the letter's Wilde persona describes this fictional acquaintance, not to mention the tour-de-force pastiche of his overwrought style, arguably closes the case on Wilde's authorship of the play. As the recipient of Wilde's confidence about a new male lover, Mrs Chan-Toon is represented as an intimate friend, close enough to be privileged with an allusion to his secret homosexual life – a piece of information that, while public knowledge in 1921, was circulating only as gossip and innuendo in 1894. In yet another moment of wish-fulfilment fantasy Mrs Chan-Toon casts herself as Wilde's adoring confidante, perhaps a version of the playwright's loyal friend Ada Leverson, who provided him with shelter during the trials and after his imprisonment. This suggestive "revelation" succeeds in associating the forger with Wilde because it confirms what the reading public already knows about him. Moreover, it does so with "*sin*uous suggestion" in stylistic terms that, as the *Hutchinson's* preface puts it, seem "characteristic" of Wilde.[50] The queer truth or essence of Wilde's life thus guarantees both the authenticity of his hand in producing the play-text and the veracity of Mrs Chan-Toon's claims about their friendship. Wilde's secrets, in other words, underwrite Mrs Chan-Toon's lies.

The Play-Text

The dedicatory letter prefacing *For Love of the King* designates it a "fairy play," an appellation that highlights its generic resemblance to a fairy tale. The original tale "For Love of the King" (1900), for its part, conforms quite explicitly to the long-ago-and-far-away generic conventions of the fairy tale. It opens, for instance, with the phrase "It was at dawn on a beautiful morning, when the world was centuries younger."[51] *For*

Love of the King ([1921], 1922) is similarly set in ancient, pre-colonial Burma, and it was initially received as something of a generic hybrid. Imagining the play as if it were an exotic bird emerging awkwardly from an egg, the *Times Literary Supplement* reviewer noted as much: "Hatched again and hatched different, *For Love of the King* might have been one of the most charming stories in 'The Happy Prince,'" which was Wilde's first volume of fairy tales.[52] This observation dovetails nicely with Gosse's estimation of the play, which he likened to Wilde's second book of fairy tales, *A House of Pomegranates*. If the image of the decadent male homosexual operates as one of the forgery's authenticatory devices, then so too does the Wilde of the fairy tales. And, as we shall see, the forgery mixes Wilde's decadence and Mrs Chan-Toon's Burmese credentials and, in so doing, expresses the forger's desire to refashion herself and to fashion her own, previously published literary work as Wilde's work. Moreover, this form of literary imposture, with its perhaps unique admixture of self-plagiarism and forgery, boldly reimagines the circuits of desire between fan and idol.

Considered as a play, *For Love of the King* relies far more on visual spectacle than on stageable action. The play-text consists mainly of stage directions, which lingeringly describe the material apparatuses of exotic luxury, interspersed with brief passages of dialogue. Act 1, for instance, opens in the palace of the king of Burmah, whom the list of characters calls "Lord of a Thousand White Elephants, Countless Umbrellas and other attributes of greatness." In the "Hall of a Hundred Doors," where "peacocks promenad[e] proudly in the blinding sunshine of late afternoon," we discover the king "seated on a raised cushion sewn with rubies":

> *Banners, propelled with a measured rhythm, create an agreeable breeze. On a great table of gold stand goblets of gold and heaped-up fruits. Everywhere will be observed the emblems of the Royal Peacock and the Sacred White Elephant. Burmese musical instruments sound an abrupt but charming discord. The poinsettia's flower punctuates points of deepest colour from out of vases fashioned like the lotus. Orchids are everywhere. The indescribable scent of Burmah steals across the footlights. The glow, the colour, the sun-swept vista sweeps across the senses.*[53]

The keynote of this scene is its attention to sensory detail; it bombards the reader with visual, aural, and olfactory stimulation to the point of overload, as if one could only apprehend ancient Burmese exoticism at the moment of being overwhelmed by it. The London *Observer* drew attention to the text's emphasis on the visual, commenting that "when Oscar Wilde wrote this masque [...] he must have had some curious foreknowledge of the cinematograph; for, while it is nothing of a play and a very indifferent masque, 'For Love of the King' would make a magnificent film."[54] The extravagant language also represents a considerable intensification in sensuous detail from the source story, thereby testifying to the laborious process of revision that Mrs Chan-Toon must have gone through in order to enhance her text's decadent markers in order to pass it off as Wilde's. In "For Love of the King" (1900), for example, the opening sequence of her short story is rendered in what we might call a vaguely Wildean manner, paying precise attention to aesthetically pleasing detail, but the campy exaggeration that defines much of the mood of the forged play is absent: "There were waving palm trees above them, and around them were birds coloured like flowers and orchids of many gay and delicate hues, on whose petals dragon flies poised, in whose cups velvet-coated bees sucked." Here, the impact of the "gay and delicate" orchids is rather attenuated, whereas in the play, in which "orchids are everywhere," it is totalizing.[55]

These freshly exaggerated stage directions, which were first published in *Hutchinson's* in 1921, are a far cry from the austere modernism depicting the afterlife in the pseudo-Wildean ghost play "Is It a Forgery?" Martin Holman, solicitor for the Wilde literary estate, wrote to Vyvyan Holland suggesting that the lavishness of *For Love of the King* made its theatrical production unlikely because it would violate both the tastes and the budgets of 1921. "For production on any stage some very strong and polished dialogue would have to be written, and the production requiring as it does four or five different scenes ... [it] would call for an expenditure which I cannot think any manager of common sense would dream of in these days."[56] Holman did not, however, suspect the play of being a fake, no doubt because the superabundance of its descriptive sequences recalls similar bursts of decadent cataloguing in genuine Wilde texts. In *Salome*, for instance, Herod tries to forestall her necrophilic demand for the head of Iokanaan by offering the princess a flock of "white peacocks," fantastically hideous lapidary treasures (including "onyxes like the eyeballs of a dead woman"), and "a garment of ostrich feathers," along with "four fans fashioned with the feathers of parrots" that have been given to him by "the King of the Indies."[57] Stylistically, the pastiche of Wilde in the stage directions of *For Love of the King* works remarkably well, crowded as they are with decadent tropes, which draw attention to sensual impressions, material objects, flowers, and an aesthete's adjectival vocabulary ("charming," "indescribable"). Although the territory (ancient "Burmah") is unfamiliar in Wilde's writings, the language evoking it certainly approximates his style. In an exotic locale suffused with "the indescribable scent of Burmah," we thus find ourselves immersed in a Burmese version of the eleventh chapter of *The Picture of Dorian Gray*, which exhaustively lists Dorian's successive collecting enthusiasms, or perhaps in the dream world of *The Sphinx*, where exotic catalogues abound.[58]

The decadent atmosphere evoked by the opening of *For Love of the King* is particularly striking if we consider the degree of effort and study that must have gone into its composition, to say nothing of the process of remediation that the original short story underwent in its transformation into a Wilde forgery. There is ample evidence of writerly labour in this work of self-plagiarism and forgery; it suggests a critical engagement with Wilde's aesthetic that amounts to something more than the production of half-baked Wildean decadence – a weakness that at times bedevils Dorian Hope. In the opening sequences of *For Love of the King*, Mrs Chan-Toon masterfully recreates the self-reflexive mood of Wilde's decadent texts. As in genuine Wilde works dating from the 1890s, *For Love of the King* articulates and exploits an awareness of its own exaggerated and accretive decadence, and its imitation of Wilde lies somewhere between homage and parody. In a 1925 article on Millard's charge of forgery against the play, John Gilmorton observes that, whatever the result of the dispute over the play's authenticity, "someone at any rate will have displayed a faculty for parody that need not be denied."[59] The play sustains a mood of decadent whimsy, which, far from acting as mere window dressing, constitutes its insubstantial core. *For Love of the King* is of a piece with the atmosphere that it attempts to evoke; it *is* mystery, illusion, fantasy. Indeed, like many of Wilde's own decadent texts – and those fashioned by other Wilde forgers – it thematizes a rejection of substance in favour of surface.

Despite all the contemporary critical dismissals of the play that echoed Lucas's "awful tosh" assessment, *For Love of the King* marks a definite artistic advance over "For Love of the King" (1900) in its sophisticated manipulation of mood – the very quality required to maintain the illusion of Wilde's authorship. We could say that Mrs Chan-Toon's "Burmese Masque" fuses, and complicates, decadence's stylistic celebration of inauthenticity with the illusory nature of literary forgery, a category of art that, as we have observed in the case of Wilde's own "Portrait of Mr. W.H.," generates seductive fantasies about authenticity and self-fashioning. In his review of the play Gosse noted that Wilde "required an atmosphere of fantasy to breathe in, and, as fortune denied him the real thing, he exhaled from his inward consciousness a scented illusion."[60] Gosse could just as easily be describing here the forgery career of Mrs Chan-Toon. In light of the information we have about her biography and literary career, two features of the play's plot stand out as especially relevant: its interest in cross-cultural hybridity, mixing the European with the Burmese; and the prominent symbolic role that it accords to birds. Judging from the focus of the paratexts on her life and on her imagined role in Wilde's, it should come as little surprise to find that the play is about her or, more to the point, her relation to Wilde. In sketching out the plot in the next section, I not only elaborate some possible biographical correspondences between forger and idol but also suggest ways by which we might assess the terms of Mrs Chan-Toon's investment in Wilde as she rewrote her own story under the name of a writer whom she admired intensely. The implications of such investment for Wilde's cultural afterlife suggest, in this case, that Wilde's legend provides a model that articulates and authorizes a mode of self-fashioning that has the power to transform the mediocre writer of forgotten stories and books into something far more exciting and glamorous: an artist-criminal.

The Play: Biofictional Allegories

For Love of the King begins with a tale of racial persecution. Mah Phru is a "girl, half Italian, half Burmese, of dazzling beauty," a description that echoes and amplifies the depiction of Mabel Cosgrove as "a girl of striking beauty" in the *Hutchinson's* preface. Mah Phru's community ostracizes her because of her mixed heritage, and she seeks help from Meng Beng, the king of Burma. (Burmese royalty, we recall, figures prominently in Mrs Chan-Toon's imagination; *For Love of the King*'s "Introductory Note" claims that her first husband was the "nephew of the King of Burmah." By the 1930s she had promoted him to the status of "Prince Chan-Toon.")[61] The king falls in love with Mah Phru and offers her protection for the two years of freedom that he will enjoy before he enters into an arranged marriage with a Ceylonese princess. They live together in the jungle, incognito, in a house whose architecture is described as "half Burmese, half Italian," where they are entertained by musicians in "semi-Venetian-Burmese costume."[62] After the lapse of these two years the king leaves Mah Phru and their two sons to return to public life and to his pre-arranged marriage. This marriage, however, produces no heirs, and Mah Phru is forced to give up her sons to the king. At this point she becomes a martyr to love and "appears as if turned to bronze – a model of restraint and dignity, blent with colour and beauty and infinite grace."[63] In order to pursue her children, she persuades a Chinese wizard to transform her into a peacock – not a peahen, curiously, but the bird's sex is only one among the play's many inconsistencies. In the guise of the bird that the stage directions describe as "royal," she infiltrates the palace gardens to see her sons and learns that the king is dying and that somehow she can exchange her life for his. Infinitely compassionate and forgiving, she embraces this destiny. In the play's final scene, unaccountably returned to human form, Mah Phru forces her way into the king's bedchamber, announces her sacrifice, and drops dead as the king recovers. The curtain falls as "jewels glitter" and "the whole world of birds sing," affording an aesthetic benediction for Mah Phru's sacrifice.[64]

The story "For Love of the King" (1900), for its part, provides the main points of the play's plot. It ends, for instance, with the protagonist's life sacrifice. Even so, a great many details change from story to play: Mah Hla (not Mah Phru) is known as "Miss Beautiful" in the short story, but there is no mention of any biracial identity; instead, the settings and characters are entirely Burmese. The wizard, who is not specified as Chinese in the story, offers to "turn her [Mah Hla] from a woman into a beautiful snowy bird," a transformation that emphasizes her purity over avian flashiness.[65] In intensifying the story's decadent exoticism for publication as a play, Mrs Chan-Toon also heightens its biographical resonances; despite the play's several disorienting inconsistencies (such as the magical bird's sex), its richer burden of detail suggests a number of interpretive possibilities, especially if we read it as biofictional allegory. Biofiction, according to Michael Lackey, refers to "literature that names its protagonist after an actual biographical figure," and the play and its introductory paratexts meet this definition.[66]

But exactly whose biography does *For Love of the King* encode? Is the peacock, whose form Mah Phru apparently chooses for purely aesthetic reasons (because "they are more beautiful") a cipher for the tragically exiled Wilde, the "Irish Peacock"[67] who was broken hearted about being estranged from his two sons after his imprisonment? (The short story's Mah Hla, by contrast, is afforded no such choice; the wizard chooses her avian form.) And how are we to read the cross-gendered, cross-species, cross-cultural figure of Mah Phru, whose protean identity is unitary only in its association with birds? Is this mysterious *female* peacock perhaps a self-figuration of the parrot-toting, Irish-Burmese Mrs Chan-Toon herself? The long-lost child of Mah Phru seems to recognize her in the bird, and their encounter might help us to arbitrate these possibilities. As he strokes her gorgeous plumage, he muses, "I shall never understand you, Queen of the Kingdom of Birds."[68] That this disguise is partly legible suggests that the ostentatious peacock invites, and ultimately repays, scrutiny. The camouflage that this "Queen" peacock affords Mah Phru foregrounds role-playing and theatricality, and this bird ultimately suggests inscrutable mystery less than the desire to perform the mysterious – and to attract attention in the process. In such capacities, this bird – unlike the non-specific "bird of exceeding grace, and an ivory hue" that we find in the short story from 1900 – signals the styles of both Mrs Chan-Toon and Wilde.[69]

Since the 1870s, peacocks and peacock feathers, which represented beauty uncontaminated by utilitarian purposefulness, had been prominent features in the symbolic lexicon of the aesthetic movement. They continued to appear in aestheticism's more decadent iterations, as we have seen in *Salome*. The peacock, also traditionally an emblem of pride, vanity, and spectacular display, functions as a hybrid symbol in *For Love of the King*. In a play where a Euro-Burmese woman becomes a showy – and martyred – male bird, Mah Phru's transformation into a peacock conflates aspects of both Mrs Chan-Toon and Wilde. This queen of a bird – beautiful, ostentatious, and simultaneously male and female – may also encode the kind of decadent male effeminacy (and homosexuality) that was associated with Wilde in the popular imagination of the 1920s. The play-text thus follows through on the precedent established in the paratexts of *For Love of the King* by merging Mrs Chan-Toon's life with Wilde's. For Mrs Chan-Toon, to forge Wilde, to write as Wilde, is to inhabit his persona. It allows her to achieve, if only between the covers of a book, an impossible aspiration: to become Oscar Wilde by means of literary performance.

Although she was clearly an astute reader of Wilde, it is in terms of the play's subject matter that Mrs Chan-Toon, as a forger, makes her major strategic error: she relies too heavily on her own expert knowledge of things Burmese. Such knowledge would not be considered a fault in a tale written "by the author of *Told on the Pagoda*," as the short story from 1900 is; it is precisely what the story's readers would expect, and those expectations are conditioned by the citation of that earlier work. But the very detailed information that can prove advantageous to a legitimate publication by a chronicler of Burmese folklore can turn into a liability in a forgery. Judging from the material she published under her own name, not to mention the precision of certain details in the play, such as the presence of betel nuts, peepul trees, and "charming Burmese girls, with huge cigars,"[70] that expertise was considerable. The spectacle of female cigar smoking appears as an element of local colour in Mrs Chan-Toon's journalistic writings about Burma; one article, for example, features two photographs of young Burmese women with cigars.[71] As early as 1901, when she was still publishing under the pseudonym "Mimosa," Mrs Chan-Toon was noted in the British press for her "gift of receiving and conveying vivid impressions of Burmese life" in her short story collection *Under Eastern Skies* (1901); according to an unnamed reviewer, it treated "the many delicate problems that arise in a land where a few Britons direct the affairs of an enormous territory and a race whose faith and ideals are foreign to us."[72] Whether as "Mimosa," "the author of *Told on the Pagoda*," or "Mrs. Chan-Toon," Mrs Chan-Toon plumed herself on her ability to bridge those cultural divides.

It is, ironically, the cultural specificity of the play's depiction of "Burmah" – notwithstanding the Chinese wizard – as opposed to, say, a generalized Orient, that impedes its success as a forgery (figure 18). In order for the forgery to sustain the fantasy of Wilde's authorship, its orientalism would have to be deployed as a decorative attribute of decadence, an evocative but unspecific background. Wilde's mouthpiece Vivian in "The Decay of Lying," for instance, praises stylistic "Orientalism" for "its love of artistic convention" and its distance from both reality and "the visible things of life."[73] Wilde's theorization of the Orient consigned the East to the realm of pure decoration. Vivian continues this line of thought in a discussion of Victorian *japonisme* when he observes that the "whole of Japan is a pure invention [...] the Japanese people are [...] simply a mode of style, an exquisite fancy of art."[74] For all its neo-Wildean, orientalist whimsy (white elephants, countless umbrellas, shimmering jewels), *For Love of the King*'s meticulous facility with Burmese names and vocabulary (the play-text is helpfully glossed with footnotes that explicate unfamiliar words) simply does not pass muster. As a writer and forger Mrs Chan-Toon is too much of an anthropologist; her novels, stories, and journalistic articles with Burmese themes dominate a literary career in which she fashioned herself as an interpreter of Burmese culture to the imperial metropole.

18 “The Chinese Wizard,” *Century Magazine*, 1921. Author’s own collection.

With all its exoticism this representation of pre-colonial Burma thus bears the distinctive imprint of Mrs Chan-Toon. "Burmah" figures as a meeting-place of European and Asian cultures and as a zone of magical birds where female peacocks are "Royal" and redemptive sacrifices are celebrated by massed bird-song. Yet *For Love of the King* is far from unique among Mrs Chan-Toon's writings for its Wildean associations. She quoted and imitated Wilde long before she forged him. During the main phase of her literary career Wilde's influence strongly marked Mrs Chan-Toon's literary output. Her 1906 story "A Man of Forty," for instance, contains a character named Mrs Cheveley (the name is borrowed from *An Ideal Husband*'s villain), who has written a book with the neo-Wildean title "The Viciousness of Virtue" and who attends a play called "The Last of the Dandies."[75] Mrs Chan-Toon's most commercially successful title, the autobiographical novel *A Marriage in Burmah* (1905), contains numerous epigrammatic passages that imitate Wilde's aphorisms, such as "the true philosophy of life is to reduce one's responsibilities."[76] In light of this pattern of Wildean imitation, Mrs Chan-Toon's forgery – which was her final book publication – represents the culmination of a literary career spent trying to inhabit and approximate Wilde and his characteristic style.

"Inspired," as the dedicatory letter claims, by the Burmese tales collected in Mrs Chan-Toon's *Told on the Pagoda*, *For Love of the King* could thus be read as an artefact of displaced or thwarted writerly ambition. Instead of writing in a manner that merely imitates and follows Oscar Wilde (as she had been doing for years), Mrs Chan-Toon invented a fantasy textual genealogy that inverted the actual relations obtaining between the two writers. Influencing Wilde with *Told on the Pagoda*, she precedes him and renders herself the textual point of origin; Wilde, according to the fake history of *For Love of the King*, imitates *her* by writing the play. He is thereby figured as the mimic and the copyist, and his imagined praise functions as a literary affirmation of Mrs Chan-Toon, the (legitimate) writer. Even if she attributes the authorship of *For Love of the King* to him, she can still claim credit for inspiring it.

By no means does such a reading of the play's biofictional coordinates intend to downplay the economic motivations that undoubtedly contributed to the play's publication. Mrs Chan-Toon had been declared bankrupt in 1910, and she was evidently in dire need of money when she negotiated with Methuen.[77] On first meeting with E.V. Lucas she pleaded that she was "very hard up" and attempted to borrow money from him, a practice she repeated in dealings with other publishers whom she approached.[78] Although she settled with the firm for £50, she attempted to extract far greater sums from the publishing house's agents once the play had been published.[79] That she regarded the forged play as an asset to be exploited as fully as possible is apparent in a short-lived profit-sharing deal that she made "for a considerable sum" with the Wilde estate on possible "Film Rights of F.L.O.T.K."[80] (Millard's exposure of the forgery scuttled the film deal.) Financial pressures prompted her to retail Wilde forgeries again in 1925, when she advertised her collection of manuscripts in the *Daily Graphic* and imprudently offered to sell fake Wilde letters to Millard. And it was her profiteering that so offended the bibliographer. As he wrote to the editor of the *Daily Graphic*, the publication of the phony poem "Opportunity" represented a violation of intellectual property rights. "If the poem were genuine," he states, "it would be a breach of the Copyright Act to publish it without the consent of Wilde's literary executor."[81] Millard was not about to countenance the exploitation of his hero's memory – or, for that matter, of his hero's heirs.

Despite such economic motivations, *For Love of the King* ultimately represents, in my view, forgery as the result of a desire or "enthusiasm" that inspires the creation of an apocryphal text that *ought* to "be incarnated in material form."[82] Mrs Chan-Toon's desire to inscribe herself into the Wilde legend leads her to fabricate a spurious text to memorialize an imagined friendship – a friendship that retroactively confers prestige onto her own, forgotten books. Like the figure of the Liar celebrated in "The Decay of Lying," the forger Mrs Chan-Toon is a teller (and writer) of beautiful untrue things.

The Parrot Text

By the time *For Love of the King* was printed under the name of Oscar Wilde, Mrs Chan-Toon was renowned for appearing in a long black cloak with her companion, a green parrot named Co-co, perched on her shoulder. The parrot went everywhere with her. In 1921, for example, Mrs Chan-Toon lived in Paris, the city of Wilde's exile and death, where she was known as "la dame au perroquet."[83] Later, in London in 1925, when she offered to sell forged Wilde letters to Millard on the strength of her connection with *For Love of the King*, Co-co accompanied her, and Millard did not fail to take notice. He wrote to Wilde's son Vyvyan Holland, describing not only the pecuniary desperation of the failed writer but also the emblematic presence of the parrot: "I found the woman," he recalled, "filthily dressed with a filthy parrot making filthy messes on her filthy shoulder in a filthy tenth-rate boarding house."[84]

Like *The Priest and the Acolyte* and other spurious texts exposed by Millard, Mrs Chan-Toon's forgeries undermined Wilde's literary reputation. Millard had spent a lifetime defending that reputation, and he was most certainly as obsessed with Wilde as was Mrs Chan-Toon. But by weaving a tissue of lies connecting her past to Wilde's celebrity and broadcasting their imaginary friendship through the press, Mrs Chan-Toon had done more damage than had previous forgers. Her interventions also threatened Millard's authority as the supreme Wilde expert. As an antiquarian book dealer Millard relied on his contacts in the bookselling world to locate Mrs Chan-Toon, who was peddling forged Wilde letters in London and Dublin. Convinced that they were spurious, and therefore that the play was also a fake, Millard pursued the peripatetic Mrs Chan-Toon, and, tellingly, he traced her by tracking the parrot. In a letter to Millard, Dublin book dealer William Figgis relayed an encounter in his store with a "rather tall and dangerous-looking woman" who was enquiring about Wilde manuscripts. "This was Mrs. Chan Toon, right enough," Figgis concluded, "and she created rather a sensation in Dublin by going about with a parrot on her arm."[85] If Millard was a literary sleuth seeking to expose a forger, Co-co the parrot was that forger's extra-literary fingerprint.

The exotic parrot, then, is the physical counterpart to representations of Burma in Mrs Chan-Toon's publications; both mark her identity in their own way. That a writer turned forger, the majority of whose texts concern intercultural encounters in colonial settings, should amplify her public persona with a tropical bird noted for verbal imitation suggests, in the first instance, that Co-co might help us comprehend better this forger's particular activities. Traditionally an emblem of exoticism, the parrot figures in post-colonial criticism as the colonized subject's capacity to mimic or approximate the language of imperial domination and cultural power. As humans' exotic "minions" whose vocal abilities have also rendered them "marvels," these speaking birds, according to Bruce Boehrer, have long been associated with "both nature's subservience to culture and the subservience of certain cultural groups."[86] And since at least the seventeenth century psittacine mimicry has been analogized to plagiarism, a kind of literary imposture that long fascinated Wilde himself.[87] In the parrot, modes of verbal imitation and of colonial subjectivity converge.

According to Boehrer, parrots are typically associated with femininity, and Co-co's intimacy with Mrs Chan-Toon would seem to affirm such a gendered troping of the bird. According to one 1924 newspaper report of the forger's movements in Scotland, this parrot was male and, at seventeen, still relatively young.[88] I want to argue that Co-co could figure (and fetishize) Mrs Chan-Toon's first husband, under whose surname she established an identity as a professional writer that she later sought to entangle with the legend of Oscar Wilde.[89] Mr Chan-Toon's celebrated legal career in the metropole casts him as an example of the colonial "mimic man" whose speech acts Homi Bhabha describes as "*almost the same but not quite*."[90] As a law student, Mr Chan-Toon attracted the notice of the London press precisely because his subordinate colonial status did not impair his ability to excel in the very field (the law) that is so closely allied to political power. Indeed, his aptitude for British language and culture in law school was such that his achievements outstripped those of his English counterparts. "Among the students of the Middle Temple called to the bar this year," writes an unnamed correspondent to *The Leisure Hour* in 1888, "was Mr. Chan-Toon, a native of Burmah. During his studentship Mr. Chan-Toon competed for the eight principal prizes open to law students and gained them all."[91] Mr Chan-Toon's career culminated in his being elevated to a judgeship in Rangoon, and he relished the prestige derived from his British education: "[A]s in England," he noted in an Anglo-Indian magazine in 1895, "a successful advocate always occupies an enviable position, and in the East there is even more glow attached to his personality."[92] Such statements suggest that he prided himself on his role as a cultural mediator of Englishness to imperial India (which included Burma); his wife, for her part, interpreted Burmese culture for English-language readers.

Although Mr Chan-Toon died in 1904, and his widow later remarried (in 1911, only to be widowed again in 1918), she continued to publish – and, indeed, to pursue an expanding literary career – as "Mrs. Chan-Toon." That name indicates a hybridized public persona, maintaining a sense of orientalist mystique along with the honorific *Mrs*, which signals the prim gentility of the Victorian lady novelist. The surname also arrogates to her identity in the literary marketplace the credibility and distinctions of her first husband. The status of Burmese royalty, which Mrs Chan-Toon sometimes ascribed to her first husband, not only attempts to offset any stigma attached to his racialized position but also constitutes an act of self-aggrandizement because it permits her to make herself into a princess.[93] Her delusions of exalted rank ("Princess Orloff" and "Princess Arakan" were identities attached to unrelated 1920s swindles)[94] thus offer imaginative compensation for her lack of prestige when the vagaries of earning a living by her pen left her living in filth, as Millard put it in 1925. Co-co the parrot, which recalls Mr Chan-Toon's successful mimicry and is the semiotic hallmark of Mrs Chan-Toon's career as a forger, encapsulates such compensatory fantasies. The forger brazenly broadcasts these fantasies with the parrot, attaching to herself a kind of prosthetic exoticism that is akin, in all its feathered opulence, to the treasures offered to Princess Salome. Wilde's was always a voice to which Mrs Chan-Toon aspired, and, if aspiration failed, then appropriation – perhaps we should call it *parroting* – would have to suffice.

Mrs Chan-Toon's parrot can also help us develop a new way of thinking about literary forgery more generally and about the relationship between forgery and authentic literature. According to Paul Carter, parrots signify "the [human] desire to communicate," but they do so in a way that emphasizes that they do not "possess" language. Instead, they merely reproduce it.[95] As a form of mimicry, parrot speech not only performs human language but also is subordinate to it. If human speech is the real thing, then parrot chatter is a fake. The fact that we can recognize parrot speech as fake confirms for human beings their position of privilege as the unique possessors of language. This subordinate relationship of the fake and imitative to the real and original has a counterpart in the world of print culture. Literary forgeries are not the authentic texts they purport to be, although some of their textual performances as "originals," like the artwork at the centre of "The Portrait of Mr. W.H.," may indeed be more persuasive – or seductive – than others. Just as the mimic man (or bird), whose linguistic performance is forever "*not quite*," imperfectly attempts to adopt the verbal register that organizes cultural power, the forger similarly attempts to simulate a form of cultural prestige: the textual register, and authority, of "authentic" literature. The "relationship between literarity and spuriosity," for K.K. Ruthven, "is framed as a binary opposition, in which literature is valorized as the authentic Self and literary forgery disparaged as its bogus Other."[96] Literary forgery, moreover, can be destabilizing to the cultural capital of literature because forgeries call into question its privileged status by upsetting "the fragile economy of literary accreditation."[97] *For Love of the King* certainly destabilized the canon of Wilde's plays, at least for a time in the 1920s. Mrs Chan-Toon and her parrot, Co-co, forged an intervention into the cultural status of Oscar Wilde at the precise historical moment of his recuperation and accreditation by the empire of British literature. Indeed, "la dame au perroquet" haunts and hybridizes the Wilde canon like no other forgers studied in this book.

Mr Chan-Toon's profession was the law, and it is one of the more delicious ironies of his wife's literary larcenies that the omnipresence of her parrot coincided with her career as a violator of laws. If colonial mimicry is to literary forgery as Queen's English is to Literature, then such mimicry is also an approximation, the act of getting near (or nearer) to something, whether it is imperial Englishness or, in Mrs Chan-Toon's case, the creative register of, and the novel place in literary history occupied by, Oscar Wilde. For Mrs Chan-Toon, whose forgery testifies to a long-held wish to establish a textual relationship with Oscar Wilde, imitation was perhaps the sincerest form of flattery. Her Wildean impersonation, though certainly exploitative, can also be more generously construed as discipleship. To Wilde, after all, the forger was the ultimate artist-criminal, an individual whose disregard for conventional laws was as valuable to society as was the critique of outworn conceptions of originality that his (or her) activities performed. To be an artist was not merely a matter of producing original work but, far more crucially, *to be an original*. And with Co-co perched on her shoulder, Mrs Chan-Toon was certainly that.

Bunk about Bernard

Mrs Chan-Toon not only has the (dubious) honour of being the most successful of the Wilde forgers; she was also the most persistent. In contrast to the Dorian Hope forger(s), for instance, whose fraudulent representations of Oscar Wilde extended over a mere two (albeit eventful) years and were eventually curtailed by their unprofitability, Mrs Chan-Toon persevered through the 1920s and into the 1930s in her attempts to conjure, and to market, an alternate-reality 1890s. Although Wilde remained at the centre of that fantasy world as the subject of her most sustained literary productions, she expanded her repertoire to include then-living Irish writers – namely William Butler Yeats and George Bernard Shaw.[98]

By the mid-1920s, with Methuen's publication of *For Love of the King* behind her, the £50 she had received from that publisher long gone, and no hope of film royalties to come, Mrs Chan-Toon redirected her forging talents towards the opportunities afforded in the rare-book market by the sale of famous writers' letters. Where she had once bundled such items with more ambitious forgeries, as she had done with the dedicatory letter appended to *For Love of the King*, she now peddled bogus letters on their own. Wilde was, of course, a highlight in her catalogue. In July 1925 Christopher Millard recorded that she had contacted him to offer, at a price of £3, "six letters written by O.W. to herself" that she was hoping "to sell [...] at a bargain for 'an immediate deal.'"[99] Millard did not fall for this scam; he was in the midst of putting together his public denunciation of her authorship of *For Love of the King*. I reiterate her approaching Millard, not only to highlight her brazenness and indefatigability (Millard was her most implacable enemy) but also to emphasize the continuation of her personal claims of affiliation with Wilde. These forged letters were ostensibly addressed "to herself," after all.

Although Millard rebuffed her, Mrs Chan-Toon seems to have met with modest success elsewhere in marketing forged letters, for she apparently persuaded London's Dobell bookselling firm into believing that she had also been in communication with another Irish poet, Yeats. Dobell's December 1925 catalogue offered for sale a set of documents that linked Mrs Chan-Toon to this Irish literary celebrity: "YEATS (W. B.) A. L. S., I p., 8vo, Jan. 8th, 1894, and a Typewritten letter signed, 1 page, 4to, Jan, 25, 1924, both addressed to Mrs. Chan-Toon, one letter relates to a portrait by Whistler which Mrs. Chan-Toon wished to present to the National Gallery, *with addressed envelopes*; also an A. L. S. of Mrs Chan-Toon, £1 1s."[100] I have not seen the "Yeats" letters, which may not have survived, but even this trace of them in a catalogue entry carries the hallmarks of Mrs Chan-Toon's grandiose imagination. In this scenario she casts herself as a patron of the arts, presenting a Whistler portrait (of whom, one wonders!) to London's National Gallery; moreover, the dates on these letters – 1894 and 1924, respectively – suggest that she has been on intimate enough terms with Yeats to receive correspondence from him over a period of thirty years. The editors of *The Collected Letters of W.B. Yeats* cautiously aver that these documents "may have been spurious,"[101] because they are traceable only to the entry in the Dobell catalogue. What I want to underscore is not merely the possible spuriousness of these fantastical missives but also the continuation of a pattern of textual desire that we have already seen on a larger scale in Mrs Chan-Toon's forged Wilde play. (This catalogue also offered, at the more modest price of five shillings, a letter apparently written to Mrs Chan-Toon's first husband from Robert Hichens, the author of *The Green Carnation*, a satire published in 1894 about Wilde and Alfred Douglas.) She has a knack for linking herself (or her first husband) with literary celebrities and for inscribing herself – retroactively – into literary history in the process.

Mrs Chan-Toon's better-documented textual larcenies involving Bernard Shaw display more boldness, or perhaps desperation, than those targeting Yeats.[102] Once released from her six-month prison sentence, she reappeared in London in 1927, only to be quickly noticed by her old nemesis, Christopher Millard. Writing to Walter Ledger, Millard notes a change of tactic (or target) on the forger's part: "Mrs. Chan Toon is in London again, trying to sell her alleged 'interview' which she pretends to have had with Bernard Shaw!" With unambiguous schadenfreude, he further tells Ledger, "I hope she will get her fingers burned again."[103] The comeuppance that Millard hoped would befall her seems not to have occurred, however, because her convoluted attempts to inveigle Shaw would not only increase in complexity but also continue for some years.

Millard died later that year and so was unable to witness the dénouement of Mrs Chan-Toon's Shavian adventure. Her supposed interview, which she entitled "A Conversation, with Some Comments," was never published. Rather than a work of journalism, it is more of a fragmentary memoir in manuscript. It records an obviously fictitious meeting between Mrs Chan-Toon and "the master writer – George Bernard Shaw."[104] In this text, now housed at UCLA's Clark Library, Mrs Chan-Toon casts herself as a breathless fan of Shaw's "extraordinary brilliancy" and seeks his assistance for a book about Oscar Wilde. (Perhaps she was trying to revive the Wilde book project that she had promoted in her 1925 interview with the *Daily Graphic*'s "Mr. London.") As ever, she is eager to embroider the past with new fictions and here places Wilde and Shaw together at school: "We had a mutual friend in your old school fellow Oscar Wilde," she tells her interlocutor. "I am writing a book about him, is it possible you would contribute a few words?"[105] Shaw, who did not attend school with

Wilde, declined to aid in this particular project, but she nonetheless managed to secure "a few words" from him. Although they were not particularly complimentary in content, in form they provided Mrs Chan-Toon with what she wanted, for they were rendered in Shaw's handwriting.

Mrs Chan-Toon clearly had not had any luck with the dealers she had approached in 1927, when Millard was last aware of her movements. The "Conversation" manuscript remained unsold, and it was still in her possession four years later when, once again living in France, she sent it to Shaw himself. Shaw did not think much of it (the interview had, of course, never happened), and he recorded his annoyance with an annotation in his distinctively spidery hand: "A string of lies from beginning to end. G.B.S. 5/12/31."[106] Then, perhaps out of misguided courtesy, he returned it to Mrs Chan-Toon at her French address. (At this stage in her life, having served a prison sentence under the name of her second husband, Wodehouse Pearse, she reverted to her first husband's name and was calling herself "Madame Chan-Toon.") Little could Shaw have known that he would be opening himself up to further correspondence with the exasperatingly tenacious forger.

By repudiating Mrs Chan-Toon's creation – others were to follow – *in writing*, Shaw unwittingly fell into the forger's trap. She managed to goad this living Irish writer into making annotations that, she believed, conferred monetary value on her manuscripts in the rare-book market. Indeed, Shaw's having read and written about Mrs Chan-Toon's imaginary "conversation" with him thereby transformed a worthless document not only into the record of a *real* conversation (of a sort) but also into a material object worth something on the market. Mrs Chan-Toon's pride did not get in the way of her commercial instincts, and she was perfectly willing to trade in autograph manuscripts that cast her in a negative light. Although another document that she had labelled "Bernard Shaw: A Tiny Sketch" was briskly retitled "Bunk about Bernard" by Shaw himself, she was eager to point out the potential value in Shaw's "most amusing interpolations & corrections."[107] On 7 September 1932 she wrote to her old victims the Dobell brothers with news of a remarkable piece of literary property: a substantial typescript entitled "With Oscar Wilde" that, like the "Conversation" and the "Tiny Sketch," had been read and annotated by Shaw. Here is her letter in its entirety (figure 19):

Tannay. Nièvre. France.

Sept 7. 1932.

Gentlemen,

Enclosed conversations, with Oscar Wilde, are taken from the Diaries, of the late Prince Chan-Toon, in Barrister-at-Law, Middle Temple – a great friend, of all the Wildes. I sent them to George Bernard Shaw a couple of weeks ago. Here is his reply. Can you make an offer, for the tout ensemble? You will observe, that he has addressed the envelope, himself! I imagine, it should prove of interest, to collectors.

Yours very faithfully

Chan-Toon

19 A letter from Mrs Chan-Toon, 1932. William Andrews Clark Memorial Library, University of California, Los Angeles.

Malvern Hotel,
Malvern.
5th Sept. 1932

This pastiche dates so remotely
that its production will resemble
a walk through the salons of Monte
Carlo dressed in the fashion of 1890.

20 A critical annotation by Bernard Shaw, 1932. William Andrews Clark Memorial Library, University of California, Los Angeles.

Tannay, Nièvre, France.

September 7, 1932

Gentlemen,
Enclosed conversations, with Oscar Wilde, are taken from the Diaries, of the late Prince Chan-Toon, Barrister-at-Law, Middle Temple – a *great* friend, of all the Wildes. I sent them to Bernard Shaw a couple of weeks ago. Here is his reply. Can you make me an offer for the *tout ensemble*? You will observe, that he has addressed the envelope, himself! I imagine it should prove of interest, to collectors.

Yours very faithfully,
Chan-Toon[108]

Affixed to the first leaf of the thirty-six-page typescript is this comment, dated "5th Sept. 1932," in Shaw's unmistakable handwriting: "This pastiche dates so remotely that its production will resemble a walk through the salons of Monte Carlo dressed in the fashion of 1890" (figure 20).[109] Communicating with her bookselling contacts almost immediately after receiving her typescript back from Shaw, Mrs Chan-Toon had lost no time in attempting to convert her latest literary endeavour into ready cash, and Shaw's comment, although dismissive, actually proffers an illuminating commentary on Mrs Chan-Toon's final piece of Wildean fan fiction. By imagining its "production," Shaw is implicitly categorizing Mrs Chan-Toon's biofiction as a period drama costumed in "the fashion of 1890."

"With Oscar Wilde" is divided into three sections, and it records the putative conversations of Oscar Wilde (who is initially called "Grandeur") and an unnamed "Prince" Chan-Toon. It is set in three locales that stitch together Wilde's biography with Mr Chan-Toon's in the manner of the prefatory paratexts to *For Love of the King*. These conversations are undated, but the names and details they unfold supply an imaginary chronology of Wilde's 1890s. The first, and longest, takes place in a "pleasant villa at Torquay," which is probably an approximation of Babbacombe Cliff, the country house of Constance Wilde's friend Lady Mount-Temple, where the Wildes stayed during the winter of 1892–3; the second setting is the Middle Temple, a centre of London's legal community and where Mr Chan-Toon "had received such signal honours […] in 1888;"[110] and the third, "In Chelsea," is Wilde's house.

"With Oscar Wilde" is, in some ways, a dispiriting document because it cannot help but record Mrs Chan-Toon's reduced creative capacities. Although it deploys the same authenticatory techniques as *For Love of the King*, their quality and effectiveness are diminished. During the Torquay episode, for instance, amid a torrent of epigrams and decadent clichés, such as hothouse flowers, indulgent extravagance, champagne, and green carnations, the putative Burmese diarist introduces his readers to a stand-in for a young Alfred Douglas, otherwise "one of Oscar's most prominent satellites. Eldest son of a well-known General, influence kept his name out of the newspapers, at the subsequent trials. Very young, tall, and fair, with a mincing and most impertinent manner, much aggravated by loud clothes and indifferent jewellery, Maurice or Sally, as he was called, presented the most extraordinary caricature of his model and patron! In his society, Oscar Wilde had for long taken great pleasure."[111] This strategy of elaborating Wilde's sexual history replicates the "Swedish Baron" section of the dedicatory letter to *For Love of the King*, but here the execution is rather cruder, and it relies more overtly on queer stereotypes (reminiscent, perhaps, of Dorian Hope) as opposed to the imaginary Swede's "sinuous suggestion." This and the later sections of "With Oscar Wilde" all but tick off a checklist of Wilde's claims to fame: he spouts epigrams ("Give me life's luxuries: one can do without the necessities!");[112] he is the friend of celebrities such as Lillie Langtry; he is attacked as a plagiarist by a newspaper; he tells a fairy-tale-like story; he is adored by his long-suffering wife, Constance. This Wilde also has prognosticatory brushes with the future: during a garden party at the Middle Temple his host (Mr Chan-Toon) identifies a legal personage in a crowd as Sir Frank Lockwood, the solicitor-general who would prosecute the case of *Regina v. Wilde* in 1895. "Is he very clever?" Oscar asks. "Better to be guilty and defended by Lockwood than innocent and prosecuted by him," Mr Chan-Toon ominously replies.[113] These are retroactively prophetic words indeed.

In contrast to the prefatory paratexts authenticating *For Love of the King*, Mrs Chan-Toon is not even mentioned in these supposed diary extracts. The friendship with Wilde (who does most of the talking) chronicled here is understood to be her husband's, and his imminent departure for "Burmah," which is mentioned more than once, serves to seal the diaristic memoir in time. After describing a quick visit to Chelsea, where Wilde gives his friend a copy of *Dorian Gray* to read on his ocean voyage, "With Oscar Wilde" concludes with four pages of "Wit and Wisdom of Oscar Wilde"; given no context, they are merely random bon mots apparently collected by the "Prince," and their approximation of Wilde's style is distant indeed. It is difficult not to feel pity for Mrs Chan-Toon when her formerly impressive talents for forgery are reduced to lines like this one: "Intense self-love is the finest absinthe in the world."[114]

Despite Shaw's assessment that this "pastiche" of faux recollections "dates so remotely" that it resembles "1890," the generic structure of the document – a series of recollected memories from a much-mythologized period in literary and cultural history – actually owes a great deal more to contemporary publications. Indeed, as Joseph Bristow points out, after the publication of Frank Harris's *Oscar Wilde: His Life and Confessions* (1918), "several writers did their best to re-embody Wilde by emulating Harris's technique of recording long conversations that had taken place many years before with the author."[115] Bernard Shaw's "My Memories of Oscar Wilde" was appended to the second volume of Harris's Wilde biography, and, in soliciting a contribution to her Wilde book from Shaw, Mrs Chan-Toon was emulating Harris.[116] Shaw's "Memories" took the form of a personal letter to Harris, annotated by its recipient, thereby providing Mrs Chan-Toon a structural precedent for a forged memoir expanded by subsequent "comments."

Other writers who contributed to the memorialization of Wilde the conversationalist, as we have seen in chapters 1 and 4, included Charles Ricketts in *Oscar Wilde: Recollections* (1932) and Laurence Housman in *Echo de Paris: A Study from Life* (1923). The content of Mrs Chan-Toon's faux-memoir, however, was more directly inspired by another title in a similar vein: Arthur Henry Cooper-Prichard's amusing and overtly fictitious *Conversations with Oscar Wilde*, which had appeared in 1931 – that is, just as Mrs Chan-Toon's final Wilde con (of Bernard Shaw) was taking shape. For Cooper-Prichard (1874–1954), who was a sometime actor, numismatic librarian, and author of a rollicking history of piracy,[117] Wilde provided an opportunity to experiment with a form of writing that we would now identify as biofiction. Unlike Housman's or Ricketts's books, Cooper-Prichard's *Conversations* opens with recollections from childhood: his affiliation with Wilde, like that of Mrs Chan-Toon, is imagined to originate in a familial acquaintanceship. "I knew him simply and naturally as a visitor to my own grandmother's house, and he knew me, at least at first, as the schoolboy nephew of my aunts."[118] The crucial difference between Cooper-Prichard's claims here and those of Mrs Chan-Toon on the one hand, and those of, say, Ricketts, on the other, is that these recollections are never meant to be understood as factual. Instead, they provide a generic framework for imaginary world-making centred on Oscar Wilde.

Wilde appears in *Conversations* as a droll sage-like figure, a sort of perpetual quotation machine, and Cooper-Prichard manoeuvres him into a variety of scenarios in order to recount the witty things he has to say. The book's chapters are contrived occasions for dialogue, some of them plausible ("Oscar Wilde and Whistler at the Opening of the [Royal] Academy"; "Oscar Wilde at a Dinner Party"), others less so ("Oscar Wilde at a Dog Show"). Although he certainly engages in Wildean myth-making, Cooper-Prichard differs from the forgers in scrupulously avoiding the salacious or exploitative; his intended audience is not looking to the Wilde legend for sex scandals. Contrived though it may be, Cooper-Prichard's book, like Shaw's "Memories," provided Mrs Chan-Toon a template for a form of forgery she had not yet tried, but whose claims of familial connection to Wilde were not dissimilar to her own. Even the title of her manuscript, "With Oscar Wilde," is identical to Cooper-Prichard's, only with the "Conversations" left out. Detached from the larger title, that noun appears instead in the letter she appended to the manuscript and sent to the Dobells. In other words, she did not merely plagiarize Cooper-Prichard's format; she plagiarized his title, too. In its sadly reduced scope, the manuscript of "With Oscar Wilde" represents all that became of the book on Wilde she apparently wanted Shaw to preface in 1931. But where Cooper-Prichard posthumously imitated Wilde's verbal style (and, at times, rather well), Mrs Chan-Toon typically only imitated the imitator. The best of the many epigrams in her forged memoir is plainly indebted to Cooper-Prichard, and both epigrams bear not only on their shared project of (re)imagining Wilde but also on this book's theme of the forgery as a beautiful untrue thing. In *Conversations with Oscar Wilde*, Cooper-Prichard ends his first chapter with Wilde observing, "Imagination is the gift of describing as fact what has not really happened."[119] Mrs Chan-Toon goes one better, having her first husband's old friend Oscar Wilde tell us, "Imagination is the faculty of believing to be true that which you know to be false."[120] Well, if anyone would know the truth of that statement, it would most certainly be she.

Conclusion

The Teacher of Fandom

In this book I have argued that, despite the economic factors that prompted their creation, the Wilde forgeries of the 1920s can also be recognized as forms of fan fiction. I have also suggested that admiration for Wilde unites two otherwise disparate groups that shaped the archival contours of his literary afterlife: the defenders of his reputation on the one hand, and the forgers themselves on the other. Despite their remarkable diversity, all the Wilde forgeries discussed so far in this study have one thing in common. They are all posthumous fabrications, having been contrived after Oscar Wilde's death in 1900, and they serve as eloquent (if at times unreliable) witnesses to the roguish creativity inspired by his extraordinary afterlife. It might come as a surprise to point out, then, that possibly the earliest Wilde forgeries date from 1898 and that they were likely produced under Wilde's personal supervision. Importantly, these first Wilde forgeries were not criminal deceptions; rather, they testify to loyalty and support for a beleaguered writer at a particularly difficult time. And they may be the work of a fan.

Although Wilde struggled, after his release from prison, to re-establish his literary career, the one new work he published in the remaining years of his life – *The Ballad of Reading Gaol* (1898) – proved massively, and surprisingly, popular.[1] Issued by the decadent publisher Leonard Smithers with the open secret of the author's name concealed under the prison number C.3.3, the *Ballad*'s first edition sold out in less than a week. Smithers followed that edition with a number of subsequent printings, eventually producing over seven thousand copies of the book in seven editions between February 1898 and June 1899. This run was supplemented by two special (and expensive) printings: an edition of thirty copies on Japanese paper priced at a guinea; and an author's edition of ninety-nine numbered copies, which were "signed by" Wilde, bound in purple cloth with a gilt design by Charles Ricketts, and priced at half a guinea. Contemplating an American printing of the poem, Wilde acknowledged that a measure of authorial anonymity would be prudent in marketing it: "I see it is my *name* that terrifies." Even so, he also cannily observed to Smithers that "the public like an open secret."[2] He was right.

According to Ian Small, the book's "popularity at the turn of the century cannot be understood in isolation from the notoriety of its author."[3] At one point in their correspondence about the design of the author's edition, Wilde complained to Smithers that the signature revealing the "open secret" of his authorship should be priced to reflect that very "notoriety." He wrote: "I think 10/6 for copies signed by the author too little. My signature should be worth more than Japanese paper."[4] Those ninety-nine signatures, which confirm C.3.3.'s authorial identity as Oscar Wilde, added commercial (and sentimental) value to each copy. They represent a confidence shared between author and reader that is uniquely inscribed into the volume and which aims to reveal, fully, the secret of authorial identity. But, whatever their market price, if we take Wilde at his word, many of those ninety-nine signatures were executed by a hand other than his own. In fact, in another letter to Smithers, Wilde suggests that most of them may be forgeries.

During his Parisian exile one of Wilde's most intimate friends (and likely a lover) was a young Frenchman named Maurice Gilbert. Nicholas Frankel records that Gilbert "would prove himself to be one of Wilde's closest, most loyal friends, nursing him through sickness, attending Wilde as he lay dying, and then days later following Wilde's corpse to its grave before placing his wreath upon it."[5] Gilbert's devotion extended to assisting with literary matters as well. According to Wilde – whose penchant for narrative embellishment does not render him a particularly reliable witness, even of his own affairs – Gilbert produced "nearly all" the signatures for the author's edition of *The Ballad of Reading Gaol*. Having received the unbound copies or "sheets" of the author's edition from his publisher on 5 March 1898, Wilde replied to Smithers two days later that he "sent off the sheets yesterday. Maurice sent them off; he was most kind and wrote nearly all the signatures, as I, I don't know why, was rather tired. He writes much better than I do, so his copies should fetch 30/- at least."[6] Is Wilde joking here, teasing Smithers as we have seen him do with Ricketts in the introduction? Perhaps. But, judging from Wilde's assessment of Gilbert's penmanship and of its capacity to pass for his or even exceed the quality of his own ("he writes much better than I do"), we will probably never know. It may be that Maurice Gilbert's "Oscar Wilde" autograph is even better than the real thing.

Christopher Millard's *Bibliography of Oscar Wilde* reproduces the salient page of the author's edition (a copy from the British Library), complete with the signature, and it certainly looks plausible (to me).[7] But what would be the result if we subjected the signature on *any* copy of the author's edition of *The Ballad of Reading Gaol* to the terse question in the title of Hester Travers Smith's ghost play: *is it a forgery*? In point of fact, a couple of provocative consequences flow from the possibility that these signatures could be forgeries, which they technically would be if Gilbert, and not Wilde, had written them.

In the first instance, there are commercial implications for the rare-book market if we cannot be certain which signatures are authentic. Wilde was correct (and prescient) in noting that his signature added value to the book. In the 2018 market, one of the ninety-nine signed copies of the author's edition of *The Ballad of Reading Gaol* was listed on a premier online antiquarian-bookselling site at a price of US$50,000. A second signed copy on the site was offered for sale at the barely less breath-taking price of US$30,000.[8] Although Wilde is more collectable (and valuable) than ever, it is intriguing to wonder what impact the impossibility of determining the genuineness of *any* of the signatures might have on the value of these expensive collectors' items. (This revelation might also influence insurance valuations for institutional collections, such as rare-book libraries.) It is, of course, beyond my remit to speculate on the fullest commercial implications of Wilde's mischievous admission to Smithers (he could, of course, be lying), but I suspect that, if confirmed, an attribution to Gilbert would exert considerable downward pressure on prices.

In the second instance, Gilbert's having written "nearly all the signatures" is perfectly in line with Wilde's own playful attitude towards forgery. With characteristic irreverence, Wilde asserts his authorial presence in an edition of his poem with a representation of his writing body that he gleefully acknowledges to be false. That the forgery is aesthetically superior to the original and thus worth more ("He writes much better than I do, so his copies should fetch 30/- at least") is also a typical Wildean move, impishly pitting aesthetic and market value against one another in an unresolvable tension. (Quibbling collectors of Wilde's autograph would thus find themselves in the cynical company of those who know the price of everything and the value of nothing.) Such commentary on the quality of Gilbert's imitation further indicates that Wilde approved of and oversaw the forging of signatures on an unknowable number of copies – "*nearly* all." And that *nearly* is crucial because it implies that, although Wilde himself executed some of the signatures, he is not telling which among the ninety-nine numbered copies have the real ones and which have the fakes. (Maybe he did not keep track or, better yet, care.) Instead, the forged and the genuine receive equal authorization. By saying, however cheekily, that he had invited Gilbert to forge signature(s) on one of his final and most deeply personal books, Oscar Wilde made of his very signature a beautiful untrue thing.

Although Gilbert's intimacy with Wilde squares awkwardly with the physical distance and emotional projection that we tend to associate with the attitude of the fan towards the object of his (or her) admiration, the affective register is the same. Like a fan, Gilbert, if Wilde is to be believed, has copied out Wilde's name dozens of times as a demonstration of love. (It must have been a tedious and repetitive task.) In chapter 1 we saw similar fannish demonstrations of affection for the writing hand of Oscar Wilde in Walter Ledger's manuscript tracings, for which Robert Ross commended the collector's "unholy" "powers of forgery."[9] But what sets these fanciful forgeries further apart from the efforts of more professional swindlers like Dorian Hope or Mrs Chan-Toon is that they are manifestly *amateur*. In Ledger's case, his amateur forgeries were neither duplicitous nor subject to commercial exchange; they were not intended for an audience of strangers unknown to their true creator. Although the author's edition of the *Ballad* was intended for sale, the non-market logic of the gift economy also clings to that volume because Wilde gave several copies to friends, including Laurence Housman.[10]

I know of two further incidents in which Wilde's name was forged by amateurs, and so I now turn to their efforts, with an eye towards illuminating the inherent theatricality of these less public forgeries. The first involves the writer and bibliophile A.J.A. Symons. Symons was a friend of Christopher Millard, and he assisted the bibliographer during his 1926 legal dispute with Methuen over *For Love of the King* by testifying on Millard's behalf in court. In a handwritten document, which contains prepared testimony to be used on the witness stand, Symons attests to his own ability to forge Wilde's autograph. Writing of himself in the third person, he remarks: "Symons is an expert forger himself, & can demonstrate in court the possibility of forgery by examples."[11]

This openly exhibited expertise is that of the amateur, however, and not the professional criminal. Two years after the *Methuen v. Millard* trial Symons again "demonstrate[d] ... the possibility of forgery" in a keepsake treasure of his own; he had his personal copy of Wilde's *Poems* custom-bound, with the signature of "Oscar Wilde" convincingly embossed in gilt on the front cover. On the flyleaf of this unique volume Symons has written: "The signature of Oscar Wilde on the cover was drawn by me: A.J.A. Symons 1928."[12] The second amateur forgery emerged in the next decade, when the Wilde collector William Andrews Clark Jr – another sort of fan – witnessed further demonstrations of amateur Wilde-signature forgery. Writing to Alfred Douglas, Clark described a book-buying trip to New York where he witnessed a forger in action:

> Sometime ago while making the rounds of the book stores in New York, I happened in the Union Square Bookshop where I found some interesting and unusual Wilde editions. The proprietor of the shop asked if I would be interested in seeing a man copy Wilde's chirography. An appointment was made for me to meet this man the next day, and it was really interesting to see how closely and how almost perfectly he copies Wilde. This man owns a book store in New York and I feel sure he is above all suspicion in connection with the great amount of Wilde forgeries on the market[,] otherwise, he would not have so openly displayed his talent.[13]

These amateur forgers (and forgeries) of the "chirography" of Oscar Wilde attest to the persistent and proliferating desire among his fans to imitate and inhabit his authorial persona into the 1930s. In Clark's telling, such forgeries also must be the work of an amateur enthusiast because of the willingness to invite guests to watch, which discounts his status as a professional forger ("I feel sure he is above all suspicion"). By such logic, he most likely forges for more personal (though here unarticulated) reasons.

From Gilbert to Ledger to Symons to the New York copyist whose chirographic talents Clark witnessed, fans who forge Wilde's signature indulge in a fantasy of proximity to and identification with the writer. This fantasy is also eminently theatrical, because every example adduced here required a performance that was subject to an audience's critical assessment. That the fan's scriptorial performance *as* Wilde invites scrutiny and evaluation is evident in the language used by all witnesses: Wilde says he admires Gilbert's "better" handwriting to the extent of preferring it to his own; Ross praises Ledger's "powers"; Symons offers to "demonstrate" his expertise in forgery on the witness stand; and the anonymous New York bookman "perfectly [...] copies" and "displayed his talent" to Clark's marvelling eyes. These Wilde fans, each in their own way, are performers engaged in what "The Portrait of Mr. W.H." designates as "a mode of acting," for which they all seek – and earn –affirmation and applause. In this not insignificant way they share the stage with the rogue's gallery of professional forgers studied in this book.

A Note on Occlusion

In 1928 A.J.A. Symons designed a cover for his copy of Wilde's *Poems* that featured a gilt-embossed Wilde autograph ("drawn by me"). Although this is a kind of forgery, the design practice itself was not unheard of, and it is possible that Symons was imitating a much splashier Wilde publication that had appeared at the start of the decade: Mitchell Kennerley's "enlarged" edition of *The Portrait of Mr. W.H.* (1921). A distinguished-looking tome, this book prominently displays Wilde's golden autograph on its front cover, a decorative flourish that visually echoes the image that serves as the book's frontispiece: Wilde's own signature in manuscript facsimile. As an authenticatory device, this facsimile aims to guarantee the legitimacy of Kennerley's edition, but in so doing it also articulates a surprisingly un-Wildean attitude towards the claims of authenticity and truth that a book – and especially this book – might make (figure 21). After all, in 1893 Wilde had wished to frame his book version of the story with a representation of the very image that the story unequivocally names a forgery: an original Ricketts portrait of the imaginary Willie Hughes. In its own way the history of this recovered Wilde text, whose publication coincided with the deluge of Wilde manuscript forgeries in the early 1920s, brings us back to Wilde's singular tale of fandom, forgery, and desire and to its remarkably generative capacity for inspiring fascination. It is with this textual history that I conclude *Beautiful Untrue Things*.

Mitchell Kennerley (1878–1950) was the publisher and gallerist whose company, the Anderson Galleries, oversaw the sale of the Oscar Wilde collection of John B. Stetson Jr in 1920. His publication of Wilde's story the following year was something of a literary spectacle. *The Portrait of Mr. W.H.* appeared in an elegant edition of a thousand numbered copies printed on handmade paper, and it was even tucked into

REDUCED FACSIMILE OF THE LAST PAGE OF THE MANUSCRIPT OF "THE PORTRAIT OF MR W. H."

THE PORTRAIT
OF MR W. H.
AS WRITTEN BY
OSCAR WILDE

SOME TIME AFTER THE PUBLICATION OF HIS ESSAY, OF THE SAME TITLE, AND NOW FIRST PRINTED FROM THE ORIGINAL ENLARGED MANUSCRIPT WHICH FOR TWENTY-SIX YEARS HAS BEEN LOST TO THE WORLD

PUBLISHED 1921 BY
MITCHELL KENNERLEY
489 PARK AVENUE
NEW YORK

21 Frontispiece and title page to Oscar Wilde's *The Portrait of Mr. W.H.* New York: Mitchell Kennerley, 1921. Author's own collection.

a slip-case. A prospectus announcing its publication reveals the fannish coordinates of Kennerley's marketing strategy and the reception that he had expected to greet this much longer version of Wilde's text – a story that the public had yet to read:

> ¶This is "the lost manuscript" described on page seven of Stuart Mason's fascinating "Bibliography of Oscar Wilde." Its recovery, after having been lost for twenty-six years, is one of the most interesting incidents in modern literary history.
>
> ¶The essay entitled "The Portrait of Mr. W.H." was published in Blackwood's Magazine for July, 1889, and caused a great deal of discussion. Shortly afterwards it became known that Oscar Wilde was working on a larger study of the same subject, and in 1893 it was announced for publication. On the day of Oscar Wilde's arrest, April fifth, 1895, his books were withdrawn from the publishers' shelves and catalogues, and the manuscript of "The Portrait of Mr. W.H." is said to have been returned to Wilde's house, Tite Street, Chelsea, since which date no trace of it has been discovered.
>
> ¶It can now be said that since Oscar Wilde completed this manuscript for the printer, it had not been seen by a living person until it was found in July, 1920, and sent to Mitchell Kennerley, who recognized it as indisputably "the lost manuscript," in Wilde's own handwriting.[14]

Kennerley figures here not only as a publisher, bibliographer, and archivist; he is just as much a Wilde fan making books for other Wilde fans. This story about the recovery of the "lost manuscript" (in 1920), and its transmission into print (in 1921), however, also unexpectedly recapitulates the narratives that we have seen surrounding the recovery of other "lost" Wilde manuscripts emanating from forgers such Mrs Chan-Toon, whose *For Love of the King* was touted as a "Remarkable Literary Discovery" when it first appeared in October 1921. Even upon its re-emergence from literary limbo, then, the new material instantiation of *The Portrait of Mr. W.H.* retains and amplifies the story's characteristic romance and mystique.

The Stetson sale of Oscar Wilde books and manuscripts, whose catalogue we explored at some length in chapter 2 as a likely source of information for Dorian Hope's forgeries, took place on 23 April 1920. The sale established that Wilde items could command impressive prices on the auction block. The catalogue also noticeably names Mitchell Kennerley as president of the Anderson Galleries on its cover, so it should come as no great surprise to learn that when, in July 1920 (and thus shortly after the sale's success) a truly lost Wilde manuscript also materialized, its custodian privately approached Kennerley. A notice included in the 17 June 1921 *New York Times* communicates some of this manuscript's provenance narrative, although the notice itself seems to be heavily cribbed from Kennerley's prospectus. In "Oscar Wilde's Lost Manuscript Found" the *Times* reported:

> On the day of Oscar Wilde's arrest, April 5, 1895, his books were withdrawn from the publishers' shelves and catalogues, and the manuscript of "The Portrait of Mr. W.H." is said to have been returned to Wilde's house, Tite Street, Chelsea, since which date no trace of it has been discovered. It can now be said that since Oscar Wilde completed this manuscript for the printer it had not been seen by a living person until it was found in July, 1920, and sent to Mitchell Kennerley, who recognized it as indisputably "the lost manuscript" in Wilde's own handwriting [...] [I]t was said that the publisher was not in the city and that no detailed information of the career of the manuscript since Wilde's arrest would be made public at present. It was asserted that the authenticity of the manuscript was beyond question.[15]

In this reiterated anecdote the mythology of Wilde's arrest once again figures as a defining event in the publishing history of his books. If much of this notice's text is borrowed from the Kennerley prospectus, Kennerley, as Ian Small points out, has himself borrowed "at times almost verbatim" from Millard's *Bibliography* the strange tale of the manuscript's secret return to Wilde's house.[16] The place of Wilde's house in this story (how many *New York Times* readers would even have heard of Tite Street?) is a detail that might suggest to those familiar with the disposition of Wilde manuscripts that – like the truly lost portrait sought by Richard Jackson, Walter Ledger, Christopher Millard, and Charles Ricketts – an expanded version of "The Portrait of Mr. W.H." would have been vulnerable to the looting and predatory bargain-hunting that attended the Tite Street sale. But this was not the case. This manuscript miraculously had escaped.

In a scrupulous editorial introduction to Wilde's *Short Fiction* (volume 8 of the Oxford English Texts' *Complete Works of Oscar Wilde*, 2017), Ian Small remarks that "Kennerley was never entirely open about how the manuscript of 'Mr. W.H.' came into his possession."[17] This is an understatement. Kennerley was actually quite secretive, not only about how he obtained the manuscript but also about what he did with it. The research of Horst Schroeder, as Small further reports, offers a fuller, but still incomplete, story of the manuscript's recovery.[18] In an abbreviated version of this account, Wilde entrusted the manuscript expansion of "The Portrait of Mr. W.H." to Frederic Chapman, the office manager of his London publisher, the Bodley Head. With its publication prevented by the chaos of the trials, it was consigned to Chapman's desk, where it apparently lay undisturbed until his death in 1918; Chapman's sister Anne found it and, in 1920, approached Kennerley. (Kennerley had also once been the Bodley Head's representative in New York.) In 1921, with the permission of the Wilde estate, Kennerley published the enlarged text in the United States and sold the manuscript (for US$3,000) to Dr A.S.W. Rosenbach, the most prominent buyer at the Stetson sale.[19] Despite his expert knowledge of the value of Wilde manuscripts, Kennerley was no profiteer in this sale, however. Like the restorative bibliographers we encountered in chapter 1, he saw himself making an altruistic intervention into literary history by reinstating a text whose manuscript had "for twenty-six years [...] been *lost to the world.*"[20] He saw an opportunity to make "The Portrait of Mr. W.H." into the beautiful book that Wilde had been unable to publish, and, according to Schroeder, he acted as an intermediary by selling the manuscript "for Miss Chapman."[21] Although Rosenbach approached Wilde collectors, such as William Andrews Clark Jr, with a view to selling the manuscript, he ended up keeping it, and it still remains in the Rosenbach Museum and Library in Philadelphia.[22]

Why does any of this matter, and how does it relate to the themes of this book? The opacity of the provenance of the Rosenbach manuscript, for starters, has tantalizing consequences. Small has established, for instance, that there are significant discrepancies between the Rosenbach manuscript and the Kennerley edition, namely that "there are portions – some textually very complex – of the Kennerley text which do not derive from the manuscript."[23] From this subtle, but momentous, observation Small draws several conclusions. First, "the Rosenbach manuscript comprises material taken from different drafts made at different times."[24] Second, in "his attempt to 'tidy' Wilde's text, Kennerley's practice is reminiscent of the work of Wilde's best-known editor, Robert Ross."[25] Third, in assembling his edition, Kennerley "was copying from a document or documents *other* than the manuscript which he later sold to Rosenbach,"[26] an *aperçu* that leads Small to the conclusion that "there must have been additional material marked for insertion [...] which is now missing, but which Kennerley had access to and printed, [and] which he either subsequently lost or failed to include when he sold the manuscript."[27] To summarize this line of reasoning, if the Rosenbach manuscript only incompletely witnesses Kennerley's printed text, then there must have been further "material" by Wilde that "has been lost" and that was nonetheless included in the 1921 volume. Having identified a significant moment in the printed text where Kennerley has silently supplied a quotation that was left blank in the manuscript by Wilde, Small suggests that this is "the most likely (but perhaps not the only) explanation" for these textual discrepancies.[28]

By this logic, the return of the "lost manuscript" thus leads to further loss, which inspires as much as it thwarts curiosity. To my mind, Small's assiduous accounting of this Wildean artefact or artefacts recalls nothing so much as the search for the lost portrait painted by Ricketts that we came across in this book's opening pages. To pursue the whereabouts of Kennerley's "additional material," we would plunge ourselves into the very realm of mystery and literary conjecture – into the depths of Small's parenthetical statement "(but perhaps not the only)" – that "The Portrait of Mr. W.H." itself so beautifully thematizes. Even in the moment of its astounding recovery, then, the enlarged version of "The Portrait of Mr. W.H." remains entangled in the legendary doom of "twenty-six years" past – that is, the date of Wilde's downfall in 1895.

How, finally, can we describe Mitchell Kennerley's actions in the early 1920s? On the one hand, he was not a forger. (It is interesting to note, however, that his representatives thought it necessary to "assert" the "authenticity of the manuscript" to the *New York Times*.) On the other hand, Kennerley's having "lost" genuine Wilde manuscript material that came into his hands looks too much like carelessness. Kennerley knew perfectly well that Wilde manuscripts could be worth a great deal of money, and his sale of the expanded manuscript to Rosenbach on Anne Chapman's behalf proves as much. The only remaining possibilities are that he deliberately destroyed what he had, or that he secreted away Wildean material as a private memento of his own. In Small's view, as an editor Kennerley wished, like Robert Ross before him, to produce a "tidy" version of Wilde. Perhaps that penchant for tidiness extended to disposing (or otherwise concealing from view) a comparatively insignificant or fragmentary manuscript? If we look carefully at the publicity surrounding Kennerley's *The Portrait of Mr. W.H.*, especially his fannish attitude about Wilde, this suggestion becomes more plausible. In this way Kennerley comes into focus as simultaneously Wilde's publisher *and* the privileged keeper of a hidden archive. Like a sphinx, he keeps his secrets well.

Mitchell Kennerley, it turns out, had a long-standing enthusiasm for Oscar Wilde. As a young man working for John Lane in New York in 1897, he indulged his fandom by producing pastiches of Wildean epigrams. Here is one particularly inventive example: "it is only dreams that really happen – and realities bore me."[29] This interest in Wilde also informed the books he published: Kennerley issued the American editions of many books about Wilde, including Robert Sherard's *Life of Oscar Wilde* (1906) and Millard's *Bibliography of the Poems of Oscar Wilde* (1908). In 1912 he published Arthur Ransome's *Oscar Wilde: A Critical Study* in the United States, and in 1916 he printed Frank Harris's equally controversial *Oscar Wilde: His Life and Confessions*.[30] When the "lost manuscript" (or manuscripts?) of the expanded "Portrait of Mr. W.H." came into his hands, the literary treasure it represented dazzled him. He told the *New York Evening Post* that holding the manuscript "was like having a million dollar banknote" that "couldn't be cashed."[31] But Kennerley did cash in on Wilde: he skilfully stage-managed the unveiling of what his prospectus hyped as "one of the most interesting incidents in modern literary history" and then sold the limited edition book, of which "no more than ten copies will be sold to a single subscriber" at the substantial price of US$10 per copy.[32] For Kennerley, then, Wilde fandom certainly did not come cheaply.

Like Kennerley, the writer Richard Le Gallienne was a British expatriate living in New York with deep ties to London's 1890s decadent milieu. But, unlike the publisher, he had known Wilde personally. In a review of Kennerley's *Portrait of Mr. W.H.*, Le Gallienne draws attention to the theatrical aspects of its recovery, spotlighting – and gently mocking – Kennerley's fannish enthusiasm for the rediscovery of the "lost manuscript." "The publisher's announcement has something like a melodramatic thrill about it, [it] almost sends a shiver down the back," he teasingly remarks.[33] Le Gallienne's insightful review, which, predictably by now, is illustrated with an uncredited image of a young man in Renaissance dress with his hand on a book, and carrying a caption that reads "The Portrait of Mr. W.H.," also promotes the uncanny capacity of Wilde's story to extend its aura to the material objects that contain it. "One can imagine," he observes, "Wilde averring with portentous gravity and unction, that the doom attaching to the transmission of his theory – as set forth in his romantic record – had evidently attached itself even to his manuscript."[34] (If only Le Gallienne had known about the Ricketts portrait!) Kennerley, who had long participated in elaborating the print record of Wilde's legend, clearly understood the value of enshrouding the expanded story in wonder and longing. His book has become another tangible representation of Wilde's extraordinary after-life. By silently intervening in Wilde's text, as Ian Small charts, and then perhaps by getting rid of the evidence, Kennerley created a mystery for future Wilde fans and bibliophiles. And he would seem to have been inspired to contrive such an unconventional tribute by none other than Wilde himself – the ultimate teacher of fandom.

Notes

Collections frequently cited have been identified by the following abbreviations.

Maggs	The collection of Maggs Bros. Ltd., London
MSS Ross	MSS Ross, Robert Ross Memorial Collection, University College, Oxford
MS Wilde	MS Wilde, William Andrews Clark Memorial Library, University of California, Los Angeles
MS Wilde Forgeries	MS Wilde Forgeries, William Andrews Clark Memorial Library, University of California, Los Angeles

Introduction

1 The Ricketts sketch is now housed in the Clark Library. See MS Wilde, box 54, folder 3, William Andrews Clark Memorial Library, University of California, Los Angeles (hereafter cited as MS Wilde).

2 Ricketts to Ledger, 14 November 1912. MSS Ross, 13/2, Robert Ross Memorial Collection, University College, Oxford (hereafter cited as MSS Ross).

3 On Wilde's emergence as a figure of myth and legend see John Stokes, *Oscar Wilde: Myths, Miracles and Imitations* (Cambridge: Cambridge University Press, 1996); Merlin Holland, "Biography and the Art of Lying," in *The Cambridge Companion to Oscar Wilde*, ed. Peter Raby (Cambridge: Cambridge University Press, 1997), 3–17; Joseph Bristow, ed., *Oscar Wilde and Modern Culture: The Making of a Legend* (Athens, OH: Ohio University Press, 2008).

4 On Wilde's constitutive place in the modern concept of "the homosexual," see Ed Cohen, *Talk on the Wilde Side: Toward a Genealogy of a Discourse on Male Sexualities* (New York: Routledge, 1993); Alan Sinfield, *The Wilde Century: Oscar Wilde, Effeminacy, and the Queer Movement*

(New York: Columbia University Press, 1994); Matt Cook, *London and the Culture of Homosexuality, 1885–1914* (Cambridge: Cambridge University Press, 2003); Dominic Janes, *Oscar Wilde Prefigured: Queer Fashioning and British Caricature, 1750–1900* (Chicago: University of Chicago Press, 2016).

5 Joseph Bristow, introduction to *Oscar Wilde and Modern Culture*, 26.

6 Ellen Crowell, "Christopher Millard's Mysterious Book: Oscar Wilde, Baron Corvo, and the Unwritten *Quest*," in *Wilde Discoveries: Traditions, Histories, Archives*, ed. Joseph Bristow (Toronto: University of Toronto Press, 2013), 349.

7 On the lengthy history of literary forgery see Arthur Freeman's catalogue *Bibliotheca Fictiva: A Collection of Books & Manuscripts Relating to Literary Forgery 400 BC–AD 2000* (London: Bernard Quaritch, 2014).

8 Harold Love, *Attributing Authorship: An Introduction* (Cambridge: Cambridge University Press, 2002), 183.

9 Ibid.

10 On the concept of the authenticatory device deployed in literary forgeries see K.K. Ruthven, *Faking Literature* (Cambridge: Cambridge University Press, 2001), 146–70.

11 Ibid., 74.

12 Ibid., 78.

13 Oscar Wilde, *The Incomparable and Ingenious History of Mr. W.H.*, in *The Short Fiction*, ed. Ian Small, vol. 8 of *The Complete Works of Oscar Wilde* (Oxford: Oxford University Press, 2017) (hereafter cited as Wilde, *Mr. W.H.*, 197). Although in the text I refer to this work as "The Portrait of Mr. W.H.," I am citing the expanded version whose proposed title "The Incomparable and Ingenious History of Mr. W.H." is employed by Ian Small in his 2017 edition of Wilde's *Short Fiction*.

14 Karen Hellekson and Kristina Busse, introduction to *The Fan Fiction Studies Reader*, ed. Karen Hellekson and Kristina Busse (Iowa City: University of Iowa Press, 2014), 5–6.

15 See, for instance, Sabine Vanacker and Catherine Wynne, eds. *Sherlock Holmes and Conan Doyle: Multi-Media Afterlives* (Basingstoke, UK: Palgrave Macmillan, 2013).

16 Daniel Cavicchi, "Fandom before 'Fan': Shaping the History of Enthusiastic Audiences," *Reception: Texts, Readers, Audiences, History* 6, no. 1 (2014): 53.

17 On Wilde and celebrity culture see Regenia Gagnier, *Idylls of the Marketplace: Oscar Wilde and the Victorian Public* (Stanford, CA: Stanford University Press, 1986); Shelton Waldrep, *The Aesthetics of Self-Invention: Oscar Wilde to David Bowie* (Minneapolis: University of Minnesota Press, 2004); Sharon Marcus, "Salomé!! Sarah Bernhardt, Oscar Wilde, and the Drama of Celebrity," *PMLA* 126, no.4 (October 2011): 999–1021; and Michèle Mendelssohn, *Making Oscar Wilde* (Oxford: Oxford University Press, 2018).

18 Michel Foucault, "What Is an Author?," in *The Foucault Reader*, ed. Paul Rabinow (New York: Vintage, 1984), 107.

19 Ibid., 108.

20 Colette Colligan's "Wilde Trials Web App" traces the global circulation of sexual information during and following the Wilde trials. See https://ccolliga.wordpress.com/a-publishers-paradise/webapp/.

21 On forgery as the central Wildean metaphor for creativity see Joseph Bristow and Rebecca N. Mitchell, *Oscar Wilde's Chatterton: Literary History, Romanticism, and the Art of Forgery* (New Haven and London: Yale University Press, 2015). See also Joseph Bristow and Rebecca N. Mitchell, "The Provenance of Oscar Wilde's 'Decay of Lying.'" *Papers of the Bibliographical Society of America* 111, no. 2 (2017): 221–40.

22 Wilde, *Criticism: Historical Criticism, Intentions, the Soul of Man*, ed. Josephine M. Guy, vol. 4 of *The Complete Works of Oscar Wilde* (Oxford: Oxford University Press, 2007), 103.

23 Wilde formulated this critique in a number of periodical pieces that appeared over a relatively short period of time. These include the essays "The Decay of Lying," (January 1889); "Pen, Pencil, and Poison" (January 1889); "The True Function and Value of Criticism" (July and September 1890), later republished as "The Critic as Artist;" and the story "The Portrait of Mr. W.H." (July 1889).

24 Wilde, *Criticism*, 143.

25 See Percy Bysshe Shelley, "To a Sky-Lark" in *Shelley's Poetry and Prose*, ed. Donald H. Reiman and Neil Fraistat (New York: Norton, 2002), 304.

26 Joseph Bristow and Rebecca N. Mitchell, *Oscar Wilde's Chatterton: Literary History, Romanticism, and the Art of Forgery* (New Haven, CT, and London: Yale University Press, 2015), 290.

27 Wilde, *Mr. W.H.*, 197.

28 According to the *Oxford English Dictionary*, two related definitions of the verb date from the fourteenth century, where it first appears in English usage. *To forge*, in the first instance, is "to make, fashion, frame, or construct (any material thing)"; in the second, "to make (something) in fraudulent imitation of something else; to make or devise (something spurious) in order to pass it off as genuine."

29 The enigmatic 1609 dedication of Shakespeare's *Sonnets* reads: "TO.THE. ONLIE.BEGETTER.OF. / THESE.INSVING.SONNETS. / MR. W.H. ALL. HAPPINESSE. / AND.THAT.ETERNITIE. / PROMISED. / BY. / OVR. EVER-LIVING.POET. / WISHETH. / THE.WELL-WISHING. / ADVENT-VRER.IN. / SETTING. / FORTH." See William Shakespeare, *Complete Sonnets and Poems*, ed. Colin Burrow (Oxford: Oxford University Press, 2002), 381. Wilde quotes the entire dedication. See Wilde, *Mr. W.H.*, 214.

30 Nicholas Frankel, "On Lying as a Way of Knowing: A Portrait of 'The Portrait of Mr. W.H.'" in *Fakes and Forgeries*, ed. Peter Knight and Jonathan Long (Buckingham: Cambridge Scholars Press), 15; italics added.
31 Paul K. Saint-Amour, *The Copyrights: Intellectual Property and the Literary Imagination* (Ithaca, NY: Cornell University Press, 2003), 106; italics in the original.
32 Frankel, "On Lying as a Way of Knowing," 17.
33 Jonathan Loesberg, "Wildean Interpretation and Formalist Reading," *Victorian Studies* 58, no. 1 (Autumn 2015): 11.
34 Wilde, *Criticism*, 163.
35 Loesberg, "Wildean Interpretation," 27.
36 Wilde, *Mr. W.H.*, 197. The three forgers under discussion were the subjects of considerable literary scandal in the eighteenth century. Macpherson forged the epic writings of "Ossian," the ancient Scottish bard; Ireland was a prolific Shakespeare forger, and Chatterton contrived the poems of a supposed fifteenth-century monk, Thomas Rowley.
37 Wilde, *Mr. W.H.*, 197.
38 Bristow and Mitchell, *Oscar Wilde's Chatterton*, 288.
39 Frankel, "On Lying as a Way of Knowing," 18.
40 Wilde, *Mr. W.H.*, 209.
41 Ibid., 204.
42 Ibid., 201.
43 Ibid., 210.
44 Ibid., 204.
45 Ibid., 205.
46 Aviva Briefel, *The Deceivers: Art Forgery and Identity in the Nineteenth Century* (Ithaca, NY: Cornell University Press, 2006), 79.
47 Ibid., 33.
48 Wilde, *Mr. W.H.*, 207.
49 Briefel, *The Deceivers*, 74.
50 Wilde, *Mr. W.H.*, 198. François Clouet was a French portraitist and miniaturist of the sixteenth century.
51 Wilde, *Mr. W.H.*, 209.
52 Frankel, "On Lying as a Way of Knowing," 21.
53 Wilde, *Mr. W.H.*, 210.
54 Ibid., 211–12.
55 Ibid., 219.
56 Ibid., 251.
57 Ibid., 234. On the constitutive role of the English Renaissance in forging ideas about homosexuality for the Victorians see Will Fisher, "The Sexual

Politics of Victorian Historiographical Writing about the 'Renaissance.'" *GLQ* 14, no. 1 (2007): 41–67.

58 Wilde, *Mr. W.H.*, 252.
59 Ibid., 253.
60 Ibid., 254.
61 Ibid.
62 Ibid., 256.
63 Ibid., 258.
64 Ibid.
65 Ibid.
66 Saint-Amour, *The Copyrights*, 108.
67 Wilde, *Mr. W.H.*, 209.
68 Ibid., 197.
69 Ibid., 207.
70 Ibid., 208.
71 The manuscript of "The Portrait of Mr. W.H." is housed at the Rosenbach Museum and Library, Philadelphia (MS EL3 W672p 921). It consists of 105 numbered and ruled foolscap pages, carefully detached from a notebook. Many are entirely in Wilde's hand, while others have printed text from the *Blackwood's* version of the story pasted onto the recto of the pages with corrections and additions in Wilde's hand.
72 Wilde, *The Complete Letters of Oscar Wilde*, ed. Merlin Holland and Rupert Hart-Davis (New York: Henry Holt, 2000), 407.
73 David Peters Corbett, *The World in Paint: Modern Art and Visuality in England, 1848–1914* (University Park: Pennsylvania State University Press, 2004), 130.
74 The expanded title appears in the Bodley Head publishers' lists in 1893 and 1894. See Stuart Mason, *Bibliography of Oscar Wilde* (London: T. Werner Laurie, [1914]), 7. For more information on the expanded title see note 13 herein.
75 On the abortive "Mr. W.H." publishing project see Josephine Guy and Ian Small, *Oscar Wilde's Profession: Writing and the Culture Industry in the Late Nineteenth Century* (Oxford: Oxford University Press, 2000), 171–6, and Small, introduction to *Short Fiction*, by Wilde, liv–lxxxiii.
76 Bristow and Mitchell, *Oscar Wilde's Chatterton*, 286.
77 Jean Paul Raymond [pseud.] and Charles Ricketts, *Oscar Wilde: Recollections* (London: Nonesuch Press, 1932), 29–30.
78 Ibid., 35.
79 Ibid., 35–6.
80 Wilde, *Mr. W.H.*, 198.

81 Corbett, *The World in Paint*, 137.
82 Wilde, *Complete Letters*, 412.
83 Ibid., 412n.
84 *16, Tite Street, Chelsea: Catalogue of the Library of Valuable Books, Pictures, Portraits of Celebrities [...] Which Will Be Sold by Auction by Mr. Bullock, on the Premises, on Wednesday, April 24, 1895* (hereafter cited as the Tite Street sale catalogue), 11.
85 Corbett, *The World in Paint*, 151.
86 Robert Harborough Sherard, *The Life of Oscar Wilde* (London: T. Werner Laurie, 1906), 361.
87 Thomas Wright, *Oscar's Books* (London: Chatto & Windus, 2008), 1.
88 Frederick Keppel's manuscript account of the Tite Street sale, dated 25 April 1895 and entitled "The Sale of Oscar Wilde's Property," is preserved in MS Wilde, K38 M3 S16 [bound].
89 Wilde's popular designation as an Apostle evangelizing the aesthetic gospel probably originates in the Gilbert and Sullivan operetta *Patience*, which satirized aestheticism and which toured North America at the same time as Wilde did. In a memorable song from *Patience* the "fleshly poet" Bunthorne, widely considered a parody of Wilde, admits to one of Wilde's famous early-career publicity stunts, confessing, "Though the Philistines may jostle, you will rank as an apostle in the high aesthetic band, / If you walk down Piccadilly with a poppy or a lily in your medieval hand." See W.S. Gilbert, *The Plays of Gilbert and Sullivan* (New York: Norton, 1976), 169. On Wilde as an Apostle during the lecture tour see Kevin O'Brien, *Oscar Wilde in Canada: An Apostle for the Arts* (Toronto: Personal Library, 1982). The phrase "gospel of intensity," used to critique the supposed excesses of aesthetic enthusiasm, followed Wilde throughout his career, from the 1882 tour to his downfall in 1895. See "The Gospel of Intensity," *Boston Evening Transcript* (10 January 1882), 2; Harry Quilter, "The Gospel of Intensity," *Contemporary Review* (June 1895), 761–82.
90 Keppel, "[N]otes made relative to Wilde's sale at a later date[:] 3/3/97," MS Wilde, K38 M3 S16 [bound].
91 Jackson's claims of friendship with Pater and his encounters with other literary worthies such as Carlyle, Rossetti, and Ruskin are recounted in the second volume of Thomas Wright's *Life of Walter Pater* (New York: Putnam, 1907).
92 *Manchester Weekly Times*, 26 April 1895, 7, quoted in Rebecca N. Mitchell, "'Cultivated Idleness': Carlyle, Wilde, and Victorian Representations of Creative Labour," *Word & Image* 32, no. 1 (2016): 113.
93 Quoted in Mitchell, "Cultivated Idleness," 113.

94 Jackson's annotated copy of "The Portrait of Mr. W.H." is housed in the William Andrews Clark Memorial Library, UCLA (PR 5819 P851 cop. 2). This note is dated 8 October 1897.
95 Jackson, Annotations to Wilde, 19 October 1897.
96 Millard to Ledger, 16 August 1911. MSS Ross 13/2, Robert Ross Memorial Collection, University College, Oxford.
97 Ricketts to Ledger, November 14, 1912, MSS Ross, 13/2.
98 Wilde, *Mr. W.H.*, 203, 204.
99 The clipping bears the title "Publisher's Disclaimer." It is pasted into the verso of the book's front cover. It is dated "11 Ap. '95," is credited to a Manchester newspaper, and quotes John Lane who was then in New York: "After seeing the papers here on my arrival last Sunday I immediately cabled to my manager to withdraw all of Wilde's books, and not merely his name, from the title pages." See Wilde, "The Portrait of Mr. W.H." William Andrews Clark Memorial Library, UCLA (PR 5819 P851 cop. 2).
100 Briefel, *The Deceivers*, 75.
101 See *A Collection of Original Manuscripts Letters & Books of Oscar Wilde* (London: Dulau & Co, [1928]), 91.
102 Joseph Bristow, introduction to *Oscar Wilde and Modern Culture*, 26.
103 I do not, for instance, discuss the Wildean representations undertaken by John Moray Stuart-Young, a queer writer and palm-oil trader in colonial Nigeria whose unusual volume of poems, *Osrac the Self-Sufficient*, was published in 1905, complete with forged facsimile letters purporting to represent Wilde's correspondence with him. Stephanie Newell's *The Forger's Tale: The Search for Odeziaku* (Athens: Ohio University Press, 2006) provides a detailed account of his career.
104 Robert Ross, "Oscar Wilde's Literary Remains," *Daily Chronicle*, 7 February 1905. Newspaper clipping, Ross Env.d.49.ii, Robert Ross Memorial Collection, University College, Oxford.

1 The Importance of Being Authentic

1 See Robert Harborough Sherard, *The Real Oscar Wilde: To Be Used as a Supplement to, and in Illustration of "The Life of Oscar Wilde."* (London: T. Werner Laurie, [1916]).
2 W. Graham Robertson, *Time Was: The Reminiscences of W. Graham Robertson* (London: Hamish Hamilton, 1931), 137.
3 Oscar Wilde, *De Profundis*, in *De Profundis; "Epistola: In Carcere et Vinculis,"* ed. Ian Small, vol. 2 of *The Complete Works of Oscar Wilde* (Oxford: Oxford University Press, 2005), 95.

4 Richard Le Gallienne, *The Romantic '90s* (London: Putnam, 1951; first published 1926), 156.
5 Crowell, "Christopher Millard's Mysterious Book," 355.
6 Jacques Derrida, *Archive Fever: A Freudian Impression*, trans. Eric Prenowitz (Chicago: University of Chicago Press, 1996), 3; italics in the original.
7 Robert Ross, quoted in Henry D. Davray, "Les apocryphes d'Oscar Wilde." *Mercure de France* 186 (March 1926): 308.
8 "The Priest and the Acolyte" originally appeared in *The Chameleon* 1 (December 1894). For the sake of consistency with the short story's (1905) appearance in book form, I use the italicized form of the title throughout this chapter.
9 Love, *Attributing Authorship*, 183.
10 Stuart Mason [Christopher Millard], quoted in Holland, "Biography and the Art of Lying," 5.
11 See Mackie, "Publishing Notoriety: Piracy, Pornography, and Oscar Wilde." *University of Toronto Quarterly* 73, no. 4 (Fall 2004): 980–90.
12 On the misattributed translations, *The Satyricon of Petronius* and *What Never Dies*, see Rod Boroughs, "Oscar Wilde's Translation of Petronius: The Story of a Literary Hoax," *English Literature in Transition* 38, no. 1 (1995): 9–49.
13 Ross, "Oscar Wilde's Literary Remains."
14 Bristow, introduction to *Oscar Wilde and Modern Culture*, 36.
15 Crowell, "Christopher Millard's Mysterious Book," 355.
16 *Catalogue of the Library of Richard Butler Glaenzer: Comprising a Complete Set of the Works of Oscar Wilde in First Editions* [1905], 26. Robert Ross Memorial Collection, University College, Oxford, d. 222.
17 Ross to Vyvyan Holland, [May/June?] 1908. Eccles Bequest, BL Add. MS 81719, British Library.
18 Richard A. Kaye, "Oscar Wilde and the Politics of Sainthood: Hofmannsthal, Mirbeau, Proust," in Bristow, ed. *Oscar Wilde and Modern Culture*, 115.
19 Mendelssohn, *Making Oscar Wilde*, 260.
20 Laura Lee, *Oscar's Ghost: The Battle over Oscar Wilde's Legacy* (Stroud, UK: Amberley, 2017), 225.
21 Alfred Douglas, *Oscar Wilde and Myself* (London: John Long, 1914), 56. Although accredited to Douglas, this memoir was mostly written by his literary collaborator T.W.H. Crosland.
22 Wilde remains the centrepiece in biographies of Ross. See, for instance, Margery Ross, *Robert Ross: Friend of Friends* (London: Jonathan Cape, 1954); Maureen Borland, *Wilde's Devoted Friend: A Life of Robert Ross* (Oxford: Lennard, 1990); Jonathan Fryer, *Robbie Ross: Oscar Wilde's True Love* (London: Constable, 2000).

23 According to Wilde's friend Reginald Turner, Wilde confided that it was "little Robbie" who had seduced him and introduced him to homosexuality. That version of events (cited in Richard Ellmann, *Oscar Wilde* [Harmondsworth, UK: Penguin, 1987], 261) has more recently been challenged by Neil McKenna, who suggests that Wilde had many homosexual encounters before Ross. See McKenna, *The Secret Life of Oscar Wilde* (London: Century, 2003).
24 Ross, "Oscar Wilde's Literary Remains."
25 Guy and Small, *Oscar Wilde's Profession*, 182.
26 Ross, preface to *De Profundis*, by Oscar Wilde (London: Methuen, 1905), v.
27 Nicholas Frankel, *Oscar Wilde: The Unrepentant Years* (Cambridge, MA: Harvard University Press, 2017), 70.
28 On *De Profundis* and the production of the Wilde myth see Nicholas Frankel, "The Typewritten Self: Media Technology and Identity in Wilde's *De Profundis*," in *Bound for the 1890s: Essays on Writing and Publishing in Honor of James G. Nelson*, ed. Jonathan Allison (High Wycombe, UK: Rivendale Press, 2006), 27–44; Josephine M. Guy, "Wilde's *De Profundis* and Book History: Mute Manuscripts," *English Literature in Transition* 55, no. 4 (2012): 419–40; and Josephine Guy and Ian Small, "Reading *De Profundis*," *English Literature in Transition* 49, no. 2 (2006): 123–49. For a reading of *De Profundis* as a "literary rant" inaugurating the "modern type," see Dina Al-Kassim, *On Pain of Speech: Fantasies of the First Order and the Literary Rant* (Berkeley: University of California Press, 2010).
29 See Ross, "A Prefatory Dedication to Dr. Max Meyerfeld," in Wilde, *De Profundis* (London: Methuen, 1908), x.
30 Wilde, *De Profundis* (London: Methuen, 1905), 11.
31 Kamran Ahmadgoli and Ian Small, "The Creative Editor: Robert Ross, Oscar Wilde, and the *Collected Works*," *English Literature in Transition* 51, no. 2 (2008): 138–51.
32 Ibid., 145.
33 Ibid., 144.
34 Ibid., 140. On Wilde's concern for the book as a work of art see Frankel, *Oscar Wilde's Decorated Books* (Ann Arbor: University of Michigan Press, 2000).
35 Millard to Ledger, 11 December 1904. MSS Ross, 13/1.
36 Ahmadgoli and Small, "The Creative Editor," 139–40.
37 On the price for the *Collected Works* see Ian Small, "What Kind of Writer Was Wilde? Editorial Practice and Canon-Formation," *Journal of Victorian Culture* 5, no. 2 (Autumn 2000), 328. I converted 1908 pounds sterling using the online UK inflation calculator www.inflation.iamkate.com, accessed 30 April 2018.

38 Ahmadgoli and Small situate the *Collected Works* of Wilde in the context of the textual editing of his literary contemporaries' writings, in which the "practice of producing a clean text was common with many of the collected or library editions of the works of major authors produced between 1880 and 1920 – such as the editions of Walter Pater and Thomas Hardy published by Macmillan, or the Cassell & Co. twenty-volume edition of *The Works of Robert Louis Stevenson*." See Ahmadgoli and Small, "The Creative Editor," 139.
39 Jacob Epstein, *Let There Be Sculpture: The Autobiography of Jacob Epstein* (London: Readers Union and Michael Joseph, 1942), 51.
40 Ellen Crowell, "Oscar Wilde's Tomb: *Silence* and the Aesthetics of Queer Memorial," in *BRANCH: Britain, Representation and Nineteenth-Century History*, ed. Dino Franco Felluga. Extension of *Romanticism and Victorianism on the Net*. Web. Accessed 10 August 2016; unpaginated.
41 Ibid.
42 On the anarchist political valence of the protest see Mark Antliff, "Contagious Joy: Anarchism, Censorship and the Reception of Jacob Epstein's *Tomb of Oscar Wilde*, c. 1913," *Journal of Modern Periodical Studies* 4, no. 2 (2013): 195–225.
43 Robert Ross, quoted in Epstein, *Let There Be Sculpture*, 55.
44 Borland, *Wilde's Devoted Friend*, 170.
45 See Crowell, "Oscar Wilde's Tomb."
46 Wilde, *The Ballad of Reading Gaol* (London: Leonard Smithers, 1898), 25.
47 Humphreys's editions of *The Soul of Man* appeared in 1895, 1907, and 1912. The text of the essay also appeared in a collection of extracts called *Sebastian Melmoth* (after Wilde's post-prison alias) published by Humphreys in 1904.
48 Robert Ross, "A Superfluous Note of Explanation," in *The Soul of Man under Socialism*, by Oscar Wilde (London: Arthur Humphreys, 1912), vi.
49 On Humphreys's role in shaping Wilde's image in several editions of *The Soul of Man* see Mackie, "Textual Dissidence: The Occasions of Wilde's 'The Soul of Man under Socialism.'" *Mémoires du Livre / Studies in Book Culture* 4, no. 2 (Spring 2013); unpaginated.
50 Ross to Millard, 23 January 1908, MS Wilde, box 57, folder 2.
51 Ross, introduction to *Reviews*, by Oscar Wilde (London: Methuen, 1908), xi; italics added.
52 Ross, "The American Edition of Oscar Wilde's Works," *Times Literary Supplement*, 10 October 1907, 307.
53 Ross, quoted in Margery Ross, *Robert Ross*, 119–20.
54 Methuen & Co., prospectus, February 1908. Wildeana Clippings, vol. I (1909), 1, William Andrews Clark Memorial Library, University of California, Los Angeles.

55 Crowell, "Christopher Millard's Mysterious Book," 348.

56 Alfred Douglas, *The Autobiography of Lord Alfred Douglas* (London: Martin Secker, 1929), 42.

57 Ibid.

58 Arthur Ransome, *Oscar Wilde: A Critical Study* (London: Martin Secker, 1912), 157.

59 Ibid., 196.

60 On the typewritten copies of *De Profundis* see *Complete Letters*, 683n, 781. See also Ian Small, introduction to *De Profundis; "Epistola: In Carcere et Vinculis,"* ed. Ian Small, vol. 2 of *The Complete Works of Oscar Wilde* (Oxford: Oxford University Press, 2005), 1–31.

61 Small, introduction to *De Profundis*, 9.

62 Laura Lee, *Oscar's Ghost*, 243.

63 Douglas, *Oscar Wilde and Myself*, 241–2.

64 Laura Lee, *Oscar's Ghost*, 269.

65 Douglas, *Autobiography*, 325.

66 Ross, "re: Oscar Wilde Deceased," [July 1908].

67 Millard to an unidentified correspondent, c. 1912, MS Wilde, box 45, folder 4. Millard wrote many letters in a similar vein. See also Millard to J. Baldwin, an Essex bookseller (1 February 1912): "The three volumes of Oscar Wilde's works which you sent in response to my application are all unauthorised pirated editions, and I am therefore putting them at the disposal of Messrs. Parker, Garrett & Co [...] solicitors to the Estate of the late Mr. Oscar Wilde [...] As a matter of fact I have noticed for some time past that you were continually offering these prints for sale [...] it is as well that you should realise that by again offering such unauthorised reprints for sale you lay yourself open to having legal proceedings taken against you" (MS Wilde, box 44, folder 1), and Millard to Edward Baker, a Birmingham bookseller (11 November 1911): "now that it seems pirated reprints are again in circulation, stringent methods will be adopted to put a stop to the sale of them" (MS Wilde, box 44, folder 1).

68 See "Pirated Oscar Wilde Books," *Westminster Gazette* (20 February 1914), Wildeana Clippings, vol. XXX (1914), 12, William Andrews Clark Memorial Library, University of California, Los Angeles.

69 Stuart Mason [Christopher Millard], "List of Editions of Works by Oscar Wilde Which May Be Offered for Sale in the United Kingdom," appended to Ross, "re: Oscar Wilde Deceased."

70 A.J.A. Symons, *The Quest for Corvo* (East Lansing: Michigan State University Press, 1955), 7.

71 Ibid., 8.

72 On Millard's life see H. Montgomery Hyde, *Christopher Sclater Millard (Stuart Mason): Bibliographer & Antiquarian Book Dealer* (New York: Global Academic Publishers, 1990); and Maria Roberts, *Yours Loyally: A Life of Christopher Sclater Millard* ([LaVergne, TN:] FeedARead.com Publishing, 2014).
73 Millard, quoted in Hyde, *Christopher Sclater Millard*, 11; italics added.
74 Millard's unfinished biographical projects, "Oscar Wilde: A Chronological Biography" [1905] and "Oscar Wilde's Life and Literary Career" [1911] are preserved in MS Wilde, box 45, folder 5.
75 See Nicholas Frankel, "Gathering the Fragments: The Role of the Collector in Remembering Oscar Wilde," *The Wildean* 22 (January 2003): 3–16.
76 On the iconography and the Wilde archive see Daniel A. Novak, "Picturing Wilde: Christopher Millard's 'Iconography of Oscar Wilde,'" *Nineteenth Century Contexts* 32, no. 4 (December 2010), 305–35.
77 See *Collection of Original Manuscripts*, 119.
78 Mason [Millard], *Bibliography of Oscar Wilde*, vii.
79 See Walter Ledger's undated and unpaginated MS notes for a prospective Wilde bibliography, MSS Ross, box 3.26.x.
80 On Millard's part in shaping the Clark archive see Bruce Whiteman, "'Some Sell, and Others Buy': Early Collectors of Oscar Wilde," in *The Importance of Being Misunderstood: Homage to Oscar Wilde*, ed. Giovanna Franci and Giovanna Silvani (Bologna: Patron Editore, 2003), 367–77.
81 Frankel, "Gathering the Fragments," 12.
82 Millard to Clark, 9 October 1922, MS Wilde, box 44, folder 2.
83 Clark followed up on Millard's prompt by sending a copy of *Wilde and Wildeiana* to Vyvyan Holland. They maintained a cordial correspondence that included exchanges of books for many years, and, despite Holland's multiple invitations to Clark to come to England to meet him and to see his books, Clark seems to have kept his distance.
84 Mason [Millard], *Bibliography*, vii.
85 Symons, *Quest for Corvo*, 18.
86 This bibliography is appended to *Miscellanies*, vol. 14 of the *Collected Works*.
87 Aldous Huxley, quoted in Frankel, "Gathering the Fragments," 12.
88 Frankel, "Gathering the Fragments," 5.
89 Ibid., 7.
90 Millard to Ledger, 26 September 1905, MSS Ross, 13/1.
91 [Christopher Millard], *Oscar Wilde: Three Times Tried* (London: Ferrestone Press, 1912), viii.
92 Ibid., iv.
93 Ibid.
94 Ross, "Introductory Note," in *Bibliography of Oscar Wilde*, by Stuart Mason (London: T. Werner Laurie, [1914]), v–vi.

95 See Holland to Clark, 19 October 1922. Clarkive Pre-1934, box 6, folder 9, William Andrews Clark Memorial Library, UCLA.

96 This description of Ledger in 1911 comes from Arthur Ransome. See Ransome, *The Autobiography of Arthur Ransome* (London: Jonathan Cape, 1976), 142.

97 Mason [Millard], *Bibliography*, viii.

98 Kaye, "Oscar Wilde and the Politics of Sainthood," 113.

99 Although Ledger's correspondence is not as extensive as Millard's, the Clark Library holds numerous Ledger letters. See MS Wilde, box 37, folder 46, and "Letters to Christopher Millard," L473L M645 1922–1927 [boxed].

100 Millard to Ledger, 26 September 1905, MSS Ross 13/1.

101 The dedication of *Impressions of America*, by Oscar Wilde, reads "To Walter Ledger: Pignus Amicitiae [Pledge of Friendship]." Robert Ross also dedicated *Miscellanies*, the fourteenth and final volume of the *Collected Works*, to Ledger.

102 Walter Ledger to P.V. Stock, 5 October 1905, MS Wilde, box 37, folder 46 (my translation). The three stories have also appeared in Spanish and German translations (my translation). According to the Millard bibliography appended to Sherard's *Life of Oscar Wilde* (1906), these stories first appeared "in an American magazine, over Wilde's name, shortly after his death," but I have not been able to trace them. They are not mentioned in any of Millard's other Wilde writings. See Sherard, *Life of Oscar Wilde*, 460.

103 See Wilde, *Le crime de Lord Arthur Savile*, trans. Albert Savine (Paris: P.V. Stock, 1905), [213] (my translation).

104 Ledger to Stock, 10 October 1905, MS Wilde, box 37, folder 46 (my translation).

105 Millard had been prompted by Ross to seek out Ledger's assistance for the projected Wilde bibliography. Millard's first letter, in 1904, asks Ledger "if you feel disposed to help me compile a complete bibliography." See Millard to Ledger, 27 November 1904, MSS Ross 13/1.

106 See Ledger, "Bibliography," in *Salomé, La Sainte Courtisane, A Florentine Tragedy* (London: Methuen, 1909), 93–109.

107 Millard to Ledger, 4 May 1905, MSS Ross 13/1.

108 Millard to Ledger, 26 September 1906, MSS Ross 13/1.

109 See "Copy of Oscar Wilde Work," MSS Ross, box 1.14, Robert Ross Memorial Collection, University College, Oxford.

110 Ross to Ledger, 13 September 1907, MSS Ross 4.

111 [John Francis Bloxam,] *The Priest and the Acolyte: With an Introductory Protest by Stuart Mason* (London: Lotus Press, 1907), 5.

112 See Ross to Millard, 27 December 1907, MS Wilde, box 57, folder 1.

113 See Millard's "Oscar Wilde: A Chronological Biography" [1905], MS Wilde, box 45, folder 5.
114 On the role of "The Priest and the Acolyte" in the trial see Merlin Holland, *The Real Trial of Oscar Wilde* (New York: Harper Collins, 2003), 67–73.
115 Carson, quoted in Holland, *Real Trial of Oscar Wilde*, 71.
116 On the publication dates for *The Priest and the Acolyte* as a stand-alone volume see James G. Nelson, *Publisher to the Decadents: Leonard Smithers in the Careers of Beardsley, Wilde, Dowson* (University Park: Pennsylvania State University Press, 2000), 350.
117 When asked by Carson "if in your opinion the piece was not immoral," Wilde replied, "Worse, it was badly written." See Holland, *Real Trial of Oscar Wilde*, 69.
118 Carson, quoted in Holland, *Real Trial of Oscar Wilde*, 81.
119 Stuart Mason, "Introductory Protest," 21–2.
120 Ibid., 24.
121 Wilde, quoted in Holland, *Real Trial of Oscar Wilde*, 16–17.
122 Wilde, *Complete Letters*, 625.
123 Timothy d'Arch Smith, *Love in Earnest: Some Notes on the Lives and Writings of English 'Uranian' Poets from 1889 to 1930* (London: Routledge & Kegan Paul, 1970), 56.
124 Mason, "Introductory Protest," 25.
125 Ibid., 6.
126 Wilde, *Complete Letters*, 1041.

2 The Picture of Dorian Hope

1 William Figgis, "Wilde MSS," undated, unpublished typescript, MS Wilde Forgeries, William Andrews Clark Memorial Library, University of California, Los Angeles (hereafter cited as MS Wilde Forgeries), box 2.
2 "Gide" to Figgis, 18 October 1921, MS Wilde Forgeries, box 2. On the Gide-Wilde connection see Jonathan Fryer, *André & Oscar: The Literary Friendship of André Gide and Oscar Wilde* (New York: St Martin's Press, 1997).
3 The accented "e" in *Salomé* here indicates the French version of the play. The unaccented title (*Salome*) indicates the English version.
4 See, for instance, Dudley Edwards, "The Wilde Goose Chase," *American Book Collector* 7, no. 5 (January 1957), 3–14; Bristow, introduction to *Oscar Wilde and Modern Culture*, 31–4; and Charles Nicholl, *Traces Remain: Essays and Explorations* (London: Allen Lane, 2011), 223–43.
5 Daniel Cavicchi, "Fandom before 'Fan': Shaping the History of Enthusiastic Audiences," *Reception: Texts, Readers, Audiences, History* 6, no. 1 (2014): 54.
6 Abigail Derecho, "Archontic Literature: A Definition, a History, and Several Theories of Fan Fiction," in *Fan Fiction and Fan Communities in the*

Age of the Internet, ed. Karen Hellekson and Kristina Busse (Jefferson, NC: McFarland, 2006), 64–5.

7 On the concept of "continuations" and "continual reading," see Carrie Sickmann Han, "Pickwick's Other Papers: Continually Reading Dickens," *Victorian Literature and Culture* 44 (2016): 19–41.

8 "Poet Holland Denies Charges of Plagiarism." *Washington Times*, 24 August 1921, 1.

9 Vyvyan Holland to William Figgis, 23 September 1955, MS Wilde Forgeries, box 2.

10 Wilde, "The Nightingale and the Rose," in *The Short Fiction*, ed. Ian Small, vol. 8 of *The Complete Works of Oscar Wilde* (Oxford: Oxford University Press, 2017), 20.

11 Ibid., 24.

12 See Joyce Kilmer, "Godlessness Mars Most Contemporary Poetry," *New York Times Magazine*, 10 December 1916, 12.

13 See "Girl Claims as Her Own 26 Poems of Dorian Hope; Mysterious Poet Vanishes." *New York Evening World*, 4 April 1921, 6.

14 In this and other news reports from 1921, Holland's first name is rendered with one "t"; later in life he was referred to as "Brett Holland." For consistency I use the latter spelling.

15 The first poetry publication by Brett Holland that I have been able to trace, entitled "Vocation," appeared in the Richmond, Virginia *Times-Dispatch* in December, 1918. Although he was eager to be known as a poet, Holland was not a particualrly talented versifier, which may account for his turn to plagiarism:

"Vocation" (for the *Times-Dispatch*)

So delicately tender,
The creature of an hour
Upon a mountain-side it grew
A gentle little flower.

It lived within the silence
Wherein its life was born;
It blossomed in the twilight,
And withered ere the morn.

Unknown it lived, unseen it died
Upon its lonely sod;
But not in vain its little life
Before the eyes of God.

See Richmond, Virginia *Times-Dispatch*, 17 December 1918, 6.

16 See "'Dorian Hope' Verse Filched by Clerk," *New York Times*, 5 April 1921, 27.

17 For Miriam Vedder see https://kihm4.wordpress.com/2013/06/07/miriam-vedder/, accessed 15 May 2017.

18 See "Dorian Hope Makes Answer to Charges Brought Against Him," *Gastonia Gazette*, 15 August, 1921, 2.

19 Wilde, *Complete Letters*, 434.

20 Herbert S. Gorman, "New Poets and Some Others," *New York Times Book Review and Magazine*, 27 March 1921, 13.

21 Wilde, "*Olivia* at the Lyceum," in *Journalism I*, ed. John Stokes and Mark W. Turner, vol. 6 of *The Complete Works of Oscar Wilde* (Oxford: Oxford University Press, 2013), 55.

22 See "Woman Impersonator Demonstrates Gas Range." *Wilmington Evening Journal*, 18 August 1916, 7.

23 See "Don't Call Me Him, For I'm a 'Her'." *Paris* [Texas] *Morning News*, 30 November 1917, 7.

24 See Richmond [Virginia] *Times-Dispatch* (March 2, 1919). 6

25 Dorian Hope to Herbert Boyce Satcher, 10 March 1920, MS Wilde, box 60, folder 6.

26 "Queen Mary" [Dorian Hope] to Herbert Boyce Satcher [postmarked 4 September 1920], MS Wilde, box 60, folder 6; italics added.

27 Eve Kosofsky Sedgwick, *Tendencies* (Durham, NC: Duke University Press, 1993), 59. Sedgwick is quoting from Neil Bartlett, *Who Was That Man? A Present for Mr. Oscar Wilde* (London: Serpent's Tail, 1988).

28 Herbert Boyce Satcher (1890–1966) was vicar of St Aidan's parish, Cheltenham, Pennsylvania, from 1924 until his retirement in 1958. He is perhaps best known for *A Bibliography of Church Music and Allied Subjects* (Philadelphia: Diocese of Pennsylvania, 1937; rev. ed. 1949). I make this assessment based on the books in his widely dispersed collection, many of which can be traced, thanks to Satcher's bookplate, through online searches of the catalogues of rare-book dealers. In the course of researching this study I purchased Satcher's copy of the 1916 autobiography *My Days and Dreams* by British proto-gay-rights pioneer Edward Carpenter, which has a telling annotation in Satcher's hand: "the author is regretably [sic] reticent regarding his personal life." On Satcher's collecting of "Uranian" poetry and photography, see Donald A. Rosenthal, *An Arcadian Photographer in Manhattan: Edward Mark Slocum* (Portsmouth: Callum James, 2011), 56.

29 Herbert Boyce Satcher, "The Dorian Hope Story," unpublished manuscript [c. 1960], MS Wilde, box 60, folder 7.

30 George Chauncey, *Gay New York: Gender, Urban Culture, and the Making of the Gay Male World, 1890–1940* (New York: Basic Books, 1994), 287.

31 Satcher, "The Dorian Hope Story."
32 Sweeney to Satcher, 15 January 1920, MS Wilde, box 60, folder 6.
33 Satcher, "The Dorian Hope Story."
34 Dorian Hope to Satcher, 10 March 1920, MS Wilde, box 60, folder 6.
35 Wayne Koestenbaum, *The Queen's Throat: Opera, Homosexuality, and the Mystery of Desire* (New York: Da Capo Press, 2001), 131.
36 Oscar Wilde, *The Picture of Dorian Gray: The 1890 and 1891 Texts*, ed. Joseph Bristow, vol. 3 of *The Complete Works of Oscar Wilde* (Oxford: Oxford University Press, 2005), 288.
37 On the Uranian poets and their ideal of pederastic, classically derived love see d'Arch Smith, *Love in Earnest*. The notion of the "profile" appears throughout Wilde's writings, often coupled to a coded interest in youthful male beauty. In "Phrases and Philosophies for the Use of the Young" (1894), for example, he opines, "There is something tragic about the enormous number of young men there are in England at the present moment who start life with perfect profiles, and end by adopting some useful profession," thereby prioritizing the aesthetically non-productive status of the "profile" over traditionally masculine utility, energy, and productivity. See Wilde, *The Major Works*, ed. Isobel Murray (Oxford: Oxford University Press, 1989), 573.
38 Hope to Satcher, 13 March 1920, MS Wilde, box 60, folder 6. The emphasis is Hope's.
39 Hope to Satcher, 17 May 1920, MS Wilde, box 60, folder 6.
40 On the ecclesiastical closet see Dominic Janes, *Vision of Queer Martyrdom from John Henry Newman to Derek Jarman* (Chicago: University of Chicago Press, 2015), 5.
41 Hope to Satcher, 5 June 1920, MS Wilde, box 60, folder 6.
42 On the formative role of the United States in shaping Wilde's career see Mendelssohn, *Making Oscar Wilde*.
43 Satcher, "The Dorian Hope Story."
44 Hope to Satcher, 13 March 1920, MS Wilde, box 60, folder 6.
45 Wilde's short story "The Canterville Ghost" satirizes American commercialism with an imaginary product called "Pinkerton's Detergent." John Sloan speculates that Lydia Pinkham's patent medicines may have inspired this flourish because Pinkham's "medical compound" "had been advertised on the same page as Wilde's portrait in the *Washington Post* in 1882, when he was on a lecture tour of America." See Wilde, *The Complete Short Stories*, ed. John Sloan (Oxford: Oxford University Press, 2010), 237n.
46 Satcher, "The Dorian Hope Story."
47 Ibid.

48 Ibid.
49 Ibid.
50 Dorian Hope's final postcard to Satcher bears a postmark of 4 September 1920.
51 Brett Holland had used this name among "friends" in New York; see "Girl Claims as Her Own 26 Poems of Dorian Hope; Mysterious Poet Vanishes." *New York Evening World*, 4 April 1921, 6.
52 See Millard to Mitchell Kennerley, 19 May 1924, MS Wilde, box 44, folder 7.
53 Alfred Douglas to Sebastian Hope, 7 October 1920 [postmark], in the collection of Maggs Bros. Ltd., London (hereafter cited as Maggs).
54 Alfred Douglas, *Collected Poems of Lord Alfred Douglas* (London: Martin Secker, 1919), 121.
55 Douglas to Hope, 7 October 1920 [postmark], Maggs.
56 Douglas to Hope, 9 October 1920, Maggs.
57 Ibid. In section 3 of *The Waste Land* ("The Fire Sermon"), Eliot's speaker relates how "Mr. Eugenides, the Smyrna merchant […] Asked me in demotic French / To luncheon at the Cannon Street Hotel / Followed by a weekend at the Metropole." See T.S. Eliot, *The Annotated Waste Land, with Eliot's Contemporary Prose*, ed. Lawrence Rainey (New Haven, CT: Yale University Press, 2005), 63. On Brighton's Metropole Hotel see 107.
58 The dedication reads: "Sebastian Hope | from | Alfred Douglas. | (First Edition of the Rossiad, published 1916.) | London. | February. 1921." In Maggs.
59 [Alfred Douglas], "A Warning to Our Readers," *Plain English* 35, no. 2 (5 March 1921): 183.
60 Dudley Edwards's "Wilde Goose Chase" offers a more detailed account.
61 William Figgis, "Wilde MSS," MS Wilde Forgeries, box 2.
62 Ibid.
63 Maggs Brothers, Ltd., to Pierre Louÿs, 1 July 1921, Maggs.
64 "Gide" to Figgis, 18 October 1921, MS Wilde Forgeries, box 2.
65 "Gide" to Figgis, 30 December 1921, MS Wilde Forgeries, box 2.
66 "Gide" to Figgis, 2 November 1921, MS Wilde Forgeries, box 2.
67 "Gide" to Figgis, 30 December 1921, MS Wilde Forgeries, box 2.
68 Ibid.
69 Ibid.
70 "Gide" to Figgis, 27 November 1921, MS Wilde Forgeries, box 2.
71 William Figgis, "Wilde MSS," undated, unpublished typescript, MS Wilde Forgeries, box 2.
72 Maggs Brothers, Ltd., to Figgis, 6 December 1921, Maggs.
73 C. Frederic Harrison to Figgis, 15 January 1922, MS Wilde Forgeries, box 2.

74 William Figgis, "Wilde MSS," undated, unpublished typescript, MS Wilde Forgeries, box 2.
75 Daniel Novak, "Sexuality in the Age of Technological Reproducibility: Oscar Wilde, Photography, and Identity," in *Oscar Wilde and Modern Culture: the Making of a Legend*, ed. Joseph Bristow (Athens: Ohio University Press, 2008), 77.
76 Wilde, *Complete Letters*, 785. Wilde had also written to Ross, from prison, about the fur coat in March 1896. See *Complete Letters*, 654.
77 "Gide" to Figgis, 13 February 1922, MS Wilde Forgeries, box 2.
78 André Gide to Figgis, 9 January 1922, MS Wilde Forgeries, box 2.
79 Figgis, "Wilde MSS," undated, unpublished typescript, MS Wilde Forgeries, box 2.
80 Ibid.
81 "Gide" to Figgis, 28 March 1922, MS Wilde Forgeries, box 2.
82 "Gide" to Figgis, 27 April 1922, MS Wilde Forgeries, box 2.
83 Millard to Figgis, 26 June 1922, MS Wilde Forgeries, box 2.
84 See, for instance, Millard to W.A. Clark Jr, 12 July 1922, MS Wilde, box 44, folder 2. Clark did not purchase any of these and was soon alerted to their status as forgeries by Millard himself once the latter had changed his mind about them. Ironically, several of the documents abortively offered to Clark now reside in the library that bears his name, only as acknowledged forgeries.
85 Figgis to Millard, 2 May 1922, MS Wilde Forgeries, box 2.
86 Figgis to Millard, 12 May 1922, MS Wilde Forgeries, box 2.
87 Millard to Figgis, 25 July 1922, MS Wilde Forgeries, box 2. See also Millard to Ledger, 26 July 1922, MSS Ross 13/4.
88 Millard to W.A. Clark Jr, 25 July 1922, MS Wilde, box 44, folder 2.
89 See "Dorian Hope Makes Answer to Charges Brought Against Him." *Gastonia Gazette*, 15 August 1921, 2.
90 *The Oscar Wilde Collection of John B. Stetson, Jr* (New York: Anderson Galleries, 1920), [1].
91 This figure comes from Walter Ledger's annotated copy of the Stetson sale catalogue (Ross d. 225) housed in the Robert Ross Memorial Collection, University College, Oxford. (Note, however, the slightly different figure cited in the *New York Times*.)
92 "Wilde Manuscript Sale Brings $46,866," *New York Times*, 24 April 1920, 32.
93 Matthew J. Bruccoli, *The Fortunes of Mitchell Kennerley, Bookman* (New York: Harcourt Brace Jovanovich, 1986), 98.
94 *The Oscar Wilde Collection of John B. Stetson, Jr*, [1].
95 Ibid., 18.

96 Ibid., 20.
97 Ibid., 22.
98 "Wilde Manuscript Sale Brings $46,866," *New York Times*, 24 April 1920, 32. Rosenbach may have overpaid, however. When he resold the *Sphinx* manuscript to William Andrews Clark Jr in 1923, he charged the collector US$1,050 – an indication that prices for Wilde manuscripts had peaked at the Stetson sale and were on the decline as the decade progressed. See Rosenbach Company Invoice (25 May 1923), Clarkive Pre-1934, box 3, William Andrews Clark Memorial Library, UCLA.
99 On Wilde's revisions, with particular emphasis on the plays, see Sos Eltis, *Revising Wilde: Society and Subversion in the Plays of Oscar Wilde* (Oxford: Clarendon Press, 1996).
100 See *The Importance of Being Earnest*, MS Wilde Forgeries, box 1, folder 21.
101 Frankel, *The Unrepentant Years*, 236.
102 Wilde's 1898 letter to Leonard Smithers sets out the precise wording for the play's dedication to Ross. See *Complete Letters*, 1110.
103 Frankel, *Oscar Wilde's Decorated Books*, 210.
104 On the poem's complex textual history, including the existence of multiple fragmentary manuscripts, see Wilde, *The Sphinx*, in *Poems and Poems in Prose*, ed. Bobby Fong and Karl Beckson, vol. 1 of *The Complete Works of Oscar Wilde* (Oxford: Oxford University Press, 2000), 305–7.
105 See Mason [Millard], *Bibliography of Oscar Wilde*, 397.
106 Wilde, *The Sphinx* (London: Elkin Mathews & John Lane, 1894), unpaginated.
107 Wilde, *The Poems of Oscar Wilde* (London: Methuen, 1908), 289.
108 *Oscar Wilde Collection of John B. Stetson, Jr*, [19].
109 See "The Sphinx," MS Wilde Forgeries, box 1, folder 23.
110 For an account of how a forger goes about contriving fake letters by famous authors see Lee Israel, *Can You Ever Forgive Me? Memoirs of a Literary Forger* (New York: Simon & Schuster, 2008).
111 "Wilde Manuscript Sale Brings $46,866," *New York Times*, 24 April 1920, 32.
112 Stuart Mason [Christopher Millard], "Forged Letters of Oscar Wilde," *Publishers' Circular*, 18 November 1911, 755.
113 This letter is one of twenty-seven mostly addressed to "Robbie" or "Bosie," in the possession of Maggs Brothers Ltd., London.
114 "Oscar" to "Bosie," 23 April 1895 [c. 1921], Maggs.
115 Carson, quoted in Holland, *The Real Trial of Oscar Wilde*, 274.
116 "Oscar" to "Bosie," 26 June 1894 [c. 1921], Maggs.
117 Examining a forgery submitted by Millard for his examination, Ledger commented: "I think the writing rather large for O.W.'s later period and

not 'Greek-like' enough." See Ledger to Millard, 28 July 1922, L473L M645 1922–1927 [boxed], William Andrews Clark Memorial Library, UCLA.

118 Just as there are exceptions to prove every rule, authenticated Wilde letters written in purple ink do exist. An undated 1898 letter to Frank Harris, for instance, makes use of this rare colour. See Oscar Wilde Collection, Box 2 Folder 6, Harry Ransom Humanities Research Center, University of Texas at Austin.

119 Vyvyan Holland to William Figgis, 23 September 1955, MS Wilde Forgeries, box 2.

120 See, for instance, the two typescripts of "Art and the Handicraftsman" held at the William Andrews Clark Memorial Library, UCLA (MS Wilde, 6721 M3 A784 [1882]b and [1882]c Bound). Typescript [1882]b has corrections and additions in purple pencil, while typescript [1882]c has passages crossed out in purple pencil, with interpolations in brown ink in Wilde's hand.

121 See "Mr. Swinburne's Poems & Ballads (3 Series)," MS Wilde Forgeries, box 1, folder 17.

122 See "Lord Arthur Savile's Crime," MS Wilde Forgeries, box 1, folder 18.

123 Edwards, "The Wilde Goose Chase," 14.

124 See "The Sphinx without a Secret," MS Wilde Forgeries, box 1, folder 26.

125 "The Sphinx without a Secret," MS Wilde forgery, Maggs.

126 Wilde, "The Sphinx without a Secret," in *The Short Fiction*, ed. Ian Small, vol. 8 of *The Complete Works of Oscar Wilde* (Oxford: Oxford University Press, 2017), 79.

127 Ibid., 81.

128 Wilde, "In the Forest" [c. 1921], MS Wilde forgery, Maggs.

129 "Pierre Louÿs" to Maggs, 3 June 1921, Maggs.

130 "Pierre Louÿs" to Maggs, 13 April 1921, Maggs.

131 "Gide" to William Figgis, 2 March 1922, MS Wilde Forgeries, box 2.

132 "Pierre Louÿs" to Maggs, undated, Maggs.

133 André Gide to William Figgis, 9 May 1922, MS Wilde Forgeries, box 2.

134 Ibid.

135 See "Dorian Hope Wanted by Police of Paris." *New York Herald*, 7 May 1922, 7.

136 According to a notice in the *Wilmington Evening Journal*, likely repeating an invention of Holland's, "[Brett] Holland was born in Bordeaux, France." See "Woman Impersonator Demonstrates Gas Range." *Wilmington Evening Journal* (August 18, 1916), 7.

137 Figgis, "Wilde MSS."

138 According to Eric W. Nye's "Pounds Sterling to Dollars: Historical Conversion of Currency" website, £138 in 1921 would be worth

approximately US$8,900 in 2018. See http://www.uwyo.edu/nuimage/currency.htm (accessed 16 April 2018). For the sake of comparison, the US$1,450 realized by the manuscript of *The Sphinx* at the Stetson sale would amount to US$18,100 today, whereas the US$7,900 realized by the cache of Wilde letters at that sale would amount to US$98,600. See www.usinflationcalculator.com (accessed 16 April 2018).

139 Figgis, "Wilde MSS."

140 See, for instance, the notices of Cravan's activities in Millard's Wildeana Clippings archive, including "Oscar Wilde's Nephew," *Modern Society*, 21 March 1914; "Oscar Wilde's Nephew Disappears," *London Mail*, 18 April 1914, Wildeana Clippings, vol. XXX (1914), 37 and 57; "A Futurist Lecture," *Evening Standard* (London), 7 July 1914; and "The Modern Aesthete," *London Mail*, 8 August 1914, Wildeana Clippings, vol. XXXI (1914), 47 and 92. William Andrews Clark Memorial Library, UCLA.

141 Millard to Figgis, 9 August 1922, MS Wilde Forgeries, box 2.

142 Millard to Mitchell Kennerley, 19 May 1924, MS Wilde, box 44, folder 7; the capital letters are Millard's.

143 See, for example, Holland's assertion, "I always understood that [Dorian Hope] was my first cousin Fabian Lloyd." Vyvyan Holland to William Figgis, 23 September 1955, MS Wilde Forgeries, box 2.

144 For investigations into the attribution of the Hope forgeries to Cravan see George Sims, "'Arthur Cravan' The Oscar Wilde Forger: A Mystery Solved?" *Antiquarian Book Monthly Review* 7 (August 1980): 398–403; and Henry Lethbridge, "The Quest for Cravan," *Antiquarian Book Monthly Review* 8 (September 1981): 336–9.

145 "A Futurist Lecture," *Evening Standard* (London), 7 July 1914, Wildeana Clippings, vol. XXXI (1914), 47, William Andrews Clark Memorial Library, UCLA.

146 Roger Conover, "Arthur Cravan," in *4 Dada Suicides: Selected Texts of Arthur Cravan, Jacques Rigaut, Julien Torma & Jacques Vaché* (London: Atlas Press, 1995), 15. On Cravan's biography see Roger Conover, "The Secret Names of Arthur Cravan," in *Arthur Cravan: Poète et Boxeur* (Paris: Terrain Vague, 1992), 25–37; Nicholl, *Traces Remain*, 223–43; and Carolyn Burke, *Becoming Modern: The Life of Mina Loy* (New York: Farrar, Straus & Giroux, 1996).

147 Mike Richardson and Rick Geary, *Cravan: Mystery Man of the Twentieth Century* (Milwaukie, OR: Dark Horse Books, 2005).

148 Nicholl, *Traces Remain*, 227.

149 See Maria Lluïsa Borras, ed., *Maintenant: Collection complète* (Paris: Editions Jean-Michel Place, 1977), 4–7, 15–17; and Cravan, "Oscar Wilde est vivant!" *Maintenant* 3 (October–November 1913): 1–11.

150 Sherard, *The Real Oscar Wilde*, 328.
151 Cravan, "Oscar Wilde Is Alive!" [part 2], *The Soil: A Magazine of Art* 1, no. 5 (July 1917): 197.
152 Ibid., 199.
153 See Cravan, "Oscar Wilde Is Alive!" [part 1], *The Soil: A Magazine of Art* 1, no. 4 (April 1917): 145–60.
154 Cravan, "Oscar Wilde Is Alive!" [part 1], 149.
155 Ibid., 151.
156 This is not to say that Cravan was oblivious to queerness or to his own capacity to engage in homoerotic seduction. In an imaginary interview with André Gide published in the July 1913 issue of *Maintenant* he purports to recall Gide's stunned reaction to his family background and attractive appearance: "J'écrivais un mot à Gide, me recommendant de ma parenté avec Oscar Wilde; Gide me recevait. Je lui étais un étonnement avec ma taille, mes épaules, ma beauté, mes eccentricités, mes mots. Gide raffolait de moi." (I wrote to Gide, recommending myself on the basis of my family relation to Oscar Wilde; Gide received me. I amazed him with height, my shoulders, my good looks, my eccentricities, my words. Gide doted on me; [my translation].) See Borras, *Maintenant: Collection complete*, 2.
157 Nicholl, *Traces Remain*, 242.
158 Ibid., 243.
159 Cravan, "Oscar Wilde Is Alive!" [part 2], 160.

3 Pen, Pencil, and Planchette

1 See George Sylvester Viereck, "Is Oscar Wilde Living or Dead?," *The Critic* [New York] 47 (July 1905): 86–8.
2 Ibid., 86.
3 Ibid., 88.
4 Ibid.
5 Wilde's attendance at a meeting of the Society for Psychical Research is recorded in an unsigned notice in that organization's journal. See "The Spiritual Outlook," *Light: A Journal of Psychical, Occult, and Mystical Research* 5, no. 216 (21 February 1885): 91.
6 Stokes, *Oscar Wilde*, 1.
7 Wilde, "The Canterville Ghost," in *The Short Fiction*, ed. Ian Small, 90.
8 Ibid., 91.
9 Cheiro [William John Warner], *Cheiro's Memoirs: The Reminiscences of a Society Palmist* (London: William Rider, 1912), 57.

10 Ibid., 61.
11 On the Gide seance see Sherard, *The Real Oscar Wilde*, 213–15.
12 See, for example, Arthur Conan Doyle, "Oscar Wilde," letter to the editor, *Occult Review* 39, no. 4 (April 1924): 235–6; and Doyle, *The Edge of the Unknown* (London: John Murray, 1930), 133–41.
13 Otis Notman, "Viereck, Hohenzollern?" *New York Times Saturday Review of Books*, 29 June 1907, 413.
14 Elmer Gertz, *Odyssey of a Barbarian: The Biography of George Sylvester Viereck* (Buffalo, NY: Prometheus Books, 1978), 77.
15 The Douglas-Viereck correspondence is part of the Eccles Bequest housed at the British Library. On the translation's dedication to Douglas see Douglas to Viereck, 6 June 1903, BL Add. MS 81704, British Library.
16 Notman, "Viereck, Hohenzollern?," 413, notes, "Mr. Viereck does not voluntarily tell the story of his descent, though he freely admitted its truth to me."
17 Douglas to Viereck, 11 November 1936, BL Add. MS 81704, British Library.
18 Viereck, *The House of the Vampire* (New York: Moffat, Yard, 1907), 48.
19 Ibid., 4.
20 Ibid., 47, 59.
21 Wilde, *The Picture of Dorian Gray*, 189.
22 Viereck, *The House of the Vampire*, 162, 158.
23 Ibid., 182.
24 Saint-Amour, *The Copyrights*, 131.
25 Viereck, *The House of the Vampire*, 130.
26 Ibid., 164.
27 Ibid., 24.
28 Ibid., 182.
29 Ibid., 186.
30 Ibid., 189.
31 Talia Schaffer, "'A Wilde Desire Took Me': The Homoerotic History of *Dracula*." *ELH* 61, no. 2 (Summer 1994): 390.
32 Ibid., 398.
33 Viereck, "Mr. W.H.," in *Glances Backward: An Anthology of American Homosexual Writing, 1830–1920*, ed. James J. Gifford (Peterborough, ON: Broadview Press, 2007), 162.
34 Gertz, *Odyssey of a Barbarian*, 226.
35 Viereck, "A Ballad of Montmartre" in *Glances Backward*, ed. Gifford, 165.
36 Ibid., 166.

37 Ibid.
38 "A Queer Story of Spiritualism," *Daily Mail* (London), 30 July 1923, 8.
39 [Ralph Shirley], "Notes of the Month," *Occult Review* 38, no. 3 (September 1923): 139.
40 See "A Queer Story of Spiritualism"; Hester Travers Smith, "The Return of Oscar Wilde," *Occult Review* 38, no. 2 (August 1923): 81–2; and Travers Smith, *Psychic Messages*, 9.
41 Edmund Bentley, *Far Horizon: A Biography of Hester Dowden, Medium and Psychic Investigator* (London: Rider, 1951), 61, 44.
42 Simone Natale, *Supernatural Entertainments: Victorian Spiritualism and the Rise of Modern Media Culture* (University Park: Pennsylvania State University Press, 2016), 123.
43 Hester Travers Smith, *Oscar Wilde from Purgatory: Psychic Messages* (New York: Henry Holt, 1926).
44 "Lazar," *The Ghost Epigrams of Oscar Wilde as Taken Down through Automatic Writing by Lazar* (New York: Covici-Friede, 1928).
45 Ibid., epigrams IV, XIX, and XXV.
46 On the spiritualism's popularity after the war see Helen Sword, *Ghostwriting Modernism* (Ithaca, NY: Cornell University Press, 2002), 3; and Jennifer Hazelgrove, "Spiritualism after the Great War," *Twentieth Century British History* 10, no. 4 (1999): 404–30.
47 See Noël Coward, *Three Plays: Blithe Spirit, Hay Fever, Private Lives* (New York: Vintage, 1999), 19, 94.
48 Sword, *Ghostwriting Modernism*, 15.
49 Ibid., 13.
50 Ibid., 30.
51 Bentley, *Far Horizon*, 40.
52 Edward Dowden, *Letters of Edward Dowden* (London: Dent, 1914), 178.
53 Elisha Cohn, "Oscar Wilde's Ghost: The Play of Imitation," *Victorian Studies* 54, no. 3 (Spring 2012): 475.
54 Ibid., 474.
55 Sword, *Ghostwriting Modernism*, 24.
56 Natale, *Supernatural Entertainments*, 121.
57 Ibid., 131.
58 See Travers Smith, *Psychic Messages*, 80.
59 Ibid., 2.
60 See Travers Smith, *Voices from the Void: Six Years' Experience in Automatic Communications* (London: Rider, 1919), 105–8.
61 Travers Smith, *Psychic Messages*, 46.
62 Ibid., 12, 44.

63 Ibid., 44.
64 Ibid., 55.
65 Stokes, *Oscar Wilde*, 6.
66 Travers Smith, *Psychic Messages*, 56–7.
67 Ibid., 163.
68 Ibid., 109.
69 Ibid., 114; italics added.
70 See Travers Smith, "The Return of Oscar Wilde," *Occult Review* 38, no. 2 (August 1923): 77–84, and *Occult Review* 38, no. 3 (September 1923): 149–54; and G.D. Cummins, "The Strange Case of Oscar Wilde," *Occult Review* 39, no. 2 (February 1924): 102–10.
71 Doyle went on to publish a book on the subject, *The Coming of the Fairies*, in 1922. On Doyle and the Cottingley fairies hoax see Douglas Kerr, *Conan Doyle: Writing, Profession, and Practice* (Oxford: Oxford University Press, 2013), 234–50.
72 Doyle to Travers Smith, 19 August 1923, Papers Relating to *Psychic Messages from Oscar Wilde*, MS Wilde, fS649 M3 P974 [1924].
73 Doyle to Travers Smith, 14 April 1924, Papers Relating to *Psychic Messages from Oscar Wilde*, MS Wilde, fS649 M3 P974 [1924].
74 Doyle, *Edge of the Unknown*, 136.
75 Elana Gomel, "'Spirits in the Material World': Spiritualism and Identity in the *Fin de Siècle*." *Victorian Literature and Culture* 35 (2007): 190.
76 Doyle, "Oscar Wilde," letter to the editor, *Occult Review*, 236.
77 See Travers Smith, *Psychic Messages*, 165–9.
78 Ibid., 81.
79 S.G. Soal to Hester Travers Smith, 2 August 1923, Papers Relating to *Psychic Messages from Oscar Wilde*, MS Wilde, fS649 M3 P974 [1924].
80 See [C.W. Soal], "A New Message from Oscar Wilde," *Occult Review* 38, no. 5 (November 1923): 269–79.
81 This journal's unwieldy title is usually abbreviated to *Psychic Science*.
82 [C.W. Soal], "The Oscar Wilde Script: A Critique by the Brother of Mr. V.," *Quarterly Transactions of the British College of Psychic Science* 3 (January 1924): 310.
83 "A Queer Story of Spiritualism," 8.
84 [C.W. Soal], "A New Message from Oscar Wilde," 269.
85 "Psychic Messages," newspaper clipping from the *Daily Sketch* (London), 27 September 1923, Wildeana Clippings, vol. LIX (1923), 84, William Andrews Clark Memorial Library, UCLA.
86 Laurence Housman, *Echo de Paris: A Study from Life* (London: Jonathan Cape, 1923), 15.

87 Dust jacket, Housman, *Echo de Paris* (New York: D. Appleton, 1924).
88 [C.W. Soal], "The Oscar Wilde Script," 304.
89 Ibid., 309.
90 Sword, *Ghostwriting Modernism*, 9.
91 [C.W. Soal], "The Oscar Wilde Script," 323.
92 Ibid., 310.
93 Ibid., 320.
94 Ibid., 312.
95 Arthur Conan Doyle, *The Sign of Four* (Peterborough, ON: Broadview Press, 2010; first published 1890), 84; italics in the original.
96 G.D. Cummins, "The Strange Case of Oscar Wilde," 106.
97 C.W. Soal, letter to the editor, *Occult Review* 39, no. 3 (March 1924): 175, 176.
98 Ibid., 176.
99 G.D. Cummins, "The Strange Case of Oscar Wilde," 108.
100 Wendy E. Cousins, "Writer, Medium, Suffragette, Spy? The Unseen Adventures of Geraldine Cummins," *Paranormal Review* 45 (2008): 6. On the *Cummins v. Bond* case see also Blewett Lee, "Copyright of Automatic Writing," *Virginia Law Review* 13 (1926–27): 22–6.
101 [C.W. Soal], "A New Message from Oscar Wilde," 275.
102 G.D. Cummins, "The Strange Case of Oscar Wilde," 110.
103 G.D. Cummins, letter to the editor, *Occult Review* 39, no. 5 (May 1924): 299.
104 Ibid., 300; italics added.
105 C.W. Soal, "The Oscar Wilde Script," *Occult Review* 39, no. 6 (June 1924): 363.
106 S.G. Soal, "Note on the 'Oscar Wilde' Script," *Journal of the Society for Psychic Research* 23 (July 1926): 112, 111.
107 S.G. Soal, "Spiritualism," in *A Dictionary of the Occult*, ed. Julian Franklyn (New York: Causeway Books, 1973; first published 1935), 267–8.
108 Travers Smith, *Psychic Messages*, 20–1.
109 Ibid., 23.
110 G.D. Cummins, "The Strange Case of Oscar Wilde," 108.
111 Travers Smith, *Psychic Messages*, 171.
112 Ibid., 173.
113 Ibid., 170, 173.
114 Ibid., 174.
115 Many spiritualist texts by dead authors feature communicators or controls emanating from the distant past; generically, they often foreground memory. According to Simone Natale, "the most common works of this kind were the memoirs of spirits, who were in a privileged position to describe their existence on earth and in the afterlife" (*Supernatural Entertainments*, 9).

116 Hester Dowden [Travers Smith], "How I Received Oscar Wilde's 'Spirit Play,'" *The Graphic* 119 (10 March 1928): 404.
117 Oscar Wilde [Spirit], "'Is It a Forgery?' A Play in Three Acts Purporting to Be Communicated by Oscar Wilde," typescript, 86 pages, in Papers Relating to *Psychic Messages from Oscar Wilde*, MS Wilde, fS649 M3 P974 [1924].
118 Bentley, *Far Horizon*, 72.
119 [Geraldine Cummins], "A Sitting with Miss Gertrude Kingston, November 4, 1925," Papers Relating to *Psychic Messages from Oscar Wilde*, MS Wilde, fS649 M3 P974 [1924].
120 Ibid.
121 Ibid.
122 Hester Dowden [Travers Smith], "How I Received Oscar Wilde's 'Spirit Play,'" 404.
123 See J.P. Wearing, *The London Stage, 1920–29: A Calendar of Plays and Players*, vol. 2, *1925–1929* (Metucken, NJ: Scarecrow Press, 1984), 930.
124 See Gertrude Kingston, *Curtsey While You're Thinking …* (London: Williams & Norgate, 1937), 289–90.
125 Gertrude Kingston to Vyvyan Holland, 1 March 1928, TCD MS 11437-1-3-13, Trinity College, Dublin.
126 Ibid.
127 Ibid.
128 Kingston, *Curtsey While You're Thinking …*, 284.
129 Lennox Robinson, quoted in Robert Tanitch, *Oscar Wilde on Stage and Screen* (London: Methuen, 1999), 267.
130 Andrew Dakers to Geraldine Cummins, 14 April 1950, Papers Relating to *Psychic Messages from Oscar Wilde*, MS Wilde, fS649 M3 P974 [1924].
131 Lennox Robinson to Geraldine Cummins, undated [c. 1949–50], Papers Relating to *Psychic Messages from Oscar Wilde*, MS Wilde, fS649 M3 P974 [1924].
132 See Wilde, *Mr. W.H.*, 208.
133 G[eraldine] C[ummins], foreword to "Is It a Forgery? A Play in Three Acts Purporting to Be Communicated by Oscar Wilde," Papers Relating to *Psychic Messages from Oscar Wilde*, MS Wilde, fS 649M3 P974 [c. 1924], 4.
134 Ibid., 11–12.
135 Hester Dowden [Travers Smith], "How I Received Oscar Wilde's 'Spirit Play,'" 404.
136 Wilde [Spirit], "Is It a Forgery?," 9.
137 The role of Mrs Garvin was apparently designed for Gertrude Kingston. See Kingston, *Curtsey While You're Thinking …*, 288–9.
138 Wilde [Spirit], "Is It a Forgery?," 38, 61.

139 Ibid., 34.
140 Ibid.
141 Ibid., 61.
142 Ibid.
143 Ibid.
144 Ibid., 64.
145 G[eraldine] C[ummins], foreword, 21.
146 Wilde [Spirit], "Is It a Forgery?," 69.
147 Bristow and Mitchell, *Oscar Wilde's Chatterton*, 306.

4 The Devoted Fraud

1 Travers Smith, *Psychic Messages*, 10.
2 Ibid., 13.
3 Millard to newspaper editors, 28 July 1925, "Who Wrote *For Love of the King*?" collection, MS Wilde, M645 W6286 [1908–26], box 2, folder 37.
4 There is very little scholarship on Mrs Chan-Toon's literary career. There is an entry for her in *Edwardian Fiction: An Oxford Companion*, ed. Sandra Kemp, Charlotte Mitchell, and David Trotter (Oxford: Oxford University Press, 1997), 62. However, it contains a number of factual errors, such as her connection to Wilde, likely derived from the bogus information that she supplied in the documents authenticating *For Love of the King*.
5 In advocating growth and change as the hallmarks of the critical spirit, Gilbert avers that what "people call insincerity is simply a method by which we can multiply our personalities." See Wilde, *Criticism*, 189.
6 The Methuen edition of *For Love of the King*, however, renders the name as two words (Chan Toon).
7 Wilde, *Criticism*, 105.
8 Perhaps the most whimsical and politically daring of Mrs Chan-Toon's adventures is recorded in a letter signed "M. Chan-Toon" that she wrote to a "London Business house" and which was reprinted in an investigative report on her movements: "Would you be so kind and courteous as to tell me where I can address myself to get in touch with the Russian government? I could be of use to them in propaganda work." See "The Woman with the Green Parrot," *Daily News* (London), 22 October 1927, "Who Wrote *For Love of the King*?" collection, MS Wilde, M645Z W6286 [1908–26], box 3, folder 10.
9 On Mr Chan-Toon's judicial appointment as First Judge in the Court of Small Causes in Rangoon see the notice on "Burmah" in *The Times*, 29 February 1892, 5.

10 For instance, the Stetson sale catalogue describes item 203, Wilde's Commonplace Book, as "An Unpublished Manuscript." See *The Oscar Wilde Collection of John B. Stetson, Jr*, 40.

11 See Wilde, *The Portrait of Mr. W.H.*, [v].

12 See "For Love of the King," by "the author of *Told on the Pagoda*," *The Idler* 17 (April 1900): 260–70.

13 Edmund Gosse, "A Vision of Burmah," in *More Books on the Table* (London: Heinemann, 1923), 373.

14 E.V. Lucas, quoted in Hyde, *Christopher Sclater Millard*, 98.

15 See "For Love of the King: A Burmese Masque in Three Acts & Nine Scenes," *Century Magazine* 103, no. 2 (December 1921): 225.

16 Evans to Millard, 7 September 1925, "Who Wrote *For Love of the King*?" collection, MS Wilde, M645Z W6286, box 2, folder 37.

17 "A Burmese Masque," *Times Literary Supplement*, 26 October 1922, 681.

18 Notice, *Evening Standard*, 19 October 1922, Wildeana Clippings, vol. LVII (1922–23), 42, William Andrews Clark Memorial Library, UCLA.

19 Gosse, "A Vision of Burmah," 373–4.

20 See "Mr. London" [Hannen Swaffer], "Wonderful London Yesterday," *Daily Graphic*, 11 July 1925, 5.

21 Millard to the editor of the *Daily Graphic*, 17 July 1925. Reprinted in *Who Wrote "For Love of the King"?* (Birmingham, UK: Frank Juckes, [1925]), [4].

22 "Mr. London" [Hannen Swaffer], "Wonderful London Yesterday," *Daily Graphic*, 17 July 1925, 5.

23 The following advertisement, describing a title "in the press," appears in the January 1924 *Catalogue of Books* published by William Rider & Son: "OSCAR WILDE AS I KNEW HIM. BY MRS CHAN TOON. Crown 8vo, illustrated, cloth, 6s. net. The author of these reminiscences was for many years intimately acquainted with the Wilde family. They throw a fresh and vivid light on the personality of a wayward genius whose position in literature has now obtained world-wide recognition." See Rider's *Catalogue of Books*, January 1924, 52.

24 "Mr. London" [Hannen Swaffer], "Wonderful London Yesterday," *Daily Graphic*, 11 July 1925, 5.

25 See Millard, *Who Wrote "For Love of the King"?* Millard further issued a "Second Edition" of this pamphlet in 1926.

26 *Methuen & Co. v. Millard*, 1926 M. No. 726, High Court of Justice, King's Bench Division, 5 March 1926.

27 Under the name Mabel Wodehouse Pearse, she was sentenced to six months' imprisonment for stealing £240 from her elderly and illiterate landlady. See "PARROT IN COURT – Woman Writer Charged with Theft of Notes," *Daily Sketch*, 6 January 1926, 2.

28 Millard to Mabel Violet Wanliss, 14 November 1926, "Who Wrote *For Love of the King*?" collection, MS Wilde, M645Z W6286 [1908–26], box 3, folder 9.
29 The existing scholarship on the play focuses almost exclusively on its status as a forgery and on the *Methuen v. Millard* libel trial. See Frances Winwar, "Some Postscripts to Oscar Wilde," *Saturday Review of Literature* 22, no. 17 (17 August 1940): 13–17; George Sims, "Who Wrote *For Love of the King*: Oscar Wilde or Mrs Chan Toon?," *The Book Collector* 7, no. 3 (Autumn 1958): 269–77; Hyde, *Christopher Sclater Millard*, 80–1, 89–103. The most detailed exposé of the forgery is Henry D. Davray's "Les apocryphes d'Oscar Wilde," *Mercure de France* 183 (October 1925): 104–17; 186 (March 1926): 308–17. See also Edward Marx, "Decadent Exoticism and the Woman Poet," in *Women and British Aestheticism*, ed. Talia Schaffer and Kathy Alexis Psomiades (Charlottesville: University Press of Virginia, 1999), 155n8.
30 Dust jacket, *For Love of the King* (New York: G.P. Putnam's Sons, [1923]).
31 See Gérard Genette, *Paratexts: Thresholds of Interpretation*, trans. Jane E. Lewin (Cambridge: Cambridge University Press, 1997).
32 Ruthven, *Faking Literature*, 43.
33 [E.V. Lucas], "Introductory Note," *For Love of the King: A Burmese Masque* (London: Methuen, 1922), [xi].
34 Oscar Wilde [Mrs Chan-Toon], *For Love of the King: A Burmese Masque* (London: Methuen, 1922), [xiii].
35 [Lucas], "Introductory Note," [xii].
36 Ibid., [xi–xii].
37 Mr Chan-Toon's books include *The Nature and Value of Jurisprudence* (London: Reeves & Turner, 1889); *Principles of Buddhist Law* (Rangoon, Burma: Myles Standish, 1894); and (with J. Bruce) *The Pawnbroker's Legal Handbook* (London: E. Wilson, 1895).
38 Her birth certificate indicates that Mary Mabel Cosgrove was born on 12 May 1873 in the city of Cork, Ireland. See "Who Wrote *For Love of the King*?" collection, MS Wilde, M645Z W6286 [1908–26], box 3, folder 8.
39 See "A Remarkable Literary Discovery: New Unpublished Work by Oscar Wilde," *Hutchinson's Magazine*, October 1921: 349.
40 Wilde, *Mr. W.H.*, 197.
41 [Lucas], "Introductory Note," [xii].
42 Newspaper clipping from *Liverpool Daily Courier*, 31 August 1922, Wildeana Clippings, vol. LVII (1922–3), 17, William Andrews Clark Memorial Library, UCLA.
43 "A Burmese Masque," *Times Literary Supplement*, 26 October 1922, 681.
44 See Wilde, *Complete Letters*, 622–5. During this time Wilde may also have been working on his unfinished blank-verse drama *A Florentine Tragedy*.

45 Oscar Wilde [Mrs Chan-Toon], *For Love of the King*, [xiii–xiv].

46 According to an unsigned 1904 obituary notice, Mr Chan-Toon "died suddenly at Rangoon from heart failure on the 9th inst., in his thirty-seventh year." See "Legal Obituary," *The Law Times* 116 (20 February 1904): 375.

47 Oscar Wilde [Mrs Chan-Toon], *For Love of the King*, [xiv]; the ellipses are in the original.

48 See Linda Dowling, *Hellenism and Homosexuality in Victorian Oxford* (Ithaca, NY: Cornell University Press, 1994).

49 See Robert Aldrich, *The Seduction of the Mediterranean: Writing, Art and Homosexual Fantasy* (London: Routledge, 1993).

50 "A Remarkable Literary Discovery," *Hutchinson's Magazine*, October 1921): 349; italics added.

51 "For Love of the King," *The Idler* 17 (April 1900): 260.

52 "A Burmese Masque," *Times Literary Supplement*, 26 October 1922, 681.

53 Oscar Wilde [Mrs Chan-Toon], *For Love of the King*, 2–3; italics in the original.

54 Newspaper clipping from the *Observer* (London), 22 October 1922, Wildeana Clippings, vol. LVII (1922–3), 44, William Andrews Clark Memorial Library, UCLA.

55 "For Love of the King," *The Idler* 17 (April 1900):, 261.

56 Martin Holman to Vyvyan Holland, 11 July 1921, "Who Wrote *For Love of the King*?" collection, MS Wilde, M645Z W6286 [1908–26], box 2, folder 23.

57 Wilde, *Salomé*, in *Plays I: The Duchess of Padua; Salomé: Drame en un Acte; Salomé: Tragedy in One Act*, ed. Joseph Donohue, vol. 5 of *The Complete Works of Oscar Wilde* (Oxford: Oxford University Press, 2013), 727, 728.

58 See Wilde, *The Picture of Dorian Gray*, 276–90; *Poems and Poems in Prose*, 180–94.

59 See John Gilmorton, "A Literary Hoax?," *The Outlook*, 8 August 1925, 88.

60 Gosse, "A Vision of Burmah," 371.

61 In an unpublished letter Mrs Chan-Toon refers to her first husband as "the late Prince Chan-Toon – Barrister-at-Law, Middle Temple – a *great* friend, of all the Wildes." Chan-Toon to unidentified correspondents, 7 September 1932, MS Wilde, box 83, folder 13.

62 Oscar Wilde [Mrs Chan-Toon], *For Love of the King*, 17.

63 Ibid., 26.

64 Ibid., 39.

65 "For Love of the King," *The Idler* 17 (April 1900): 266.

66 Michael Lackey, "Locating and Defining the Bio in Biofiction," *a/b: Auto/Biography Studies* 31, no. 1 (2016): 3.

67 Oscar Wilde [Mrs Chan-Toon], *For Love of the King*, 29. I borrow the term *Irish Peacock* from Wilde's grandson Merlin Holland. See Holland, *Irish*

Peacock and Scarlet Marquess: The Real Trial of Oscar Wilde (London: Fourth Estate, 2004).

68 Oscar Wilde [Mrs Chan-Toon], *For Love of the King*, 33.

69 "For Love of the King," *The Idler* 17 (April 1900): 266.

70 Oscar Wilde [Mrs Chan-Toon], *For Love of the King*, 7.

71 See Mrs Chan-Toon, "A Burmese Festival," *English Illustrated Magazine* 42, no. 84 (March 1910): 586–93.

72 See "Stories of Burmah," *The Sketch*, 6 November 1901, 118.

73 Wilde, *Criticism*, 86.

74 Wilde, *Criticism*, 98.

75 "A Man of Forty" appears in the short-story collection *The Triumph of Love, and Other Stories* (London: Greening, 1906). "The Last of the Dandies" tells of the famous early-nineteenth-century French dandy, the Count d'Orsay, whose love affair with the Anglo-Irish Countess of Blessington is chronicled in Mrs Chan-Toon's article "The Romance of the Countess of Blessington." *The Lady's Realm* 16 (July 1904).

76 Mrs Chan-Toon, *A Marriage in Burmah* (London: Greening, 1905), 32.

77 In a bankruptcy notice in *The Times* she is described as an "authoress" and "widow." See "The London Gazette, Tuesday, Nov. 8.," *The Times*, 9 November 1910, 22.

78 "Plaintiff's Departmental Memoranda" [in *Methuen v. Millard*], "Who Wrote *For Love of the King*?" collection, MS Wilde, M645Z W6286 [1908–26], box 3, folder 5.

79 Shortly after *For Love of the King* was published, Mrs Chan-Toon wrote to Frederick Muller, agent for Methuen: "I write to you to say that I am willing to part with all rights in FOR LOVE OF THE KING for the sum of £1000 cash [...] it is a great chance for any one." See M. Wodehouse Pearse to Muller, 7 November 1922, "Who Wrote *For Love of the King*?" collection, MS Wilde, M645Z W6286 [1908–26], box 2, folder 17.

80 Vyvyan Holland to Millard, 30 July 1925, "Who Wrote *For Love of the King*?" collection, MS Wilde, M645Z W6286 [1908–26], box 2, folder 24.

81 Millard, *Who Wrote "For Love of the King"?*, [4].

82 I borrow this language about forgery from Frankel's "On Lying as a Way of Knowing," 15.

83 This description comes from Boris de Skossyreff, the president of a Paris-based Wilde fan club and a keen observer of Mrs Chan-Toon's Parisian movements. See Skossyreff to Millard, 4 September 1925, "Who Wrote *For Love of the King*?" collection, MS Wilde, M645Z W6286 [1908–26], box 1, folder 5.

84 Millard to Holland, 28 June 1925, "Who Wrote *For Love of the King*?" collection, MS Wilde, M645Z W6286 [1908–26], box 2, folder 24.

85 Figgis to Millard, 30 July 1925, "Who Wrote *For Love of the King*?" collection, MS Wilde, M645Z W6286 [1908–26], box 2, folder 37.

86 See Bruce Thomas Boehrer, *Parrot Culture: Our 2,500-Year-Long Fascination with the World's Most Talkative Bird* (Philadelphia: University of Pennsylvania Press, 2004), 7–8.

87 See Boehrer, *Parrot Culture*, 68–9. Beyond the scope of this essay, another habit of thought, popularized by Robert Louis Stevenson's *Treasure Island* (1883), aligns the parrot with piracy: like Cap'n Flint on the shoulder of Long John Silver, the parrot completes the romanticized figure of the pirate. For a discussion of the pirate in colonial discourse, with an emphasis on "piracy" in print culture, see Srinivas Aravamudan, *Tropicopolitans: Colonialism and Agency, 1688–1804* (Durham, NC: Duke University Press, 1999), 71–102.

88 On the bird's sex see "The Lady with the Parrot," *Aberdeen Press and Journal*, 1 March 1924, 4. Most of the few contemporary descriptions of Co-co, however, render the bird an "it." An unsigned newspaper report of Mabel Wodehouse Pearse's arrest for theft in 1926 notes her appearance in court with that "famous parrot." "It," the report states, "can speak English and French, and is very intelligent" ("Parrot in Court," 2). Stevenson's Cap'n Flint exists in a similar state of indeterminacy: although the parrot was named for an infamous male pirate, Long John Silver informs Jim Hawkins that his pet is female. See Stevenson, *Treasure Island* (Oxford: Oxford University Press, 1998).

89 An account of the "Woman and the Green Parrot: A Curious Tale," in the *Daily News* (London), 22 October 1927, which traces Mrs Chan-Toon's movements in the 1920s, indicates that she continued to employ her first husband's name, even though her new married name was Wodehouse Pearse. By the early 1930s, long after she had been widowed for a second time, her letters confirm that she had returned to the name of Mrs Chan-Toon.

90 Homi Bhabha, *The Location of Culture* (London: Routledge, 1994), 89; italics in the original.

91 "A Distinguished Burmese," *The Leisure Hour* 37 (1888): 710.

92 See [Mr] Chan-Toon, "Hints to Indian Law Students," *Indian Magazine and Review* 295 (July 1895): 350.

93 Arrested in Mexico in 1908, she gave her name as "Princess Chantoon." See "Princess in Mexico Prison," *New York Times*, 8 June 1908, 5.

94 Her impersonation of Princess Orloff, a White Russian exile, has been traced by Davray ("Les apocryphes," 316). Her stint as "Princess Arakan" is recorded in "Woman and the Green Parrot." See press clippings, "Who

Wrote *For Love of the King*?" collection, MS Wilde, M645Z W6286 [1908–26], box 3, folder 10.

95 Paul Carter, *Parrot* (London: Reaktion Books, 2006), 8.

96 Ruthven, *Faking Literature*, 3.

97 Ibid., 4.

98 Another target of Mrs Chan-Toon's larcenous imagination was the Irish fantasist Lord Dunsany (1878–1957). In 1924 she had attempted to inveigle a woman named Mabel Violet Wanliss by claiming an acquaintanceship and a correspondence with Dunsany. The scam went awry when Wanliss managed, through family connections, to contact Dunsany. After hearing about the outcome of the *Methuen v. Millard* trial, Wanliss wrote to Millard to offer her support. See Mabel Violet Wanliss to Millard, 11 November 1926, "Who Wrote *For Love of the King*?" collection, MS Wilde, M645Z W6286 [1908–26], box 1, folder 20.

99 Millard to Ledger, 1 July 1925, MSS Ross 13/5.

100 See *Dobell's Catalogue of Autograph Letters, Manuscripts &c.* [December 1925], item 391; italics in the original.

101 John Kelly and Eric Domville, eds. *The Collected Letters of W.B. Yeats*, vol. 1, *1865–1895* (Oxford: Clarendon Press, 1986), 375n.

102 A fascination with Irish authors remained a consistent touchstone throughout Chan-Toon's writing career. See also "Falsifiers and Fabricators; or, the Gift of Irish Wit," *Rangoon Times* 33 (1 April 1903): 3.

103 Millard to Ledger, 4 April 1927, MSS Ross 13/5.

104 [Mrs Chan-Toon], "A Conversation, with Some Comments" [1931?], MS Wilde, box 83, folder 12.

105 Ibid. The phrase "your old school fellow" has been crossed out, apparently by Shaw himself.

106 Ibid.

107 [Mrs Chan-Toon], "Bernard Shaw: A Tiny Sketch" [1932?], MS Wilde, box 83, folder 12. See also Mrs Chan-Toon to Mr Dobell, 9 October 1932, in the same folder.

108 Chan-Toon to unidentified correspondents, 7 September 1932, MS Wilde, box 83, folder 12. Although the recipient of this missive is not identified, a later letter of 9 October addressed to Mr Dobell about further Shaw correspondence in "Bernard Shaw: A Tiny Sketch" strongly suggests that she is dealing with the same firm.

109 [Mrs Chan-Toon], "With Oscar Wilde" [c. 1932], MS Wilde, box 83, folder 12.

110 Ibid., [18].

111 Ibid., [6].

112 Ibid., [9].

113 Ibid., [20].
114 Ibid., [33].
115 Joseph Bristow, "Picturing His Exact Decadence: The British Reception of Oscar Wilde," in *The Reception of Oscar Wilde in Europe*, ed. Stefano Evangelista (London: Bloomsbury, 2010), 37.
116 See Bernard Shaw, "My Memories of Oscar Wilde," appended, with separate pagination, to vol. 2 of Frank Harris's *Oscar Wilde: His Life and Confessions* (New York: Frank Harris, 1918), 7–32.
117 Although not a great deal is known about Arthur Henry Cooper-Prichard, he was an Englishman who worked for some time in the United States. He is recorded as working as an actor for a travelling theatre company in Los Angeles in 1910. He also served as the American Numismatic Society's first librarian in New York in 1911. His history of pirates, *The Buccaneers* (London: Cecil Palmer) appeared in 1927. Two sections of *Conversations with Oscar Wilde* had appeared in print before they were collected under that title; see "Reminiscences of Oscar Wilde," *Cornhill* 68 (February 1930): 144–54; and "Oscar Wilde at Afternoon Tea," *Cornhill* 69 (November 1930): 590–6.
118 Cooper-Prichard, *Conversations*, 2–3.
119 Ibid., 21.
120 [Mrs Chan-Toon], "With Oscar Wilde," [c. 1932], MS Wilde, box 83, folder 12, [30].

Conclusion

1 On the publication history of *The Ballad of Reading Gaol* see Guy and Small, *Oscar Wilde's Profession*, 183–98; and Nelson, *Publisher to the Decadents*, 173–208.
2 Wilde, *Complete Letters*, 1011.
3 Small, introduction to *Poems and Poems in Prose*, by Wilde, xxvi.
4 Wilde, *Complete Letters*, 1031.
5 Frankel, *Unrepentant Years*, 209.
6 Wilde, *Complete Letters*, 1032.
7 See Mason [Millard], *Bibliography of Oscar Wilde*, 421.
8 This copy was offered for sale on AbeBooks.com by a dealer in California: https://www.abebooks.com/servlet/SearchResults?an=wilde%2C+oscar&bi=0&bx=off&ds=30&recentlyadded=all&sortby=1&tn=ballad+of+reading+gaol&xpod=on&yrh=1898&yrl=1898. (Accessed 10 May 2018.)
9 Ross to Ledger, 13 September 1907, MSS Ross 4.
10 See Wilde, *Complete Letters*, 1032n.

11 See Symons, [Prepared Testimony in *Methuen v. Millard*], "Who Wrote *For Love of the King*?" collection, MS Wilde, M645Z W6286 [1908–26], box 1, folder 15.
12 Wilde, *Poems* (London: Methuen, 1928). This volume is now held by the Clark Library, PR 5811 F28 1928.
13 William Andrews Clark Jr to Douglas, 28 August 1932, MS Wilde, box 10, folder 70.
14 "The Portrait of Mr. W.H. as Written by Oscar Wilde" (New York: Mitchell Kennerley, 1921), [unpaginated publisher's prospectus]. Pilcrows appear in the original.
15 "Oscar Wilde's Lost Manuscript Found," *New York Times*, 17 June 1921, 9.
16 See Small, introduction to *The Short Fiction*, by Wilde, lxxiii.
17 Ibid., lxxiv.
18 Ibid., lxxii–lxxvi.
19 According to Matthew J. Bruccoli, "before the discovery was announced, Kennerley sold the manuscript […] to Dr. Rosenbach for $3,000. The Doctor was unable to dispose of it at $5,500 and kept it in his collection." See Bruccoli, *The Fortunes of Mitchell Kennerley*, 141–2.
20 Wilde, *The Portrait of Mr. W.H.*, [ix]; italics added.
21 Quoted in Horst Schroeder, *Oscar Wilde, "The Portrait of Mr. W.H." – Its Composition, Publication and Reception* (Braunschweig, Germany: Technische Universität Carolo-Wilhelmina zu Braunschweig, 1984), 38.
22 The Rosenbach Company offered the manuscript to William Andrews Clark Jr, and he presumably declined. See Percy E. Lawley to Clark, 10 March 1921, Clarkive Pre-1934, box 8, William Andrews Clark Memorial Library, UCLA.
23 Small, introduction to *The Short Fiction*, by Wilde, lxxvi.
24 Ibid., lxxix.
25 Ibid., lxxx.
26 Ibid., lxxxi; italics added.
27 Ibid., lxxxiii.
28 Ibid.
29 Kennerley, quoted in Bruccoli, *The Fortunes of Mitchell Kennerley*, 13.
30 On Kennerley's arrangement with Harris see Bruccoli, *The Fortunes of Mitchell Kennerley*, 40–1.
31 "'W.H.' a Boy Actor, Wilde's Theory," *New York Evening Post*, 20 June 1921, 7.
32 "The Portrait of Mr. W.H. as Written by Oscar Wilde" [unpaginated publisher's prospectus].
33 Richard Le Gallienne, "The Lost 'Portrait of Mr. W.H.,'" *New York Times Book Review and Magazine*, 24 July 1921, 3.
34 Ibid.

Bibliography

Collections

Clarkive. William Andrews Clark Memorial Library, University of California, Los Angeles.
Eccles Bequest. British Library.
Harry Ransom Humanities Research Center, University of Texas at Austin.
Maggs Brothers Ltd. London.
MSS Ross. Robert Ross Memorial Collection, University College, Oxford.
MS Wilde. William Andrews Clark Memorial Library, University of California, Los Angeles.
MS Wilde Forgeries. William Andrews Clark Memorial Library, University of California, Los Angeles.
Papers Relating to *Psychic Messages from Oscar Wilde*. MS Wilde. William Andrews Clark Memorial Library, University of California, Los Angeles.
Rosenbach Museum and Library, Philadelphia.
TCD MS. Trinity College, Dublin.
Wildeana Clippings. William Andrews Clark Memorial Library, University of California, Los Angeles.

Other Sources

A Collection of Original Manuscripts Letters & Books of Oscar Wilde. London: Dulau [1928].
Ahmadgoli, Kamran, and Ian Small. "The Creative Editor: Robert Ross, Oscar Wilde, and the *Collected Works*." *English Literature in Transition* 51, no. 2 (2008): 138–51.
Aldrich, Robert. *The Seduction of the Mediterranean: Writing, Art and Homosexual Fantasy*. London: Routledge, 1993.

Al-Kassim, Dina. *On Pain of Speech: Fantasies of the First Order and the Literary Rant* Berkeley: University of California Press, 2010.

Antliff, Mark. "Contagious Joy: Anarchism, Censorship and the Reception of Jacob Epstein's *Tomb of Oscar Wilde*, c. 1913." *Journal of Modern Periodical Studies* 4, no. 2 (2013): 195–225.

Aravamudan, Srinivas. *Tropicopolitans: Colonialism and Agency, 1688–1804*. Durham, NC: Duke University Press, 1999.

"The author of *Told on the Pagoda*" [Mrs Chan-Toon]. "For Love of the King." *The Idler* 17 (April 1900): 260–70.

Bartlett, Neil. *Who Was That Man? A Present for Mr. Oscar Wilde*. London: Serpent's Tail, 1988.

Bentley, Edmund. *Far Horizon: A Biography of Hester Dowden, Medium and Psychic Investigator*. London: Rider, 1951.

Bhabha, Homi. *The Location of Culture*. London: Routledge, 1994.

[Bloxam, John Francis]. "The Priest and the Acolyte." *Chameleon* 1 (December 1894): 29–47.

– *The Priest and the Acolyte*. London: privately printed, 1894 [actually 1905].

– *The Priest and the Acolyte: With an Introductory Protest by Stuart Mason*. London: Lotus Press, 1907.

Boehrer, Bruce Thomas. *Parrot Culture: Our 2,500-Year-Long Fascination with the World's Most Talkative Bird*. Philadelphia: University of Pennsylvania Press, 2004.

Borland, Maureen. *Wilde's Devoted Friend: A Life of Robert Ross*. Oxford: Lennard, 1990.

Boroughs, Rod. "Oscar Wilde's Translation of Petronius: The Story of a Literary Hoax." *English Literature in Transition* 38, no. 1 (1995): 9–49.

Borras, Maria Lluïsa, ed. *Maintenant: Collection complete*. Paris: Editions Jean-Michel Place, 1977.

Briefel, Aviva. *The Deceivers: Art Forgery and Identity in the Nineteenth Century*. Ithaca, NY: Cornell University Press, 2006.

Bristow, Joseph. Introduction to *Oscar Wilde and Modern Culture: The Making of a Legend*, edited by Joseph Bristow, 1–45. Athens: Ohio University Press, 2008.

– ed. *Oscar Wilde and Modern Culture: The Making of a Legend*. Athens: Ohio University Press, 2008.

– "Picturing His Exact Decadence: The British Reception of Oscar Wilde." In *The Reception of Oscar Wilde in Europe*, edited by Stefano Evangelista, 20–50. London: Bloomsbury, 2010.

Bristow, Joseph, and Rebecca N. Mitchell. *Oscar Wilde's Chatterton: Literary History, Romanticism, and the Art of Forgery*. New Haven, CT, and London: Yale University Press, 2015.

– "The Provenance of Oscar Wilde's 'Decay of Lying.'" *Papers of the Bibliographical Society of America* 111, no. 2 (2017): 221–40.

Bruccoli, Matthew J. *The Fortunes of Mitchell Kennerley, Bookman*. New York: Harcourt Brace Jovanovich, 1986.

Burke, Carolyn. *Becoming Modern: The Life of Mina Loy*. New York: Farrar, Straus & Giroux, 1996.

"Burmah." *The Times*, 29 February 1892, 5.

"A Burmese Masque." *Times Literary Supplement*, 26 October 1922, 681.

Carpenter, Edward. *My Days and Dreams*. London: George Allen & Unwin, 1916.

Carter, Paul. *Parrot*. London: Reaktion Books, 2006.

Catalogue of Books. London: William Rider, 1924.

Catalogue of the Library of Richard Butler Glaenzer: Comprising a Complete Set of the Works of Oscar Wilde in First Editions [1905]. Ross d. 222, Robert Ross Memorial Collection, University College, Oxford.

Cavicchi, Daniel. "Fandom before 'Fan': Shaping the History of Enthusiastic Audiences." *Reception: Texts, Readers, Audiences, History* 6, no. 1 (2014): 52–72.

Chan-Toon [Mr]. "Hints to Indian Law Students." *Indian Magazine and Review* 295 (July 1895): 350–1.

– *The Nature and Value of Jurisprudence*. London: Reeves & Turner, 1889.

– *Principles of Buddhist Law*. Rangoon, Burma: Myles Standish, 1894.

Chan-Toon [Mr], and J. Bruce. *The Pawnbroker's Legal Handbook*. London: E. Wilson, 1895.

Chan-Toon, Mrs [Mabel]. "A Burmese Festival." *English Illustrated Magazine* 42, no. 84 (March 1910): 586–93.

– "Falsifiers and Fabricators; or, the Gift of Irish Wit." *Rangoon Times* 33 (3 January 1903): 13.

– "A Man of Forty." In *The Triumph of Love, and Other Stories*. London: Greening, 1906.

– *A Marriage in Burmah*. London: Greening, 1905.

– "The Romance of the Countess of Blessington." *The Lady's Realm* 16 (July 1904): 357–63.

Chauncey, George. *Gay New York: Gender, Urban Culture, and the Making of the Gay Male World, 1890–1940*. New York: Basic Books, 1994.

Cheiro [Warner, William John]. *Cheiro's Memoirs: The Reminiscences of a Society Palmist*. London: William Rider, 1912.

Cohen, Ed. *Talk on the Wilde Side: Toward a Genealogy of a Discourse on Male Sexualities*. New York: Routledge, 1993.

Cohn, Elisha. "Oscar Wilde's Ghost: The Play of Imitation." *Victorian Studies* 54, no. 3 (Spring 2012): 474–85.

Conover, Roger. *4 Dada Suicides: Selected Texts of Arthur Cravan, Jacques Rigaut, Julien Torma & Jacques Vaché*. London: Atlas Press, 1995.
– "The Secret Names of Arthur Cravan." In *Arthur Cravan: Poète et Boxeur*, 25–37. Paris: Terrain Vague, 1992.
Cook, Matt. *London and the Culture of Homosexuality, 1885–1914*. Cambridge: Cambridge University Press, 2003.
Cooper-Prichard, A.H. *Conversations with Oscar Wilde*. London: Philip Allan, 1931.
– "Oscar Wilde at Afternoon Tea." *Cornhill* 69 (November 1930): 590–6.
– "Reminiscences of Oscar Wilde." *Cornhill* 68 (February 1930): 144–54.
Corbett, David Peters. *The World in Paint: Modern Art and Visuality in England, 1848–1914*. University Park: Pennsylvania State University Press, 2004.
Cousins, Wendy E. "Writer, Medium, Suffragette, Spy? The Unseen Adventures of Geraldine Cummins." *Paranormal Review* 45 (2008): 3–7.
Cowan, Robert Ernest, and William Andrews Clark Jr. *Wilde and Wildeiana: The Library of William Andrews Clark, Jr.* San Francisco: John Henry Nash, 1922.
Coward, Noël. *Three Plays: "Blithe Spirit," "Hay Fever," "Private Lives."* New York: Vintage, 1999.
Cravan, Arthur [Fabian Lloyd]. "Oscar Wilde est vivant!" *Maintenant* 3 (October–November 1913): 1–11.
– "Oscar Wilde Is Alive!" *The Soil: A Magazine of Art* 1, no. 4 (April 1917): 145–60; 1, no. 5 (July 1917): 195–200.
Crowell, Ellen. "Christopher Millard's Mysterious Book: Oscar Wilde, Baron Corvo, and the Unwritten *Quest*." In *Wilde Discoveries: Traditions, Histories, Archives*, edited by Joseph Bristow, 343–65. Toronto: University of Toronto Press, 2013.
– "Oscar Wilde's Tomb: *Silence* and the Aesthetics of Queer Memorial." *BRANCH: Britain, Representation and Nineteenth-Century History*, edited by Dino Franco Felluga, n.p. Extension of *Romanticism and Victorianism on the Net*. Web. Accessed 10 August 2016.
Cummins, G.D. Letter to the editor. *Occult Review* 39, no. 5 (May 1924): 297–300.
– "The Strange Case of Oscar Wilde." *Occult Review* 39:2 (February 1924), 102–10.
D'Arch Smith, Timothy. *Love in Earnest: Some Notes on the Lives and Writings of English "Uranian" Poets from 1889 to 1930*. London: Routledge & Kegan Paul, 1970.
Davray, Henry D. "Les apocryphes d'Oscar Wilde." *Mercure de France* 183 (October 1925): 104–17; 186 (March 1926): 308–17.
Derecho, Abigail. "Archontic Literature: A Definition, a History, and Several Theories of Fan Fiction." In *Fan Fiction and Fan Communities in the Age of the*

Internet, edited by Karen Hellekson and Kristina Busse, 61–78. Jefferson, NC: McFarland, 2006.

Derrida, Jacques. *Archive Fever: A Freudian Impression*. Translated by Eric Prenowitz. Chicago: University of Chicago Press, 1996.

"A Distinguished Burmese." *The Leisure Hour* 37 (1888): 710.

Dobell's Catalogue of Autograph Letters, Manuscripts &c. [December 1925].

"Don't Call Me Him, For I'm a 'Her'." *Paris* [Texas] *Morning News*, 30 November 1917, 7.

"Dorian Hope Makes Answer to Charges Brought Against Him," *Gastonia Gazette*, 15 August, 1921, 2.

"'Dorian Hope' Verse Filched by Clerk." *New York Times*, 5 April 1921, 27.

"Dorian Hope Wanted by Police of Paris." *New York Herald*, 7 May 1922, 7.

Douglas, Alfred. *The Autobiography of Lord Alfred Douglas*. London: Martin Secker, 1929.

– *Collected Poems of Lord Alfred Douglas*. London: Martin Secker, 1919.

– *Oscar Wilde and Myself*. London: John Long, 1914.

– *The Rossiad*. London: [R. Dawson], 1916.

[Douglas, Alfred]. "A Warning to Our Readers." *Plain English* 35, no. 2 (March 5, 1921): 183.

Dowden, Edward. *Letters of Edward Dowden*. London: Dent, 1914.

Dowden [Travers Smith], Hester. "How I Received Oscar Wilde's 'Spirit Play.'" *The Graphic* 119 (10 March 1928): 404.

Dowling, Linda. *Hellenism and Homosexuality in Victorian Oxford*. Ithaca, NY: Cornell University Press, 1994.

Doyle, Arthur Conan. *The Edge of the Unknown*. London: John Murray, 1930.

– "Oscar Wilde." Letter to the editor. *Occult Review* 39, no. 4 (April 1924): 235–6.

– *The Sign of Four*. Peterborough, ON: Broadview Press, 2010. First published 1890.

Edwards, Dudley. "The Wilde Goose Chase." *American Book Collector* 7, no. 5 (January 1957): 3–14.

Eliot, T.S. *The Annotated Waste Land, with Eliot's Contemporary Prose*. Edited by Lawrence Rainey. New Haven, CT: Yale University Press, 2005.

Ellmann, Richard. *Oscar Wilde*. Harmondsworth, UK: Penguin, 1987.

Eltis, Sos. *Revising Wilde: Society and Subversion in the Plays of Oscar Wilde*. Oxford: Clarendon Press, 1996.

Epstein, Jacob. *Let There Be Sculpture: The Autobiography of Jacob Epstein*. London: Readers Union and Michael Joseph, 1942.

Fisher, Will. "The Sexual Politics of Victorian Historiographical Writing about the 'Renaissance.'" *GLQ* 14, no. 1 (2007): 41–67.

Foucault, Michel. "What Is an Author?" In *The Foucault Reader*, edited by Paul Rabinow, 101–20. New York: Vintage, 1984.

Frankel, Nicholas. "Gathering the Fragments: The Role of the Collector in Remembering Oscar Wilde." *The Wildean* 22 (January 2003): 3–16.

– "On Lying as a Way of Knowing: A Portrait of 'The Portrait of Mr. W.H.'" In *Fakes and Forgeries*, edited by Peter Knight and Jonathan Long, 14–26. Buckingham, UK: Cambridge Scholars Press, 2004.

– *Oscar Wilde: The Unrepentant Years*. Cambridge, MA: Harvard University Press, 2017.

– *Oscar Wilde's Decorated Books*. Ann Arbor: University of Michigan Press, 2000.

– "The Typewritten Self: Media Technology and Identity in Wilde's *De Profundis*." In *Bound for the 1890s: Essays on Writing and Publishing in Honor of James G. Nelson*, edited by Jonathan Allison, 27–44. High Wycombe, UK: Rivendale Press, 2006.

Freeman, Arthur. *Bibliotheca Fictiva: A Collection of Books & Manuscripts Relating to Literary Forgery, 400 BC – AD 2000*. London: Bernard Quaritch, 2014.

Fryer, Jonathan. *André & Oscar: The Literary Friendship of André Gide and Oscar Wilde*. New York: St Martin's Press, 1997.

– *Robbie Ross: Oscar Wilde's True Love*. London: Constable, 2000.

"A Futurist Lecture," *Evening Standard* (London), 7 July 1914. Wildeana Clippings, vol. XXXI (1914), William Andrews Clark Memorial Library, University of California, Los Angeles.

Gagnier, Regenia. *Idylls of the Marketplace: Oscar Wilde and the Victorian Public*. Stanford, CA: Stanford University Press, 1986.

Genette, Gérard. *Paratexts: Thresholds of Interpretation*. Translated by Jane E. Lewin. Cambridge: Cambridge University Press, 1997.

Gertz, Elmer. *Odyssey of a Barbarian: The Biography of George Sylvester Viereck*. Buffalo, NY: Prometheus Books, 1978.

Gide, André. *Oscar Wilde: A Study from the French of André Gide*. With introduction, notes, and bibliography by Stuart Mason. Oxford: Holywell Press, 1905.

Gilbert, W.S. *The Plays of Gilbert and Sullivan*. New York: Norton, 1976.

Gilmorton, John. "A Literary Hoax?" *The Outlook* (London), 8 August 1925, 88.

"Girl Claims as Her Own 26 Poems of Dorian Hope; Mysterious Poet Vanishes." *New York Evening World*, 4 April 1921, 6.

Gomel, Elana. "'Spirits in the Material World': Spiritualism and Identity in the *Fin de Siècle*." *Victorian Literature and Culture* 35 (2007): 189–213.

Gorman, Herbert S. "New Poets and Some Others." *New York Times Book Review and Magazine*, 27 March 1921, 13.

"The Gospel of Intensity." *Boston Evening Transcript*, 10 January 1882, 2.
Gosse, Edmund. *More Books on the Table*. London: Heinemann, 1923.
[Grolleau, Charles.] *The Trial of Oscar Wilde: From the Shorthand Reports*. Paris: privately printed [Charles Carrington], 1906.
Guy, Josephine M. "Wilde's *De Profundis* and Book History: Mute Manuscripts." *English Literature in Transition* 55, no. 4 (2012): 419–40.
Guy, Josephine, and Ian Small. *Oscar Wilde's Profession: Writing and the Culture Industry in the Late Nineteenth Century*. Oxford: Oxford University Press, 2000.
– "Reading *De Profundis*." *English Literature in Transition* 49, no. 2 (2006): 123–49.
Han, Carrie Sickmann. "Pickwick's Other Papers: Continually Reading Dickens." *Victorian Literature and Culture* 44 (2016): 19–41.
Harris, Frank. *Oscar Wilde: His Life and Confessions*. New York: Frank Harris, 1918.
Harris, Frank, and Lord Alfred Douglas. *New Preface to "The Life and Confessions of Oscar Wilde."* London: Fortune Press, 1925.
Hazelgrove, Jennifer. "Spiritualism after the Great War." *Twentieth Century British History* 10, no. 4 (1999): 404–30.
Hellekson, Karen, and Kristina Busse. Introduction to *The Fan Fiction Studies Reader*. Edited by Karen Hellekson and Kristina Busse, 5–6. Iowa City: University of Iowa Press, 2014.
Holland, Brett. "'Vocation' (for the *Times-Dispatch*)." *Times-Dispatch* (Richmond, Virginia), 17 December 1918, 6.
Holland, Merlin. "Biography and the Art of Lying." In *The Cambridge Companion to Oscar Wilde*, edited by Peter Raby, 3–17. Cambridge: Cambridge University Press, 1997.
– *Irish Peacock and Scarlet Marquess: The Real Trial of Oscar Wilde*. London: Fourth Estate, 2004.
– *The Real Trial of Oscar Wilde*. New York: Harper Collins, 2003.
Hope, Dorian [pseud.] "If Thou Wilt Be." Forgery. Collection of Maggs Bros. Ltd., London.
Housman, Laurence. *Echo de Paris*. New York: D. Appleton, 1924.
– *Echo de Paris: A Study from Life*. London: Jonathan Cape, 1923.
Hyde, H. Montgomery. *Christopher Sclater Millard (Stuart Mason): Bibliographer & Antiquarian Book Dealer*. New York: Global Academic Publishers, 1990.
"Irish-Burmese Authoress in America." *The Day* [New London, CT], 16 January 1908, 1.
Israel, Lee. *Can You Ever Forgive Me? Memoirs of a Literary Forger*. New York: Simon & Schuster, 2008.

Janes, Dominic. *Oscar Wilde Prefigured: Queer Fashioning and British Caricature, 1750–1900*. Chicago: University of Chicago Press, 2016.

– *Vision of Queer Martyrdom from John Henry Newman to Derek Jarman*. Chicago: University of Chicago Press, 2015.

Kaye, Richard A. "Oscar Wilde and the Politics of Sainthood: Hofmannsthal, Mirbeau, Proust." In *Oscar Wilde and Modern Culture*, edited by Joseph Bristow, 110–32. Athens: Ohio University Press, 2008.

Kelly, John, and Eric Domville, eds. *The Collected Letters of W.B. Yeats*. Vol. 1, *1865–1895*. Oxford: Clarendon Press, 1986.

Kemp, Sandra, Charlotte Mitchell, and David Trotter, eds. *Edwardian Fiction: An Oxford Companion*. Oxford: Oxford University Press, 1997.

Kerr, Douglas. *Conan Doyle: Writing, Profession, and Practice*. Oxford: Oxford University Press, 2013.

Kilmer, Joyce. "Godlessness Mars Most Contemporary Poetry." *New York Times Magazine*, 10 December 1916, 12.

Kingston, Gertrude. *Curtsey While You're Thinking …* London: Williams & Norgate, 1937.

Koestenbaum, Wayne. *The Queen's Throat: Opera, Homosexuality, and the Mystery of Desire*. New York: Da Capo Press, 2001.

Lackey, Michael. "Locating and Defining the Bio in Biofiction." *a/b: Auto/Biography Studies* 31, no. 1 (2016): 3–10.

"The Lady with the Parrot." *Aberdeen Press and Journal*, 1 March 1924, 4.

Lazar [pseud.]. *The Ghost Epigrams of Oscar Wilde as Taken Down through Automatic Writing by Lazar*. New York: Covici-Friede, 1928.

Ledger, Walter. "Bibliography." In *Salomé, La Sainte Courtisane, A Florentine Tragedy*, by Oscar Wilde, 93–109. London: Methuen, 1909.

Lee, Blewett. "Copyright of Automatic Writing." *Virginia Law Review* 13 (1926–7): 22–6.

Lee, Laura. *Oscar's Ghost: The Battle over Oscar Wilde's Legacy*. Stroud, UK: Amberley, 2017.

Le Gallienne, Richard. "The Lost 'Portrait of Mr. W.H.'" *New York Times Book Review and Magazine*, 24 July 1921, 3 and 22.

– *The Romantic '90s*. London: Putnam, 1951. First published 1926.

"Legal Obituary." *The Law Times* 116 (20 February 1904): 375.

Lethbridge, Henry. "The Quest for Cravan." *Antiquarian Book Monthly Review* 8 (September 1981): 336–9.

Loesberg, Jonathan. "Wildean Interpretation and Formalist Reading." *Victorian Studies* 58, no. 1 (Autumn 2015): 9–33.

"London, Mr." [pseud. Hannen Swaffer]. "Wonderful London Yesterday." *The Daily Graphic*, 11 July 1925, 5; 17 July 1925, 5.

"The London Gazette, Tuesday, Nov. 8." *The Times*, 9 November 1910, 22.

Love, Harold. *Attributing Authorship: An Introduction*. Cambridge: Cambridge University Press, 2002.

[Lucas, E.V.] "Introductory Note." In *For Love of the King: A Burmese Masque*. London: Methuen, 1922.

Mackie, Gregory. "Publishing Notoriety: Piracy, Pornography, and Oscar Wilde." *University of Toronto Quarterly* 73, no. 4 (Fall 2004): 980–90.

– "Textual Dissidence: The Occasions of Wilde's 'The Soul of Man under Socialism.'" *Mémoires du Livre / Studies in Book Culture* 4, no. 2 (Spring 2013); unpaginated.

Marcus, Sharon. "Salomé!! Sarah Bernhardt, Oscar Wilde, and the Drama of Celebrity." *PMLA* 126, no. 4 (October 2011): 999–1021.

Marx, Edward. "Decadent Exoticism and the Woman Poet." In *Women and British Aestheticism*, edited by Talia Schaffer and Kathy Alexis Psomiades, 139–57. Charlottesville: University Press of Virginia, 1999.

Mason, Stuart [Millard, Christopher]. *Bibliography of Oscar Wilde*. London: T. Werner Laurie, [1914].

– *Bibliography of the Poems of Oscar Wilde*. London: E. Grant Richards, 1907.

– "Forged Letters of Oscar Wilde." *Publishers' Circular*, 18 November 1911, 755.

– "List of Editions of Works by Oscar Wilde Which May Be Offered for Sale in the United Kingdom." Appended to Ross, "Re: Oscar Wilde Deceased." [London: privately printed, 1908.]

– *Oscar Wilde, Art and Morality: A Defence of "Dorian Gray."* London: J. Jacobs, 1908.

– *Oscar Wilde, Art and Morality: A Record of the Discussion Which Followed the Publication of "Dorian Gray."* London: Frank Palmer, 1912.

– *The Oscar Wilde Calendar*. London: Frank Palmer, 1910.

McKenna, Neil. *The Secret Life of Oscar Wilde*. London: Century, 2003.

Mendelssohn, Michèle. *Making Oscar Wilde*. Oxford: Oxford University Press, 2018.

Methuen & Co. *Prospectus, February 1908*. Wildeana Clippings, vol. I (1909). William Andrews Clark Memorial Library, University of California, Los Angeles.

Methuen & Co. v. Millard. 1926 M. No. 726. High Court of Justice. King's Bench Division.

Millard, Christopher Sclater. *Who Wrote "For Love of the King"?* Birmingham, UK: Frank Juckes, [1925].

–, compiler. Wildeana Clippings, 1909–27. 56 vols. William Andrews Clark Memorial Library, University of California, Los Angeles.

[Millard, Christopher Sclater]. *Oscar Wilde: Three Times Tried*. London: Ferrestone Press, 1912.

Mimosa [Mrs Chan-Toon]. *Told on the Pagoda: Tales of Burmah*. London: T. Fisher Unwin, 1895.

Mitchell, Rebecca N. "'Cultivated Idleness': Carlyle, Wilde, and Victorian Representations of Creative Labour." *Word & Image* 32, no. 1 (2016): 104–15.

"The Modern Aesthete." *London Mail*, 8 August 1914. Wildeana Clippings, vol. XXXI (1914), William Andrews Clark Memorial Library, University of California, Los Angeles.

Natale, Simone. *Supernatural Entertainments: Victorian Spiritualism and the Rise of Modern Media Culture*. University Park: Pennsylvania State University Press, 2016.

Nelson, James G. *Publisher to the Decadents: Leonard Smithers in the Careers of Beardsley, Wilde, Dowson*. University Park: Pennsylvania State University Press, 2000.

Newell, Stephanie. *The Forger's Tale: The Search for Odeziaku*. Athens: Ohio University Press, 2006.

Nicholl, Charles. *Traces Remain: Essays and Explorations*. London: Allen Lane, 2011.

Notman, Otis. "Viereck, Hohenzollern?" *New York Times Saturday Review of Books*, 29 June 1907, 413.

Novak, Daniel A. "Picturing Wilde: Christopher Millard's 'Iconography of Oscar Wilde.'" *Nineteenth-Century Contexts* 32, no. 4 (December 2010): 305–35.

– "Sexuality in the Age of Technological Reproducibility: Oscar Wilde, Photography, and Identity." In *Oscar Wilde and Modern Culture: The Making of a Legend*, edited by Joseph Bristow, 63–95. Athens: Ohio University Press, 2008.

O'Brien, Kevin. *Oscar Wilde in Canada: An Apostle for the Arts*. Toronto: Personal Library, 1982.

The Oscar Wilde Collection of John B. Stetson, Jr. New York: Anderson Galleries, 1920. Also in Ross d. 225, Robert Ross Memorial Collection, University College, Oxford.

"Oscar Wilde's Lost Manuscript Found." *New York Times*, 17 June 1921, 9.

"Oscar Wilde's Nephew." *Modern Society*, 21 March 1914. Wildeana Clippings, vol. XXX (1914), William Andrews Clark Memorial Library, University of California, Los Angeles.

– "Oscar Wilde's Nephew Disappears." *London Mail*, 18 April 1914. Wildeana Clippings, vol. XXX (1914), William Andrews Clark Memorial Library, University of California, Los Angeles.

"Our Portraits." *The Graphic* 69 (27 February 1904): 282.

"Pirated Oscar Wilde Books." *Westminster Gazette*, 20 February 1914. Wildeana Clippings, vol. XXX (1914). William Andrews Clark Memorial Library, University of California, Los Angeles.

"Poet Holland Denies Charges of Plagiarism." *Washington Times*, 24 August 1921, 1.

"The Portrait of Mr. W.H. as Written by Oscar Wilde." Unpaginated publisher's prospectus. New York: Mitchell Kennerley, 1921.

"Princess in Mexico Prison." *New York Times*, 8 June 1908, 5.

– "Psychic Messages." *Daily Sketch* (London), 27 September 1923. Wildeana Clippings, vol. LIX (1923). William Andrews Clark Memorial Library, University of California, Los Angeles.

"A Queer Story of Spiritualism." *Daily Mail* (London), 30 July 1923, 8.

Quilter, Harry. "The Gospel of Intensity." *Contemporary Review*, June 1895, 761–82.

Ransome, Arthur. *The Autobiography of Arthur Ransome*. London: Jonathan Cape, 1976.

– *Oscar Wilde: A Critical Study*. London: Martin Secker, 1912.

Raymond, Jean Paul [pseud.], and Charles Ricketts. *Oscar Wilde: Recollections*. London: Nonesuch Press, 1932.

"A Remarkable Literary Discovery: New Unpublished Work by Oscar Wilde." *Hutchinson's Magazine*, October 1921, 349.

Richardson, Mike, and Rick Geary. *Cravan: Mystery Man of the Twentieth Century*. Milwaukie, OR: Dark Horse Books, 2005.

Roberts, Maria. *Yours Loyally: A Life of Christopher Sclater Millard*. [LaVergne, TN:] FeedARead.com Publishing, 2014.

Robertson, W. Graham. *Time Was: The Reminiscences of W. Graham Robertson*. London: Hamish Hamilton, 1931.

Rosenthal, Donald A. *An Arcadian Photographer in Manhattan: Edward Mark Slocum*. Portsmouth: Callum James, 2011.

Ross, Margery. *Robert Ross: Friend of Friends*. London: Jonathan Cape, 1954.

Ross, Robert. "The American Edition of Oscar Wilde's Works." *Times Literary Supplement*, 10 October 1907, 307.

– Introduction to *Reviews*, by Oscar Wilde. London: Methuen, 1908.

– "Introductory Note." In *Bibliography of Oscar Wilde*, by Stuart Mason, v–vi. London: T. Werner Laurie, [1914].

– "Oscar Wilde's Literary Remains." *Daily Chronicle*, 7 February 1905. Ross Env.d.49.ii, Robert Ross Memorial Collection, University College, Oxford.

– Preface to *De Profundis*, by Oscar Wilde. London: Methuen, 1905.

– "A Prefatory Dedication to Dr. Max Meyerfeld." In *De Profundis*, by Oscar Wilde. London: Methuen, 1908.

– "Re: Oscar Wilde Deceased." [London: privately printed, 1908.]

– "A Superfluous Note of Explanation." In *The Soul of Man under Socialism*, by Oscar Wilde, v–x. London: Arthur Humphreys, 1912.

Ruthven, K.K. *Faking Literature*. Cambridge: Cambridge University Press, 2001.

Saint-Amour, Paul K. *The Copyrights: Intellectual Property and the Literary Imagination*. Ithaca, NY: Cornell University Press, 2003.

Satcher, Herbert Boyce. *A Bibliography of Church Music and Allied Subjects*. Philadelphia: Diocese of Pennsylvania, 1937; rev. ed. 1949.

– "The Dorian Hope Story." Unpublished manuscript, [c. 1960]. MS Wilde, box 60, folder 7, William Andrews Clark Memorial Library, University of California, Los Angeles.

Schaffer, Talia. "'A Wilde Desire Took Me': The Homoerotic History of *Dracula*." *ELH* 61, no. 2 (Summer 1994): 381–425.

Schroeder, Horst. *Oscar Wilde, "The Portrait of Mr. W.H." – Its Composition, Publication and Reception*. Braunschweig, Germany: Technische Universität Carolo-Wilhelmina zu Braunschweig, 1984.

Sedgwick, Eve Kosofsky. *Tendencies*. Durham, NC: Duke University Press, 1993.

Shakespeare, William. *Complete Sonnets and Poems*, edited by Colin Burrow. Oxford: Oxford University Press, 2002.

Shaw, George Bernard. "My Memories of Oscar Wilde." Appended, with separate pagination, to vol. 2 of *Oscar Wilde: His Life and Confessions*, by Frank Harris. New York: Frank Harris, 1918.

Shelley, Percy Bysshe. "To a Sky-Lark." In *Shelley's Poetry and Prose*, edited by Donald H. Reiman and Neil Fraistat, 304. New York: Norton, 2002.

Sherard, Robert Harborough. *The Life of Oscar Wilde*. London: T. Werner Laurie, 1906.

– *The Real Oscar Wilde: To Be Used as a Supplement to, and in Illustration of "The Life of Oscar Wilde."* London: T. Werner Laurie, [1916].

[Shirley, Ralph.] "Notes of the Month." *Occult Review* 38, no. 3 (September 1923): 129–40.

Sims, George. "'Arthur Cravan' the Oscar Wilde Forger: A Mystery Solved?" *Antiquarian Book Monthly Review* 7 (August 1980): 398–403.

– "Who Wrote *For Love of the King*: Oscar Wilde or Mrs Chan Toon?" *The Book Collector* 7, no. 3 (Autumn 1958): 269–77.

Sinfield, Alan. *The Wilde Century: Oscar Wilde, Effeminacy, and the Queer Movement*. New York: Columbia University Press, 1994.

16, Tite Street, Chelsea: Catalogue of the Library of Valuable Books, Pictures, Portraits of Celebrities […] Which Will Be Sold by Auction by Mr. Bullock, on the Premises, on Wednesday, April 24th, 1895. N.p., n.d.

Small, Ian. Introduction to *De Profundis; "Epistola: In Carcere et Vinculis,"* edited by Ian Small. Vol. 2 of *The Complete Works of Oscar Wilde*. Oxford: Oxford University Press, 2005.
– "What Kind of Writer Was Wilde? Editorial Practice and Canon-Formation." *Journal of Victorian Culture* 5, no. 2 (Autumn 2000): 323–33.
Soal, C.W. "The Oscar Wilde Script." *Occult Review* 39, no. 6 (June 1924): 361–3.
[Soal, C.W.] Letter to the editor. *Occult Review* 39, no. 3 (March 1924): 175–7.
– "A New Message from Oscar Wilde." *Occult Review* 38, no. 5 (November 1923): 269–79.
– "The Oscar Wilde Script: A Critique by the Brother of Mr. V." *Quarterly Transactions of the British College of Psychic Science* 3 (January 1924): 299–326.
Soal, Samuel George. "Note on the 'Oscar Wilde' Script." *Journal of the Society for Psychic Research* 23 (July 1926): 110–12.
– "Spiritualism." In *A Dictionary of the Occult*, edited by Julian Franklyn. New York: Causeway Books, 1973. First published 1935.
"The Spiritual Outlook." *Light: A Journal of Psychical, Occult, and Mystical Research* 5, no. 216 (21 February 1885): 91–2.
Stevenson, Robert Louis. *Treasure Island*. Oxford: Oxford University Press, 1998. First published 1883.
Stokes, John. *Oscar Wilde: Myths, Miracles, and Imitations.* Cambridge: Cambridge University Press, 1996.
"Stories of Burmah." *The Sketch*, 6 November 1901, 118.
Stuart-Young, J.M. *Osrac, the Self-Sufficient, and Other Poems, with a Memoir of the Late Oscar Wilde*. London: Hermes Press, 1905.
Sword, Helen. *Ghostwriting Modernism*. Ithaca, NY: Cornell University Press, 2002.
Symons, A.J.A. *The Quest for Corvo*. East Lansing: Michigan State University Press, 1955. First published 1934.
Tanitch, Robert. *Oscar Wilde on Stage and Screen*. London: Methuen, 1999.
Travers Smith, Hester. *Oscar Wilde from Purgatory: Psychic Messages*. New York: Henry Holt, 1926.
– *Psychic Messages from Oscar Wilde*. London: T. Werner Laurie, [1924].
– "The Return of Oscar Wilde." *Occult Review* 38, no. 2 (August 1923): 77–84; and *Occult Review* 38, no. 3 (September 1923): 149–54.
– *Voices from the Void: Six Years' Experience in Automatic Communications.* London: Rider, 1919.
Vanacker, Sabine, and Catherine Wynne, eds. *Sherlock Holmes and Conan Doyle: Multi-Media Afterlives*. Basingstoke, UK: Palgrave Macmillan, 2013.
Viereck, George Sylvester. "A Ballad of Montmartre." In *Glances Backward: An Anthology of American Homosexual Writing, 1830–1920*, edited by James J. Gifford, 165–7. Peterborough, ON: Broadview Press, 2007.

– *The House of the Vampire*. New York: Moffat, Yard, 1907.
– "Is Oscar Wilde Living or Dead?" *The Critic* (New York) 47 (July 1905): 86–8.
– "Mr. W.H." In *Glances Backward: An Anthology of American Homosexual Writing, 1830–1920*, edited by James J. Gifford, 162. Peterborough, ON: Broadview Press, 2007.
Waldrep, Shelton. *The Aesthetics of Self-Invention: Oscar Wilde to David Bowie* Minneapolis: University of Minnesota Press, 2004.
Wearing, J.P. *The London Stage, 1920–29: A Calendar of Plays and Players.* Vol. 2, *1925–1929*. Metucken, NJ: Scarecrow Press, 1984.
"'W.H.' a Boy Actor, Wilde's Theory." *New York Evening Post*, 20 June 1921, 7.
Whiteman, Bruce. "'Some Sell, and Others Buy': Early Collectors of Oscar Wilde." In *The Importance of Being Misunderstood: Homage to Oscar Wilde*, edited by Giovanna Franci and Giovanna Silvani, 367–77. Bologna: Patron Editore, 2003.
Wilde, Oscar. "Art and the Handicraftsman." MS Wilde 6721 M3 A784 [1882]b and [1882]c bound. William Andrews Clark Memorial Library, University of California, Los Angeles.
– *The Ballad of Reading Gaol*. London: Leonard Smithers, 1898.
– "The Canterville Ghost." In *The Short Fiction*, edited by Ian Small. Vol. 8 of *The Complete Works of Oscar Wilde.* Oxford: Oxford University Press, 2017.
– "Chatterton" [c.1886]. In *Oscar Wilde's Chatterton: Literary History, Romanticism, and the Art of Forgery*, edited by Joseph Bristow and Rebecca N. Mitchell, 333–409. New Haven, CT: Yale University Press, 2015.
– *The Collected Works*. 14 vols. Edited by Robert Ross. London: Methuen, 1908.
– *The Complete Letters of Oscar Wilde*. Edited by Merlin Holland and Rupert Hart-Davis. London: Fourth Estate, 2000.
– *The Complete Short Stories*. Edited by John Sloan. Oxford: Oxford University Press, 2010.
– *Le crime de Lord Arthur Savile.* Translated by Albert Savine. Paris: P.V. Stock, 1905.
– *Criticism: Historical Criticism, Intentions, the Soul of Man*. Edited by Josephine M. Guy. Vol. 4 of *The Complete Works of Oscar Wilde.* Oxford: Oxford University Press, 2007.
– *De Profundis*. London: Methuen, 1905; 1908.
De Profundis. In *De Profundis; "Epistola: In Carcere et Vinculis,"* edited by Ian Small. Vol. 2 of *The Complete Works of Oscar Wilde.* Oxford: Oxford University Press, 2005.
– Impressions of America. Edited by Stuart Mason [Christopher Millard]. Sunderland: Keystone Press, 1906.

– *The Incomparable and Ingenious History of Mr. W.H.* In *The Short Fiction*, edited by Ian Small, 197–258. Vol. 8 of *The Complete Works of Oscar Wilde*. Oxford: Oxford University Press, 2017.
– "The Nightingale and the Rose." In *The Short Fiction*, edited by Ian Small, 20–4. Vol. 8 of *The Complete Works of Oscar Wilde*. Oxford: Oxford University Press, 2017.
– "*Olivia* at the Lyceum." In *Journalism I*, edited by John Stokes and Mark W. Turner, 54–6. Vol. 6 of *The Complete Works of Oscar Wilde*. Oxford: Oxford University Press, 2013.
– "Phrases and Philosophies for the Use of the Young." In *The Major Works*, edited by Isobel Murray, 572–3. Oxford: Oxford University Press, 1989.
– *The Picture of Dorian Gray: The 1890 and 1891 Texts*. Edited by Joseph Bristow. Vol. 3 of *The Complete Works of Oscar Wilde*. Oxford: Oxford University Press, 2005.
– *Poems*. London: Methuen, 1928.
– *Poems and Poems in Prose*. Edited by Bobby Fong and Karl Beckson. Oxford: Oxford University Press, 2000.
– *The Poems of Oscar Wilde*. London: Methuen, 1908.
– "The Portrait of Mr. W.H." Manuscript. MS EL3 W672p 921. Rosenbach Museum and Library, Philadelphia.
– "The Portrait of Mr. W.H." *Blackwood's Edinburgh Magazine*, July 1889, 1–21. PR 5819 P851 cop. 2, William Andrews Clark Memorial Library, University of California, Los Angeles.
– *The Portrait of Mr. W.H.* New York: Mitchell Kennerley, 1921.
– *Salome*. In *Plays I: The Duchess of Padua; Salomé: Drame en un Acte; Salome: Tragedy in One Act*, edited by Joseph Donohue, 707–31. Vol. 5 of *The Complete Works of Oscar Wilde*. Oxford: Oxford University Press, 2013.
– *The Sphinx*. London: Elkin Mathews & John Lane, 1894.
– *The Sphinx*. In *The Poems of Oscar Wilde*, edited by Robert Ross, 289–314. Vol. 9 of *The Collected Works of Oscar Wilde*. London: Methuen, 1908.
– *The Sphinx*. In *Poems and Poems in Prose*, edited by Bobby Fong and Karl Beckson, 180–94. Vol. 1 of *The Complete Works of Oscar Wilde*. Oxford: Oxford University Press, 2000.
– "The Sphinx without a Secret." In *The Short Fiction*, edited by Ian Small. Vol. 8 of *The Complete Works of Oscar Wilde*. Oxford: Oxford University Press, 2017.
Wilde, Oscar [Mrs Chan-Toon]. "For Love of the King: A Burmese Play in Three Acts and Nine Scenes." *Hutchinson's Magazine* 5, no. 28 (October 1921): 349–56.
– "For Love of the King: A Burmese Masque in Three Acts & Nine Scenes." *Century Magazine* 103, no. 2 (December 1921): [225–42].

– *For Love of the King: A Burmese Masque*. London: Methuen, 1922.
– *For Love of the King: A Burmese Masque*. New York: G.P. Putnam's Sons, [1923].
Wilde, Oscar [Spirit]. "'Is It a Forgery?' A Play in Three Acts Purporting to Be Communicated by Oscar Wilde." MS Wilde fS 649M3 P974 [1924]. William Andrews Clark Memorial Library, University of California, Los Angeles.
"Wilde Manuscript Sale Brings $46,866." *New York Times*, 24 April 1920, 32.
Winwar, Frances. "Some Postscripts to Oscar Wilde." *Saturday Review of Literature* 22, no. 17 (17 August 1940): 13–17.
"Woman Impersonator Demonstrates Gas Range." *Wilmington Evening Journal*, 18 August 1916, 7.
"The Woman with the Green Parrot." *Daily News* (London), 22 October 1927. MS Wilde, M645Z W6286 [1908–26], box 3 folder 10, William Andrews Clark Memorial Library, University of California, Los Angeles.
Wright, Thomas. *Life of Walter Pater*. New York: Putnam, 1907.
Wright, Thomas. *Oscar's Books*. London: Chatto & Windus, 2008.

Index

The abbreviation OW refers to Oscar Wilde. Page numbers with (f) refer to illustrations.